TEHRAN CHILDREN

TEHRAN CHILDREN

≡

A Holocaust Refugee Odyssey

Mikhal Dekel

W. W. NORTON & COMPANY
Independent Publishers Since 1923

Tehran Children is a work of nonfiction. Certain names of individuals have been changed.

Copyright © 2019 by Mikhal Dekel

For information about permission to reproduce selections from this book, write to Permissions, W. W. Norton & Company, Inc., 500 Fifth Avenue, New York, NY 10110

For information about special discounts for bulk purchases, please contact W. W. Norton Special Sales at specialsales@wwnorton.com or 800-233-4830

Manufacturing by Worzalla
Book design by Chris Welch Design
Production manager: Julia Druskin

Library of Congress Cataloging-in-Publication Data

Names: Dekel, Mikhal, 1965-author.
Title: Tehran children : a Holocaust refugee odyssey / Mikhal Dekel.
Description: First edition. | New York : W.W. Norton & Company, 2019. | Includes bibliographical references and index.
Identifiers: LCCN 2019020829 | ISBN 9781324001034 (hardcover)
Subjects: LCSH: Jewish refugees—Iran—Tehran. | Refugee children—Iran—Tehran. | Jewish children—Iran—Tehran. | Jewish children—Poland. | Jews—Poland.
Classification: LCC HV640.5.J4 D45 2019 | DDC 940.53/1809253095525—dc23
LC record available at https://lccn.loc.gov/2019020829

W. W. Norton & Company, Inc., 500 Fifth Avenue, New York, N.Y. 10110
www.wwnorton.com

W. W. Norton & Company Ltd., 15 Carlisle Street, London W1D 3BS

1 2 3 4 5 6 7 8 9 0

For Hannan and Rivka'le

Contents

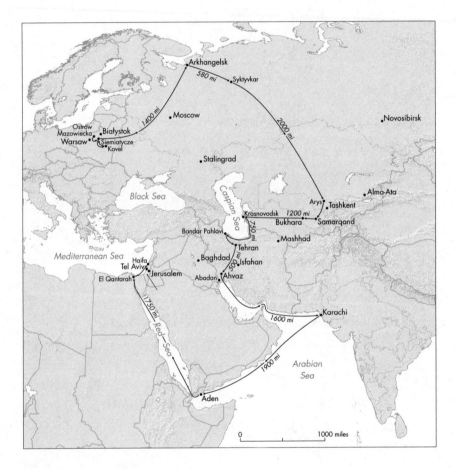

Arkhangelsk
580 mi
Syktyvkar
1400 mi
Moscow
2000 mi
Novosibirsk
Ostrów
Mazowiecka
Białystok
Warsaw
Siemiatycze
Kovel
Stalingrad
Caspian Sea
Black Sea
Arys
Tashkent
Alma-Ata
Krasnovodsk
1200 mi
Bukhara
Samarqand
Bandar Pahlavi
750 mi
Mashhad
Tehran
Mediterranean Sea
Haifa
Tel Aviv
Jerusalem
Baghdad
500 mi
Isfahan
El Qantarah
Abadan
Ahvaz
1750 mi
Red Sea
Karachi
1600 mi
1900 mi
Arabian
Sea
Aden

0   1000 miles

NEW YORK CITY, 2007

My search for the history of the Tehran Children began the day I met Salar Abdoh. Not exactly met. We had eyed each other many times before, not without curiosity, in the mailroom, in department meetings, along the corridors of the North Academic Center, the windowless, drab transplant in the grand old Gothic campus of the City College of New York, where we both taught in the English department. We might have even exchanged a few words. But the last day of the 2007 academic year was our first real conversation, the first of hundreds.

The few years that preceded my meeting with Salar were the hardest of my life. I had an infant who turned toddler but never slept, a shapeless doctoral dissertation, and many classes to teach. I had little paid help and no extended family in New York. Three afternoons a week I would drift into the North Academic Center to teach my classes and drift right back home to my son. At night I wrote my dissertation between feedings.

But one academic year passed, then another. My dissertation somehow came together. Climbing the stairs of Columbia University's Kent Hall on my way to the defense, I ran into my mentor, the late literary theorist Eve Kosofsky Sedgwick, who nodded at me with approval. I felt an unbelievable lightness. At the end of May, I would be marching in doctoral robe and cap at Columbia; in September, my position at City College would change from Instructor to Assistant Professor, which meant I would teach less and earn more. The April spring was gorgeous, with clear blue skies and crisp air. I taught the last class of the semester outdoors, sitting with my students on the freshly mown lawn of Shepard Hall, talking with them quietly about Melville and Freud. On the way back from class I ran into Salar, who invited me and a few others to toast the end of the school year in his office.

Salar's office was lovely, with floor rugs, lamps, and kilims that covered the walls and diffused the blandness of the institutional building, and a sort of sitting area, where a few of us lounged drinking red wine and trading bits of college gossip. I remember noting Salar's old-world mannerisms, a cordiality and decorum that I knew in my father and grandfather but in no one of our generation. I noted that among our colleagues, he was the most curious about Israel, where I grew up, and the least moralistic. When our conversation turned to our love of Middle Eastern seashores—Salar's family had owned a house on the Caspian before the Islamic Revolution—I told him I believed my father had crossed the Caspian on his way to Iran during World War II. I knew my father had also spent time in Tehran then, that he and his sister had been among a group of refugees known as the "Tehran Children," but I didn't know much more.

Salar got up, typed a few words on his keyboard, and called me to his computer screen. On the display was a February 23, 2006, issue of *The Iranian*, an online magazine of Iranian affairs and culture, and on its front page was an op-ed titled "Revealing Errors—Iran, Jews and the Holocaust: An Answer to Mr. Black" by Abbas Milani. I read the words on the screen:

> In early January of this year, a prominent American journalist published a strangely inaccurate attack on Iran, making the country complicit in the crimes of the Holocaust. . . . He claims that if we look at Iran's "Hitler-era past" we will discover "that Iran and Iranians were strongly connected to the Holocaust and the Hitler regime." The facts of history are just the opposite of what Mr. Black has claimed. As early signs of the murderous Final Solution became visible, the Iranian government of the time convinced the Nazi race experts in

Germany that Iranian Jews had lived in Iran for over twenty-five hundred years and were fully assimilated citizens of Iran and must be afforded all the rights of such citizens. The Nazis accepted this argument and the lives of all Iranian Jews living under the Nazi yoke were saved. . . . Moreover . . . when the Nazi killing machines began their slaughter of innocent Polish Jews, 1388 Jews, including 871 children were moved to Tehran where they lived in relative safety till they moved to Israel. . . . *History of Contemporary Iranian Jews* has provided an account of what are called the "Tehran Children."[1]

I stared at the screen for a long time, then back at Salar, then sat down and read the piece more carefully. The Tehran Children, including my father Hannan (Hannania), his sister Rivka (Regina), and their cousin Noemi (Emma) were Polish-born child refugees who in 1943 came to Palestine via Iran. But until that moment I had never thought of the *Tehran* in that phrase as an actual place. That my father was a Tehran Child, I had always taken for granted as simply a fact about who he was, like the fact that he had straight, slightly coarse black hair that he combed back, and small, slanted blue eyes; or that he died on October 10, 1993, a year after he retired from the Israeli Air Force, where he had served for forty-eight years.

And though I am a scholar of comparative literature and trained to read across national boundaries, until that moment I could not imagine the story of the Tehran Children in any other context than the one I had internalized while growing up in Israel: as a successful rescue mission of Jewish children by the World Zionist Organization. My father's story was an Israeli story, a part of the country's mythology, and therefore it could not figure in the historical narrative of any other nation—not least one that had become, more recently, a political antagonist. I didn't even think of my father as a Holocaust survivor. Survivors had a muted aura of shame and anxiety in the Israel of my youth, but Tehran Children were Israelis: kibbutzniks, army generals, media personalities, industrialists. They were not Europe's rejected but Israel's desired, the "lucky ones" who had been rescued by the burgeoning Jewish state. Growing up, whenever I was asked if my father was a survivor, I would answer, "No, he was not. He was a Tehran Child."

The leading scholars in my field of comparative literature—René Wellek, Erich Auerbach, and others—had been refugees. Wellek was born in Vienna and escaped to the United States in 1939; the German born Auerbach was a refugee in Turkey and later the United States. They did not write about the refugee experience but composed, as refugees, odes to national literatures and to a unified, stable European canon. The two foremost twentieth-century historians of the nation, Eric Hobsbawm and Ernest Gellner, were also refugees. Hobsbawm was born in Alexandria, Egypt, to Jewish parents from Poland and Austria, spent his early childhood in Vienna and Berlin, fled to London in 1933, and served during the war in the British Royal Engineers and Royal Army Corps. Gellner was born in Paris, raised in Prague and escaped to St. Albans, England, in 1939. It was from the position of the "mobile and the rootless," as Gellner had called it, that Auerbach wrote *Mimesis: The Representation of Reality in Western Literature* while in exile in Istanbul and that Gellner began to study nations. "When I first saw Berber villages of the central Atlas, each building clinging to the next, the style wholly homogeneous, the totality crying out that it was *Gemeinschaft* I knew at once that I wanted desperately to know, as far as an outsider ever could, what it was like *inside*," Gellner explained.[2]

I was born into the *Gemeinschaft*. I knew what it was like inside. But my inside wasn't a centuries-old Berber village—it was a two-decade-old nation-state with unsettled borders, perpetual conflict, and a population full of citizens who like my father were born elsewhere. That elsewhere—the Diaspora—had no place in my childhood. It was "negated," as the early-twentieth-century Zionist writer Yosef Hayyim Brenner had declared. On account of this negation, Israel became my only home. Part of Israel's raison d'être was to give rise to a child who was a tabula rasa, a child without a painful Jewish past. I was that child. I had no framework for thinking about my father's relationship to Iran or to any of the other places he had lived in or passed through before becoming an Israeli. I didn't even have a framework for understanding his life in prewar Poland, where, as I would later discover, his family had lived for eight generations, a life that had been erased so completely that it seemed not even to have existed in *his* memory. In nearly every sparse apartment in the quiet neighborhoods of the Mount Carmel of my youth was a life that had been lived elsewhere before the war, a complex story of survival, and an entire other family—parents, siblings, sometimes former children and former spouses—who had existed before the war. Nobody talked. Everything was negated.

"You should write your father's story," Salar said. "No," I laughed, "but *you* could write it. You were born in Iran. You're not implicated by the Holocaust. You are heir neither to the victims nor to the perpetrators. And you know more about refugees than I do." Salar and his teenage brothers, as he told me, had fled to the United States after the 1979 Islamic Revolution. Soon I noted similarities between him and my father, microscopic traits and habits, detectable only to one trained by a lifelong cohabitation with a refugee: the way he cut a paper towel sheet in half and saved the second half for later; the way he ate everything off his plate; his slightly anxious relationship to food and to the cold, the caution, the aloneness.

"My father has no story," I told Salar. " 'His portrait I essay, but shall never hit it,' " I used to say to people, quoting Melville, when they asked about him. He was a quiet, ordinary man from a sleepy northern Israeli town, and in 2007, fourteen years after his death, the image I had of him was blurry and impersonal: a cordial, reserved man, a bit severe, prone to occasional bouts of anger. I knew nothing of his family history; nor did I think it could reveal much about him. Words like *trauma, displacement,* and *forced migration*—even, strangely, the word *refugee* itself—did not come to mind in relation to him either. I thought of him mostly as a workingman, a man who lived in a kind of grueling present tense and who fulfilled responsibilities, day in and day out. He showed little emotion and cried only once in my presence, while watching Christopher Walken being pawned by the Vietcong in a game of Russian roulette in *The Deer Hunter*. We watched the film at home on television, my father, my brother, and I, and I remember looking at him—if I recall correctly, it was winter and, as always, slightly chilly in our Haifa apartment—and seeing that his blue eyes were red and tears were rolling down his cheeks.

We had been six at home: my parents, my siblings, and my paternal grandmother Rachel (Ruchela), whom we used to call Achel; a petite, thin woman with pale, wrinkly skin and sharp, slanted blue eyes, like my father's. Hannan had been separated from his mother during the war, and when she arrived in Israel years later, she moved in with him, then with my mother and him, then with all of us. For as long as I could remember, until her death in 1981, she lived in a little room off the kitchen in our quiet apartment atop Mount Carmel in Haifa. We did not speak much to her, and she spoke little either to us or in general, spending most of her days reading in her room or listening to the radio. My mother, who cooked and cleaned for her and washed her clothes, resented her. My father, who would often lash out at my mother and sometimes at us without apparent reason, treated her always with kindness and care. At times, Achel would stay in her room all day, venturing out only when he came home. I recall no fights between my father and his mother, no tension, nothing except a deep, delicate harmony. There were always two teams: him and her, my mother and us children.

When I was six or seven and had just learned to write, I composed a letter to my father, asking why he loved his mother more than us. I tucked it under his pillow in my parents' bed and waited anxiously. When Hannan found the letter, he was furious, scolding me that he would never have dared to write such a letter to *his* father. I remember well the guilt, the shame, the desperate wish that I could take my words back, feelings that plagued me for years. My father did not speak a word to me for a long time after that, and though a lifetime of shared moments, many of them happy, followed, we were never completely at ease together again.

In New York, where I moved in 1992, life became lighter. I married a lighter man, set up a brighter home, began to study literature. My father sent me letters—lovely, well written, surprisingly warm—in which he talked about a possible visit to New York and other plans for his retirement. But that year, after returning from a trip to his hometown in Poland, where he had not been in fifty-three years, he fell ill. He died the next year, at sixty-six, suddenly and shockingly, from the degenerative brain disease Creutzfeldt-Jakob.

I flew in to see him before his death. He could still drive then, though much more recklessly than usual, and we drove down the steep curves of Haifa's Derekh Ha'Yam to Carmel Beach, where we had been together years earlier. Unlike the beach excursions of my childhood—a big, tense, potentially explosive production of towels, tents, coolers, sandwiches, and five bodies crammed into a tiny, un-air-conditioned military-owned Renault 4—it was just the two of us now, each with a small towel, in something like intimacy, even leisure, but not without the tinge of estrangement that had settled between us since I was six or seven. When we got very near the water, he stripped down to his swimwear, folded his clothes meticulously, and placed them and his polished brown sandals neatly on his small towel. He floated in the Mediterranean for a long time, his eyes shut, looking peaceful. *Eize yam*, What a sea, he said, as he used to always say when the water was a blue plateau without a ripple. My father was a man of few words, and now he had even fewer. On our drive home he said, without being prompted, that he was having a few memory problems lately.

When I flew to Israel again a month later, he was speaking Polish—a language I had never before heard him speak—smiling sweetly and calling my mother *siostra*. "Is she your sister?" I asked him. "Of course," he said, perplexed by the question, casually digging into the omelet my mother had just served him on the same small, cluttered, sticky kitchen table where we had taken our meals since I was born. He looked mild and soft, as if the tension and intensity that had been etched into his features for an entire lifetime had simply melted away, revealing the sweet, calm, slightly vacuous face of a Polish-speaking child. Six weeks later he was lying comatose

in the neurology unit at Carmel Hospital, his body convulsing and twitching, his mouth agape as if in pain, and a month later he died.

During the week of the shiva, we flipped through old photos of him:
a chubby boy in a cap, jacket, and long socks, walking ahead of his sister
Rivka, whose name then was Regina, and their parents, Zindel and Ruchela,
on a cobblestone street in their hometown of Ostrów Mazowiecka, Poland;
a tanned, slimmed-down adolescent riding a pony in Kibbutz Ein Harod.
He was chubby again as a mustached Israeli Air Force cadet; he beamed
at his wedding to my pretty young mother—he was thirty-four, she was
twenty-three—as he cut their wedding cake; he appeared on the beach with
a toddler me, and in photos from our trips to American national parks,
taken in the years 1977 to 1980, when Hannan was in charge of Israeli F-15
technical staff training at McDonnell Douglas, the defense contractor, in
St. Louis. Hannan smiling elusively, the enigma of Hannan.

"Had he always been like this?" I asked his cousin Noemi, whose original
Polish name had been Emma. Like this: cordial, distant, aloof. "Or did the
war make him that way?" "Always, he was always like this," she said. "It has
nothing to do with the war." Noemi-Emma, five years my father's junior,
had traveled from the Soviet Union to Iran and from Iran to Palestine with
my father and nearly one thousand other child refugees. I was relieved by
her answer, proud, in a way, of my father's resilience, still unaware that her
response was simply generic: like nearly all Tehran Children, Noemi—who
was seven when the war in which she would lose her mother, father, and
only brother broke out—dismissed the notion that the past had marked
her or her cousins. "We overcame the war," she said. "We became Israelis."

I recounted the conversation with Noemi to Salar when he asked about
my father. "I can't think of what she said without a measure of skepticism," I said, "about 'overcoming,' about becoming Israeli completely." In
the liberal academic circles in which we both moved, Israel was increasingly questioned, shunned even, and often I found myself defending,
halfheartedly, what I called home and what many of my friends called
"the Zionist project."

And the longer I lived in New York, the more I found myself missing life in Israel—its smells, its blue skies, its beaches at sunset—while increasingly troubled by its politicians and its policies, and worried for its future. It wasn't just Israel but the whole notion of national belonging and national identity that I was no longer able to take at face value, having adapted, like other students trained at American universities during the 1990s, the political scientist Benedict Anderson's insight that nations were not historic, ancient entities but "imagined communities" bound together by shared texts, images, and dates on the calendar. Like many doctoral students, I had spent years identifying how such communities were "constructed," "imagined," and "manipulated." That model suddenly seemed inadequate for understanding my father's refugee experience or even for making sense of how my own life had turned out.

"Nations can be beautiful things," Salar said. "And so are national rituals and national belonging, especially when you lose or never had them."

"It's not that simple," I replied, but I was also grateful for his comment. I wondered if my father had shared his life with friends, with strangers, with people other than us. Dori Laub, a survivor-psychiatrist, writes that the absence of empathy in bystanders and fellow victims during the war shaped many Jewish survivors' postwar lives of isolation and friendlessness. I began to wonder whether something like that had also shaped my father's life and in turn my own, which had been influenced so profoundly by his detachment. I still did not know how Salar's investment in my father's history, my investment in his history, and subsequent investments, of me in others' histories and of others in mine—as I began to research my family's past and discovered the interconnected complexity of the pasts it touched—would shape the book that I did not yet know I would write. I still did not know it would be the source of that book's hope, as well as its heartbreak.

But the mention of the Tehran Children in *The Iranian* piqued my curiosity. It was the first time it occurred to me that Tehran was not only the place from where my father was delivered but also the place where he had actually lived during the war. Which immediately raised other questions: How had he ended up in Iran? Had Iran really welcomed the Tehran Children, as Abbas Milani claimed, or was their arrival there arbitrary? The name *Iran* is derived from "Aryan," the Aryans of the East. Did these Persian Aryans have something to do with my father's survival?

And so I began, very gradually, to trace my father's journey from Poland to Iran. I read, and I made plans to travel to my father's hometown of Ostrów Mazowiecka, and from there to some of the other places where he found himself after fleeing across the Soviet border at the onset of the war. I traced his path through the Soviet border towns, to his deportation to a Siberian "special settlement," and to Uzbekistan, from where, as I discovered, he sailed to Iran, then to India and finally journeyed to Mandatory Palestine, where he arrived with his sister and cousin on February 19, 1943. They had crossed thirteen thousand miles from Poland to Palestine, half the earth's circumference. I began to follow that odyssey slowly, carefully, without a theory, a model, a road map, "following the actors"—as the sociologist Rogers Brubaker would put it—rather than presupposing anything. I followed the Tehran Children not on a journey from the "wretched diaspora" to "salvation," not from point A to point B, but on a path in which every point of transit could also have been, and often was for others, a point of arrival. I tried to retrace their route as they lived it, looking at each place they had been, teasing out also the *could* and *would have beens*.

It wasn't, of course, possible to simply reach back into the well of my father's past and retrieve it whole across the bar of seven decades of silence, across the bar of the erasure caused by the Holocaust, across half a century of Communist revisionism, across present-day politics in Israel, Iran, Russia, Poland, Uzbekistan, and the United States—politics that were consequences of the past, but that also shaped its retelling. It also wasn't easy to uncover a history of refugees, who leave little trace and fall outside the memory and memorialization work of nations. And it wasn't only my father's history.

Nearly all European Jews who were not murdered during the war became refugees. "Contemporary history has created a new kind of human beings," the political philosopher Hannah Arendt, herself a refugee, wrote in an essay that she published in New York on the same month and year my father arrived in Jerusalem: "the kind that are put in concentration camps by their foes and internment camps by their friends." "A refugee used to be a person driven to seek refuge because of some act committed or some political opinion held . . . but we committed no acts and most of us never dreamt of having any radical opinion. With us the meaning of the term 'refugee' has changed. Now 'refugees' are those of us who have been so unfortunate as to arrive in a new country without means and have to be helped by Refugee Committees."[3] She was right, of course, but as I would soon discover, there were also different types of refugees, and different routes of refuge: shorter or longer, brutal or a little friendlier.

Most of the Polish Jews who eluded Nazi extermination—roughly 250,000 out of the roughly 350,000 who remained alive after the war—survived, like my father, through deportations in the Soviet Union and then as exiles and refugees in Central Asia, Iran, India, and Palestine. Hundreds of thousands of Catholic Poles, Ukrainians, Lithuanians, and displaced Russians traveled the same roads as they did. Residents of the places where he and other refugees arrived—Russians, Uzbeks, Kazakhs, and Persians, Jews and non-Jews—were affected as well by contact with the refugees, as were rescuers and local and foreign aid groups. The history of the Holocaust refugees was not just their own; it was the history of Poland, Russia, Uzbekistan, Iran, Israel, and to an extent even the United States, which supplied refugee aid. Their fate became entangled with dynamics still playing out today: relations between Poles and Jews; between Iran, Jews, and Israel; between "Eastern" and European Jews; between refugees and citizens; between Jews, Christians, and Muslims. Little had been written on this history, in part because until recently, archives in Russia, Poland, and Central Asia were unavailable; in part because for a long time, and despite decades of Holocaust research and a boom of Holocaust stories in popular culture, the history of those who fled the Nazis into the Soviet Union and the Middle East still did not fall under the category of "Holocaust history." And so I began to write it.

1

"EACH OF US FEELS AS IF HE IS BORN AGAIN"

Iran, August 1942

Seated in her apartment in Tehran, a middle-aged, blue-eyed, sunburned woman named Anna Borkowska tells, in essence, my father's story. Born in Warsaw and still living in Tehran, Borkowska recounts her ordeal from the beginning of the war, when she escaped with her mother from Warsaw to the Soviet side, to her deportation to Siberia, her migration to Uzbekistan, and her eventual evacuation to Iran. She plays a Chopin nocturne on her piano with her eyes half shut, and talks about her carefree childhood in Poland and her arrival in Iran in August 1942, the same month, perhaps even on the same boat, as my father and the thousand other children known in Israel as the Tehran Children.

A couple of years after our initial conversation about my father's wartime stay in Tehran, after returning from a summer visit to Iran, Salar brought back with him a copy of *The Lost Requiem*, a 1983 Iranian documentary on the Polish refugees in Iran, in which Borkowska is the main protagonist. The film, by Khosrow Sinai, does not directly mention Jewish refugees but refers to all the refugees as "Poles who came to Iran." It begins with a scene in a cemetery, a man walking along rows of identical gravestones, simple but not unkempt, with a bouquet of flowers, as the camera slowly pans across gravestones carved with Polish orthography in the Polish section of Doulab, Tehran's Catholic cemetery. In *Pole-e-Firuzeh*, a Persian-language quarterly that Salar brought as well, director Sinai wrote that he began to work on the film after accidentally stumbling on the gravestones

while attending a memorial service for a Christian friend in 1969. "I saw
. . . gravestones etched with strange names. The dates of the deaths were all
between 1941 [and] 1945. . . . I was curious. . . . [The people who were at the
cemetery] knew nothing. At last the priest walked over and said: 'These are
the graves of the Poles who came here from Siberia during World War II.
By the time they arrived in Iran they had endured so much hunger and
sickness that they were dying in droves. But the Iranians were very kind
to them.'" The film tells the story of this "kindness."

Two years into our first conversation about the Tehran Children in
Salar's office, we decided to write a book about them together. I was banned,
as an Israeli citizen, from traveling to Iran, but Salar traveled there often
and could research whereas I, and most others, couldn't. I liked our collaboration; it felt like a buffer between the pain of my father's past and my present. It felt like a way of enlarging the usual lens through which I was used to
looking at the Jewish past, which I welcomed, politically, intellectually, and
emotionally. It seemed like a way that I might overcome ahistoric categories
like "anti-Semitism" and vexed oppositions like Jew/ Christian/ Muslim, a
way of sidestepping the deep and deepening impasse between Israel and
the Islamic Republic. It was good to have the company of a compassionate
observer who wouldn't unravel under the weight of Jewish history.

Together we read the English translation of a Polish-language book
of testimonies by Tehran Children, *Dzieci Syjonu* (*Children of Zion*),
collected and edited by Henryk Grynberg, a Polish-Jewish writer, and
together we visited Grynberg in his home in McLean, Virginia, where he
now lived. I had never before met, or even conceived of, a Polish-Jewish
writer who wrote in Polish—all the Polish-Jewish writers I had known
in Israel wrote in Hebrew—and I had not known Grynberg's connection
to the story of the Tehran Children. My father's sister Rivka, who had
read *Children of Zion* in Israel in its Hebrew translation, told me she had
been shocked by how faithfully it recounted her experiences.

Grynberg's other books—*The Jewish War*, *The Victory*, and *Drohobycz,
Drohobycz and Other Stories*—which Salar and I also read before our
meeting with him, are fictional works based on his experiences inside

Nazi-occupied Europe, with which I was more familiar, nearly all written from the perspective of a child narrator. In contrast, *Children of Zion* was a work of non-fiction, a collage of what are called the "Protokoły Palestyny" (Palestine Protocols): transcripts of interviews with Polish-born Jewish refugees who during the war had journeyed to Palestine via Iran. The interviews, Grynberg explained to us, had been conducted in Jerusalem in 1943 by the Polish Centrum Informacji na Wschód (Polish Information Center), mostly in Polish.[2] The Polish Information Center was an arm of the Polish government-in-exile, a representative body of Polish citizens in occupied Poland and abroad, which was established after the Nazi occupation of Poland and was recognized by the Allies.

Based first in Paris, where a large part of Poland's political and military elites had first fled, then in London, this coalition of the Polish Peasant, Socialist, Labor, and National parties, which was established under the leadership of Władysław Sikorski, a former general and politician who served as its prime minister, was, as I suddenly understood, my father's government when he arrived in Palestine. After the war, Grynberg said, the testimonies, which were collected by the Polish Information Center from thousands of Polish-born Jewish and Catholic refugees, were sent from Jerusalem to England, where the Polish government-in-exile resided. From there they were transferred to Ireland—one of two countries that continued to recognize the government-in-exile after the war—and later to the Hoover Institution at Stanford University. There, Grynberg told us, they sat undisturbed until the mid-1980s, when an Eastern European historian, Norman Naimark, found them and sent Grynberg copies, thinking he might use them for a book. Grynberg compiled the testimonies collected from Jewish children in Palestine into *Dzieci Syjonu*, which was translated into German, Hebrew, and English as *Children of Zion*.[3] In *Children of Zion*'s concluding pages was a list of "Polish citizens evacuated from the Soviet Union and Iran to Palestine," and in this list I found my father, his sister, and their cousin: "Teitel Hannania, lat 14, Ostrów Mazoweicka"; "Teitel Regina, lat 11, Ostrów Mazowiecka"; and "Perelgric Emma, lat 10, Warszawa." Teitel, or 'Tejtel' in its Polish spelling, was my father's surname until he Hebraized it to "Dekel" in the 1950s. Dekel is a direct translation of Teitel. It means "palm tree."

That my Israeli father was listed as an evacuated Polish citizen who might have given testimony in 1943, in Polish, to a Polish Information Center in Jerusalem, was as disorienting as reading the piece by Abbas Milani in Salar's office. And Grynberg himself was like no Polish-Jewish man I had ever met. He and his mother had neither fled nor were deported to a concentration camp during the war but remained in Poland under a false Catholic identity. "I experienced the Holocaust as both a Jew and a Catholic," he said to Salar and me with a sad, nervous smile, "and I know exactly what happened with Jews and Poles in Warsaw." He made us tea, which we drank in the quiet, orderly living room of his Virginia ranch house, and brought up from the basement the pile of original testimonies that had been the source of *Children of Zion*. The testimonies did not include my father's.

After the war, Grynberg said that some of his classmates in Poland were refugees who had returned from the Soviet Union, but he did not know much about them. No one talked in Poland either, and his own wartime and postwar experiences, including the horrific murder of his father by a Polish neighbor, began to be the core of his autobiographical fiction only in the late 1950s. But today, he said, he regretted fictionalizing those experiences, even ever so slightly, for the sake of his readers, which is why he made sure to publish the testimonies he received from Stanford verbatim. I told him that my aunt had recognized herself in his book. We searched, unsuccessfully, for her testimony too in his pile. But on the cover of the German edition of his book, called *Kinder Zions*, I saw her. My aunt Rivka Binyamini—then Regina Teitel—a bony child with blue eyes and pale, thin lips, dressed in an oversize wool jacket that must have once belonged to a middle-aged woman, her hair covered with a scarf. She looked like a Gypsy child, a Bosnian, a Pole, a German even: a generic, fair, blue-eyed child refugee. But I immediately recognized the face, which much later would shed its youthfulness and its anxiety but was distinctively my aunt's: the intense, intelligent gaze, the protruding cheekbones, the pale shade of blue of her eyes, identical to my father's.

"You should do everything to find their testimonies," Grynberg said as he handed me an autographed copy of *Kinder Zions* to give to my aunt. "You will learn a lot. Children do not manipulate information; they tell it as it is." The testimonies he had compiled in his book seemed indeed to be simple, straightforward accounts of the children's experiences, mostly of what had happened before they arrived in Iran. To read them was to read a litany of horrors—flight, bombings, deaths, violence, thefts, starvation, forced labor—devoid of much context. I could not quite take their details in, not yet anyway. They were too overwhelming.

"Let's go visit my friend Homa," Salar suggested, and within an hour we were seated on a low lounging sofa in a Washington, D.C. suburb, at the heels of a fireplace, a glass of wine in hand, laughing with Homa and Lida, a Persian-born Jewish woman whose family was spread across Los Angeles, D.C., Tehran, and Tel Aviv. Lida's sister, who was married to a Muslim man, still lived in Tehran. The rest of her siblings were in Israel, where she too used to live. Once, when she worked there as a waitress, she chanced on then Defense Minister Moshe Dayan. "I didn't wash the hand that shook his for days," she said. We laughed hysterically. Most Persian Jews were Zionist; most left Iran after the 1979 Islamic Revolution; some had been arrested, tortured, or even executed. But Lida's relationship to her birthplace, Iran, seemed far less complex than Grynberg's, or my father's relationship to Poland. The four of us had a fantastic evening together. And shortly after, in July of 2009, Salar and I each left for the Middle East, to look for additional materials on the refugees.

=====

In every household in Israel, Iranian President Mahmoud Ahmadinejad could be heard on TV, rallying the crowds on Quds (Jerusalem) Day: "The pretext for the creation of the Zionist regime is false. . . . It is a lie based on improvable and mythical claims." This was 2009, the year of the Iranian protest movement in the wake of Ahmadinejad's bid for a second term.

The Iranian president had uttered enough Holocaust denials and calls for Israel's erasure that he had become the obsession of Israeli media, which covered news of Iran with little nuance and growing alarm. I was suspicious of mainstream Israeli media coverage, but in New York, when I had searched the keywords *Iran* and *Zionism* at Columbia's Butler Library, publications of Bustane ketab-e Qom, the world's largest center of Shi'a scholarship, popped up with titles like *Jews and Zionism: Research on a Calamity* and other Persian-language variations of the *Protocols of the Elders of Zion*, only more outlandish. "The Zionists export to Muslim countries seven types of gum that not only impede virility but cause infertility," etc.

It was, nonetheless, something of a summer of hope. In Tehran, rather than rallying against Israel on Quds Day, the Iranian opposition mobilized protesters against its own government. In Tel Aviv, Iranian and Israeli flags and the words *Kan Tipatakh Bekarov Shagrirut Iran Be'yisrael* (The Iranian Embassy in Israel Will Open Here Soon) were painted on a ten-foot billboard and hung overnight near Rabin Square. And in Jerusalem, an artists' collective called the Flood announced it was creating its own Iranian "cultural embassy," which would feature works by Iranian artists and "show a different face [of Iran] than the one the media is feeding us."[4]

Salar interviewed Khosrow Sinai in the director's home in Tehran. His interest in the Polish refugees dates back to 1970, Sinai told him, when he began interviewing Catholic Poles who were still living in Iran. But he had no funding ("World War II did not interest the Iranian public then") and abandoned the project. In 1974, after the shah of Iran met with some former Polish refugees who thanked him profusely "for the humanity and hospitality of the Iranians," Sinai was encouraged to finish the film. But he hesitated, fearing to appear to be a lackey of the shah, who demanded to be the film's centerpiece,[5] so he postponed making the film indefinitely until, as he put it, "fate in the form of the [Islamic] Revolution made the decision for me." *The Lost Requiem*, funded by the Ministry of Culture of the Islamic Republic, opened in 1983 to an audience of

Polish-born Iranians and their descendants at a church on Neauphle-le-Château, the street named after the French town that had harbored the exiled Ayatollah Khomeini.

A quarter century later, I was watching *The Lost Requiem* in my childhood home in Haifa, amid my father's photos and his air force memorabilia—tiny framed wings of an F-15 fighter, various certificates of honor—listening to Anna Borkowska and other former refugees praise the "hospitality," "humanity" and "kindness" of Iran. The film was about one nation extending its help to another: "Lest no nation endure what the Polish nation had endured and be forced into exile," its narrator declares, rather bombastically, in its final scene. Sinai was not aware, he told Salar, that there had been Jews among the Polish refugees, and even now that knowledge did not seem to mean much to him either. For me too, with the little I yet knew about relations between Catholics and Jewish refugees in Iran, the difference between my father and Sinai's protagonists, most of whom were Polish women who had married Iranian men, seemed less like a schism between a Catholic and Jewish story as it was a difference in how Borkowska's and my father's stories ended. For him, Iran had been a way station; for her, a final destination. It became her home, as it did, historian Lior Sternfeld claims, for as many as five thousand of the Polish refugees in Iran.[6] She was a Polish-born Iranian.

≡

Back in Israel, I began to seek former Tehran Children: my aunt and her cousin and others who were dispersed across the country. Most remembered little about their time in Iran; one, who had been older, had flickers of memories of visiting Tehran's city center and spending the Sabbath at the home of a local Iranian-Jewish family. But in Jerusalem, I found a treasure. A former child refugee, Ilana Karniel, born Alina Landau, gave me a copy of a travel diary her older brother, Emil Landau, had kept on their journey. The siblings were fifteen and ten when they arrived in Iran, the same age as my father and his sister, Regina. They had been born in Warsaw to a pianist mother and spoke and wrote only in Polish.

Alongside the diary, which was translated into Hebrew by an Israeli novelist friend, was a map of their journey that Emil had drawn. Its precision was extraordinary.

The first detail Emil Landau notes in his first Iran entry, as he describes how his ship, pulled by tugboats, nears the southern shores of the Caspian Sea, is the "rows of Studebakers and Chevrolets" parked in the port. Hundreds of thousands of Allied troops were in Iran. Iran circa 1942 was full of American trucks that were being shipped to them. Drawings of Studebakers blowing the scarves of Persian women as they race against the backdrop of the rock reliefs of Persepolis and Shiraz appeared in *Life* magazine ads continually that year. "Long lines of big, multi-drive Studebaker military trucks rumble past the sites of ancient Persian cities in Iran," said the accompanying ad copy. "Wherever our troops arrive, Studebaker trucks from home are there to greet them."[7] Emil Landau was mesmerized, and his enthusiasm about Iran echoed, at least initially, that of Sinai's interviewees.

On the historic day of August 16, 1942 . . . a small ship with a Persian flag came near the Kaganowich. . . . In forty degrees and some weather, the first group of passengers leaves on the tugboat's dock and after a half hour sail gets to the small port Bandar Pahlavi. Difficult to transmit in writing the first impression. Each one feels as if he is born again, has come to a place out of this world. The port's waters are littered with colorful boats; the surroundings are mowed lawns and flowerbeds; rows of impressive Chevrolets and Studebakers wait for transport, and everything seems good and beautiful, everything smiles together with the Persians, and with the Indian soldiers who gaze at the arrivers with pity. After we are on shore everyone hugs everyone.

Emil and Hannan's first point of contact with Iran was the port town of Bandar Pahlavi, now Bandar-e Anzali, a town on the southeastern shores of the Caspian Sea that in contrast to the Iran of the Studebaker ads in *Life* magazine, was no desert. A Persian photographer who took photographs of the arrivers and is interviewed in *The Lost Requiem* had captured Pahlavi's luscious green mown lawns, and through his lens I could see it through my father's eyes. I had imagined it something like the dusty Egyptian coastal towns I had visited in my youth: the stalls and the storefronts of Sharm el-Sheikh, the busy, lively, disorganized pulse of the Middle East. But Pahlavi was subtropical, more like Southeast Asia; calm and elegant, with winding marble stairways that led from the beach to a manicured park, two marble lions at its entrance. Pahlavi was the first city my father encountered since the beginning of the war that had not been ravaged by war and hunger.

"To us . . . it is a heaven," Dr. Hayim Zeev Hirschberg, a rabbi and scholar who arrived in Iran at the same time as my father, wrote in an article I would later discover, of his first impression of the port town.[8]

"Iran welcomes us," Krystyna Wartanowicz, a Polish refugee in her early thirties, wrote in a diary I would find quoted elsewhere.[9]

There were many such iterations.

$$=$$

The Iran my father reached in the summer of 1942 was, perhaps not unlike today, a highly complex country: a constitutional monarchy concurrent with a succession of repressive dynasties; an Islamic nation that had not fully dissolved its Zoroastrian origins; an oil-rich country courted by and meddled with by the Russian and British empires yet never fully colonized; a poor country in rapid modernization that in 1942 had a mandatory education system, a national university, newly built roads and bridges, and a Trans-Iranian Railroad that connected the Persian Gulf with the Caspian.

The country's bridges and railroads were built in the 1920s and '30s by German engineers. Iranian engineers, including Salar's uncle Yahya, were educated in Germany. German expertise was preferred by Iran's king to that of the Soviets and the British, which already held a stake in the country through the Anglo-Persian Oil Company. Hitler's rise to power did not weaken this German-Persian alliance. In the spring of 1942, when my father arrived in Iran, Uncle Yahya graduated as a chemical engineer from the University of Dresden and went to work for the chemical manufacturer I. G. Farben, infamous as the producer of Zyklon B and as a close collaborator with the Nazis. Nazi Germany needed oil, and Iran needed an ally against Soviet and British pressure.

Der Mythus des zwanzigsten Jahrhunderts (The Myth of the Twentieth Century), a book second only to *Mein Kampf* in its popularity among German readers of the 1930s, draws parallels between "Aryan Persia" and "Germanic Europe": "Aryan Persia constructed for us the religious Myth from which we still draw substance. . . . And Germanic Europe gave mankind its most radiant ideal," the Nazi philosopher Alfred Rosenberg wrote.[10] In 1933, *lran-e Bastan* (The Ancient Iran), a racist Persian magazine financed by pro-Nazi Iranian intellectuals and devoted to propagating notions of the superiority of the two nations, was launched, arguing that Iran was the chosen race of Asia as Germany was the chosen race in Europe.[11] In 1936 the name *Iran*, Aryānām, literally meaning "the Land of the Aryans," officially replaced *Persia*. Aryānām was a nickname that until then had been used only internally. Now the Reich cabinet issued a special decree exempting Iranians (along with a few other non-Germanic groups) from the restrictions of the Nuremberg Racial Laws on the grounds that they were pure-blooded Aryans.

That same year German-Jewish refugees began petitioning the Persian embassy in Berlin for entrance visas to Iran, and the Iranian government, concluding that "it was possible to make use of their presence," began admitting "doctors, engineers, agricultural specialists, foremen, architects, mechanics, musicians, and artisans."[12]

Erica Busse, a pharmacist born in Bavaria in 1911 and trained at Berlin's Kaufmännische Privatschule, received an entry visa to Iran, as did Hans S. Grossmann, a lawyer born in 1902 who possessed a doctorate of law from the University of Leipzig. Elizabeth Kottler and her industrialist husband arrived from Berlin in 1933 with a considerable sum. They imported, traded, and lost, living out the war in Tehran. Joachim (Joshua) Pollock, a young member of the Berlin-based Adass Jisroel, a Modern Orthodox community, arrived with little but ended up doing good business with the Soviets and the British while becoming increasingly religious in Iran.[13]

In a petition from October 18, 1938, "fifty Austrian Jews" appeal to the Iranian Foreign Ministry, which then forwards their letter to the Interior Ministry:

We are . . . very much like any other Austrians. Most of us are well educated. Three of us are engineers, two are architects, one is a doctor, and several are farmers and workers of various kinds. We are respectfully asking that you allow us into your country on a permanent basis. We are about fifteen to twenty families and we would like to be exemplary citizens of your country. . . . We would like to work with you and we have no intention of competing with anyone in your country. Our engineers are experts in a variety of industrial and city planning areas. And they will be able to help you in building governmental buildings. Needless to say we will also be able to help your local laborers and teach them our expertise. We announce ourselves as under the laws of your county already. We are putting our faith upon you to allow us to work in your country and to give us a piece of land so that we can make it flourish. We await your reply.
[Signature unreadable][14]

The petition, which must have been passed on to the Interior Ministry, was included in a book of documents from the Iranian Interior Ministry, which Salar brought back with him from Iran. He returned after a summer of protests, at the end of which Ahmadinejad was reelected president of the Islamic Republic and sworn in with Ayatollah Khomeini's blessing. The research he had attempted for me in the national archives, which had no central database or any decipherable order, yielded little besides old newspaper clippings. But Salar found this book of documents, and in a makeshift archive of Polish documents, located in the basement of a shoe store on Enqelab Avenue in Tehran, some photos and other artifacts. Mr. Nikpour, who owned the store, was an Iranian who had married a Polish refugee. These days, he told Salar, their son Ramin and his family were living in Warsaw, having obtained Polish citizenship after the fall of Communism, while his youngest, Reza, was collecting documents on Polish refugees in Iran inside the archive he had created in the basement.

Back in New York, Salar and I hovered quietly over the petition of the "fifty Austrian Jews," wondering what their odds had been. By 1938 it was, of course, a question of life and death. The wording of the petition suggested that someone intimately familiar with Persian policies and culture had helped write it. The targeted list of professions, the emphasis on non-competition with the locals, and above all the final sentence, "We declare ourselves to be under the laws of your county already and under your protection [*zir e panāh e shomā*]," showed that the letter had been carefully crafted to conform to what the writer believed was needed. "We are putting our faith upon you" was a submissive appeal to an authority that was at once religious, legal, and moral. Salar said it would have spoken keenly and deeply to the Persian mind.

But there was no reply to the petition in the collection of documents, only the petition's translation into Farsi and a note from the Interior Ministry to Prime Minister Mahmoud Jam:

11/1/1938
Dear Honorable Prime Minister,
Fifty Jews from Vienna have written a letter requesting that they be allowed to "permanently move to Iran and that a piece of land be given to them so that they can work on it and make it thrive." Attached you will find the translation of their letter. We ask that whatever decision you make about their request be relayed to us so that we can answer them.
Signed: Abolghasem Foruhar

The Interior Ministry's cover note hardly appeared enthusiastic. Yet the petition had not been tossed aside but was sent in less than a fortnight to Prime Minister Jam, who was known as a level-headed, pragmatic politician.

There were other documents related to Jewish refugees in Salar's book. In a memo dated September 1937 from Jam's office to the Interior Ministry, Jam instructs that a police force be sent to Khorasan Province "to keep Jews from entering Iran" (through the Soviet border). Those who had already entered "should be told that it is not in their best interest to remain there and better for them if they went to Baghdad and awaited their circumstances and fate there. But if they are not convinced . . . it is not necessary to bother them and give them difficulties." Jews from Bukhara, Iraq, and the Caucasus had been quietly living in Iran since the early 1930s. Had the Iraqis been "convinced" to return to their country, their "circumstances and fate" could very well have thrust them into the clutches of the pro-Axis Iraqi prime minister Rashid Ali al-Gaylani, an Arab nationalist who on April 3, 1941, would launch a coup d'état of his government, followed by a two-day pogrom—the Farhud—against thousands of Baghdadi Jews.

In another memo, the Interior Ministry warns the regional police in Khorramshahr Province, on the Iraqi border, about "a number of Jews in Khorramshahr [who] are involved in smuggling [refugees]" and asks that they be sent "to the interior of the country." Officials hardly showed enthusiasm for the refugees, but the policy and its enforcement did not seem all that harsh.

"They give typical Persian instructions," Salar laughed while translating the memos. "We are flexible people, we always go both ways."

"Better to go two ways than only one—bad—way," I said, thinking about the refugee-carrying *St. Louis*, which the United States would turn away *during* the war.

But the pendulum in Iran kept shifting between Axis and Allied affiliation. On March 20, 1939, Adolf Hitler reportedly sent Reza Shah a greeting for Nowruz, the Persian new year.[15] On September 4 Iran declared its neutrality, continuing its commerce with Nazi Germany. A month later, on October 26, Prime Minister Mahmoud Jam was replaced by the pro-German Ahmad Matin-Daftari, who ordered that Persian Jews no longer be employed in government offices or the railway company. To the degree that Matin-Daftari was genuinely pro-German, or mostly anti-British, he rejected hundreds of entry petitions of Lithuanian Jews. Eight months later he was replaced by Ali Mansour, a pro-British politician.

All the while, all borders of the world were closing on Jewish refugees, yet they were still entering or passing through Iran. On May 9, 1941, "Consul Hersh Cynowicz at the Hotel Lalezar" wrote a letter to the Joint Distribution Committee (JDC) in New York, on behalf of fifty-eight refugees. He detailed the ordeal of refugees who had come to Tehran from Vilna, Lithuania, via Moscow. They had originally been in possession of Japanese transit visas to Vladivostok, but the Japanese government annulled their visas. The British embassy in Moscow, which had issued them visas to Palestine, could not transfer them there because transit through Syria for Polish citizens was barred. Then, they wrote, "the Persian consul in Moscow came to our aid and issued transit visas to all of us through Iran." The visas were valid for five days, but due to transit problems, the refugees remained in Tehran for five weeks. The "attitude of the local authorities" is "favorable," the consul wrote, but they had no means of subsistence.[16]

Salar sent me before-and-after photos of the Lalezar, the now decrepit neoclassical hotel from where Consul Hersh Cynowicz petitioned on behalf of European refugees. He called Lalezar Street "the Champs-Elysées of Tehran."

By 1941, Iran had an ultranationalist party, Ḥezb-e Pān Irānist, which advocated an anti-Semitic agenda with explicit echoes of Nazism. It had German workers and engineers. (It also had Iranians in Germany who, like Salar's Uncle Yahya, were waiting to capitalize on their German education as heads of an Iranian I. G. Farben and the like.) German-language Nazi propaganda was broadcast from Berlin, and local Germanophiles were "waiting for the Wehrmacht to punch through Soviet Caucuses and into Persia," as Salar wrote me from Tehran. There was sympathy for Hitler among Shiite clerics, even a rumor that Hitler had secretly converted to Islam and would reveal himself as *haidar* (hero) after the war. There was a large, nervous, yet untouched local Jewish population. "The Jews here are anxious," an observer wrote from Iran in a letter I found quoted in a book on Iran and the Jews. "The front is getting closer and it affects the local population. There have been instances of violence, and rumors of distribution of Jewish property after the enemy comes."[17] Jews were dismissed from the governmental, academic, and military positions they had been allowed to occupy only thirty-five years earlier. Things could have perhaps taken a different, much starker turn for both refugees like my father and the Jews of Iran. But they did not.

On August 25, 1941, two months after the Wehrmacht marched into the Soviet Union and the Soviets joined forces with the Allies, Anglo-Soviet troops invaded Iran, deposed and exiled Reza Shah, jailed Ahmad Matin-Daftari, and anointed the shah's more amenable son Muhammad Reza Pahlavi in his stead. A combination of factors had spurred the invasion, not the least fears that the Iranian oil fields, which had been under the control of the Anglo-Iranian Oil Company since 1909, would be diverted into German hands. Both the British and the Soviets now carved out spheres of influence in Iran, the former in southern Iran, and the latter in the north. Eight months later my father arrived there. By then, and despite continual, low-grade attacks by pro-German Persian groups, Iran had become a center of gravity for British, Indian, Russian, and Polish soldiers, and an array of refugees from various countries. It became a bit of a cosmopolitan center.

In Pahlavi, where my father and other refugees disembarked, he received "wonderful food" from "hospitable Persians," as children reported in the culminating pages of Grynberg's *Children of Zion*.[18] In his diary, Emil Landau wrote that more than once during their first week in Iran, "a well-dressed man, seemingly wealthy," would buy "the entire contents of a sweet or pancake stall" and distribute them among the children.

Sir Reader Bullard, the British ambassador to Iran, attributed the Persians' initial embrace of the refugees to their status as victims of the Soviet Union, whose meddling in Iran they resented. Mona Siddiqui, an Islamic Studies professor, links hospitality to the Qur'anic commandment to "do good" to parents, relatives, orphans, the needy, "the near neighbor" (jāri dhī l-qurbā), and "the neighbor farther away" (l-jāri l-junūbi), a category that at least according to some commentators included non-Muslims.[19]

I was skeptical about both explanations: of Bullard's outright cynicism, but also, though I knew laws and traditions mattered, of thinkers who drew direct lines from religious texts to actions.[20] I did not know whether Iranian Jews were involved in the reception of European Jews. In truth, I knew little about this ancient Persian-Jewish community and how it functioned within the largely Shi'a Iranian society. I learned only that initially at least, my father arrived in Iran and was warmly welcomed. In the beginning that was all I needed to know.

From the multiple volumes on the history of Iranian Jews, I learned that Shi'i Imami Islam, Iran's dominant religion since the seventeenth century, regarded Jews and other religious minorities (*dhimmies*) as impure (*najes*). This belief was "rationalized and substantiated," as the historian Daniel Tsadik puts it, by allusions to these groups in the Qur'an and the *hadith* (the collection of the Prophet Muhammad's statements and actions). The Qur'an sometimes lumps Jews together with Christians as *ahl al-kitdb* (People of the Book) and at other times refers to them separately as *banu isra'll* (Children of Israel) or *yahuid*.

Yahuid, or People of the Book, are sometimes referred to with enmity and at other times with a call for tolerance. The principle, especially in Imami Shi'i literature, is the superiority of the Shia to all other human beings, non-Imami Muslims included.[21] Those who accepted their inferior status received a measure of legal protection under the shelter of Islam; in exchange, they were submitted to conditions, regulations, and laws that demonstrated their submission: "Jews may not buy fresh fruit"; "If a Muslim curses a Jew, the Jew must remain silent and bow his head"; "He who kills a Jew shall go free upon a small payment of blood money"; and so on.

There were limitations on commerce with Jews, for instance, on the purchase of shoes "and other similar things" made of leather. *Dhimmies* were specially prohibited from harming a Muslim; from displaying the "abominable," as in drinking wine in public; from building buildings taller than those of Muslims; and so on.[22] The regulations varied and were applied inconsistently in the different cities and regions of decentralized

Iran; they were also, for the most part, aimed not only at Jews but at all *dhimmies*.

In her book of travels through Iran in the 1880s, the English explorer and naturalist Isabella L. Bird describes how the "Jews of Hamadan [a town 300 kilometers northwest of Tehran] are daily kicked, beaten, spat upon in the streets" and "are regarded as inferior to dogs."[23] The historian Bernard Lewis, outlining the harsh living conditions of Jews of the Ottoman Empire writes that still, "compared to the Jews of Iran," they "were living in paradise."[24] Things improved in 1906, when a constitutional revolution in Iran granted full citizenship rights to all religious minorities, including Jews, but in Tehran's Mahalleh-ye Juhunda (Jewish Quarter), or the Mahalleh, as the Jews called it, residents' conditions remained dismal. "I saw the Mahalleh," Polish-born refugee Dr. Hirschberg would write about his visit there in 1942: "its poor residents, its homes that were nearly sunk to the ground, its small doors, which you cannot enter unless you bend down completely. I was told that they were built this way on purpose—to make self-defense easier during attacks. . . . Many families lived in basements, in caves really, without light and air. Sickly, pale children with all kinds of skin diseases looked at us visitors with curiosity."[25]

But there were others, I learned, who were increasingly living outside the Mahalleh, including a doctor who, before the year is over, will die treating the refugees. Dr. Ruhollah Sapir, a thirty-one-year-old internist with a receding hairline, wearing a fitted gray suit and black tie in group photos in the books of histories of Iranian Jews, was attending to patients at Darmangah-e Mahalleh (Mahalleh Clinic) when he heard of the Polish refugees who had landed at Bandar Pahlavi and were en route to Tehran. Born in 1910, four years after the Constitutional Revolution gave him equal rights of citizenship, Sapir was raised in the budding ideology of Westernization, secularization, and nationalism of Reza Shah and educated at Alliance Israélite Universelle, a European-based Jewish school chain. He was committed to the medical profession in an idealistic but also confident and carefree manner that was attributable not only to the political moment but also to the special status that Jewish physicians had held over the centuries in Persia. "The physicians of Kashan sit in repose, calmness and tranquility, their maintenance ample . . . and all the people of the city obey them, even the gentiles," as a traveler wrote in 1860.[26]

In 1860, the Alliance Israélite Universelle, which Dr. Sapir attended before university, was founded by Parisian Jews under the banner of "working everywhere for the emancipation and moral progress of world Jewry." Its first Iranian school, directed by a French Jew named Joseph Baruch Cazes, opened in Tehran in 1898, followed by schools in Hamadan, Isfahan, Shiraz, Sanandaj, and Kermanshah soon afterward. The schools' explicit purpose, as expressed in a letter to the Iranian ambassador to Paris, was to mold Iran's Jewish population into loyal, productive Iranian citizens: "We take great pride in announcing the opening of a school for Jewish children in Tehran. . . . His majesty's equity and justice lend us hope that the government officials will provide the requisite assistance in this charitable undertaking. We are confident that by educating the Jews, we are providing a service to Iran."

In Tehran, after reportedly witnessing the mistreatment of a Jewish patient in local hospital, Dr. Sapir founded the Darmangah-e Mahalleh, a low-cost medical clinic whose stated mission was "to treat each patient with the utmost dedication, never discriminating against anyone for any reason."[27] It was located inside the destitute, crammed Mahalleh, where Sapir and the other members of Kanun-e Javanan-e Isra'el-e-Iran (Center for the Young Jews of Iran), many of whom were physicians, thought it would be more accessible to those most in need. Sapir himself lived outside it.

By early 1942, the success of the Darmangah-e Mahalleh had encouraged Dr. Sapir and several others to establish the Kanun-e Kheeyrkhah (Goodwill Center), a charitable Jewish organization that would help build Jewish hospitals, medical clinics, and Jewish orphanages in Shiraz, Mashhad, Hamadan, and Isfahan, where the situation of Jews was far worse than in Tehran. It was one of only a handful of self-run Jewish charities that predated my father's arrival in Iran, where care for individuals among Jews and Muslims was assumed to be the exclusive responsibility of the extended family, and one of the first homegrown Jewish organizations. Another had been a small Zionist movement that on November 2, 1917, after Britain declared its support for "the establishment in Palestine of a national home for the Jewish people," spontaneously sprang to life in Iran.

Zionism came naturally to Persian Jews, some of whose family lines hailed back to 597 BCE, when they were exiled from Judea to Babylonia. Six biblical books—Isaiah, Daniel, Ezra, Nehemiah, Chronicles, and Esther—contain references to the life of these original refugees, who continued to live in their own communities across the Kingdom of Persia but never completely severed their connection with the Land of Israel. Since at least the ninth century, Persian Jews had returned to Jerusalem to settle or for pilgrimage, taking the title "Haji," like Muslim pilgrims who after the rise of Islam traveled to Mecca. In 1894, a "Haji Synagogue" was consecrated in Tehran with a stone from Jerusalem. In the wake of the Balfour Declaration, which Persian Jews learned about via a telegram from the Jewish community of St. Petersburg, this practice turned political.

In late 1917, a modest Zionist organization was founded along with the Zionist paper *Ha'geula* (The Salvation). In early 1918, Ebriyat Hamziqat Sefet Eber, the association "for the strengthening of the Hebrew language," began holding monthly meetings at the home of Aziz Haim Ishaq (known as Haji Aziz Elghanian after traveling to Jerusalem). By 1922 it spread to twenty-seven cities across Iran.

Less than four years later, under the banner of creating a centralized, secular government, Reza Shah banned all Zionist activities (and all nonreligious assemblies by any minority group). The Zionist activist Shmuel Chaim was arrested on charges of anti-shah activities and executed, after which all Zionist organizing stopped completely. During the next decade and a half, scores of other political activists were executed or imprisoned. The Anglo-Soviet invasion spurred their release and brought about an atmosphere of freedom that made it possible for Zionism to reemerge. It also, much more prominently, gave birth to Tudeh, a Marxist party whose inception on September 29, 1941 marked the first occasion in which Jews had equal membership in an Iranian political party.

Tudeh's internationalist Marxist agenda, which created a public space for Jews and Muslims to interact as equals, was a magnet for young professional Persian Jews who comprised nearly half of its members and the majority of its journalists and pamphleteers. It also colored the character of Kanun-e Javanan-e Isra'el-e-Iran, which was created under a Jewish yet universalist and socialist banner. Its orientation was nonetheless explicitly and publicly Jewish, with a stated purpose of providing assistance to those in need and helping raise standards of living in the Mahalleh. It was into this Persian-Jewish world that Hannan arrived.

═══

By the time my father arrived there, Iran's Jewish population consisted of other Jewish groups as well: Polish-Jewish refugees who had come from Central Asia with earlier transports; German and Austrian "refugees from Hitler," as one testifier described them; a "large number" of Bukharan Jews who had escaped the Soviets after the Revolution; "Jews from the Caucasus who used their Persian citizenship to exit the Soviet Union and settle in Tehran"; "a community of 'Ashkenazi' Russian Jews who had moved [to Iran] after the Revolution"; Iraqi refugees, including "wealthy Iraqi merchants who sat in Tehran for their business"[28]; and Jews from Palestine: 450 skilled and unskilled workers, engineers, foremen, construction workers, engravers, mechanics, plumbers, accountants, and clerks who traveled by trucks from Palestine to Iran as members of the Jewish labor battalion Solel Boneh.

In early 1942, Burma fell to the Japanese, making Iran one of the only sources of oil for the Allies. The Anglo-Iranian Oil Company, which needed to accelerate production at its oil-refining facilities in Abadan, was short on manpower and expertise, and so Winston Churchill, who was apprised of the situation declared that "the Jews of Palestine will do the work."[29] Solel Boneh, which had been founded as a Jewish construction

company in 1924, had been building infrastructure for the British in Palestine for nearly two decades. Now its workers were dispatched as part
of the Allies' war efforts across the Middle East. Some Solel Boneh workers who had been sent to Iran arrived in Palestine only months before;
some had British Palestinian citizenship; some discovered their Zionism
in Iran; some opposed Zionist activities and even sought to thwart them;
several were outright imposters, traveling to Iran in the guise of being
Solel Boneh employees but actually working on behalf of Mossad LeAliyah Bet, an organization that during the war sought to bring Jewish refugees to Palestine clandestinely.[30]

Iran in 1942, as far as I knew, was "point zero," a tentative moment
in which events could have unfolded in many directions, a moment and
a place in which many people would cease to be one thing and would
become another.

In 1942, the Persian-Jewish community began to organize, forming
the Tehran Committee for Jewish Refugees with members from the
different Jewish groups in Tehran. Among them were a Persian-Jewish
merchant and member of the former Tehran-based Zionist group, a
physician, a pharmacist, two Iraqi refugees, and a Berlin-born German-
Jewish refugee.[31]

American Jewish and Zionist aid organizations arrived in Iran in 1942
to assist my father and the other Jewish refugees. They connected with
Dr. Sapir and others on issues of care for refugees and would continue
supporting the Mahalleh Clinic and other institutions for decades after
the war ended.

In 1942, representatives of Solel Boneh and later of the Jewish Agency
for Palestine, the governing body of the Jewish population of Palestine,
first arrived in Iran and made contact not only with Polish-Jewish refugees but also with local Persian Jews. They also made initial contact with
the Persian king, sowing the seeds of the extensive collaboration between
Iran and Israel that would begin after the war and continue until the 1979
Islamic Revolution.

Though I still did not know it, 1942 Iran was the place where my father ceased to be a "Polish Jew" and began his initiation into a Jewish-Israeli identity, the only one by which I knew him. In a photo of him in Tehran, he looks petite and haggard, standing in the third row of a group of malnourished-looking refugee boys—but his eyes are smiling.

Group photo in Tehran. Hannan is standing fifth from left.

2

"A LIBERAL FAMILY"

Ostrów Mazowiecka, Poland, 1939

I found four photos of my father from before the war. In my favorite one, he is walking with his parents and sister on Warszawa Street, away from the family brewery and home. His posture is erect. His arms are folded behind his back. He is wearing his school uniform from Tarbut, the network of Hebrew-language schools that operated in Eastern Europe during the interwar years: a black-gray jacket, matching knee-high pants, and a cap. His sister Regina, to his left, is in a long-sleeved, knee-high dress and a bonnet. Behind them are their parents: Ruchela is wearing a form-fitting skirt suit, gloves, and hat; Zindel, bespectacled, is in a suit and tie, a cigarette between his fingers, as in every photo I have of him. A tall, muscular, hatless man walks behind them like a bodyguard. I do not know and have not been able to identify him. There's another man whose back is turned to the camera as if looking at others who are coming. The photo is undated, but from the size of the children, it couldn't have been taken before 1937 or so. They look contented, well dressed, and comfortable, their eyes smiling.

Photos lie, of course, but there are ways in which they don't. This isn't a studio photograph; it is a photo of their lives. Their street is wide and immaculately clean; their clothes look rigidly pressed. My father at ten or eleven looks bigger here than in the photo taken of him in Iran years later. He is nearly as tall as his father, and in all other family group photos, Zindel's arm is on his shoulder.

Hannan, Regina, Ruchela, and Zindel Teitel, Ostrów Mazowiecka

I do not recognize this proud, relaxed boy, and I cannot see in him the man I knew as my father.

The boy in the photo is my father before the Holocaust, before the word *Holocaust* was even invented. He speaks Polish and Yiddish, languages I do not know. He does not appear to dread his birthplace in the way I had somehow learned to do, without knowing anything about it. It wasn't just me; every contemporary historian of Jewish life in Poland must now read the Jewish prewar past in Poland across the bar of the Holocaust and the subsequent decades of Communist and post-Communist historical amnesia and revisionism. Everything in that photo—the fabric of the child Hannan's daily life—was annihilated by the Nazis, and its memory was annihilated by nearly half a century of Communism and its aftermath. The Zionist historiography on which I was reared described "the Diaspora" as inherently moribund. When I brushed that aside and reached for the work of non-Zionist, mostly German historiographers of Eastern Europe,

I found myself reading through their biases, internalizing their portrait of a traditional, backward Polish-Jewish society, "waiting for agents of modern, Western enlightenment to deliver them from their abysmal, primitive state."[1] I am a Westerner, and I inherited these notions of Poland as well.

Hannan's years as a refugee shaped him, but I have little photographic evidence: there is a gap between Poland and Palestine, between the Ostrów and the Haifa photos. With the exception of that group photo taken in Tehran, I have no photos of my father, Regina, or any other Teitel family member during their years as refugees. Nor did I have public, widely circulated images that I could consult, such as the iconic photo of the surrendering boy of the Warsaw Ghetto, or the one of the liberated prisoners in Buchenwald, which Art Spiegelman superimposed on a family album in *Maus*.

No iconic photos of the era's million plus refugees existed.

The boy who was my pre-refugee, pre-Israeli father could be known to me only by the place from which he came: a town of about ten thousand. Ostrów's 1857 census lists 2,412 Jewish residents out of a total population of 3,972 (62 percent); and 5,910 out of a total of 7,914 (75 percent) in 1897, a not-atypical growth rate in northeastern Polish towns.[2] At the beginning of the twentieth century, nearly half of Poland's urban population was Jewish. Urban life—the stores, the stalls, the inns, especially in smaller towns like Ostrów—was Jewish. Already by the mid-nineteenth century, Ostrów was what historian Gershon Hundert calls "a community large enough to support the living of the dailiness of life in a Jewish universe."[3] It is a little misleading to call Jews a minority group in nineteenth-century Ostrów and in many other Polish towns. Yet this is the way they are remembered in Poland, Israel, and the United States today.

There is no shortage of books and photos of prewar Ostrów, even of the Teitel brewery and of other Teitel family members. We have population records, birth and death certificates, school graduation diplomas, and *yizkor* (memorial) books. The *Ostrów Mazoweick* volume in the *Kehilot Yisrael* (Communities of Israel) series lists my great-grandfather Michel Teitel among "Persons of Upper Ostrów": "wealthy and the son of the wealthy"; "gentle and noble"; "a true public figure"; "an educated man who knew languages yet remained loyal to the Torah and the Commandments"; "a perfect family man"; "a democrat"; "a man who distinguished himself for his generosity to individuals and the community."[4]

Of course everyone shines in memorial books, but still the ways in which they shine vary. The Ostrów Mazowiecka *yizkor* book remembers Michel as "a person of gentle character": "On the one hand, a perfect family man deeply attached to . . . his family and on the other hand, a true community worker willing to devote all his time and energy to public and individual needs." It commends him for his erudition ("familiar with modern literature and current affairs"), his "pleasant combination of qualities," his propensity for public service ("his involvement in any public activity ensured its success").[5]

In a photo of my great grandfather Michel and his wife, Fejge Teitel, he is looking away from the camera, wearing a long dress coat with buttons, pants that are tucked into his boots, and a military-like cap in the "Russian" style that was permitted by the 1850 prohibition on traditional Jewish dress and typically preferred by Orthodox Jews.[6] He does not wear a yarmulke, though a small knitted skullcap could have been hidden under his cap.

Hannan's grandmother Fejge wears a wig, which was prohibited by law, and looks directly at the camera. Wide-faced and pale-skinned, with large, alert blue eyes, she appears bold and not exactly modest, quite different from the Orthodox women one sees today in New York or Tel Aviv. Her children, Pesja, Icok, Zindel, and Sura, were raised piously. But in their photos, they are dressed in the "German style," more or less according to the standards of Western fashion, clean-shaven, in shorter and dressier coats than their father and in sexier gowns than their mother.

A man who chose German style over Russian style could not, by law, grow a beard. Such a man communicated to the world that he belonged to the middle-upper classes of acculturating Jews, barely distinguishable from Poles of the same class. Looking closely at Icok and Zindel's photos, their dress nonetheless seems slightly antiquated, a less than perfectly cut suit. They seemed like the members of a provincial aristocracy, neither pious and secluded, nor assimilated "Poles of the Mosaic Faith," as the urban Jewish elite of Warsaw and Krakow was called. Their sister Sura, who would leave Ostrów for Warsaw at twenty—unlike her brothers, she was not groomed to work at the brewery—looks smarter in her photos. In Warsaw she would marry an accountant, Adam (Abram) Perelgric, and have two children—Danek (Daniel) and Emma. In the photos that Emma gave me when I met her in Tel Aviv, her mother shows no traces of her pious upbringing: she is gorgeously made up, with thick dark hair, large dark brown eyes, red-hot lipstick, and high heels. She had a good address—Sienna 72—good furniture, and good clothes, and rarely visited Ostrów, where only her young daughter would be sent to summer with the Teitel clan.

Several years later, an Ostrów-born Polish historian, Magda Gawin, would tell me that it was well known that the Teitel family was deeply rooted in Ostrów. They were, I discovered, among the three wealthiest and well-respected families in town, along with the Nutkiewiczs and the Frejmowiczs. My prewar father was much richer than me.

$$=$$

Nearly three and a half million Jews lived in prewar Poland, in the largest and most politically and socially autonomous Jewish community in Europe—9.5 percent of Poland's total population was Jewish. In prewar Germany, by comparison, Jews constituted 0.75 percent of the population; in France, 0.6 percent. But I had not known, until receiving a copy of the Teitel family tree from the genealogical organization Ostrów Mazowiecka Research Family, that Hannan had been born into a clan: eight generations, each birthing up to seven children in a town much smaller than Haifa, the small Israeli city in which I was born. Michel Teitel—born 1771, died 1845, Ostrów Maz—was the first member of the family to appear in Ostrów's records. Michel, Mikhal. My male namesake.

The Poland into which the first Michel Teitel arrived in the late eighteenth century from somewhere in the Austro-Hungarian Empire, was a conglomerate of autonomous regions controlled by local noblemen and priests. This loosely knit federation expanded and shrank, was invaded and annexed, and at some point ceased to exist as an independent kingdom altogether. And for 150 years, during wars and famines, anti-Jewish laws and reprieves and shifting borders and rulers, the Teitel family remained in Ostrów.

Their brewery, the Teitel Broca Browar, was a family-run business, managed by Hannan's grandfather Michel Teitel and later by his uncle Icok, a graduate of the Münchner Brauerakademie—a school for beermakers—in Munich, and his father Zindel, who served as his deputy. Other members of the Teitel clan worked as account and middle managers; some, like my father's family, lived in apartments inside the brewery's compound. In one of our interviews, my aunt Regina, who had worked as a draftswoman in an architectural firm in Jerusalem, drew me a diagram of the compound. In the middle was the brewery's main building, the underground malting area, offices. Around it was a tower with a drying facility and a lightning rod, and storage spaces for barley, bottles, and corks. On the left was a one-story house where Zindel, Ruchela, Hannan, and Regina lived; on the right was a two-story redbrick building where Icok, Hannan's uncle, lived with his wife and four children beneath Fejge's and Michel's second-floor apartment. There were a few miscellaneous buildings in the front, and a parking space for wagons and trucks that loaded beer, ice, and lumber. The children, my aunt told me, would play hide-and-seek in the yard, amid the logs and containers or in the garden in the back. (She recalled vines of green beans and apple trees.) They were not farmers, but they had a few horses, sheep, and cows, and large quantities of barley, a summer crop that was dependent on temperate weather and required a quick and exceedingly clean process of storing, malting, drying, grinding, and extracting.

There was no way to know Hannan outside this clan of highly educated farmers, not because it was ideal or lacking in conflict—Regina had told me that in 1939 they did not even celebrate Passover together—but because it was the source of their and therefore his sustainability. By age twelve, he had already stirred the malted beer, helped carry sacks of barley, and ridden on a few rounds with the drivers. Had there not been a war, my father would most likely have worked at the brewery alongside his uncle's oldest son Ze'ev (Wolf) Teitel. "Hannan loved to walk around the factory and talk to the workers and the drivers. Everyone in the brewery loved him: he was a kind, smiling child," Regina told me. She herself was less friendly as a girl ("our nanny Nanja Aslanova hated me but loved your dad"), with a stormy temperament. Her moods and tantrums gave her the reputation of a monster and made her nanny fear her. She interacted little with the workers and with people outside the family. She rarely exited the brewery's grounds and had never left Ostrów before September 6, 1939, when she was ejected into the wide world all at once.

In the first months of the German occupation, according to Polish sources, approximately 1.2 million Polish citizens crossed the border into the Soviet Union: Jews, middle- and upper-class Poles, the Polish intelligentsia, Ukrainians, Belarusians, and Lithuanians, some of whom had fled in the reverse direction, from Russia to Poland, during the First World War. The decision to choose the Soviet side, which in the 1910s and '20s had brought equal if not greater misery to the region than the German side, was not obvious. Bracha Mandel, a former Tehran Child and a current friend of Regina's, hid with her parents in a forest near their house for over a month, sneaking home every night for supplies and food and waiting to see how events would unfold.

On September 6, 1939, even before the Nazis entered their town, the Teitels fled Ostrów. They packed what they could into two Chevrolet trucks and left behind what had been built over eight generations. September 6, 1939, was the end of Hannan and Regina's childhood, and of their childhood selves, and in their stead emerged tiny adults—the persons I knew as my aunt and father—quiet, responsible, intelligent, taking up as little space as possible, as if they were still squeezed into an overpacked truck.

From the moment they left, they became migrants, tiny particles in the huge tide of refugees that swelled on Poland's roads by foot, cart, wagon, car, and truck. September 6, 1939, was the first of 1,277 days that Hannan and Regina would be refugees, and of nearly five thousand such days for their parents.

$$=$$

Poland was a wound, my father's, my aunt's and mine, by inheritance. That the "Poles were as bad as the Germans" is knowledge I had internalized without ever hearing it explicitly uttered by anyone. But not everyone I talked to shared my apprehension of Poland. Stanley Diamond, a Canadian lawyer and founder of Ostrów Mazowiecka Research Family, the organization that sent me Ostrów's population censuses and my father's family tree, told me that his experience working with Ostrów's municipality archives had been "wonderful." Ilana Karniel, the former child refugee who gave me her brother Emil's diary, told me she missed her Polish childhood every day. Miryam Sharon, another former refugee, said she "felt a strange familiarity" on a recent visit to Poland: "I felt that I know [the Poles], that I forgive them, that they too suffered, that I've always been there, that I grew up on these streets and never left them, that I belonged to this place. I felt no estrangement; I felt I had returned home after sixty years."[7]

My aunt, a generally mild and reasonable person, was not impressed. "The brewery's Polish workers cheered when we left Ostrów," she said. "They shouted 'now the browar will be ours!'" In 1992, a year after the Communist Polish People's Republic of Poland completed its transition to the democratic Third Polish Republic, she and Hannan and their spouses visited Poland. They obtained copies of their birth certificates in Ostrów, tried unsuccessfully to find out about reparations for their lost property, and left feeling depressed. A year later my father died, speaking Polish on his deathbed.

In 2011 I traveled to Poland for the first and what I then thought would be the last time, planning to visit Ostrów Mazowiecka briefly en route to Siemiatycze, where my father's family briefly took refuge after fleeing. In my mind Poland belonged to my father's prewar past—and was largely irrelevant, as far as I was concerned, to the story of the refugees. But as soon as I arrived in Warsaw, I realized that my father's history, including his history of refuge in Central Asia and Iran, was an active part of Poland's present. My hotel in Warsaw, the Ibis, was on Andersa Boulevard, named after General Władysław Anders, the commander in chief of the Polish army-in-exile with whom Hannan and Regina traveled to Iran. Just outside the Ibis, on the site of the former Jewish ghetto, was the Monument for the Fallen and Murdered of the East: a huge, bronze wagon packed with hundreds of crosses, representing Polish citizens who died in World War II while on flight in the Soviet Union. Amid the large crosses was a tiny tombstone with a Star of David to represent the Jews, who in reality had made up at least half of the refugees, among them my father.

That Poland was a tense array of museums and memorials, each with a double Polish-Jewish meaning, was apparent even before the 2015 election of the revisionist Law and Justice Party brought these conflicts to the forefront. There was even a guide, Elzbieta Janicka's *Festung Warschau* (Fortress Warsaw), to sites of Warsaw's Jewish history that were replaced by the city's numerous memorials to Polish victimization. In some cases, like the Monument for the Fallen and Murdered of the East, it was a question of skewed proportions. In Ostrów Mazowiecka, I would soon find out, it was complete oblivion.

And yet, Poland, land of my father's mythical prehistory, was surprisingly pleasant. Salar, who was traveling from Tehran to New York, offered to stop and meet me in Warsaw, from where a Polish guide, Krzysztof Malczewski, would drive us together to Ostrów Mazowiecka. In my imagination, Ostrów was black, brown, or gray, the bleak nothingness of a decrepit, nondescript post-Communist town. But on the crisp June afternoon we traveled along the Grzybowka River from Warsaw to Ostrów, it was green and luscious and sweetly lazy. In a light stream of 1970s cars, we passed sporadic stalls, stores, and wild green grass on the highway side barriers.

On the way, the friendly Krzysztof ("call me Kris") told us he was among other things an importer of Israeli irrigation systems: "the anti-Semitic farmers don't want machines made in Israel, but all other systems break down so they have no choice." His Catholic mother had hidden his Jewish father during the war, he told us when we stopped, at his insistence, to eat pierogi and *gołąbki* at a local gas station. They were exquisite.

In 1900 a routine dip in the Grzybowka River resulted in the fatal illness and rapid death of Pesja, my grandfather Zindel's oldest sister. Two years later a thunderbolt hit the Teitel brewery and caused a fire that destroyed it. But the Teitels managed to hang on, at times even to thrive. Pesja was buried in the Teitel plot in Ostrów's Jewish cemetery, next to her many ancestors. The brewery was rebuilt with a tower and a lightning rod, and on a much larger scale. During World War I, Ostrów—situated at the heart of what the historian Timothy Snyder calls "the bloodlands," the region extending from central Poland to western Russia where the battle between German and Russian ambitions was most violently fought—was occupied first by the Russians, then by the Germans. The Germans requisitioned all food products, brass doorknobs, copper frying pans, kerosene, barley from the Teitel brewery, and finally the brewery itself. The family moved to another Ostrów building, owned by Hannan's grandmother's family.

When the city overflowed with an endless, hungry stream of refugees, thousands of Russians who had been evicted from border cities and fled westward, Fejge Teitel and others organized the charity Hakhnasas Orhim (Hospitality of Guests) to feed them. When an epidemic of typhus erupted, they organized Linas Hazedek (Charity Home), which cared for the sick under the supervision of a doctor and a pharmacist they brought from Warsaw. Then a fund was created to provide loans to retailers and artisans whose livelihood was wiped out by the war.

Several *yizkor* book entries identify Michel Teitel as Ostrów's wartime deputy mayor, who "did much to alleviate the suffering of its residents." Another said Hersz Teitel "served as deputy mayor under the German Occupation." Whatever the case, they became involved in caring for their town's refugees, extending the support of their existent charities to guests and strangers and creating new charities as needed. *Tzedakah* (charity)— "equal in importance to all other commandments combined," as the Talmud says—seems to have been hardwired into their faith and something they had always practiced. But it was mainly during the war years that Jewish communities across Poland, Ostrów included, began to organize large-scale charity work.

Four months after the advent of the war, an American, nonpolitical Jewish relief organization—the Joint Distribution Committee—was founded in New York with the explicit purpose of providing financial and medical assistance to Jewish refugees displaced by the war. Shortly afterward American doctors and medications were sent to Poland, partnering with local charities and philanthropic families like the Teitels across Poland's Jewish world.

When the First World War was over, the Teitels reclaimed the brewery. Hannan's uncle Icok returned from his studies in Germany and assumed its management. The Hapsburg monarchy collapsed, and a Polish revolutionary, Józef Piłsudski, seized power, pushing for an independent Polish state, which was announced on November 11, 1918. Ostrów was now, for the first time since the earliest known Michel Teitel arrived there in the late eighteenth century, part of an autonomous Polish nation-state. They were nervous, yet not entirely unhappy citizens. Piłsudski was regarded as tolerant and pragmatic, and for businesspeople like the Teitels, an independent Polish nation-state was preferable to a Bolshevik Poland. Three months later a new front was opened, again thrusting them deep into the bloodlands, this time between Poland the USSR.

Again the town was occupied, this time by Soviet troops who remained in Ostrów for nearly two years, drinking beer out of the Teitel barrels and working to bring Lenin and Trotsky's revolution to Poland. Under their wing, idealistic young Bund activists organized the town's first trade unions of woodworkers, carpenters, tailors, porters, bakers, and employees of the Teitel sawmill, owned by another branch of the family. They founded a theater, hosted lectures, held teach-ins on the writings of Karl Kautsky, and were executed by the Poles as soon as the Soviets were defeated and the Red Army was evacuated from Ostrów. They were hanged from a tree on Ulica Malkińska, an execution that Ostrów's chief rabbis were ordered to attend while the rest of its Jewish residents stayed home.

Within Poland's new borders now lived five million Ukrainians, a million Belarusians, and over three million Jews, minorities that received political representation in the new Polish government. Ostrów was now bigger, more modern, and more interesting than ever, with new schools, a new library, and a new electric power station. The horses and carts that had delivered Teitel beer for generations were replaced with four-cylinder Chevrolet trucks and Czech Škodas. The younger Teitel children—Hannan and his cousins—began to attend Tarbut, a coed, Zionist-oriented Jewish elementary school chain whose local branch was built in 1922 inside the Teitel sawmill compound. Teachers at Tarbut, recently arrived Galicians displaced by the Polish-Russian war, were cultivated and demanding, bringing to Ostrów's Jewish schoolchildren the standards of Russian education that had shaped their own education.

In 1926, thirty-year-old Zindel married Ruchela Averbuch, a twenty-four-year-old graduate of Ekaterynoslavsky University in what is now Ukraine. In their photos, Zindel, looks attractive and mild: a little heavyset, a little whimsical, with a constant grin, his hand invariably resting on his children's shoulders. Ruchela, boney, sharp-chinned, and carefully dressed, appears older, more elegant, and more severe than him when she in fact was younger and poorer. In Siemiatycze, Ruchela's hometown, which had been Russian and was now Polish, her widowed mother was an importer of fabrics from Krakow. Within a year of their marriage Hannan was born, and four years later Regina.

═══

No trace of Jewish life remains in Ostrów Mazowiecka today, our guide Krzysztof told us, and I had to take him at his word as he speedily drove us on a tour of the invisible prewar city: the auto garage had been a synagogue, the nursery school had been a yeshiva. Nearly all the public and residential buildings that had belonged to Jews before the war—on Plac Ksienznej Anny Mazowieckiej, the old market street, and on Brokowska, Chausée Brokowska, Miodowa, Pułtuska, Rożanska, Koza Jagielońska, Nurski, Solna, Ostrołęcka, Jatkowa, Batorego, and Warszawska streets—were gone, set, I was told, on fire on November 9, 1939. Nothing remained of Ostrów's Jewish past. There was no collision between the town's Jewish and Catholic pasts as there was in Warsaw—no haunting, only plain, uncontested erasure.

Homes on "mixed" streets like Ulica 3^{go} Maja, Malkińska, Pocztowa, Kosciuszki Alley, Ugniewska, Cmentarza, Lubiejewska, and Piaskes were demolished. Ostrów's Jewish cemetery, where eight generations of Teitels had been buried—"more than most of the Poles," my aunt Regina told me on the phone the night before my trip—had been razed and was now a livestock market.

The Teitel brewery was gone as well, and in its stead stood a large, freshly painted middle school whose students were on summer vacation. We walked around the school's grounds, looking for traces that weren't there. From a small stone house adjacent to it, a red-haired woman walked out; "she heard from the house's previous owner," Krzysztof translated, "that every Easter Teitel used to gift beer bottles to his Polish neighbors."

At the entrance to the schoolyard a small stone monument was carved with the inscription:

To MIEJSCE ZOSTAŁO UŚWIĘCONE PRZEZ MĘCZEŃSKĄ KREW
POLAKÓW WALCZĄCYCH O WOLNOŚĆ PODCZAS OKUPACJI
HITLEROWSKIEJ W LATACH 1939–1944.
*(This place was sanctified by the martyr blood of Poles fighting for
freedom during the Hitlerite occupation of 1939–1944.)*

There was no mention of the brewery or its owners. "After your family left," Krzysztof told me, "the Gestapo moved in, and the brewery became Gestapo headquarters. When the Nazis retreated in 1944, they blew it up with dynamite. The name of the street where the *browar* had stood for three generations had been changed from Warszawska to Partyzanci Street. The street, I assume, had been renamed for the partisans who were interrogated and tortured and killed inside the *browar*. Ostrów had written a new history for itself, and someone, presumably me, would have to protest it, to fight for the plaque that would hang next to the monument for the Martyr Blood of Poles Fighting for Freedom and read HERE STOOD THE TEJTEL BROCA BREWERY, 1856–1939.

Ze'ev (Wolf) Teitel, the tall, blond, and apparently brilliant older cousin whom the child Hannan worshipped, had spent the first twenty years of his life at the brewery and would have been next in line to manage it. On his deathbed in Haifa, at eighty, he wrote a detailed account of the Teitel beer-making process, down to the temperature in which the malt was fermented (67 degrees C); the name of the Polish supervisor (Schwintowsky); who did the stirring and how (by hand); the German counting song the stirrers sang; the sweet and sticky yellow liquid that was extracted and sold as a nonalcoholic drink (kvass); and many other details that at the time I read with no particular interest, unsure why he bothered to convey a craft that none of us children, for whom his memoir was written, knew or cared about. Only now in Ostrów, in the face of the absence of everything that had been theirs, did I suddenly realize that he and Hannan were probably the only people in the world to have retained the memory of the Teitels' beer making skill, a craft the family had developed for generations. "Traumatic realism" is what the Holocaust scholar Michael Rothberg calls random details such as Wolf describes: disembodied, unmoored, yet concrete details of a lost past that bring that past alive but also accentuate its absence. The details of the beer making skill remained in my uncle's words, but there was no longer a brewery or brewers in Ostrów.

Not only the Teitel boys' youth but the youths of dozens of other men and boys were tied to the brewery: the laborers, the artisans, the

Icok, Zindel, Hannan, and Regina in front of the Teitel brewery

mechanics, the drivers, the welders, the cleaners: generations and some-times entire families worked at the *browar*. The artisan who hand-carved the wooden beer caps had apprenticed with his father and inherited his job at the *browar*; he carved tiny chess sets for Hannan and Wolf, which the children adored.

Still in Ostrów I could glimpse my father's prewar self: the ice skating in the pond adjacent to the brewery, the mushroom hunting in Ostrów's pine forests on Saturday afternoons, the Jewish holidays, the family's stature, his prescribed destiny at the *browar*, his school, Tarbut, and what would have been his high school, the Liceum Ogólnokształcące im. Mikołaja Kopernika w Ostrowi Mazowieckiej.

As it turned out, the neoclassical building of the Liceum Ogólnokształcące was the only indirect remnant of the Teitel family in Ostrów.[8] "Apart from the many negative aspects concerning the coexistence of the two communities, there were also some positive ones," Andrzej Pęziński, an elderly resident of Ostrów, wrote in an unpublished manuscript on Ostrów and later confirmed to me in person. "Some of the rich Jews—Teitel and others, financially supported the construction of the *gymnasium* building in Ostrów, where their children studied."

Salar, Krzysztof, and I walked over to see the neoclassical *gymnasium* building, much of which remains intact today. On its front outer wall, the words "Built in 1928" were engraved. At its entrance was a granite memorial, "to the teachers who led secret teaching during World War II."

Later that night we visited another elderly Ostrów resident, eighty-seven-year-old Riczard Ejchelkraut, in his crumbling Communist-style apartment complex. He climbed into a crawl space and brought down stacks of *gymnasium* yearbooks. In their rosters were the names of multiple Teitels: Sura Teitel, Berek Teitel, and Wolf Teitel, as well as other Teitel names I did not know. Riczard, guileless and flirtatious, sat under the sunken ceiling and peeling walls of his living room and leafed through the yearbooks with me as Salar filmed us exchanging hand gestures. In the corridor was a large map of old Ostrów. On the walls were old volumes of a local journal, of which Riczard had been an editor. "It's eerie," I said to Salar as we walked into the near-silent Ostrów night, "how huge brick buildings evaporate and paper records—birth certificates, school diplomas, yearbooks—seem to remain forever."

≡

The Teitels did not leave Ostrów in the 1920s, despite the nasty tide of Polish nationalism and sporadic attacks on Jewish property ("pogrom-chiks," as Regina called them), and despite a national emigration policy that strongly incentivized the emigration of Jews and other minorities. Many Jewish residents, including some Teitels, had already emigrated, pushed out by a combination of anti-Jewish violence, Polish emigration policies, and a new, sophisticated industry of obtaining entrance visas to the United States and Australia. For the first time in nearly a century, the ratio between Jews and non-Jews tipped, and Catholics were now a majority in town.

By the early 1930s, Roman Dmowski, co-founder and chief ideo-logue of the right-wing National Democracy Party Endecja and the liberal Józef Piłsudski's chief rival, had local supporters in Ostrów who began to organize occasional boycotts of Jewish businesses and stir up tension. All the while the Teitel Broca Brewery, the sawmill, and other Teitel businesses continued to operate and thrive, and by the mid-1930s they were cultivating more expansive and ambitious busi-ness opportunities than ever. With Prohibition waning in America, where they now had a steady base of relatives and townspeople who could serve as liaisons, Icok and Zindel began preparing to export their beer overseas. If they had made plans or tried to leave Poland, I did not know them.

At night over schnitzel and beer at Usługi Hotelowe, among a crowd of truck drivers and itinerant farmers, Krzysztof and I asked Salar about his father, Ali Abdoh, who had fled Iran after the outbreak of the Islamic Revolution and was forced to leave behind his many assets. Other mem-bers of the Abdoh clan, who were less successful than him, had managed to smuggle their assets out of the country long before January 1979, and so they did well in America, while Ali, angry, died in Los Angeles of a heart attack six months after fleeing Iran. "He thought he was invincible," Salar said. "He was sure he could negotiate with the government." I doubted the Teitels thought themselves invincible, but I knew that even in the late 1930s they did not imagine the worst.

On January 30, 1933, Adolf Hitler was appointed chancellor of Germany by the president of the democratic and parliamentary Weimar Republic.

In September 1933, when Hannan entered first grade at Tarbut, Prohibition in the United States was lifted, and the Teitel brewery prepared for production on a much larger scale for export.

In mid-1934 in Poland, the far-right Obóz Narodowo Radykalny (ONR, National Radical Camp) was formed, and in October of that year members destroyed the tents that Jewish residents of Ostrów had erected for the harvest holiday of Sukkot.

On May 12, 1935, Józef Piłsudski died and with him fell the last stronghold of a pragmatic, liberal Poland. Jews across Poland mourned him, but he was buried in a ceremony attended by Hitler. ONR had its own party in Ostrów by now, headed by a man named Radwansky, who spearheaded and orchestrated a takeover of the town's fabric industry, which had been entirely Jewish-owned. "With the help of ONR, three Polish residents of Ostrów began buying fabrics from a Jewish retailer in Warsaw and selling them in their own store," Wolf Teitel wrote in his memoir, "but they soon went bankrupt and were forced back to buying fabrics from Jewish stores, where even Radwansky shopped, sneaking there on Sundays through the back door."

In 1936, after Wolf was denied admission to the Politechnika Warszawaska despite achieving the necessary grades, the family decided he would further his studies in Belgium. Wolf refused, insisting that if he must leave home, he would sail to the Jews in Palestine and study civil engineering at the Technikum in Haifa. On the day of his departure, the Teitels assembled in the brewery's yard for a group photo: Wolf, tall and slim, in a beige travel suit, is perched between his parents Icok and Leja, who look tense but not despondent. Zindel, Ruchela, Regina, and a chubby nine-year-old Hannan are also there. It is the only family group photo I have of them.

=

3

BORDER CROSSING

From Hitler to Stalin

August 1939 was the tensest month. All that summer Hannan's parents, Zindel and Ruchela Teitel, his grandmother Fejge, his uncle Icok, and all the Teitel relatives and townspeople had been glued to the radio, to the *Gazeta Polska*, and to the Yiddish *Haynt* that arrived in Ostrów Mazowiecka from Warsaw each day. Acutely aware of Hitler's government and the possibility of war, they were skeptical of the *Gazeta*'s calming assurances that the Polish army was prepared and capable of defeating Germany within three months. Yet barley continued to be delivered to the Teitel brewery each week, malted in the underground *mälzung* and dried inside the drying tower. Laborers—half the Teitel brewery's employees were Catholic Poles—continued to stir the fermenting liquid inside the boilers. Bottles of beer continued to be loaded onto Chevrolet trucks and shipped to vendors across Poland. The Teitel children, Hannan and Regina and their cousins—two of Icok's four children, thirteen-year-old Szulamit and seventeen-year-old Pesja, lived inside the Teitel compound and another cousin, seven-year-old Emma Perelgric, was summering with them from Warsaw—continued to play in the front yard and in the vegetable garden in the back. But at nights the adults weighed the odds and considered the options.

On September 6, 1939, six days after the German invasion of Poland, the Teitels fled Ostrów in two of the brewery's 133 HS Chevrolet trucks (the same type my father would encounter nearly three years later in

Iran). They filled the trucks to the brim with breads, cheeses, fruits, vegetables, cartons of eggs, and every nonperishable food they could get their hands on. Heavy winter coats, blankets, pillows, and some clothes. Soap and towels. Cash, jewelry, watches, anything gold or silver. They took their *cancartas*—national identity cards—and their Polish *gymnasium* diplomas, deeds of their properties in Ostrów, including the brewery and five apartments, their marriage and birth certificates, and a photo album.

My aunt Regina described the scene to me in the first of my many interviews with her during my summers in Israel. She was reluctant to talk at first ("*izvi*"—"leave it"—"let's talk about you"), but the more I learned and the more precise my questions became, the more details poured out of her. We would meet at her spacious home in a new tower in Ramat HaSharon, a suburb of Tel Aviv, where she would serve me chicken soup, fruit, and cookies, then sit, very focused and serious, trying to give the best, most precise answers. When she hesitated, she said, "I think it was *x*," or "I'm not sure it was on *x* day." She never second-guessed or filled in the blanks when she didn't know but said, "I was a little girl, I don't remember," or, "Your father would have remembered." When she was sure of a detail, she never wavered, and every time I was able to corroborate what she said, I found that she was right.

As her father and uncle were loading the trucks, she said, dozens of Jewish townspeople trickled into the brewery, offering stacks of cash in exchange for a ride. But there was no extra room. Twelve-year-old Hannan and eight-year-old Regina and their parents took the smaller truck. In the large truck were all the rest: their grandmother Fejge Teitel, seventy-seven; Noemi Perelgric, seven; two relatives, Berek Teitel and his wife, Chaja; and their uncle Icok, with his wife, Leja, and their two youngest daughters. (Icok's oldest child, Ze'ev Teitel, twenty-four, was at the Technikum, a technical university in Palestine, for three years, and the second-oldest, Ruchela, twenty-one, was with her fiancé in Warsaw). The young children sat on blankets atop boxes in the back of the truck. Chaja and Berek were squashed in the middle row amid cartons of eggs. When Chaja complained about the seating arrangement, Fejge set her bulging blue eyes on her and said coldly: "This is a war now and everything has changed." Regina remembered her grandmother's gaze and words vividly.

Their trucks rolled through the large metal gates engraved with the words *Teitel Broca Browar*. They turned left onto Warszawa Street, then a right, another left in the direction of Białystok, and they never saw their home again.

Though Regina (now Rivka), and to a degree her cousin Emma (now Noemi) were excellent sources of information, I was desperate to also find the testimony my father had given to the Polish Information Center in Jerusalem, the one that was missing from Henryk Grynberg's book of testimonies, *Children of Zion*. I assumed that at fifteen—the age that he was when he arrived in Palestine—he would have almost certainly been interviewed. But his testimony was nowhere to be found. I searched for it repeatedly but I did not find it at Stanford's Hoover Institution, where I discovered hundreds of other Polish-language testimonies and thousands of documents of the Polish government-in-exile, including a file folder that contained a smaller blue folder with a Star of David on its upper right corner, the meaning of which I could not fathom. I also did not find my father's testimony at the Sikorski Archive in London, or at the United States Holocaust Memorial Museum, or at Yad Vashem in Jerusalem.

And then I found it, or more accurately it found me, on a snowy afternoon in Boston. I was listening to a conference panel on "Children's War Testimonies" when I heard a panelist read from a testimony of a fifteen-year-old boy named "Chananja Teitel" who described his mother as "a woman a bit over 40 years old, with university education, who graduated from the University of Yekaterinoslav." The testimony was the presenter's primary example in a paper on "Descriptions of Parents in Children's War Testimonies." The rest of the panel was a blur.

The panelist, University of Maryland historian Eliyana Adler, told me she had found my father's testimony at Ginzakh Kiddush Hashem (Sanctification of the Name), a tiny, messy, strangely fascinating archive at the heart of the Gur Hasidic community in Bnei Brak, Israel, a place that, as she put it, was run by "yeshiva *bochers*"—Orthodox scholars—"who don't look you in the eye." Your father's testimony, she said, was one of a small group of testimonies given in Yiddish, not Polish. She did not have a full copy of Hannan's testimony, only a summary, as the archive did not have a copier and did not release material to scholars, only to family members. That night I sent a Hebrew e-mail message to Ginzakh Kiddush Hashem in Bnei Brak identifying myself as Chananja Teitel's daughter, and in the morning a reply arrived with an attached photo of eight yellowing pages. The heading was "PRATAKAL NOM. 26: fon Khanina Taytel," typed in Yiddish.[1]

My father's testimony, as I discovered when I visited the small, homey archive that was lodged inside a Gur Hasidic yeshiva the next time I was in Israel, was part of the collection of David Flincker, the Polish-Jewish journalist who had been his interviewer. I did not know why or how Flincker, a descendent of a Gur Hasidic family and former editor of the Warsaw-based Polish-language Jewish daily *Echo Żydowskie* and the Yiddish *Tageblatt Yiddish Daas*, came to be my father's interviewer on behalf of the Polish Information Center in Jerusalem. And I wondered why, unlike most Tehran Children testimonies, his interview had been conducted in Yiddish. (Had it been his small act of rebellion to demonstrate that he had now switched nations and loyalties? Was it simply Flincker's choice of language?). But I was elated, and surprised, to read the Yiddish testimony, which was riddled with witticisms and idioms—like *es helft vi a toytn bankes* ("it helped like applying cupping glasses to a corpse")—much different from the succinct, laconic Hebrew style I associated with my father.

PROTOCOL NUMBER 26
GINZAKH KIDDUSH HASHEM
TESTIMONY OF CHANANJA TEITEL, 15 YEARS OLD, BORN IN
OSTRÓW MAZOWIECKA, SON OF ZINDEL TEITEL, CO-OWNER OF
THE OSTRÓW MAZ BREWERY
Arrived in Israel from Russia through Tehran in 1943

First paragraph:

> On the 6th day of the war, before the Germans even entered Ostrów
> Maz, we—father, mother and little sister—escaped town. The roads
> were filled with refugees; there was terrible panic. My father, who
> was a *nagid* (a prominent person) in town and who owned a beer
> factory and was well known by all Jews and gentiles, had even more
> to fear than others. We escaped anywhere we could.

Hannan's father and his uncle Icok drove the two trucks in the direction
of Białystok, one hundred kilometers east of Ostrów. Throngs of refugees
walked on the road alongside Polish army tanks and jeeps, herded to the
sidelines by panicked Polish soldiers. Thirteen days earlier a secret adden-
dum to the Molotov-Ribbentrop Pact had divvied up Poland between the
Soviet Republic and Germany. The German Third Army, which had invaded
Poland from East Prussia on September 1, was making its way north toward
Masovia, and *Einsatzgruppen*—SS paramilitary death squads—were
already executing "threatening" civilians, Poles and Jews, along the way.

They stood in traffic. Along the main route from Warsaw to Białystok,
Wojska Lądowe, Polish Land Forces, were encircling and barricading
Ostrów and other eastern towns as German Luftwaffe pilots dropped
bombs directly on them and on the convoys of refugees, killing and
wounding scores and sending ripples of panic among the wave of moving
bodies, already brittle after just days of war. Other children's testimonies
were more detailed than Hannan's succinct one:

> Day after day they bombed our town, so we loaded our things onto
> a cart and started on our way. But just outside town the army com-
> mandeered our cart and we had to go on foot with our bundles
> on our backs. The soldiers chased us off the highway, saying that
> our bundles were like signals to the German planes. We trudged
> to Bochnia at one in the morning. The next morning the planes

returned. They dipped down low, dropped incendiary bombs, and fired machine guns. We hid in a bombed-out house. When things died down, my father bought a horse and cart, and we moved on. But we did not know where to go: whatever place we got to, the Germans immediately closed in, as if they were hunting us down.[2]

From the time I first started reading them, the "Protokoły Palestyny" told an altogether different Holocaust story than is typically known: not the story of survival within the confines of the perverse, rigid logic of the death camp, but the story of being vomited out from the tentative safety of home into a vast, impoverished, ferociously dangerous world. A story that began with the act of fleeing.

On Friday, September 1, panic broke out. Poles, Jews, anyone who could was running away in the direction of Lwow. My father did not want to run away. How could he just set off into the wide world with six children and no money. . . . But when people began saying that the Germans were already in Podhajce and that the last train was about to leave, my father changed his mind. There was a terrible crush on the train. There was no place to sit or stand. People were walking on top of people; children were trampled. New passengers got on at every station, and fights broke out between newcomers and those who were already there. When airplanes approached, the train would stop and people would trample over each other to jump out and take cover in ditches. When the air raid was over, they would cram themselves back into the train, losing relatives and belongings in the process. All the while you could hear shrieking from people who had been robbed, children crying, people shouting. For two days and nights we traveled like this to Lwow.[3]

The children's testimonies varied, but the details were more or less the same. All the children remembered the first days of flight more vividly than any that would follow.

≡

When I interviewed Regina, she remembered one story in particular. The one of Hannan sleeping through a German bombing that collapsed the ceiling of the enclosed terrace in Małkinia Górna, where the family spent their first night away from Ostrów. It was a typical anecdote, a version of which other former refugees I interviewed would often choose to share: a moment of comic relief or good luck, a fateful decision that turned out well, any situation in which parents had made a choice, even a bad one, or did something rather than having something done to them. I imagined they were terrified. Before the war, Hannan had spent a night outside Ostrów only once, for a tonsillectomy in Warsaw, while Regina had barely left the brewery's compound. Now they were thrown into the wide world at once, and in a frantic escape from the Wehrmacht.

During the seventeen days that passed between the Nazi invasion on September 1, 1939, and the Soviet invasion of September 17, in towns designated for Soviet control under the Molotov-Ribbentrop Pact, German soldiers entered to loot, humiliate, maim, and kill, shouting slogans along the line of "Jews, go join your Bolshevik brothers," then retreat a few days later. In Ostrów, one child reports in his "protocol," German soldiers randomly arrested his eighteen-year-old brother, took him and others to a Polish officers' compound nearby, made them kneel in the mud for three days without food or water, and shot any of them who moved. On the fourth day, those who survived were ordered to pave a road, and only on the fifth day were they given bread and water and released.[4] In other testimonies, children describe witnessing people's beards cut off along with "parts of their faces"; old people who were made to stand for hours holding their hands up in the air; holy books that were ripped and trampled on in synagogues; people, including family members, who were ordered to douse one another with gasoline and were burned alive.[5]

I did not know what Nazi violence my father had encountered—he mentioned none in his testimony, and I fantasized that he might have escaped early and fast enough to somehow avoid it. But he had not. During the first days of the war, as I would learn a few years into my research from Yuval Bdolach, a Jerusalem-based gynecologist, Hannan witnessed the murder of an Ostrów family: a mother and four daughters. The woman, Chana Weiss, was Bdolach's great-aunt. "When your father arrived in Jerusalem in 1943, he recounted the murder of her sister and her nieces to my grandmother. Your father saw everything at close range; his was the only testimony," Bdolach said.

German Fieseler Fi 167 bombers, undeterred by the half-obsolete Polish fighter planes that took clumsy shots at them, continued to dive low and target the moving throngs. Within weeks, half of Poland's air force was destroyed, and the other half retreated to France. Most of Poland's navy and infantry decamped soon afterward, some joining other Allied armies. With the military gone, only throngs of civilian refugees were left on the roads of northeastern Poland. The bodies of the dead, like the Weisses, were hastily swept to the roadsides by new waves of refugees. *Yizkor* books and monuments are attached to a town, a nation, a fixed site; there is no memorialization of people who die in between towns and nations, no record of the deaths of the Weisses or the scores of others who died in the first weeks of the war along those one hundred refugee-blanketed kilometers between Ostrów and Białystok.

Roughly one-and-a-half million Polish Jews—nearly half of the entire Polish-Jewish population—as well as ethnic Poles, Lithuanians, and other minorities, ended up within Soviet borders in the first months of the war, whether because their towns fell under Soviet occupation, or, like the Teitels, they fled east to escape the Wehrmacht.

After crossing into the Soviet Union, Zindel and Ruchela Teitel and their children decided to peel off from the rest of the family, which was headed to Białystok, and drive to Siemiatycze, Ruchela's hometown. Ruchela's mother, Esthera Averbuch, and her younger brother Daniel still lived there, running a small textile shop. Ruchela's older married sister, Masha Halberstadt, lived with her husband and two children nearby. Siemiatycze had belonged to the Russian Empire, then to the Soviet Union, and since 1921, to the Polish Republic. Now after a brief but brutal Nazi occupation, from September 11 to 13, 1939, it was returning to Soviet hands.

Siemiatycze's Polish administration collapsed on September 15. On September 17 Red Army troops entered. And by the end of September, the town's administration, schools, and institutions were fully Sovietized, as the town filled with thousands of refugees, its population tripling within the first months of the war. It was a fate that was replicated across all the border towns of Soviet-controlled Poland.

On a beautiful and crisp June morning, having visited Ostrów the day before, Salar and I, seated in the back of a Polish taxi, traveled on the road the Teitels had taken from Ostrów to Siemiatycze. It took us an hour and a half; it had taken them days. Along the way they ran out of gas and had to abandon their Chevrolet truck, replacing it with a horse-driven cart for which Zindel paid a fortune. (*Mamom ve-damim*, a Talmudic phrase, was what my father used to describe the exorbitant cost in his testimony.) They had to abandon most of their belongings as well. Less than two weeks after fleeing, they owned a trunk, a cooking pot and utensils, four winter fur coats, a king-size down blanket, cash, jewelry, watches, and documents. They were now migrants, and their former life was entirely gone.

$$\equiv$$

Unlike in Ostrów, traces of Siemiatycze's Jewish past have remained: Yiddish signs in the long, dilapidated strip of small businesses; a gorgeous eighteenth-century synagogue turned community center that had a strange exhibition of "Jewish life" (one yarmulke, one shofar); a partially intact Jewish cemetery restored by "the Gutman family of Florida"; and elderly Polish neighbors who lived next to the cemetery and happily offered recollections of the Jewish funeral processions they used to watch from their window. Sixty-one percent of prewar Siemiatycze's five thousand residents had been Jewish, according to a 1921 population census.

Hannan's family of four moved into the already cramped family apartment above the Averbuch textile shop in Siemiatycze and remained there for several months. By January 1940, the Soviets placed a statue of Lenin in the town square; imposed a nightly curfew; changed crosses for red stars, photos of Polish politicians for photos of Soviet politicians, and street names from Latin to Cyrillic. They hung banners with inscriptions and substituted the ruble for the Polish zloty at an equal value. They restricted the sale of goods, capped prices, and penalized hoarding, measures that were taken to control not only the local population but also the Red Army, whose starving and ill-dressed soldiers were dazzled by Siemiatycze's plentiful stores and quickly began to devour their inventories.

Acquisition turned to theft, requisition, and finally expropriation of state-owned and private businesses, including the Averbuch textile store. Within a few months, the material basis of existence had been undercut for nearly everyone, from landowners to small storekeepers like Ruchela's family. Ruchela's older sister Masha, along with her husband Yosef Halberstadt and her children Sarah and Hannania, each slightly older than my father and Regina, escaped their now-German-controlled hometown of Siedlce and moved into the grandmother's tiny home in Siemiatycze as well. Then Red Army soldiers expelled all three families—Averbuch, Halberstadt, and Teitel—to a nearby village, forcing them to leave their furniture and belongings inside the cramped home that the soldiers were now seizing.

Zindel decided to head to Kovel, a much larger industrial town nearly three hundred kilometers to the southeast of Siemiatycze. He decided alone, without consulting or sharing his thoughts, still retaining the habits of the man he had been two months prior: "My dad was silent and did not let us say a word," Hannan wrote in his testimony. Before leaving, and despite all the tensions and misery, they celebrated Hannan's Bar Mitzvah. They drank the last Teitel Broca beer bottle they had brought with them and sang together, and my father recited his *aliyah*, or Torah reading, for which he had trained months before in Ostrów. When the children woke up the next morning, a horse and wagon were waiting to take them to Kovel, where they arrived with a sea of other refugees in mid-April 1941.

Kovel turned out to be worse than Siemiatycze. Entire factories had been transported to inland Russia; most finished products—from furniture to food to hospital and school equipment, anything useful—had been carted away. The lines to the mostly empty stores, which are mentioned in every refugee testimony, extended entire blocks. There were murderous fights over food lines, which Zindel largely avoided by shopping on the black market. "There was no work, so that no one could make a living in Kovel," Hannan wrote.

> In the meantime the prices increased every day. . . . As for the stores, one would have to stand in queue [*ogonkes*] the whole day and often return with nothing. The bitterness, both among the Jews and the Poles increased, but one was afraid to utter a word. . . . The little money that we had brought with us from home, and on which we had lived the entire time, began to run low, and there were no prospects for improvement.

The questions that the Polish Information Center asked of Hannan and of other Polish-born refugees in Jerusalem, Iran, and elsewhere focused almost exclusively on the hardship of life under the Soviets. They were assembled, as I would later learn, for a reason: to create a paper-trail documentation of Soviet abuse of Poles, which would thwart the creation of a Bolshevik Polish state after the war. But the testimonies exceeded their original purpose. They contained glimpses of individual lives ("my father went around . . . depressed") and even of friction in relations between Jews and Poles, which the Polish Information Center wished to display in the best light possible. It appears that the testimonies were not, or not entirely, edited.

My father's protocol documented the decline of his father. Zindel was unable to adjust to the new situation, and his class, his skills, his ideology, and his expertise were in direct opposition to the street smarts that were needed in this new situation. He had no ties to the Communists or the Bundists (members of the Jewish labor movement)—in fact, he deplored them. His clothes and manners were a liability, marking him as a bourgeois target for local Communist militias. "My father, who had never been used to the speculation business and was unable to be idle, went around depressed," Hannan wrote. "He didn't allow us to talk, and he himself would not blurt out a word." "Our mother was the one who functioned from that point on," Regina told me, but Ruchela, who was fluent in Russian is rarely mentioned in my father's testimony.

In mid-November 1939, Zindel received a reassuring letter "from the other side of the Bug River, where the Germans were and where my father had his business property," as Hannan wrote. An uncle from Sokołów Podlaski, a town to the south of Ostrów, reported that "the [High] Holidays passed by for him quite all right" under the *Generalgouvernement* (German-controlled Poland). Zindel began contemplating going back to Ostrów. First the Teitels returned to Siemiatycze, then when posters appeared calling for people who wished to return to the *Generalgouvernement* to register at a local government office, they began to consider returning home.

"Perhaps we will succeed in crossing the border" back to the German side, Hannan wrote in his testimony, in the future tense.

$$=$$

From Siemiatycze, Salar and I continued to Białystok, the road that was not taken by my grandfather but was taken by his brother Icok and the family members who fled with him. The two families, each in its own truck, had parted ways hastily in the pretty, sleepy, nondescript town of Zambrów, which Salar and I passed along the way. Zindel had turned south to Siemiatycze, Icok north to Białystok, and the two never saw each other again.

Białystok was the natural place for the Teitels to head when the war broke out. It was the largest town in northeastern Poland, with a Jewish majority (41,900 out of a population of 66,000 in a 1897 population census; around 51,000 in 1939), and it had a strong and wealthy Jewish merchant elite, including a franchise and many clients of the Teitel brewery. It was an epicenter of Zionism and Jewish institutions, with a

Sholem-Aleichem Library containing over twenty thousand Yiddish books; a gorgeous Choral Synagogue; and the Hebrew *gymnasium*, which was now an insurance company that Salar and I passed on our walking tour of the city. It was a Mitteleuropean thing of beauty, with an aura that immediately swallowed us when we drove into town in the early afternoon, as gold light fell softly on the neoclassical buildings and the streets and the center's cafes filled with people.

Our Białystok guide, Lucia (Lucy) Gold, a petite, blond, chain-smoking woman whom we arranged to meet at Hotel Branicki, was a representative of the town's Jewish organization. She was, as she put it, the town's Jewish organization, fighting single-handedly to preserve and commemorate Białystok's grand Jewish past. Like our Ostrów guide Krzysztof and nearly all Jews we would meet in Poland, Lucy was half-Jewish, a descendant of that rare group of Jews who had managed to remain in or return to Poland not only after World War II but also after the anti-Semitic waves of the late 1950s and the 1960s. But unlike Krzysztof, she publicly and openly identified as Jewish, and perhaps for this reason she was less upbeat, more cautious and circumspect, and a bit of a depressive; her office door, Lucy told us as she stewarded us around town with downcast eyes and a tired smile, sometimes got covered with swastikas. On the day of our arrival, a festival featuring Jewish food, books, and music that Lucy had organized ended with the massively attended concert of an Israeli punk rock band. When its heavily tattooed members came to bid her goodbye, her eyes lit softly.

Our tour of Białystok revealed the richly sinister history of every corner of the town's elegant, spacious boulevards. The alluring Viennese café in Kościuszko Square, with its mouthwatering display of *Kaiserschmarrn* and apple strudel, which we devoured, was located precisely on the spot where *Einsatzgruppen* had executed hundreds of Jews less than two years after Icok Teitel's arrival. But on the lazy ordinary June 2012 day when we ate there, nothing, nothing even hinted at that particular Nazi horror, nor at the town's growing refugee crisis in October 1939, when Icok Teitel and his family—including Hannan's grandmother Fejge and his cousin

Emma, who could not be returned to her parents in Warsaw after the war broke out and therefore remained with her uncle—arrived.

Białystok was changed by the Soviet occupation even more dramatically than Siemiatycze or Kovel. Within just a couple of months, its centuries-old textile and leather industry had been transported east in its entirety. Heaps of uncollected piles of garbage piled up everywhere, and scores of refugees continued to flow—and eventually were smuggled—into town.

> When we arrived in Białystok the town was full of refugees, and we barely managed to find a little corner in a school.

> In Białystok it was not easy to get into the synagogue, which was full of refugees who did not want to let new people in. Fortunately we met some friends there.

> We trudged through the streets of Białystok before finding a corner in the overcrowded synagogue on Jerusalem Street.[6]

By early 1940, Białystok was the largest migrant city in Soviet Poland. That spring nearly all refugees were expelled into nearby villages, where land was redistributed, and were ordered to remain one hundred kilometers from the German border. But Icok managed to stay in Białystok and did not think of returning to Ostrów.

Perhaps it was his business acumen that made him recognize much more quickly than Zindel—in the music that blasted in the streets, in the propaganda broadcasts, in the destroyed lawns and sidewalks and the dead flower beds, which were in full bloom again as Salar and I walked through Białystok—that their world had irrevocably changed, and the quicker they adjusted, the better. Or perhaps as Białystok filled with new refugees, Icok had a more accurate picture of life under the *Generalgouvernement*. Perhaps escaped Ostrowers even told him about the mass shooting of Ostrów's Jewish residents—nearly five hundred men, women, and children—on November 11, 1939. Whatever the reason, Icok made the opposite choice from his brother Zindel. He chose not to return to Ostrów. Instead he relinquished his and his family's Polish citizenship for Soviet citizenship, and within a couple of months he was appointed superintendent of beer breweries in the Białystok *voivodeship*.

≡

"I was not entirely accurate when I told you that Hannan never spoke about the war," I told Salar when we headed toward the train that would take us from Białystok back to Warsaw; some Israeli punk rock musicians were waiting at the station as well. In fact, there was always one repeated story: the tale of two brothers who had made two choices during the war. One had made the "wrong" choice—to return to Nazi-controlled Poland—yet survived; and the other had made the "right" choice—to remain in the Soviet Union—and did not survive. It was a story relayed to my siblings and me not as testimony or history but as a grim moral lesson: the understanding of life as fundamentally ironic, human agency as largely futile, and rational choices as meaningless in the face of the greater forces of the universe. It was a philosophy at once stoic and defeatist, by which my father did not consciously live but which perhaps unconsciously hindered his career advancement or at the very least consoled him against the detrimental (though not life-endangering) professional and personal choices he had made throughout the years.

Salar told me about his family members who left Iran early enough or already had portions of their fortunes abroad, whereas his father stayed. In February 1979 revolutionary forces seized Persepolis, Ali Abdoh's soccer team, along with the American-style sports club he had built in Tehran and the rest of his real estate holdings. Shortly thereafter his name was added to a list of candidates to be apprehended. In May, Ali showed up at Wellington boarding school in England, where Salar and his brothers, Sardar and Reza, studied alongside other wealthy children of the Middle Eastern moneyed elite, ordered them to pack up, and flew them to Los Angeles. But the stress had already gotten to him, and he suffered a fatal heart attack within months, leaving the Abdoh boys homeless and penniless, illegal wanderers across America. "You get used to it quickly," Salar said as we walked through Białystok's empty, pretty streets. "You don't even think about it. You just start to scope out the new lay of the land and to do the things you need to do to survive." Was there a figure of a "child refugee" that cut across historical periods and nations? I wondered, or was there no comparison between survival during wartime, in a land of secret police and no food products, and survival in abundant 1980s Los Angeles?

"America had food," Salar said, "but for a long time we had no clue how to get it." He was a teenage boy. Teenage boys, as my father had been during the war, as my own son now was, were hunger—bottomless pits of hunger. Salar and his brothers worked at odd jobs and found food (never enough) but also trouble on the streets of L.A. "It was harsh, but nothing like your father's situation," he said, though neither of us was aware yet how much worse my father's "situation" would become.

"What did it feel like at first? Did you grasp that life as you knew it was over?" I grilled Salar about his transition from his privileged, if moderately miserable life as a rich Persian boy at a British boarding school, to his life as a homeless teenage refugee in America, trying to imagine how long it had taken my father to relinquish the habits of the wealthy, proud boy of his Ostrów photos. "I grasped it immediately. When you are in the middle of it, you don't think about how rotten things are. You do. But first you have to get by from one day to the next. You have to find shelter. Basic things. That sort of thing. You don't cry over what you've lost. There's no time for that. Or maybe you're just too young to fathom the enormity of what's hit you."

≡

When a campaign for Soviet passportization began in April 1940, hundreds of thousands of Jews and other Polish citizens chose to leave Soviet- for German-occupied Poland. Some distrusted and even hated Soviet Russia with an intensity that was deep and deepening; some feared that if they relinquished their Polish citizenship, they would be trapped in the

Soviet Union forever; and some were so beaten down by the refugee life and by the deteriorating conditions in the border towns that they imagined a return home must be preferable.

> My father . . . would not accept a Soviet passport. He said the Soviet air was stifling him.

> My father did not want a Soviet passport and, like all our neighbors from the synagogue, registered to go back home.

> When we had to decide whether to accept Soviet passports, my parents decided not to since that would mean remaining in Russia forever.

> My father saw that life in the Soviet Union was getting more and more difficult and decided to register us to go back home.

> My father registered us, because we received news from the other side that the situation was improving and people were able to eat and on our side things were getting worse and worse.

And in Protocol 26, my father's:

> The Russians hung posters in the street that one should come and get registered and everyone who wants to go home will be sent home to the place he desires. So my father didn't ponder much and filled a registration form where he noted that he wanted to be back on the German side in Ostrów Mazowiecka.

"Our father hated the Communists," my aunt Regina said to me, as if her father's choice had been merely ideological, principled albeit misguided. She did not say, as Hannan's testimony suggested, that Zindel had fallen into a deep, apathetic depression, or that he lacked the skills to survive in the cutthroat world of refugees in the Soviet Union.

Hundreds of thousands of Polish citizens weighed the pros and cons of Germany versus the USSR, using considerations and knowledge deduced from their old lives and their old wars. They balanced rumors of German atrocities against their memories of the relative "civility" of the German occupation during World War I, when a member of the Teitel clan had even served as mayor, and they assessed their prospects for survival in Stalinist Russia.

After a talk I gave in Paris in 2016, the daughter of a former Polish refugee told me that her father, some of whose family survived and some of whom were killed, was tormented his whole life by the wrong choices those murdered had made. "The refugees' self-narration is always one of right, or wrong choices," I told her, but as I was coming to learn, the fates available to the refugees were determined much less by their own will than they thought, and much more by larger, and largely arbitrary forces.

A Russo-German Boundary and Friendship Treaty, a second (secret) supplement to the Molotov-Ribbentrop Pact, stipulated that anyone who wanted to move from the Soviet side of Poland to the *Generalgouverne-ment* would be able to do so. On June 1, 1940, ten months after his family fled Ostrów, Zindel Teitel went to an office of the German Repatriation Commission that was formed to aid these reverse migrants and filled out the application to return, adding his and the names of his wife and children to the list of hundreds of thousands of Poles, Ukrainians, Belarusians, and Jews who had already registered to return to their hometowns.

In the coming week, the application was passed to a Soviet court in Bielsk Podlaski, a town southwest of Siemiatycze, where on July 5 the Teitels were tried in absentia. On July 6 their banishment decrees—handwritten index cards bearing the name, birthdate, place of residence, occupation, nationality, education, and place of exile of each of them—were produced.

Months earlier, on February 19, 1940, B. Bashev, head of the All-Union Timber Amalgamation (AUTC) and the USSR NKVD had signed an agreement stipulating that the latter would supply ten thousand new slave laborers to the former. The AUTC was in need of fresh lumber workers, their corps having been diminished by the Soviet-Finnish war. And so between May and July 1940, five thousand families were deported from the western regions, and 4,250 additional ones, the Teitels included, were to be transported north by the end of that year.[7]

On the night of July 7, 1940, four NKVD men knocked on the Teitels' door at two a.m., to fetch them. Hundreds of thousands would have the identical fate.

> On Friday evening armed NKVD men came into our home and ordered us to pack our things, saying we were going to Warsaw.

> On Friday at midnight there was a violent knock on the door and NKVD men with revolvers drawn ordered us to get dressed quickly.

> At two o'clock in the morning four NKVD men came in, carrying revolvers. One stood by the door, another by the window, and they informed us that we were going to Germany.[8]

Each family was awakened in the middle of the night on its own, packed on its own, was shocked and horrified on its own, but all the accounts are identical. It was always on a Friday, the night of the Sabbath. Always in the middle of the night. Always four armed NKVD men. "The science of arrest is an important segment of the course on general penology and has been propped up with a substantial body of social theory," Aleksandr Solzhenitsyn would write two decades later in *The Gulag Archipelago*. "The sharp, nighttime ring or the rude knock at the door, the insolent entrance of the unwiped jackboots of the unsleeping State Security operatives. . . . Everyone living in the apartment is thrown into a state of terror by the first knock on the door. The arrested person is torn from the warmth of his bed. He is in a daze, half-asleep, helpless, and his judgment is befogged."[9]

The State Security men who entered Hannan's apartment informed Zindel that his family would be "going home in special cars" and ordered them to dress and pack their bags. They then drove them by truck to the train station and herded them into a red cattle car (a "Red Cow," as these cars became known in the history of transports). It was already full, with nearly fifty people. As opposed to Stolypins, railcars that transported prisoners on ordinary train routes, Red Cows did not need to follow regular train schedules and could therefore go anywhere and nowhere, into emptiness itself. The passengers—prisoners—could be told they were going anywhere, or they could not be told at all.

The Teitels were told they were going to Warsaw. The brutal overcrowding on a Stolypin would have been bad enough—people lay on top of each other, with corpses dying under their feet. But Red Cows were worse. One thousand people would be loaded at once into twenty-five or so cars, a procedure that could take hours, even days. Those inside could see little—the small windows had been barred. Outside every exit, convoy guards stood with machine guns. "We were all one piece of filth," my father wrote in his testimony. "The children cried and the adults pounded on the walls, begging for food and water. When they finally fell asleep, at 1 a.m. the next night, Red Army soldiers brought in soup and some pieces of bread." It was

Refugees loaded on Red Cows

the standard transport routine: never enough food and drink and always distributed at night.

Between 1929 and 1931, the Soviet Union had exiled a million peasants aboard Red Cows, which set out from Moscow daily and from other provincial capitals weekly. Germans of the Soviet Volga Region and other national and minority groups living in the Soviet Union had been exiled this way, and now it was the Poles: Catholic and Jews, including Hannan, Regina, Zindel, and Ruchela. Though they did not know it, Ruchela's sister Masha Halberstadt, her husband Yosef, and their children Sarah and Hannania, with whom they had been living in Siemiatycze, were deported as well, on a different train, on a different day.

Emma Perelgric, Hannan's and Regina's younger cousin, who had been vacationing with the Teitels and had fled east with them, and her father, Adam, were also deported. On September 6, when Emma left with her uncles, Adam was in Warsaw with his wife, Sura, and their son. In late September 1939, he too crossed to the Soviet side in order to fetch his young daughter from Białystok and return with her to Warsaw. In Białystok they were detained a fortnight by Emma's illness, then caught with their smugglers on their return trip. According to their banishment certificates, Adam was arrested, sentenced on June 29, 1940, and banished on July 10, and Emma was banished three days earlier, on July 7, though in my interviews with her, Emma insisted that she and her father were sent away together.

By the time the Teitels, the Perelgrics, and the Halberstadts were deported, with the exception of several dozen tailors, mechanics, gardeners, and other specialized workers who had been kept alive to service the town's Nazi administration in Ostrów, there were no Jewish residents left in Ostrów. Warsaw, where Sura Perelgric and her son Daniel remained, was now under Nazi occupation. They stayed put in their apartment at 72 Sienna Street and were later moved to Marszałkowska, inside the Warsaw ghetto.

As for the deportees: their train would typically begin to move in the early morning hours, and it did not take long for them to realize they were heading not west toward Warsaw or Ostrów Mazowiecka but east to an unknown destination, a day or a month ride away.

4

UKAZNIKS

Laborers in Arkhangelsk and Komi, USSR

They loaded us into dark train cars.

They loaded us into train cars with no windows.

They packed us into freight cars, which were then sealed.

They packed us in, eighty people to a car, and sealed the doors.

They packed us into cars that were cramped and dirty and we lay on top of each other.

They kept us for twenty-four hours without giving us anything to eat or drink.

We stood at the station all day and all night without bread and water.

The cars were sealed and we stood in the station for two days and two nights.

The train was standing for Friday and Saturday, and we were given nothing to eat or drink.

In the night the train set off. [1]

Hannan traveled in utter darkness, standing up or half seated, while the younger children slept huddled on the railcar's floor. Around four a.m., as his train passed through Baranovichi, in Belarus, lights flickered through the cracks in the boarded doors and windows, but he could not decipher them. At dawn, when the Red Cow stopped at Minsk station, locals sneaked up to the train and told his parents where they were. "Sooner or later in life," Primo Levi wrote, "everyone discovers that perfect happiness is unrealizable, but there are few who pause to consider the antithesis: that perfect unhappiness is equally unattainable." Levi had experienced "perfect unhappiness" for the first time in his life when he was deported to Auschwitz. Hannan's first nine months as refugee—the upheaval, the decline of his father—had been terrible, but the ride inside the airless Red Cow, for an unknown duration and to an unknown destination and without food and water, must have been, I thought, his first experience of perfect unhappiness. "We could have starved the whole day, begged in tears for something to eat, and it helped like cupping glasses to the dead," *es vet helfn vi a toytn bankes*, he wrote in his testimony. "You could cry your eyes out after a tiny piece of bread. The children were starving the entire days and the adults, who witnessed the lament of the children, wept with them."

Locals who tried to sell or even sneak bread into the trains during stops at stations were driven away. The hole that had been cut in the floor for the disposal of excrement was insufficient. After a week of travel, all were sick with dysentery, unable to make it even to the one hole that was their toilet and over which everyone fought. A terrible stench, which many former refugees recall in their testimony, rose from the living bodies and the corpses, which remained in the cars until they were hauled out, sometimes at the next stop, sometimes only at the end of the journey. "When they unloaded a trainload from the Leningrad prisons in Solikamsk, the entire embankment was covered with corpses and only few got there alive. . . . There were many occasions when they found out who was still alive and who was dead only when they opened up the car

after arriving at the station. Those who did not come out were dead,"
Solzhenitsyn writes in *The Gulag Archipelago*. He called the Red Cows
"Slave Caravans."[2]

Unlike his aunt Sura Perelgric, who was ensnared in Nazi-occupied Warsaw, my father, in his weeks of travel on the Red Cow in July 1940, experienced suffering that was not uniquely Jewish. Centuries before Hannan
boarded the Red Cow, Russia had practiced transport to remote places of
exile as a way of removing (and killing off) political opponents and ethnic
populations. In 1649, Russia's Code of Law created the authority to con-
demn fugitive serfs, rebels, robbers, thieves, religious dissenters, counter-
feiters, beggars, and others (including "anyone who drove his horses into
a pregnant woman and caused her to miscarry") to "eternal exile" in Siberia. During the reign of Peter the Great (1682–1725), many who opposed
the tsar's modernization program were exiled for reasons of state. In 1928–
29, during the campaign against "socially alien elements, pre-Revolution
"bourgeois," former nobles, imperial officers, and intellectuals were
deported from Moscow and Leningrad to the Russian North. Between
1929 and 1933, during the campaign of collectivization, dispossessed peasants who were deemed *kulaks* (wealthy farmers) were deported from the
motherland to Siberia—1,803,392 in 1930–31 alone. The years 1935–40 saw
the deportation of national groups: Germans, Chechens, Baltic nations,
and also Kalmyks, Balkars, Karachays, Turks, Far East Koreans, and
Poles. In 1939–41, some 1.2 million Polish citizens were deported, among
them roughly 600,000 ethnic Poles, 200,000 Ukrainians and Belarusians, and 400,000 Jews, according to Polish sources.[3]

In her 1951 *The Origins of Totalitarianism*, Hannah Arendt called the
fate of the millions of victims of this system a "symmetrical phenomenon" to Nazism. Only there was less documentation of the experience
of entrapment in the cruel, colossal, yet impersonal Soviet machine of
human subjugation than there was in the machine that had been designed
primarily for the elimination of Jews. There was no Primo Levi of Polish-
Jewish exiles, no K. Zetnik, no Aharon Appelfeld. There were no images

of skeletal humans behind barbed wires. There were the "protocols," which revealed how each adult and child lived the shock and suffering of their new incarceration.

> We thought we were going home, and only after some time did we realize we had been deported to Russia.
>
> Everyone started to cry. When we children saw the grown-ups weeping we began crying even louder.
>
> We started to cry and to bang on the door with our fists.[4]

When they stopped at Passazhirskaya station in Moscow, Ruchela tried to plead with a Soviet soldier in her native Russian. He said to her squarely, "You will never get out of where you are going. You and your children will die there and no one will know where you were." After leaving Moscow, the children began to sing a Yiddish tune—its lyrics went, "Mama, I want to remember who I am and where I came from and who my parents were / Mama, this is no country for me"—then fell into dead silence as they rode through denser and denser landscape and alongside endless forests, feeling as if they were being taken off the earth.

$$=$$

In the summer of 2013, I traveled from New York to Russia and Uzbekistan with the goal of retracing my father's transport from Siemiatycze to Siberia. Preparation for the trip, which began months earlier, brought me into contact with places and people I never knew existed in New York City: a Russian travel agency on Kings Highway in Brooklyn where everything was doable and attainable within minutes and for cheap; a Bukharan professor who supposedly was collecting data on Polish refugees in Central Asia but whose credentials I could never find online; and a man who went by multiple names—Viktor Aslanov, Viktor Pirozhkov—the Moscow-based father of my Russian babysitter, who volunteered to accompany me on my trip to Siberia. The sitter, a warm, sharp, enterprising girl of twenty, had suggested that her father, whom she described as a well-connected businessman, could open more doors for me in Russia than any professional tour guide. Viktor spoke little English, so she suggested she come along as my translator.

Traveling from Poland to Siberia turned out to be harder than I expected. I had underestimated the distance, and there were no direct passenger trains to my destination, no Red Cows that could travel to any random point on the vast Russian map. I had not enough time at my disposal to traverse these huge distances by multiple trains. The longer I stared at the map of Russia, the more discouraged I became.

I also did not know the precise location of Hannan's place of exile. (Only later would I procure his, Regina's, Zindel's, and Ruchela's banishment cards, which identified it as Posiołek Ostrowsky in Arkhangelsk.) I grilled Regina and Emma, trying to extract a name, a place, and an account of their transport. Did you travel ten days or two weeks? Were there high or low fences at their place of banishment? What was the precise temperature? Like all questers and genealogists, I was obsessed with precision, an obsession that was a little absurd: Was it this hut? Was it wooden? At some point Regina mentioned something like "Posolok Ostrovsky" ("I'm not sure. Maybe. I can't really remember"), but I could not locate this name on any map, of gulags or otherwise. Perhaps it was a "nickname," I asked her, for a camp where many "Ostrowers" had been exiled? She wasn't sure, nor was she sure of "Arkhangelsk," which she thought all the exiles had used as a figure of speech for a place far off and remote. She repeatedly said she did not know for sure and hated saying things unless she was certain. "Tell me about the landscape you saw on the way." "How many days did it take you to get there?" "Many days?" "A month?" "A fortnight?" "I don't know, I don't know."

In June 1940, the month of Hannan's and Regina's banishment, there were three categories of internment under which they could have been exiled.

There were "regular" prisons like Lubyanka, the former KGB headquarters and prison in Moscow, where high-profile inmates like Raoul Wallenberg and General Władysław Anders were imprisoned, tortured, and often murdered.

There were the gulags of the Gulag Archipelago: corrective labor camps for "political dissidents." On the eve of World War II, the Glavnoye Upravleniye Lagerey (Main Camp Administration) already housed roughly a million and a half inmates. Approximately one hundred thousand Polish deportees labeled as "political prisoners" were sent there.

And there were *posiołki*, "special settlements": the forced exile colonies that were devised during tsarist Russia and perfected by Stalin, and whose main purpose was populating the far reaches of the Soviet empire. You take a population—an entire ethnic group, or so-called minor "subversives" like Zindel Teitel; transport them and their families to an un- or little-populated area; and there, through their sheer desire to survive, they will create a stronghold. Some of these *ukazniks*, or slave laborers, would be used for specific projects of industrialization and nation building, such as the All-Union Timber Amalgamation's building and expansion of railways in the northern Soviet Union. Between May and July 1940, the NKVD "supplied" the AUTA with 4,844 Polish families (out of the requested 5,000), of which 1,040 went to the Arkhangelsk region, 850 to Komi, and the rest to Siberia.[5] Among them were Hannan and his family. Technically they were not prisoners—*posiołki* were not encircled by barbed fences and guards—but in reality they had nowhere to escape.

The greatest concentration of Polish citizens, according to the United States Holocaust Memorial Museum's map of special settlements and gulags, seems to have been in Komi, a central northern plateau at the foot of the Ural Mountains, east of Arkhangelsk and west of the Siberian Plain. The Komi region was "settled" primarily during World War II, though ethnic Komi people had lived there long before. It was at the same latitude as Arkhangelsk, as well as, by some quirky coincidence, the birthplace of Viktor Aslanov, who offered to travel with me to Syktyvkar, capital of the Komi Republic. The distance from Siemiatycze to Syktyvkar was 2,432 kilometers. Viktor suggested we fly from the midpoint, in Moscow: 1,297 kilometers, a two-hour flight. Let's take the train, I wrote him through his daughter: twenty-eight hours during which I'll experience, however lamely, a fraction of my father's trip. Two days before Viktor's daughter and I were to depart for Moscow together, the sitter confessed to me, crying and apologizing frantically, that her Russian passport had expired and she was bailing out.

Salar, who already had other commitments, could not go either, although we agreed to meet for the second half of my trip, to Uzbekistan. In Russia I would be on my own then, or more precisely in the hands of Viktor Aslanov: the tall, pale, bald businessman in black Prada flip-flops, a large silver cross, and a bandanna, who greeted me with a bouquet of white roses at the exit of Vnukovo Airport in Moscow on June 2, 2013.

A fortnight after the Teitels were shut up in their Red Cow, the doors were opened, and Hannan, Regina, and their parents were let off in an unknown station. They were driven by cart twenty kilometers to a small settlement with a few dozen barracks. Russian *kulaks*—wealthy farmers—who had been exiled before them had built the barracks where they had then been housed, eight people or two families to a room. Thereafter the *kulaks* had either died—between 1929 and 1932, 51 percent of the three hundred thousand special settlers in Arkhangelsk alone had died of infectious diseases or starvation—or been removed or promoted as supervisors.

Still, within the gulag universe, and only within it, the Teitels could be said to be lucky. They were lucky to have arrived in July, the warmest month of the year. They were lucky to have brought their coats, which would mitigate the frost and minus-50-degree-Celsius temperatures that would arrive in winter. They were lucky to be housed with veteran slave laborers: a Jewish family from Warsaw that had been exiled two months earlier showed them how to drive away the armies of fleas, lice, mice, mosquitoes, and flatworms, and how to fend off the starving wolves and bears that roamed the forests and repeatedly neared their barracks for food. They were lucky to have had only eight people in their barrack—in some settlements there were thirty, fifty, or even eighty to a barrack. In some settlements there were no beds, and exiles had to build them. In some settlements, there were no barracks, and exiles slept on the earth until each had built a barrack for his family. Some were not allowed to build barracks and slept in tents in the rain and the snow. Hannan had been lucky and would continue to be lucky, a miserable joke.

On the night of their arrival, they were greeted with the slogan "Whoever will not work will not live." In the morning Hannan, Ruchela, and Zindel were marched to the forest and Regina to a makeshift Soviet school; according to Soviet regulations, children over thirteen were required to work and under thirteen to study.

=

Sitting at the wheel of his black BMW X5 SUV, with soft techno music playing in the background, Viktor Aslanov listened as I told him my father's story and did not appear particularly moved. Nor did he seem to comprehend exactly the purpose of my trip. He would have much preferred, I understood quickly even with his broken English, to show me around Moscow and St. Petersburg, his beautiful cities, than to travel to Komi. He would come along on the train ride to Syktyvkar, but only after we spent a day and a half in Moscow. When I asked him about our departure time to Syktyvkar, he answered, "Elvis and Sinatra," at which point I began to suspect he'd understood nothing of what I'd said.

"Everything is good, don't worry," was his mantra, and he appeared totally happy and at ease—quite the opposite of the friendly young Russian woman who'd sat next to me on my surprisingly excellent Transaero flight from New York to Moscow. She had been talkative and helpful on the plane, but as soon as we landed in Russia, she got anxious and quickly disappeared. "Russians had been thrown into gulags for so much as looking at a foreigner and quickly learned to avoid them," I read in Anne Applebaum's 2005 book *Gulag*, which I took with me on the trip.

It seemed that at least in this regard, in placing myself under a wealthy, seemingly well-connected Muscovite, I had chosen well.

Viktor's apartment was in one of Moscow's swanky new towers that protruded in their glitter high above dirt roads, decaying Soviet-era apartment buildings, and unkempt, sad-looking playgrounds. It boasted floor-to-ceiling windows; a marble cooking island with a Nespresso coffee machine and a set of Wüsthof kitchen knives; a black granite bathroom with plush gray towels; a cream-colored master bedroom with black satin sheets and velvet covers; a pink-themed second bedroom ("for my daughter"); and a music streaming system that played when you switched on the lights. The walls had been painted by an artisan whom Viktor had flown in especially from Ukraine, and the chandeliers were imported from Germany. "You cannot get rich in Russia without government ties, which is why many government people own in my building," he said causally, as we passed by what looked like a SWAT team of armed commandos who greeted Viktor with a nod of recognition inside the lobby of his slick, black granite tower. "Just doormen," he said. "Don't worry. Everything is good."

In part, Viktor lacked interest in Hannan's history because exile and forced labor was every Russian's history, including his own—his mother had been sent from Moscow to work in a special settlement in Komi, and like most Russians, he possessed only fragments of knowledge about her and the country's mammoth and quite recent past. "In a quarter of a century, we have not tracked down anyone," Solzhenitsyn wrote in 1973 about the absence of any criminal prosecution of those responsible for the transports and exiles, the starvation and exploitation, the injuries and deaths of millions. Nor has anyone been tracked down in the decades since.

But Russia's past wasn't exactly forgotten, I thought, staring at the unidentified neo-Baroque office building at Lubyanka Square, which was flanked by camera-wielding tourists. The former All-Russia Insurance Company building–turned–KGB headquarters and prison now housed a KBG Museum and a KGB Café, where diners ate on "bureau" desks. But it also continued to house the KGB's successor, the FSB—Federal Security Services of the Russian Federation—and to serve as a prison. Russia's past continued to live in the present in a mixture of selective memorialization, manufactured nostalgia, and erasure, while its present was being lived without a coherent past.

"But why rake up the past?" Solzhenitsyn had written. "Why reopen the old wounds of those who were living in Moscow and in country houses at the time, writing for newspapers, speaking from rostrums, going off to resorts and abroad? Why recall all that when it is still the same even today?"[6]

I had thought of Hannan's life in the Soviet Union as a terrible yet circumscribed chapter that ended as soon as he and other exiles made it outside the country's borders to Iran. But only in Russia I realized that it continued as reality for millions of other men, women, and children. I read Arendt's *The Origins of Totalitarianism* as an analysis of a dark period that had passed, but at the time when she published it in 1951, Stalin was still living and the Red Cows still delivering slave laborers across the USSR. "I had never heard of or studied in school anything of what Arendt or Solzhenitsyn write about," Nataliya Kolmogorova, a twenty-something exchange student from Moscow, had told me after we read both books in a graduate seminar. Aside from his own life in the Soviet Union, Viktor too knew little.

Despite Viktor's protestations, I was bent on visiting Moscow's Gulag Museum, where there was little about the gulag and lots about the life of Leon Trotsky: a collection of undated, decontextualized photographs. I wondered who was funding this expensive piece of real estate, which was nestled among the Gucci and Prada shops of Aslanovska Street, secured by armed guards and plainclothes policemen. A few German tourists were meandering around, but with the exception of Viktor, no locals. We ate sushi at Arbat and had dinner at Café Pushkin, an upscale tsarist-style restaurant that was hugely expensive and full of wealthy foreigners in designer jeans and suits. Café Pushkin featured a traditional menu, nineteenth-century decor, and waiters dressed to look as if they were cut out of a Tolstoy novel, though the restaurant was merely seven years old.

Moskovsky Metropolitan—the 207 miles of subway stations, statues, etchings, and sublime woodwork that Viktor and I had used to travel between Krasnoselskaya station and Red Square—had been built by slave laborers like my father and his parents. It was awe-inspiring and beautiful, severe in its architecture, starkly different from the filthy, energetic feel of New York subways. "Scores died tunneling deep under Moscow. They are pretty much forgotten now, but their work is the pride and glory of Moscow and of Russia, probably the world's most bizarrely beautiful, most efficient, busiest and cheapest underground system," I read in a *Guardian* article that night, lying on my pink velvet bed in Viktor's guestroom. Sebastião Salgado's photographs came to mind, thousands of antlike bodies employed in a single labor. Hannan Teitel, my father: an ant, a body, a serf of the Soviet empire.

=

The alarm rang at two a.m., announcing that the prisoners were to start loading the wood that had been chopped the day before onto trucks that would transport it to train cars. Failure to perform an "excellent job" would result in a "deed" that carried the threat of a six-month imprisonment. The alarm did not stop ringing until the loading was done. No one—not even a young child—was allowed to return to the barracks. Then Zindel and Ruchela were marched to the woods to chop, saw, and drag their day's work back to the barracks.

All families deported to Komi and Arkhangelsk were employed in timber, M. Konradov, head of the Department on Special Settlements of the USSR, noted in his report from that year. To get to the heart of the forest, which was thirteen kilometers away, Zindel and Ruchela had to make their way through thorns and bushes that cut deep creases in their legs and arms. When they cleared the bushes, they startled snakes and rats, and mosquitoes swarmed them, biting every exposed part of their bodies. They and other newcomers, mortified accountants, lawyers, artists, writers, and business owners like Zindel, yelled at the NKVD guards to send them home, to which the standard answer was "You'll go home when the entire forest is chopped." But the forest, along which Viktor and I were about to ride for twenty-eight hours and fifty minutes on railways that had been built by forced laborers, was endless.

On the morning of our trip, Viktor sealed a car sale deal (a nondescript office; a bearded, unkempt buyer from the provinces; a voluptuous blond secretary whom Viktor and his business partner scolded for the speed with which she delivered Nescafe). After we strolled past the blank-faced soldiers patrolling the Kremlin, the grand Bolshoi Theater, and the "Starlite Diner" (an "American café from the fifties"), we headed to Yaroslavskaya station where we boarded, despite my desire to take a third-class coach, a first-class sleeper car. It was luxury, Russian style: a small, stuffy, un-air-conditioned unit, a table, two bunk beds, two rough but clean white sheets, and two military-style blankets.

Viktor had thought of everything to bring for our twenty-eight-hour ride, from slippers to tiny salt and pepper shakers, tablecloths, and all manner of meats and cheeses, which he had crammed into a huge portable cooler. He relied on no one and was always prepared, he said. I had wanted to relive at least a tiny fraction of Hannan's miserable transport to nowhere, for an unknown period of time, in a boarded-up cargo car with no toilets, no money, no connections, no knowledge of how long his train ride would be, starving and scared. But for Viktor, our ride was to be an abundance to counter the misery of his poor childhood in Communist Komi, where his siblings still lived, and of his own mother, an internal Russian exile. Viktor's mother's place of deportation was the place he now called his home, where he had been raised and where his mother was buried, while for Hannan and for me, "Arkhangelsk" was remembered only as a cursed way station, a point en route to a destination, if it was remembered at all.

Each *ukaznik* at Ostrovsky Oblast was required to cut a minimum of three cubic meters of wood per day, a quota that was impossible to fulfill for most deportees. In turn, they received only a fraction of their full salary:

thirteen rubles for every fifteen working days, eighty-seven kopecks per day. After a 30 percent deduction—10 percent for NKVD "protection"; 5 percent for "culture"; 10 percent for the Red Army; 5 percent for "small expenses"—at best they were left with sixty kopecks a day. A kilo of bread cost 105 kopecks, a price that was determined by the forces of the free market, and that had been driven higher and higher by the severe food shortages caused by the Soviet-Finnish war (November 1939–March 1940). But the salary of an *ukaznik* was determined by Moscow.

And the regulations that governed the daily routines of life for my father and his family, even in this small, seemingly forsaken settlement, were a series of strict laws wholly dictated from above: an eight-hour workday, seven days a week; a 25 percent pay reduction for lateness of twenty minutes or under (lateness of over twenty minutes counted as an absence); and a food ration that ranged from 800 grams of bread for the highest class of workers to 400 grams for children. By 1940, a food card system had been instituted for all "residents" in the Soviet Union, who, with the exception of the class of persons charged with the distribution of produce, generally starved. Yet exiles at special settlements who were not defined as "residents" did not even qualify for these meager allowances. During the workday they received a ration of one piece of "bread"—dough that had been soaked in water—and a bowl of "soup." For sustenance during off-hours, they were required to use their salary, which was insufficient to purchase any food product.

Hannan was too weak to chop down trees and "too old" for school. He was therefore assigned with other children to "lighter" tasks: inserting wood trims into the barracks to preserve the heat, delivering food to adults working farther in the forest, harvesting hay while buried to the waist in mud, and lighting fires around groups of laborers in order to fend off malaria-carrying mosquitoes. Roughly 220,000 to 250,000 children— a quarter of the Polish deportees were fourteen or under[7]—built barracks, plucked roots, collected twigs, hunted for mushrooms and berries, peeled tree bark, or burned branches. In other settlements, older children carted coal from mines, set bricks for railroads, or worked in factories. Their daily quotas, like the adults', were unattainable: plucking 60 roots a day with bare hands, burning 2.5 square acres of wet branches with one box of matches. Hannan received, at best, 400 grams of bread, if he did not have 25 percent deducted for lateness.

In hundreds of settlements across the Soviet Union, Polish citizens— Jews and Catholics—endured the same fate as Hannan and his family. In Posiołek 18 in Poyaminka, Arkhangelsk, Emma Perelgric recited the tenets of Communism, while her father Adam labored. In another settlement, Hannan's aunt on his maternal side, Masha Halberstadt, also chopped down trees with her husband and older son, while their young daughter Sarah "studied." Each day followed the next in a mundane, body-crushing routine with no end in sight.

=

Present-day Russia as an investor's heaven was the first topic of conversation during Viktor's and my twenty-nine-hour trip north: "Thirteen percent income tax, thirteen percent interest on money in the bank," as he put it. "My apartment is worth two million dollars, and I can rent it for ten thousand dollars a month. But for tax purposes it was valued at one hundred thousand dollars. The government people who have apartments in the building need to make their money." He grinned. It was hard to gauge where he stood on everything, appearing to be a critic of both the Soviet Union and modern Russia, but also a player who had benefited from both systems.

Viktor's father, an ethnic Komi, had been a principled, unwavering party man, and so Viktor had passed his childhood in perpetual hunger. Then in the early 1980s, at sixteen, he began buying overstocked, expired medicines from pharmacies and reselling them on the black market for a 25 percent profit. With these profits he started buying American jeans in Moscow and reselling them in Komi, making so much cash by seventeen that he could secretly support his mother and two sisters and buy cake at the town's single café. There he met Yakov, the Leningrad-born son of a prominent Jewish journalist, twenty years his senior, who became a lifelong friend and mentor. "Yakov is a 100 percent Jew," Viktor said as we were nearing Syktyvkar. The wave of official Soviet anti-Semitism in the wake of the 1967 Arab-Israeli war had made him unemployable in Leningrad, Yakov would tell me a day later, and so he ended up in Komi: "No one would hire a Jew in Leningrad, not even in cleaning, but in Komi they didn't care."

A year under the urbane Yakov's tutelage convinced Viktor that he must spread his wings beyond Komi, and at eighteen, having already married a dancer he had impregnated, he made his move toward Leningrad and eventually Moscow, where he expanded his businesses. "My wife's father was a government official in Komi. He didn't approve of my activities, but he saw that his daughter had what to eat." Viktor grinned again over the *pelmeni* and vodka he had brought from home. He was distrustful of the train's cleanliness. "I raise a glass to my friend Yakov's honor." He drank his shot of vodka and immediately disappeared to wash our cups.

When it became clear to Hannan and his parents and other recent arrivals at Posiołek Ostrowsky that adherence to its rules and regulations could lead either to slow death by starvation or a fast death by exhaustion, accident, or disease, they began to protest. After a week, a Jewish woman, Jarzembiak, who was about to be imprisoned for six months for failing to complete her work, grabbed a knife and threatened to stab the commandant, who in turn grabbed a revolver. Hannan and the rest of the camp's inhabitants gathered around them, sure it would end in bloodshed. But after an hourlong standoff, Jarzembiak was sent to prison. From that point on, assembly for any reason other than a scheduled "lecture" or mandatory camp event was forbidden.

Then came pleading and bargaining by Russian-speaking Ruchela as she tried to negotiate a reduced quota for her husband, Zindel, who began to have chest pains and cough incessantly. The commandant, respectful and polite in Ruchela's presence, advised her to tell her husband to carry on. "If you don't endure, you and your family will die." She received the same answer from the camp's doctor, an exile like them, who refused to release my grandfather from work. "No one is exempt," he told Ruchela, "not even pregnant or old women," Hannan reported in his testimony. The doctor was polite and firm.

The Ukrainian *kulaks* who had been exiled here before them, some of whom were now their guards were anti-Semitic, anti-Polish, and in general hardened by camp life. They would herd the Poles and Jews to the forest and inform on them whenever they could. Except for the commandant and a handful of NKVD, most of those in charge were themselves exiles whose relative positions of power were tenuous. For everyone who held a superior position, however slight, the supreme goal was to keep the machine going continuously and without a glitch.

On July 9, 1940, an inspector named Sukharov wrote a memo to the Ministry of Health in which he detailed the "very bad" conditions in the special settlements of Komi: falling barrack ceilings and leaking roofs; 1.5 square meters of living space per person; people sleeping on double-planked bunks; the absence of laundry and washing devices; mosquitoes swarming small children; people going without bread for two days; no milk and sugar for babies; many cases of mushroom poisoning; and an outbreak of typhus. (Sukharov reported that he had seen six cases, four of whom were fatal in the four days he visited the settlements.) There was no way, he wrote, to separate the sick from the healthy, as they all lived and worked in the same area. He requested isolation material and funds for building a new school and houses. There was no reply to this or to a subsequent memo that called for the AUTC to release twelve million rubles to build proper accommodations for laborers. Nothing was ever changed or improved, nor was it expected to be, even by Inspector Sukharov, whose job it was to produce a report, not to attend to its implementation.

The twenty-nine-hour train ride from Moscow to Komi's capital Syktyvkar passed quickly and pleasantly. I stared out the window at the masses of Siberian pines and birches and spruces and larches—forests that my grandparents and millions of others had chopped down—gliding by. I filmed them initially, then gave in to boredom and monotony. Komi's main industry was still timber. At every station were containers of wood beams, and every gift I would receive from Viktor's local friends— engraved spoons, pencils, boxes—was made of wood. His friends—Yakov, a bespectacled, stocky seventy-year-old with a good mane of brown hair and a perpetual grin, and Lidiya, an extremely made-up childhood friend and former lover—were warm, effusive even, when they met us at the Syktyvkar station. But everyone else looked anxious and unsmiling. The city's drab Soviet residence buildings, its sad, lackluster shops, the scores of drunks who rolled on sidewalks, benches, and even outside my expensive, "American-style" Hotel Syktyvkar, weighed on me immediately. The city had given rise to a slew of orphanages, which until recently, I was told, were besieged by foreign adoptive parents, to whom my hotel catered.

From roughly 6,000 Komi farmers, cattle breeders, fishermen, and hunters at the beginning of the twentieth century, the city's population had been increased by deportation of exiles to 235,000.

Mikhail Rogachev, a local historian whom Viktor had procured in advance to help me with my research, was already seated at the café of the Hotel Syktyvkar when we got there. A tan, slender man in his late fifties, in a T-shirt and close-cropped hair, hunched forward, he looked a little bewildered when I walked into the lobby with a beaming Viktor, a grinning Yakov, and sweet, shy nineteen-year-old Stasya, who was to be my translator.

On Mikhail's right sat an Arizona State doctoral student who, as it turned out, was researching the exiles in Komi and staying at my hotel. Rogachev was the head of the "Komi Republic Not-for-Profit Foundation for Those who Suffered Political Repression" and editor of the multivolume anthology *Repentance: The Komi Republic's Martyrology of the Victims of Political Repression*. He had been a collector and publisher of former exiles' memoirs since 1996.[8]

Two men, seated on a sofa in the hotel lobby, stared at us as we arrived and throughout that evening and night and all other days I remained in

Komi. "Plainclothes policemen," Viktor said indifferently, when we exited the hotel a few hours later. "Here in the north it's still the Soviet Union." Everywhere I went, my two plainclothes companions followed. "Don't worry about it," Viktor said. "They'll do nothing. Everything is good."

Access to Syktyvkar archives was limited and sporadic—the American Ph.D. student told me he had been hanging around in Syktyvkar for over three weeks and still had not been able to gain entrance to them. Residents held their cards very close to their chest, afraid or reluctant, I couldn't tell which, to divulge what they knew. Mikhail seemed to me circumspect as well. "What about Mikhail?" I asked Viktor. "He has no problems. His office is open," he dismissed me with a wave of the hand, clearly enjoying his status as the benevolent protector of us all.

There had been three waves of deportations: a Jewish deportation on July 24, 1940; a Polish deportation on February 10; and a deportation from Arkhangelsk to Komi in August or September 1941. "The majority of 'Polski Hebrai' were sent to special settlements, not to gulags," Mikhail said, "and it was easier for them because they came in warm time. They had small plots and had some time before winter to plant something. They tried to settle themselves. Polacks, they came already in winter so they did not have time." It was a theme I would hear repeatedly throughout my journey: the "advantage" of Jews over regular exiles. "The work in settlements was very hard because most Polish Jews were city people and had to do what they were not used to and could not do. They had enough power, but they did not know how to do the work. This influenced their salary. They could not get any food. They did not have enough houses. When they had clothes, they traded with the Komi," he continued. "Komi people liked their fancy clothes. They never saw European clothes before. Most Polish women, they exchanged underwear for food."

At Regina's school, children would have been allowed to speak only Russian, Mikhail said. Some classes were mixed with locals. Others were for Poles only. He called both Jews and Catholics "Polish people." "Polish people did not want their kids to go to this school, but the government told them they had to. Poles organized their own underground schools. There were teachers among them. And some children—Poles and Jews— were sent to boarding schools in Komi. Here in Syktyvkar were 21,000 Polish Jews, out of 100,000 total population."

"How many families lived on average in a settlement?" I asked Mikhail.

"From fifty to five hundred. The commandant did not know exactly how many people will come. For example, in Syktyvkar there was stone factory; the government would ask them: How many people will you need? Then they send them. In Komi there are documents how and why they settled them, but it's hard to find and hard to translate." Mikhail had created an index of names of people who were exiled to Komi, when and why they were sent there, and when and if they died. "Three thousand out of the 21,000 Jews died in the first years," he said. Mikhail himself was not an exile but a Lithuanian who had come to Syktyvkar after the fall of the Soviet Union to research special settlements and stayed. I did not know the source of his numbers, nor the source of funding for his projects. "Only in Komi we have such research," he said.

In one of the testimonies quoted in Henryk Grynberg's book, the residents of Komi are described as "half-savage people who would entrap animals and eat them raw." In another, a child had written that "we would run to the wild Komi people to ask for meat and eat it raw like them. They suggested that we eat tree bark. We dried and grinded the tree bark and mother made noodles with it." But most of the exiles' contact with the outside world was with freed *kulaks*, the landed farmers who had been exiled years before them and had by now set up small farms in nearby *kolkhozes*. The *kulaks* were the rulers of the black market, having at their disposal crops that they grew, perhaps even a cow and some poultry, while the rest of Komi and Arkhangelsk starved. As my father had written, they sold a kilo of rotten tomatoes for five rubles and a glass of milk for forty, Ruchela's and Zindel's combined monthly salary. But as Mikhail had told me, everyone gladly took European clothes or fabrics in exchange for food.

By September 1940, fabrics began arriving in their settlement in parcels from Siemiatycze, where Ruchela's mother and brother remained. The Soviet government, which censored the post, encouraged exiles to write their relatives and request goods and supplies, which Zindel did almost immediately. Soon afterward lard wrapped in newspaper and bottles of beer arrived from Zindel's brother Icok Teitel, now a superintendent of beer breweries in Łomża, near Białystok.

In Posiołek Pomminka, two postcards even arrived from Sura Perelgric in Nazi-occupied Warsaw. The first, dated September 5, 1940, was sent on the occasion of Emma's eighth birthday:

My most dearest little daughter, soon you will celebrate your birthday—
on September 22 you will turn eight, my dearest Emusia. Your father
will perhaps remember to make you happy. I did receive your postcard
from August 10 of the current year. May God grant good news from you!
Everything is all right with us. We live only because of thoughts of you, my
dears. [Cut off words]. I wish you, my dear child, good health [cut off word]
and to your Father. Danek [Noemi's brother, Daniel Perelgric] left so I am not
going to have him sign.
Your mother, Sura[9]

Sura's postcard was addressed to "Adam and Emusia" in Arkhangel'skaya Oblast, Kargopolskiy rayon, Novokovzenskoye p/o, Posiołek Pomminka 18, suggesting that the father and daughter who were exiled separately had ended up together. It arrived on September 29, a week after Emma's birthday, and bore the insignia of both the German and the Soviet censor, each of whom had crossed out words. In the crossed-out sentence, the words *mother, family,* and *brother* were legible. I wondered where "brother" "Danek" had gone. I wondered if Adam had wondered.

Still, for Emma, the sight of her mother's handwriting and particular style of expression made her even happier than the lump of sugar she had received on her birthday from her father, as she told me. She loved him in an abstract, more distant way, having been raised primarily by a nanny and her mother. Her father, she said, a white-collar worker his entire life, was mystified by the need to feed, care for, and keep a little girl clean and healthy, a task for which he had no prior experience. Exile had bound the child and father in an unprecedented physical closeness that was awkward for both, and Emma was relieved to feel her mother's mediating presence, if only for a day and through a postcard that had been written in the family apartment on Sienna Street where Emma had lived from birth.

Two and a half months later, Sura wrote a second and last postcard from within the Warsaw Ghetto. It arrived at the settlement six months later.

Warsaw, March 10, 1941.

My dearest Adam and Emusia,

I am very happy that you are receiving my letters. Write to the address I am giving you on the reverse. Sometimes [when] I have an occasion, I will write you longer letters, but I prefer to write postcards. They arrive faster. Mr. Józik Sztejnb wrote about you. I regret that he couldn't help you. His mother wrote to him to send you. . . . You will write me when you receive this. I will be happy. Liza wrote me that Mr. Raffons sent you a package. Is it so? I am very anxious about you. I sense that you are tired with work. Perhaps Mr. Józik could unburden you. He supposedly established himself well in the city. . . . Probably, your parents, Adam, moved, we don't know where yet. Sals (?) is trying to find out their new address. I was also supposed to change the apartment, but I am staying for now, and I am very pleased with it, understandably.

Mr. Stanisław did not receive any letter from you. He lives in N. 76, the third house from me. We often communicate. I will write again. Meanwhile, I am sending my regards. Everybody sends their regards to you. The latter does not work there anymore either, but he helped me find work.

Emma: Remember your name is Noemi [נעמי, in Hebrew letters, appeared to be scratched out]. It is the name I gave you.

The letter was signed "Your mother, Sarah," not Sura.[10] Emma—whom I knew as Noemi—showed me her mother's postcards for the first time in

2011, several years after I began interviewing her. She has refused to give them to the Israeli Holocaust Museum Yad Vashem or any other archive or even to let me Xerox them in a nearby shop. "They are my worthiest possessions," she said, "my mother's will." She never conclusively deciphered the names or the postcards' cryptic message. Did Sura mean by the words "I was also supposed to change the apartment, but I am staying for now, and I am pleased with it, understandably" that she would soon be attempting to escape the ghetto that by the date of the letter had been surrounded by a nine-foot fence and cut off from the world? Did the ominous sentence "Remember your name is Noemi: It is the name I gave you" mean: *Remember me by the Hebrew name I gave you*?

In exchange for gifting the commandant with a bottle of beer that was sent by his brother Icok, Zindel was able to secure a fortnight of reduced workload for the entire family. From the issues of *Pravda* in which Icok's lard was wrapped, they got a bit of sense, if not exactly reliable, about the advancement of the war. The parcels from Siemiatycze and Łomża had saved the Teitels' lives, as they admitted them to a black-market system that flourished alongside the Soviet propaganda, which was pumped into them consistently and daily in mandatory lectures by the same commandant they would later bribe. Within two or three months, their lives in Posiołek Ostrowsky, as in hundreds of settlements across the Soviet Union, fell into a miserable, cynical routine that they no longer rebelled against.

＝

No special settlement is memorialized or marked in present-day Komi. "We know where they were," Mikhail Rogachev told me the day we drove to look at remnants. "But after people moved, the barracks crumbled and there is nothing there." He offered instead to take me to a former gulag, "where many Jewish suffered," as he put it. I hesitated, unsure I wanted to veer into details and places that were irrelevant to my father's story. "This is relevant," Mikhail said.

Approximately two hundred thousand Polish citizens—Jewish and Catholic—were imprisoned in Soviet prisons and gulags during the war: prisoners of war of the Polish army, including the former commander of the Nowogródzka Cavalry Brigade, General Anders, and roughly twenty thousand officers; Jewish and Catholic intellectuals and educators like the futuristic poet and publisher Aleksander Wat and the philosopher-activist Emil Sommerstein; religious and clerical figures like Warsaw's Great Synagogue's chief rabbi Dr. Moses Schorr; leaders and activists of all Zionist movements, including Bund leaders Henryk Ehrlich and Wiktor Alter; and many, many more. Their experiences, if they survived, are drenched in blood and well documented by Solzhenitsyn, Eugena Ginzburg, and others: the whippings, the hangings, the mock executions, the isolation cells, and the starvations.

David Lauenberg, a member of the socialist Zionist movement Ha'shomer Ha'tsair and a former Jewish cadet of the Polish army (who in 1942 would become the Tehran Children's supervisor in Iran), testified that men were suspended from ceilings and kicked and stabbed to death, or tied to carts and dragged across stones until death. Lauenberg himself, at his Karelia Republic gulag in northwestern Russia, was at one point tied to a tree and left to die without food and water, to be devoured by mosquitoes. "Dachau was a sanitorium in comparison to the gulag," a prisoner who had escaped from Dachau, only to be arrested and deported to the gulag, told him.[11]

Transportation arrangements to the former gulag in Komi were a problem. Viktor's friend Sergei, who was to be our driver, had still not materialized from his bout of summer drunkenness ("It can last up to a week," Viktor said), and hiring a professional driver, as I suggested, would have been a personal insult to Viktor's status as power broker in this town. In the end, he procured another friend whom he introduced as Lev, a curly-haired man in his mid-thirties whose business was "fixing computers."

The day was spectacular, sunny with the lightest chill, and the mood was jovial inside Lev's black four-wheel-drive Nissan. Mikhail, seated in

front in his T-shirt and aviator glasses, seemed much freer and more animated than he had been at the hotel, dispensing driving directions with
both hands. Beside me in the back seat, Stasya the translator and Viktor Aslanov chatted in Russian. We drove alongside modest farmhouses,
forests, and sporadic piles of logs for no more than twenty minutes from
Syktyvkar's main street when we arrived at Plesmek, a gulag that housed
roughly twenty thousand people, including many Polish POWs who had
been captured after the Soviet invasion.

The gulag continued to operate until 1956. Its commandant's barrack,
which was built of stone, was still intact. Some of the boarded-up barracks
were there as well. A farm of livestock, patches of a wooden fence, and
remnants of structures that had been a prison and a court all remained.
"Could prisoners escape from here?" I asked Mikhail. The place did not
seem to have been very well fenced. "Some tried, but there was nowhere for
them to go. They would have been caught and executed down in that forest," he said, pointing to the thick expanse of trees to the east of the camp.

The executioners—former camp security people—continued to live in
their gulag residences even after 1956, later selling them as dachas, summer homes for city people.

In nearby Posiołek Jerome, newly built, spacious dachas were nestled
between the deserted old slave laborer barracks and miscellaneous agricultural machines in a kind of grassy, lazy, half-deserted, totally unmen-
acing rural scene. "Lower your voice," someone said when we passed a
large, quaint redbrick house. The sons of the head administrators of the
camp still lived there. At Jerome, a blue brick building that had been the
orphanage where Viktor's mother was placed while his grandmother
worked as an exiled slave laborer was now a boarding school that looked
well equipped and cheerful, its handsome wood interior undergoing ren-
ovations while the children were on their summer break. Russian construction workers, friendly and polite, gladly showed us the original walls
and ceilings of the building they were renovating. They had no idea about
its former function. "When it was a special settlement school, there was
just one fireplace and no other heating," Mikhail said. No one responded.

Many former inmates of Jerome, including Viktor's grandmother, built a neighborhood of decent-size brick houses a few kilometers away once they were released from slave labor.

A chunky, elderly lady in a wool hat and black sunglasses, a neighbor of his grandmother's, recognized Viktor and stopped us. Her parents had been professors in Tver, a pretty provincial city 180 kilometers northwest of Moscow, when they were deported to Jerome in 1941, Stasya translated. But when I asked the neighbor more questions, she turned around and disappeared in the direction of the nearby Sysola River, where for seven years her professor parents had loaded timber onto barges that carried it off to the western Soviet Union.

Komi was home to seventeen gulags and more than one hundred special settlements. Though remnants of some, like the ones we had visited, still existed, none were identified with an official sign or a plaque. Their memory was kept alive in the memoirs and letters of former prisoners and laborers, which Mikhail Rogachev had been collecting for twenty-five years, and in grassroots memorials. I noticed one of them on our drive back, a large chunk of limestone engraved with the words PRISONERS OF FOREST CAMPS, beneath which was a green tire filled with flowers. "There are 189 such grassroots memorials in Komi," Mikhail said, "more than in any other region." This one was erected by a German woman whose grandfather, an ethnic German Soviet, had been exiled to and died in Komi. "The authorities gave her no trouble," Mikhail said, anticipating my question.

Ninety percent of Komi's current population, including the president of the Republic of Komi, were deportees and their descendants. "Every year students make expeditions to the Komi Republic. They write down testimonies of deportees, and on the thirteenth of every October they attend a ceremony," Mikhail said. Still, the available data focused on technicalities—measurements, numbers, dates—not on repression or on responsibility.

"Only after 1939 barbed-wired fences began to be used in gulags," Mikhail said as we drove past what he called "a real *Lager,*" a camp, whose electric station still stood intact. "It was a *Lager*, but different from the German," he said. I assured him I was not comparing (though I was). He looked tense. A year later, when I had the documents in his collection *Repentance* translated, my Russian émigré translator called them "bureaucratic mumble jumble," referring to the busywork of midlevel administrators pretending to "do something" about a situation for which they knew full well that nothing could be done.

Still, Mikhail's documents—reports about numbers of laborers in each camp and in each barrack; official complaints about food shortages and about the number of square meters each laborer was allocated; requests for payments and an increase in budget—painted a slightly more complex picture than that of indifferent oppression. Many of the administrators at special settlements were locals; they too were more or less conscripted, Mikhail told me. Perhaps he signaled to me quietly that in a land that was full still of the descendants of the ones who had labored and the ones who had whipped them into laboring to fill production quotas established in Moscow, it was useless, if not dangerous, to assign blame.

$$\equiv$$

In December 1940, the temperatures in Hannan's settlement reached minus 50 degrees Celsius. (He had written minus 60 in his testimony, but the records showed otherwise.) Berries, mushrooms, and all kinds of leaves and shrubs that provided sustenance in the spring were now buried under many feet of frost and snow, and the potatoes the laborers had begun to grow had frozen. In certain patches along their daily route, snow was five meters deep. At night Zindel, Ruchela, Hannan, and Regina worked, slept, and huddled together, wearing all their clothes, and took turns staying up to add logs to the fire. The frost caused Hannan to lose sensation in his fingertips, a sensation he never regained, though I had not previously known when it happened. Others had to have frozen limbs amputated. Many were ill, including the woman with whom they shared their barrack: for eight days she lay feverish while her husband frantically and unsuccessfully tried to secure a cart to take her to a hospital. The cart was needed for hauling lumber and would be available only on Sunday, the day she died. She was buried in the forest patch they used for burying deportees. Her four young children carved her initials on a nearby tree and on the next day sold her clothes to the *kulaks*. There were many such testimonies of illness, death, and burial in the settlements.

Death in a special settlement was a private affair, witnessed and recorded by no one except the deceased's family, if at all. It was recounted in almost every refugee testimony:

> My brother Hirsch fell ill, and we didn't know what it was. Since there was no medical help he died after a few weeks and we buried him in the middle of the forest.

> When my two brothers . . . came down with measles . . . they were wrapped in blankets and taken by sledge [to the hospital]. They [caught] a cold, and died three days later. . . . With the help of my older brother, my father dug a grave and buried them together.

> My father was a healthy man. I don't recall him being sick before the war. . . . One day he felt weak at work, but the supervisor said he would be all right. He died in the forest before everyone's eyes. His body was brought back in the evening after work. All night long we and Mama stayed by him and chased the mice away. At dawn we sewed a garment for him from a couple of shirts and wrote his first name, last name, and the date on a board.[12]

I could find no reliable data on the number of deaths in special settlements. Soviet records suggest one-fifth to one-quarter of all laborers died in exile. Jewish and Polish sources claim higher numbers. Jewish sources put the death rate during 1941–42 at 22 to 28 percent.[13]

Driving back to Syktyvkar to the sound of Sting ("I'm an alien, I'm a legal alien") booming out of Lev's speakers, we began our return from the land of the gulags, past small, brightly colored wooden "dachas," more or less well maintained, which may or may not have been former settlements. I asked Mikhail if there were any burial grounds we could visit. He resisted at first ("there are no cemeteries; there's nothing now, just forests"), then signaled to Lev to turn into a nearby forest, where we continued to drive, still jovial and chatty, for half a mile, zigzagging between enormous pine trees and marshes in a wild, serene nature scene. Then the smell hit me, a distinct, slightly sweet odor, and after that the mosquitoes, a thick blanket of insects that hovered above us from the moment we exited the jeep into the forest clearing.

In the middle of the clearing was a large rusty metal cross, lit momentarily by a beam of afternoon light that darted through the trees. The ground on which we stood was uneven, and in every direction I saw mounds of earth that seemed to stretch on with no end in sight. The dead were gulag prisoners, Mikhail said. Prisoners, not family members, buried other prisoners in gulags. "Every day they would cart the day's dead and bury them together in a single hole. Those who died of hunger would be shot in the heart before they were buried, to make sure they were dead." Stasya, the teenage translator who had been upbeat all day, began translating Mikhail's words more solemnly and hesitantly. She was seventeen, lived less than a half an hour away, and had never known such places existed. The mosquitoes that zoomed overhead were merciless. Mikhail lit a cigarette.

I began walking, and I walked for half an hour atop masses of corpses. Mikhail and Viktor stayed behind in the clearing. Stasya leaned against the jeep and cried. There were small mounds for individual graves and large mounds indicating mass burials. I lost my sense of direction and orientation. There were no names, no gravestones, just the raw earth and a handful of strewn crosses. Once in a while there would be an empty hole, where perhaps the bones had been dug out. Individual gravestones were forbidden in the gulags and the special settlements, though occasionally a distinct number would be carved next to a burial site on a nearby tree, or a "wooden pyramid," the half of a Star of David that was the secret sign that Jewish deportees sometimes made for their dead. In one area, a handwritten sign that said SPECIAL SETTLEMENT CEMETERY 1942–1944 was hammered into a tree.

"Sometimes people come to search for the burial place of a relative," Mikhail would tell me later that night. The Israeli former coach of the British soccer team Chelsea, Avram Grant, had been there last year, flying in a helicopter to scout for his grandmother's burial place, which he couldn't find, Mikhail said. Every June 20, Russian, Litvak, and Polish descendants and relatives meet here for a modest ceremony, he told me, nearly a thousand of them still living in the Komi Republic. He said he did not know whether there were "Polack Hebrai" among them.

Komi and Arkhangelsk, it suddenly hit me, were one gigantic, unmarked burial ground where my father and his family could have also ended their lives without a trace. I turned to look for Lev's jeep but saw only a huge expanse of mounds closing on me from all directions, and for a moment I felt as if I were drowning, blurry-eyed and gasping for air. Then Viktor came toward me and walked me back to the jeep with a gentleness I didn't know he had. A surge of warmth and gratitude toward him overtook me as we drove back to Syktyvkar in silence.

=

Relations between Polish Jews and Catholic Poles in Posiołek Ostrowsky were "heartfelt," as Hannan described them in his testimony to the Polish Information Center in Jerusalem. "Jews and Poles helped each other in anything they could," he said. It was a sentiment repeated in many testimonies and in regard to many settlements, especially those that were predominantly Jewish. When Jewish exiles skipped work on the first day of Passover, April 11, 1941, and prayed together inside a barrack in defiance of the Soviet prohibition against religious ceremony, my father wrote that their Polish neighbors did not inform on them or complain that only they worked that day. Some children reported on fights between Poles and Jews, and on cases where veteran Polish refugees refused to allow Jewish newcomers into their barracks.[14] But others described bonding over a common language and a common desire to return to Poland where, as Hannan reported, both Jews and Poles were repeatedly told they would never return. ("Just as you will never see your ears, you will never again see Poland," the commandant used to say to Zindel.)

> In the *posiołek* were many Poles who were friendly to us, helped us settle in, and gave us useful advice.

> In the *posiołek* there were thirty Poles for six hundred Jews, and relations with them were very good. Among them was a high Polish official—a devout Catholic and an anti-Semite—who became friendly with my father. They would have long conversations and became convinced that religion was the only consolation in that terrible situation.[15]

Catholic and Jewish Polish citizens also bonded around religious practice, which many attempted to continue illegally. In several settlements, both Jewish and Catholic Polish worshippers were imprisoned or exiled to gulags. In one, five NKVD men barged into a barrack that had been secretly made into a makeshift synagogue in the middle of prayer and dragged three elderly worshippers out by their collars. Yet the arrests, which reduced productivity and sometimes led to the halting of nearly all work, eventually resulted in the turning of a blind eye to religious activity. On Passover 1941 Zindel joined the minyan and prayed as Hannan and other boys stood guard at the door, on the lookout for the commandant. He did not go to the forest on the first day of Rosh Hashanah and Yom Kippur. The religiosity that he had begun to slowly abandon in Poland was his and others' rebellion, a link to a former life whose memory was dissipating.

But it was mostly, it seemed to me, a way to mark time and break the tedium of identical days lived in cruel repetition. "I would spend eight hours by the canal. During this time there was one self-propelled barge which passed from Povenets to Soroka and one, identical in type, which passed from Soroka to Povenets. Their numbers were different, and it was only by their numbers that I could tell them apart and be sure that it was not the same one as before on its way back. Because they were loaded altogether identically: with the very same pine logs," Solzhenitsyn had written.[16] By Passover 1941, ten months had passed since Hannan was exiled: three hundred identical days.

≡

Anton Beck, a mustached and heavyset Russian of German ethnicity, wearing a plaid shirt and pressed jeans in the style of an aging American Marlboro Man, sat across from me in the offices of Mikhail Rogachev. His parents had been deported to Komi from Saratov in the Volga Republic, where nearly eight hundred thousand Germans had been living since the mid-eighteenth century. Catherine the Great had offered them land, exemption from military conscription, and religious freedom for their Catholicism in exchange for developing the region. In July 1941, having already worked for three years as slave laborers, Anton was born in the settlement where the family would remain for fourteen more years. In 1955 they were rehabilitated and became teachers in Syktyvkar, where Beck, now retired, became a news reporter.

"Why did you choose to stay in Syktyvkar?" I asked Beck, who had come especially to meet me in Mikhail's office. "Aren't you angry at what was done to your family?" In response, Beck took out a double-spaced typed document he had prepared in advance: a tedious, very general description of life in the special settlements to which I listened gloomily, knowing there was no hope of stopping him. When I tried to intervene with questions, he increased his reading speed, waving his finger at me at dramatic moments. "You could not run away from the special settlement. If you tried, they sent you away for hard labor for twenty years." He ended on a high note: "I am a Russian. Why should I leave?" Since his retirement, he had been devoting his time to keeping the memory of the German deportations alive ("in the Soviet years we were scared for our families and did not speak") and to writing a memoir ("to show this true history to our children"). Many such memoirs have been published in

Germany, Beck said, where nearly three million ethnic German Russians, including nearly all his family, now lived. Some 460,000 have remained in Russia, several hundred of them in Komi, where they were exiled. "I do not speak German," he told me. "I feel myself a Russian."

My father could have been Beck, I realized in Komi. His family could have remained in Posiołek Ostrowsky as Anna Borkowska remained in Iran. He could have been imprisoned for fourteen years, and been released when he was twenty-seven, at which time he might have not been able to leave the Soviet Union. He could have remained in Syktyvkar or Arkhangelsk City, or perhaps, if he were as enterprising as Viktor—which he was not—he could have lived as a Russian Jew in Leningrad or Moscow, from where he might have been forced by 1970s anti-Semitism to return to the Urals as Viktor's Jewish friend Yakov had.

But Hannan did not become Beck.

On June 22, 1941, German forces invaded the Soviet Union, putting pressure on the Red Army, already depleted by a continual Soviet-Finnish war. In response, the Soviet Union, having less than two years prior cooperated with Germany in invading Poland, joined the Allied forces.

On July 30 the USSR and Poland signed a treaty for the resumption of diplomatic relations, turning enemies to allies overnight. It was signed by Władysław Sikorski, prime minister of the Polish government-in-exile, and Ivan Maysky, Soviet ambassador to the United Kingdom in the presence of Winston Churchill and his secretary of state for war, Anthony Eden. On August 12, the treaty was affirmed "by the presidium of the Supreme Soviet" in Moscow, and its terms were publicly announced: A Polish army-in-exile would be established on Soviet soil, to fight with the Allies against the Nazis; a Polish government-in-exile embassy would be established in Moscow; and all who had been Polish citizens on September 17, 1939—gulag prisoners, Polish army POWs, and special settlers—would be released from Soviet gulags, prisons, and special settlements.

For a brief moment in late 1941, the Soviet government, which did not regard "Ukrainian, Byelorussian, Lithuanian, and Jewish" Polish citizens as Polish nationals, was on the defensive. The Teitels and the Perelgrics and the Halberstadts and at least three hundred thousand other Polish-born Jews fell under the July 30 treaty for the release of Polish citizens. It was questionable whether Icok Teitel and others who had consented or were forced to relinquish their Polish citizenship regained it through the treaty; for those like him and his family, who had not succeeded in fleeing the Wehrmacht as it marched into the USSR, it did not matter.

On the day I left Syktyvkar, I received a call from the Moscow office of the Joint Distribution Committee (JDC) that the Teitels' and the Perelgrics' deportation cards had been found in a Red Cross database in Moscow and would be scanned and e-mailed to me immediately. I now had in my possession scans of the brown handwritten cards that each of the Teitels and the Perelgrics received:

Teyzhel Zindel M.
(Name variant: Teitel, name variant: Zundel)
Born in 1896. Jewish.
Lived: Białystok region.
Verdict: Banishment in the Arkhangelsk region. 08.07.40, Plesetsk district,
Ostrovsky Special Settlement.
Released by the USSR Supreme Soviet decree "On Clemency of Polish
Citizens," September 5, 1941

Teyzhel Rachel Hananovna
(Name variant: Teitel)
Born in 1902, Semyatichi. Jewish. University education.
Lived: Białystok region.
Verdict: banishment in the Arkhangelsk region. 08.07.40, Plesetsk district,
Ostrovsky Special Settlement.
Released by the USSR Supreme Soviet decree "On Clemency of Polish
Citizens," September 5, 1941

Teyzhel Rivka Zindelevna
(Name variant: Teitel)
Born in 1931. Jewish. Education: 2.
Lived: Białystok region, Belsk.
Verdict: Approx. to banishment in the Arkhangelsk region. 08.07.40, Plesetsk district, Ostrovsky Special Settlement.
Released by the USSR Supreme Soviet decree "On Clemency of Polish Citizens," September 5, 1941

Teyzhel Hannan Zindelevich
(Name variant: Teitel)
Born in 1927. Jewish. Education; 3.
Lived: Białystok region.
Verdict: banishment in the Arkhangelsk region. 08.07.40, Plesetsk district, Ostrovsky Special Settlement.
Released by the USSR Supreme Soviet decree "On Clemency of Polish Citizens," September 5, 1941

Perelgrits Abram Haskelevich
(Patronymic option: Haskilevich)
Born in 1900 in Warsaw. Jewish. Higher education, an accountant.
Lived: Białystok region.
Sentenced: June 29, 1940. Refugee.
Verdict: Evicted July 10, 1940, to banishment in Vologda Region, Velikoustiugskii district, Poldarsky.
Released by the USSR Supreme Soviet decree "On Clemency of Polish Citizens," September 9, 1941

Perelgrits Noemi Abramovna
Born in 1930 in Warsaw. Jewish.
Lived: Białystok region.
Verdict: banishment in the Arkhangelsk region. 07.07.40, Kargopolsky district, Poyaminka Special Settlement.

Released by the USSR Supreme Soviet decree "On Clemency of Polish Citizens," September 6, 1941

I now knew the place and date of Hannan's exile: Posiołek Ostrowsky in Arkhangelsk. My aunt had been right all along.

I knew that their nationality was registered as "Jewish," not as "Polish," and that their Jewish names were used on the cards: Rachel for Ruchela; Rivka for Regina; Noemi for Emma; Abram for Adam.

I knew that though their citizenship did not appear on their cards, the only one of the six who was explicitly labeled *bezhenets* (refugee) was Adam Perelgric. He had been tried for a "graver" offense than the Teitels—not for requesting to return to the German side, but for attempting to illegally cross the German-Soviet border—and his Polish citizenship had been revoked. Adam Perelgric's was also the only one that did not have the words *special settlement* on it. He had been banished not to a special settlement but to a gulag. Father and daughter were exiled not only on different dates but, now I knew, to seemingly different destinations: he to the Vologda region, she to Arkhangelsk.

But I knew that Emma had not exactly been wrong either. Her settlement was very possibly located near her father's camp. Archangelsk oblast bordered Vologda on the north; the Yertsevo camp complex, where Adam was likely sent, spanned both regions. Yertsevo, managed by Ispravitelno-Trudovoy Lager, the Central Gulag Administration, is described in a survivor memoir as a camp whose work conditions were so brutal that prisoners would chop off their own fingers to avoid work and would live for an average of only two years.

Both Teitels and Perelgrics were released roughly three weeks after the amnesty was publicly announced, fourteen months after they were exiled.

Not all Polish citizens were released. Aside from the larger disputes between the Soviet and the Polish governments, smaller, arbitrary facts determined the release of one and the detainment of another.

"There were many different releases," the Arizona State graduate student whom I had met with Mikhail on my first day in Syktyvkar, told me when I met him in the lobby of our hotel. "Sure, there was the agreement, but there was no blanket amnesty, no moment when they were all told: 'Now you can go.'" He was researching precisely this topic, but "not very successfully," as he put it. "The archives seem to be perpetually closed to me," he complained, proud and morose and declining Viktor's insistent offers to help him.

Some refugees were eligible for "clemency" but were never informed of it by their camp commandants, who wished to keep production going in their settlements.

"In some *posiolki*, workers were so cut off from the world that they did not know of the outbreak of a Soviet-Nazi war or the clemency," the student said, "and no one notified them they were free to leave."

Some learned about it from newspapers that wrapped parcels they received from their relatives, and they showed the news to their commandants.

Many were told that clemency applied to Poles but not to Jews, in which case they had to apply to higher authorities to be released.

Some workers went on strike after commandants refused to release them.

Nearly everywhere, workdays got longer, guards and supervisors became more vigilant, and wages declined.

Nearly all workers, even after they were released, were lured to stay: the war was still waging, the quotas still needed to be filled, and wedding the Polish refugees to their places of exile would hasten their "Sovietization":

> When the news of the amnesty came they tried to hold on to us with the promise of potatoes, wood to build a house, and a cow for each family.

> After the amnesty was announced for Polish citizens a senior NKVD official came and asked us to stay. He promised land, tools,

and seeds and assured us that no one would take our Polish citizenship away, but nobody would listen to him.

After the amnesty was announced they asked us to stay and promised things would be better, but we did not want to.[17]

I had not imagined the possibility that refugees had remained in their
places of exile until I realized that the testimonies in my possession were
all written by the people who had left. Yet some deportees were never
freed. Some were freed but conscripted to a limited radius nearby. Some,
especially those with large families and young children, did heed the
promise of land and better conditions and remained. Some simply did not
wish, or were too exhausted, to travel any farther and stayed in the vicinity of where they had been exiled. Some waited too long, and on January
16, 1943, the clemency was revoked.

"One thing I know for sure," the American student said, "many deportees
were forced to stay here despite the amnesty, and some even chose to stay."

One family that was released by "the USSR Supreme Soviet Decree on
Clemency to Polish Citizens" yet remained in Komi was that of Dmitry
Nesarelis, who would go on to become a prominent Russian anthropolo-
gist and a renowned ethnographer of the Komi people. Nesarelis's parents
were Polish Jews who were exiled to Komi in July 1940, the same month
and year as my father. He received a Ph.D. in cultural anthropology from
the State University of Arkhangelsk and became a popular public figure
who helped found Natsionalnyy Muzey Respubliki Komi, the National
Museum of the Komi Republic in Syktyvkar, which Viktor and I visited
on my third day in Komi.

As we walked to the museum, we passed the Monument of Eternal
Glory on Kommunisticheskaya Street, with its three twenty-foot-high
bronze women (the mother, wife, and daughter and of a fallen soldier)
and the city's newest clothing shops, which Viktor gleefully admired.

We entered the pretty, empty museum that boasted a four-story exhibition of taxidermy of bears, reindeers, pike, and ducks (holy animals

to the ancient Komi), as well as displays of spears, sleds, and fur coats and photos of hunters and gatherers. The museum did not feature any objects related to exiles like Nesarelis, who had written himself out of its narrative, creating instead a story of origin for Komi that was rooted in its indigenous past. And he was not only an inventor and preserver of this story, but an advocate for its transmission to locals, fighting for the center of study of the Komi people to remain in Syktyvkar and not be moved to Western Europe.

In the paths of refugees, points of departure for some are points of arrival for others. In Komi I finally grasped the simple yet profound insight that what gets labeled as a point of transit or a "home" is determined only in retrospect.

On my last day in Syktyvkar, I was invited for an interview with a journalist at Radio Syktyvkar, who like everyone else seemed to be aware of my presence in town. Lively and hip in a cropped haircut and a black T-shirt, my interviewer was also the granddaughter of a deportee. "Why did you decide to come to this area?" she asked, and Viktor, having practiced his English in recent days, translated. "When was the first time you heard this story?" "How do Americans view Stalin? As a tyrant or as the person who built the Soviet Union?"

"Depends," I said cautiously. "More of a tyrant, I suppose. But there are admirers. And how do Russians view Stalin?"

"The deportations are a big part of the story of all families, not only in Komi but in all Russia," she said, also cautiously. "Komi is an island of gulags. My family was deported, and several people who were political prisoners were murdered by the NKVD. There are still many children of deportees in Komi, but also of guards and NKVD. . . . But nobody will tell you 'we come from a family of camp guards.' Some security people were forced: soldiers were conscripted, and some local people did not want to do it. But in any case, everybody is the same today, regardless if they were free or prisoners."

"It's strange," I told the reporter. "I began by writing my father's history, a Jewish history, but when I came to Komi, I realized that what happened to him during deportation was everybody's history: yours, mine, Viktor's."

"From this past we are related." She smiled at me sweetly. "But tell me, was the story of the deportation told in your family as a tragedy?"

"It wasn't really told," I said, "but most Polish Jews who survived in the USSR do not regard their deportations as the worst tragedy because in a sense they were saved by Stalin. It saved them from being murdered in Treblinka."

"What's Treblinka?"

"I AM A JEW"; "I AM AN UZBEK"

Their release from hard labor at Posiołek Ostrowsky did not lift Zindel and Ruchela's mood. They were intermittently ill and considerably weakened by two years of chronic semistarvation. They no longer received packages from their relatives in Białystok and Siemiatycze and did not know why; they no longer had many sellable belongings from Ostrów or entertained thoughts of returning there. The only thought they now had was to stay alive.

They did not know that Nazi troops had invaded Białystok and Siemiatycze and were pushing eastward toward them. They knew that though they were freed from slave labor, they were still trapped in the USSR. They did not know where their next meal would come from, nor anything about where they were heading. Still, when they were told they could leave Posiołek Ostrowsky for an unknown destination in Central Asia, they chose to go. Two decades earlier they had read *Tashkent: Korob Khlebny povest* (Tashkent: City of Bread), Aleksander Neverov's best-selling 1923 novel about a starving boy who travels to Tashkent, where at last he finds food for his family. The book had been translated into Polish, Yiddish, and Hebrew in the 1920s and was a hit among Jewish readers. Tashkent was everyone's desired destination.

Nearly all released Polish citizens on Soviet soil—urban and provincial, socialist and bourgeois, intellectual and mercantile—headed to the five Soviet Muslim republics of Central Asia: Uzbekistan, Turkmenistan, Tajikistan, Kazakhstan, and Kyrgyzstan.

According to the Polish government-in-exile, the Soviet government was to release 1.2 million Polish civilian citizens, at least a quarter of them Jewish:[1] 600,000 deportees; 400,000 "resettled peasants"; 100,000 state officials and functionaries and their families; and additional Polish citizens in prisons, labor camps, and the Red Army.[2] "Well over a million and a half to a million eight hundred thousand . . . [including] 500,000 Jews if not more," was the number given by the Polish ambassador in Washington.[3]

For its part, the Soviet government gave the number of "Polish citizens deprived of freedom" as only 387,932, of which it announced it would release 345,511 within two months of the amnesty.[4] It was unclear whether Poland's ethnic minorities—Jews, Belarusians, Lithuanians, and others—were included in this count.

Jewish sources, noting the extreme variance in the numbers given by the Polish and Soviet governments, estimated that the Polish citizens on Soviet soil who were Jewish numbered between 350,000 and 500,000.[5]

On September 5, 1941, Zindel, Ruchela, Hannan, and Regina stood in line at the commandant's barrack alongside dozens of Polish and Polish-Jewish families like themselves: filthy, emaciated, and holding tight to their bundles. They were still swaddled with the down blankets they had brought from Ostrów. Once they were inside the barrack, they handed their banishment records to an NKVD man, who handed them to the commandant, who wrote in black ink across each certificate, "Released by Special Settlements Amnesty 05.09.41."

A day later, on September 6, unknown to the Teitels, Emma Perelgric was released "on amnesty" from Pomminka; her father, a broken man, was released "by the USSR Supreme Soviet Decree on Polish Citizens" two days after that, on September 8, as were the family of Ruchela's sister Masha Halberstadt.

Column of refugees marching to Central Asia

In accordance with Soviet policy, those released from gulags and prisons received a free railway pass and a stipend of fifteen rubles a day, but former inhabitants of special settlements, who technically "had not been shut away in camps and prisons," received no pass and no stipend once they were outside their settlement.[6] From the moment Hannan's family was released from Posiołek Ostrowsky, they were on their own.

General Władysław Anders, who had been imprisoned at Lubyanka in Moscow, was released a month before Hannan. The Protestant son of a Polonized German family (he would later convert to Catholicism), Anders had been born in the Russian Empire and served in the tsarist military as a young officer. With Poland's 1918 independence, he joined the Polish military. As commander of the Nowogródzka Cavalry Brigade, he fought in three battles against the Soviets, but in October 1939 he was captured while retreating to the Romanian border and taken prisoner. He was interrogated, tortured, and dumped into solitary confinement, first in a Lwów prison and then in Lubyanka.

Then one evening in early August 1941, as the historian Norman Davies tells it, the door to his cell swung open, and a gaunt and emaciated Anders was taken to a newly appointed Polish ambassador, who told him he had been chosen to command a Polish army-in-exile. "For nearly two years I had lived in prison cells," Anders wrote in his memoir. "Now the fresh air, the noise of the streets and the traffic almost intoxicated me. How strange it was to be free again."[7]

No other former Polish prisoner's fate had been overturned as dramatically as that of Anders. He might have died like many others at Lubyanka, but instead he was received with pomp and ceremony by Joseph Stalin. "Anders still looks wretched, but declares he feels well," the Polish ambassador in Moscow wrote to the Polish prime minister in London. In their meeting, Stalin reportedly asked Anders about his treatment in Soviet prisons, to which Anders replied that it was "exceptionally bad" and Stalin answered, "Well, it couldn't be helped; such were the conditions."[8] The day of their meeting, September 5, was also the day of my father's release from Posiołek Ostrowsky.[9]

Much of the Polish army was decimated or in exile in France and Britain; twenty thousand were said to have been captured by the Soviets and unaccounted for. Anders was thus instructed to assemble a new army, an army in exile, from among recently released Polish citizens. To recruit them, Anders was to head immediately to Siberia and to Central Asia, where, he was told, over a million Polish citizens were making their way. A call for enlistment would be distributed in the settlements, and divisions of the newly created Polish army would assemble in Tatishchevo, Buzuluk, and other areas in southwestern Russia, bordering Kazakhstan.

Among those released by the amnesty, along with Anders and families like my father's, were a number of writers, intellectuals, and public figures: the poet Władysław Broniewski; the writer and editor Aleksander Wat; leaders of the Bund, the Jewish labor movement; members of the socialist Zionist movement Ha'shomer Ha'tsair, and others. These figures were, to borrow a term from Primo Levi, "privileged witnesses": they were more networked and had a larger frame of vision than "ordinary" refugees like my father but shared with them a common fate.

There wasn't much scholarly research on the post-amnesty Polish refugee experience; Soviet archives had been sealed off for decades and were still not fully accessible; few memoirs were published, none of them well known; and no films had been made. The Polish Information Center testimonies provided facts without any context. It was a history for which there was no frame of reference, for which *I* would be writing the frame of reference: I was writing, I increasingly came to realize, a new kind of Holocaust history, a new kind of second-generation memoir of my father's Holocaust. My guides were the writings of "privileged witnesses," the writings about them, and the slew of archival material that would teach me, by analogy and by contrast, what happened to Hannan after his release from Posiołek Ostrowsky. But how to tell it when even its background details were unknown?

Numerous children of Nazi victims have written memoirs. But most of them do not focus on historical detail, in part because the historical contours of the transports and concentration camps are by now generally known, in part because they focus on the second generation: their parents' silences and postwar neuroses, the children's dread of their parents' pasts, and their inability to know those pasts. More recent Holocaust memoirs have tended to be less psychologically conflicted and more evidence-based but are still grounded narrowly in testimonies or in a few relevant details, as if searching for a plethora of knowledge about the Holocaust would overwhelm both writer and readers. A line divided historians from psychologists and memoirists, an underlying assumption that intense historical focus in a memoir makes it less personal, obscures the survivor, and causes a "failure of empathy."[10]

I too had begun in this way, treating historical research as an exigency and a means to an end—I would conduct just enough to allow me to write my father's memoir responsibly. But increasingly the knowledge of historical detail was making me listen more shrewdly but also more empathically. The more I knew, the more I read, interrogated, and compared accounts and testimonies, the broader, deeper, and more precise my understanding became, the more I "heard" the voices of my father and others. I read accounts of others to piece together the puzzle of my father, and gradually his past, and theirs, which had been dead, began speaking to me.

I read *My Century*, Czesław Miłosz's interviews with Aleksander Wat, about Wat's refugee experience in Kazakhstan and Uzbekistan. Wat, born Aleksander Chwat, was a contemporary of my grandfather Zindel Teitel, born like him to a prosperous, observant Jewish family. But Wat, unlike Zindel, abandoned Jewish Orthodoxy and went on to publish and edit a Communist literary monthly, and rise to the center of Warsaw's cultural circles. Then he abandoned Communism[11] and became a Polish loyalist who was disheartened by the rise of 1930s anti-Semitism: "I had the same feeling that every Jew, even the most assimilated, had: the absolute certainty that as soon as you turned around your friends would say, 'That Jew!'," he writes.[12] After fleeing east from Warsaw, Wat was arrested and imprisoned in Lubyanka, where he and his Polish and Ukrainian cellmates were interrogated and tortured by the NKVD. At nights his cellmates would sing hymns to the Virgin, which strongly moved him—"I felt enormous envy for them. I sat in my corner and wept." He converted to Catholicism in jail, was released by Amnesty, and weighing one hundred pounds, set off in the direction of Kazakhstan's capital Alma-Ata (now Almaty), where many other intellectuals and artists also headed. [13]

And I read the poems of Władysław Broniewski, an interwar poet. His 1939 manifesto "Bagnet na broń" (Bayonet On)—"Hey boys, mount the bayonet"—called for all Poles to unite against their common enemies. He wrote poems during and about his refugee years. Broniewski too was imprisoned in Lubyanka, and after his release traveled to an Anders recruitment center and joined the Polish army.[14]

And I read writings by and about Ha'shomer Ha'tsair members, particularly the movement leaders Mordecai Rozman and Motek Rottman, who did not "flee" to the Soviet side as my father did but rather "crossed" under movement orders. (Other leaders were instructed to remain in

Nazi-occupied Poland and eventually fought and died in the Warsaw Ghetto Uprising.)[15] Rozman was caught, imprisoned and tortured in an NKVD prison. After his release under the amnesty he wrote an under-ground pamphlet—"For the existence of the Movement, for the existence of humanity, in order to plan operations and tackle life a little, we must wait together in some corner"—which he tried to disseminate in Uzbeki-stan, hoping to connect with fellow Ha'shomer Ha'tsair members who, like the Teitels, were flocking toward Tashkent and Samarqand.[16]

≡

Also moving through the Soviet interior in these years, in addition to the "amnestied" Polish refugees and greatly outnumbering them, were Soviet *evakuirovannyy* (evacuees). They were intellectuals, artists, and scientists; members of the Soviet Academy of Arts and Sciences; famous screen actors, actresses, and directors; government officials; top industri-alists; members of the cultural and political elite of Moscow and Lenin-grad; factory workers from the western USSR who were evacuated along with their factories, dismantled piece by piece; refugees from the western USSR fleeing the Nazis; former Polish citizens like Icok Teitel who had fled Nazi-occupied Poland and accepted, or were forced to accept Soviet citizenship; and entire government offices, prisons, and cultural institu-tions like ballets and theaters. Approximately 16.5 million Soviet citizens were evacuated to the country's interior between June 1941 and autumn of the next year.[17] In Uzbekistan, the majority of them—63 percent—were Jewish, according to imperfect data from late 1941.[18]

Population transfers and deportations were an old phenomena that predated the Soviet Union, but the evacuation of prominent persons and entire industries was entirely new. On June 24, 1941, only two days after the Nazi invasion, an Evacuation Council of top-ranking officials was cre-ated to designate segments of the population and institutions that would be especially endangered should the Nazis reach Moscow and Leningrad. It then arranged for their transfer into the country's interior. Among the evacuees were the biggest names in interwar culture and some of my own literary heroes: the poets Anna Akhmatova, Nadezhda Mandelstam, and Korney Chukovsky; the novelists Aleksey Tolstoy and Boris Pasternak; the film director Vladimir Aslanov; the Russian formalist critic Viktor Shklovsky; the Yiddish theater master Solomon Mikhoels; the historian Boris Romanov; Elena Bulgakova, wife of the recently deceased novelist Mikhail Bulgakov; and many, many others.

The evacuation's stated purpose was to avoid an uncontrolled exodus of people, but its unstated purpose, as the historian Rebecca Manley put it, was to shape the modern Soviet Union by "generating, organizing, and categorizing migration." "At its core," Manley writes, "the operation aimed to retain control over Soviet space, threatened, in the eyes of the state, not only by German forces, but by 'enemy elements' and internal dissolution." As the result of the "operation," much of the Jewish USSR was evacuated into its Central Asian Muslim republics, which in 1941 became a land of Jews and Muslims.[19]

"Uzbekistan Soviet Republic Becomes New Home for Hundreds of Thousands of Evacuated Jews," reported the Jewish Telegraphic Agency in February 18, 1942. Putting their number at "millions," the story labeled the evacuated Jews not as "evacuees," "migrants," or "refugees" but as "settlers": "sparsely populated, the Uzbekistan Soviet Republic offers unlimited opportunities in the agricultural and industrial field and is able to absorb millions of new settlers."[20] "This was also a Jewish war, not only a Russian one," Wat wrote in his memoir. "In that sense the Jews' patriotism was incredibly dynamic. . . . All Jews who were active people, especially industrial engineers, performed miracles. They worked twenty hours a day, and the rapid transfer of industry into the depths of Russia, to Asia, was, to a tremendous extent, owing to Jewish organizational ability and dynamism."[21]

The conditions of transport for the prominent *evakuirovannyy* were radically different than for the *deportatsiya*: Akhmatova was flown from Moscow to Tashkent. But together with the refugees, they constituted an ocean of transmigrating people heading to the Soviet interior, most of them to Central Asia. I had at first thought of my father's story as unique, then as one story among hundreds of thousands of Polish refugees. But the story of his migration to Central Asia was one of millions, part of the largest-scale population transfer in Soviet history.[22]

===

The line at the check-in desk for Uzbekistan Air flight 642 from St. Petersburg to Bukhara was a clot of haggard, sunburned Uzbek laborers in loose, dusty clothing, middle-aged men who immediately gave way when they saw me. I hesitated to simply pass to the head of the line. "Go on," whispered Salar, who had flown to St. Petersburg to meet me. The men encouraged me with hand gestures, pointing to the desk. I was the only female passenger on the flight, surrounded by the humble, worn-out faces. Immediately after Salar and I boarded, the steward seated us in the empty back seats of the plane and away from the laborers, where he served us better food and real coffee in exchange for helping him practice his English. Once in a while, he shot disgusted glances at the neatly but shabbily dressed laborers whom he reluctantly served.

Seventy-one years earlier, my father and his family had arrived in Uzbekistan, much more haggard and shabbily dressed than my Uzbek flight mates. Still, I thought, this was their daily life today and everyday, not just in wartime.

Salar and I arrived in Uzbekistan on June 9, 2013, on a collaborative research grant we had won a year earlier. Visiting Bukhara and Samarqand, centers of Muslim pilgrimage and Persian architecture second only to Mecca and Medina, had been an old dream of Salar, who was conversant in the Persian-based Tajik language spoken in those cities. I had only my narrow agenda: to find the house where Hannan had lived in Samarqand, the kolkhozes (collective settlements) where he, Regina, their cousin Emma, and their families had labored, the hospital where they had been treated for typhus and malaria, the orphanage where they were placed before being shipped to Iran, the landscape they arrived in.

Planning a trip to Uzbekistan was harder than I thought. There were no links to universities, no information on archives, not even reliable information on hotels and transportation for independent researchers. A friend of a friend who had worked as a policy analyst for a sustainable agriculture organization in Samarqand said that the country functioned like a police state, and research that involved talking to people was difficult. "I imagine archival work could also be tricky," she wrote. "As for the country itself, it is magical to visit. A real treat to go."

A CCNY historian who specialized in Central Asia told me that because of the worsening political situation, she had not been able to travel there in years. A Mr. Shvili, chief librarian at the Tashkent National Archives with whom she connected me, did not answer my e-mails.

Finally, just weeks before our trip, I landed a contact. At the bottom of an online list of 152,000 Central Asia deportation cards published by the United States Holocaust Memorial Museum was the line "compiled by Professor Oybek Bozorov." I couldn't find Bozorov's contact information or university affiliation anywhere online or through the Holocaust Museum, but my Russian host Viktor Aslanov, with his widespread connections across the former Soviet Union, managed to nonetheless find his address and phone number in Bukhara. On the phone, through a translator, Bozorov sounded effusively friendly and said he would be happy to assist me with all my research needs once I got to his country.

When I called Bozorov again a week before my trip, the person who picked up the phone, presumably his wife, said he was gone for an indefinite time. I did not know whether he would be there when we arrived in Uzbekistan. And my trip's still-unplanned logistics needed to be finalized, in a country for whom all I could find were guided tours with names like "Uzbekistan's Silk Road Cities" or "Uzbekistan: Heart of Central Asia." I did not want to see "the Silk Road that has played host to waves of conquerors and nomads"; all I wanted was to follow the footsteps of my father and the Polish citizens who had flocked to Central Asia after being released from the Siberian gulags and special settlements.

In the end, an Israeli businessman who "worked with the Uzbeks," as he put it, helped me. "Under no circumstances should you travel to Uzbekistan as an independent researcher," he said. "You go around the country as a regular tourist." The man hooked me up with a Tashkent-based travel agency that was owned by the daughter of a government official. "You will have no problems in Uzbekistan if you travel with a guide from her agency," he said, and within twenty-four hours, a private "tour" of Bukhara, Samarkand, and Tashkent was arranged, including a guide, a driver, and hotels and meals, all paid for through a money transfer to a bank in Thailand. A week later, checking "tourism" as "purpose of your visit" at the Bukhara International Airport, Salar and I stepped into the early morning Uzbek sun and the open arms of a gregarious, heavyset, middle-aged woman covered in a loose, flowery scarf: our guide Kamara. The Hyundai jeep's boyishly polite driver, Bilol, quickly loaded our bags and drove us into the city.

Bukhara was a shock. Otherworldly majestic structures rose from empty stretches of land. Mosques, mausoleums, Sufi madrassas, and palaces were adorned in turquoise and gold and orange; the roads were yellow sand. It was all so radically different from the snowy gray of Komi, from the Polish green forests, from the intensity of New York and Tel Aviv, from the religious tensions of Jerusalem. Bukhara was a place of breathtaking beauty, though its grandeur, it goes without saying, was never mentioned in any refugee testimony I had read.

The Soviets did not ban religious practice entirely in Uzbekistan, whose population was 80 percent Muslim—there were something like sixty-five registered mosques and as many as three thousand active clerics during the Soviet era. But they weakened it through massive campaigns to "liberate" Muslim women, raise literacy, discourage traditional art forms, dress, and customs, replace Uzbek words of Arabic, Persian, and Turkic origin with Russian ones, and shift the Uzbek language from the Arabic to the Latin and from the Latin to the Cyrillic alphabet. A Muslim board that governed the practice of the Muslim faith during the Soviet era consisted of clerics screened for their reliability and loyalty. Praying was reluctantly tolerated, and religious teaching was forbidden.

But the madrassas and mosques that overwhelmed me with their beauty as we rode past them to the Sasha and Son hotel in old Bukhara were nonetheless preserved. They had been restored during the interwar period, in massive Soviet campaigns of renovation, after falling into dis-repair in previous centuries. And by the time of my father's arrival, they stood majestic, humongous, yet empty—one of the reasons, my contact Oybek Bozorov would later hypothesize, that so many refugees were sent to Uzbekistan: there was ample room to house them in the vast, empty madrassas and mosques.

By the time my father arrived in Uzbekistan, it had been a Soviet Socialist Republic for seventeen years. Three-quarters of its farm house-holds had been organized into *kolkhozes*; most of the former Uzbek polit-ical leadership and cultural intelligentsia had been exiled or executed and replaced with more pliant, Soviet-leaning leadership; and the Russifica-tion of Uzbek culture was in full force, though it did not completely dom-inate local customs.

$$=$$

The distance between Posiołek Ostrowsky in Arkhangelsk and Kolkhoz Octoyber in Kazakhstan (the collective farm to which the Teitels were eventually assigned) was roughly four thousand kilometers. They had received no funds and were provided with no organized means of trans-portation. So they walked, along with the roughly two hundred former laborers of Posiołek Ostrowsky, to the nearest train station, Yemtsa, and traveled by rail from there to Arkhangelsk. At the Arkhangelsk station, there were already thousands of refugees and evacuees like themselves, from Moscow and elsewhere, all trying to head south, and hundreds more were arriving daily. The trains were full, and Hannan and his fam-ily had to make their own way.

After a week of sleeping at the train station, atop the down blanket they had carried since Ostrów, they boarded a cargo train headed in the direction of Kazakhstan. It took them six weeks to traverse the four thou-sand kilometers to their destination. Along the way, their paths crossed those of multitudes of other refugees and evacuees. "All of Russia was on the move," Wat had written, by train, truck, car, wagon, plane, and foot. Emma and her father Adam Perelgric were also on their way from the Vologda to Uzbekistan, carrying their bundles on the sides of roads, knocking on farmhouse doors along the way and begging for food.[23]

Judging from other testimonies, memoirs, archival documents, and interviews, I can imagine that my father and Regina begged Red Army soldiers for a bit of their bread ration. Or else, when the train stopped, they ran into the fields to pick cabbages, wild plants, and whatever else was on the ground. They would have, for the second time in their lives, traveled amid corpses and people dying of hunger or thirst. "Every day [the Russians] go up and down the train taking out the bodies," Joanna Synowiec, a twelve-year-old Polish girl who had been with my father at Posiołek Ostrowsky, reported.[24] They would have spent weeks in train stations along the way. Sometimes local Jews would have helped them, and elsewhere they would have managed to trade or buy something with whatever they had left.

"The journeys of these people are marked by tragedy," Władysław Kot, the newly appointed Polish ambassador-in-exile to the Soviet Union, wrote in an urgent telegram to the Polish Foreign Ministry in London, pleading for help. "Above all they are being decimated by hunger and disease, a kind of hunger dysentery. Death occurs on many of the transports, and the travelers bring with them seriously ill cases, who often end their lives at the railway junctions. In one of the transports from the north there were sixteen corpses."[25]

The Soviet Evacuation Council's plan to manage the mass migration, maintain hierarchies, and use the deportees and evacuees as a tool of economic development fizzled within days. With no food rations or transportation, everyone and everything fell into chaos. Within weeks, what had been envisioned as an organized transfer to and resettlement in Soviet Central Asia disintegrated into an uncontrolled, savage exodus of millions. But even amid the chaos, the released Polish citizens stood out in their misery: they traveled for weeks without food, without adequate clothing, without the local language, without knowledge of the laws and regulations. Both the Teitels and the Perelgrics survived the journey: Hannan and his family arrived at Arys station in southern Kazakhstan, while Emma and Adam Perelgric arrived at Bukhara's Kagan station in November 1941.

Bezhenets, the Russian word for "refugee," connotes movement. "It signifies run, anxiety, fear, half-broken breathing, and the beating of a heart that seems to be jumping out of one's chest," writes historian Olga Medvedeva-Nathoo, who has collected data on lives of Polish-Jewish refugees in Kazakhstan.[26] In Soviet archives, newcomers to Central Asia are mostly described not as *bezhenets* but as *evakuirovannyy* (evacuees), implying a transfer between two steady geographical points. But movement was a key feature of Hannan's and millions of others' wartime ordeal.

In Moscow, the newly appointed Polish ambassador, Kot, raised the issue of the fate of thousands of Polish refugees "wandering en masse from north to south in tragic conditions" with the Soviet government.

> At first we thought it would be possible to influence the control of the transports and the settlement of the people. Unfortunately, war events, which have caused a mass evacuation of Soviet citizens from the west and the south, have rendered all planned operations impossible. . . . At present everybody is being unorganizedly directed towards Tashkent and because of this influx, nobody is able to prepare. . . . There is no accommodation for them, nor food, nor work, nor feeding points at the railway stations. . . . A very considerable number of them consists of children, women and old people. They lack suitable clothing, as they had to dispose of it when they travelled to the south, and many of them are ill. . . . We have got to work out together a detailed plan for solving this lack of planning and the chaos which is arising in connection with the release of Polish citizens from prisons, camps, and places of compulsory settlement.[27]

The Soviet government, Kot reports he was told, could not support those in transit or who did not work. Payment for this group should be undertaken by the Polish government.

"The Polish government? But we have no resources, we have no money," Kot writes that he replied. "The Polish people didn't go to the USSR of their own free will. You have torn them away from their organized normal life, their farms, their workshops; you flung masses of human beings into incredibly difficult conditions."[28]

The refugees would receive no aid at this point, from either the Polish or the Soviet government.

≡

Sergey Kim, a "research assistant" on behalf of Professor Bozorov, was seated in the lobby of Sasha and Son, the surprisingly gorgeous small pearl of a hotel in old Bukhara. Sergey was a third-generation Korean Uzbek, as he put it. He was fluent in Russian, Tajik, Uzbek, and English but knew nearly no Korean. At "the professor's request," he said, he had been researching my father's history. Before we even checked into our rooms, he presented me with Hannan's, Regina's, Ruchela's, Zindel's, Emma's, and Adam's deportation cards, which noted that the Teitels had been assigned to Kolkhoz Octoyber in Kazakhstan and the Perelgrics to Kolkhoz Dimitrov in the Samarqand region. Sergey had found them in the KGB archive in Tashkent. "In the KGB archives, there are big, big books with the names of all refugees and evacuees; the cards were made out of the information in these books. In one book it is written that your grandfather was a 'beer maker,'" Sergey said. "But I could not get everything I wanted, the people at the archive ask too many questions."

Sergey had found that the Teitels had entered Uzbekistan through Arys station, the gateway to the Trans Aral Railway, which ran a route from Kazakhstan to Tashkent. He had also seen many written requests of Polish refugees asking to go from Arys station to Tashkent. "The distance from Arys to Vreskt—the train station of the Tashkent region, which is now in the city of Yangiyo'l—was less than one hundred kilometers," he said. "But at least initially Tashkent was off limits to refugees and allowed only for a certain class of evacuees." When I asked him to clarify, he reiterated: "The refugees and even the evacuees could not choose where they were going. You are talking about the Soviet State. No one had freedom of choice, not even the most prominent evacuees."

Every former Tehran Child whose memoir I had read, and everyone I interviewed, presented their migration to Central Asia as a matter of choice and volition. The goal of escaping the "terrible cold" was a repeated theme. My aunt Regina said she thought her father Zindel chose to head to Central Asia in search of warmer weather. Another former Tehran Child, a friend of my aunt, told me her "terrible asthma" had propelled her father to seek a warmer, drier climate. Others said they had relatives in Central Asia ("we knew we had family who were already in Tashkent and we had to try to find them"), or that their parents had long-term plans ("my parents thought that we might be able to go to Palestine from Uzbekistan"). These explanations all turned on free will and agency, usually of the interviewee's parents acting to better the situation of their children.

"Of course, this cannot be true," Sergey said in a hushed voice, his face contorting in discomfort. The lobby of Sasha and Son was quiet and empty with the exception of the receptionist, who kept looking our way. Outside, our guide Kamara was waiting. "Let's get out of here through the back door to talk," Sergey whispered. "And please, Professor, turn off your camcorder."

We walked out into dusty Eshtoni Pir Street. "It's so strange," I said to Sergey as we continued toward the lovely Eshtoni Pir Madrassa. "The deportation cards I received in Komi listed a first place of exile—Arkhangelsk—and now I know the second—Kolkhoz Octoyber, Kazakhstan. But only now when I hear it from you does it click for me that my father's release from Posiołek Ostrowsky was in fact a second *deportatsiya*."

"Of course," Sergey said. "All the documents at the KGB archive say: 'Yosef go in this direction,' 'Hayyim go in that direction,' that's what the documents say, I saw it with my own eyes." The archive's director had not granted Sergey permission to copy documents, so he had typed notes that he would give me on a password-encrypted USB drive, he said, and he had memorized many facts about the Jewish migrants that he could share with me. "Because somehow my whole life has been related to Jews, and I love the Holy Land," he added, "and many of my friends in Tashkent had been Jews. The school I studied in in Tashkent was unofficially a kind of

Jewish school, where all the children of evacuees and refugees studied." In Tashkent he knew a man, Palikovsky, "very, very old and very, very poor," who was collecting materials for an encyclopedia of well-known Jewish people in Uzbekistan. "He has completed only one volume," Sergey said. "I got to know him through my friends in Eben Ezer, a small organization that helps people with Jewish origins go to Eretz Yisrael." Everyone who worked at Eben Ezer was an ethnic Korean Uzbek.

"Why would they work at such an organization?" I asked, totally confused.

"Because they are very religious, and Eben Ezer is not a Jewish organization but belongs to descendants of very religious Christians who saved Jews in Sweden. They persuade Uzbek Jews that according to the Bible they should go to Eretz Yisrael." Sergey pronounced the last two words in unaccented Hebrew.

Sergey, a graduate of the National University of Uzbekistan in Tashkent with a degree in economics, was also very religious. He had formerly been a Soviet-style atheist and a drinker, but when "a tragedy hit him," as he put it—his son was born with cleft lip—he "met with the God of Abraham, believed in him and went in his way."

"A Presbyterian in a Muslim country sounds precarious," I said.

"Yes," he whispered. "But I am a citizen of Uzbekistan; I have nowhere else to go. I'm not like my Jewish friends."

Most of Sergey's friends left for Israel after the collapse of the Soviet Union and the beginning of Uzbek independence. "Do you keep in touch by Facebook?" I asked stupidly, still unaware that except in some hotel rooms, the Internet was unavailable in Uzbekistan.

Sergey said nothing.

"Were any of your school friends former Polish refugees?" I tried again: after Russia, I was no longer surprised that a good portion of the refugees here remained in their place of exile.

"I don't know where they came from, but all of them were Ashkenazi Jews: Dabravistaky, Shpaliansky, Viberman. As I know from state archives, a large group of people stayed here in Uzbekistan. This was the

Soviet Union," he said for the third time. "They told you where to go and whether you could leave. When your family arrived here, they would have had to present their documents and receive a placement to a *kolkhoz*—in their case Kolkhoz Octoyber—before they were allowed to leave Arys station." He was whispering emphatically, as if I weren't getting it. "I saw it with my own eyes. They were assigned to specific addresses, to stay with specific Uzbek families: Abram Velovic goes to Karima Blah-Blah-Blah; Zindel Teitel goes to Akmal So-and-So."

"Did the Uzbeks consent to this?" I asked.

Sergey stared at me, exasperated. "Everybody was forced. The Hebrew people were forced to go to the *kolkhozes,* and the Uzbek people were forced to take them. This was the Soviet system. No choice, no freedom!"

≡

Arys station, where Hannan, Regina, and their parents arrived in November 1941, became, within weeks after their release from the settlement, a permanent encampment for thousands. "Peasant men and women, whole families, middle-class people, workers, intellectuals, all on the miserable floor of the train station; entire families with their bundles waiting a day, two, three," Wat recalled in *My Century.*[29] Outside the station, NKVD men prevented the people inside from exiting until they presented the necessary paperwork and were dispatched accordingly. The more the attempt to control migration disintegrated into a mass uncontrolled movement of people, the harder the state tried to confine people to their place of deportation and region of resettlement.

Inside, there was no food. The bread distribution centers that were commissioned by the Evacuation Council to local distributers had not yet been set up, and in the black market system that immediately emerged, the refugees, unlike the evacuees, had nearly nothing left to bargain with. Refugees subsisted on what they had hoarded, and they sat, as the Teitels did, weakened and sullen-faced, atop their blankets and bundles, as Regina told me.

A couple of weeks before the Teitels arrived at Arys station, eight-year-old Alina Goldlust and her five-year-old brother Janusz had passed through. Their parents, Jacob and Jonina, had died in Siberia, and somehow they had made it south with the great wave of migrants. Ten months later Janusz and Alina would be shipped to Iran alongside my father. Three decades later Janusz would command the Israeli Defense Forces' Seventh Armored Brigade against the Syrian invasion in the Golan Heights. Seven decades later, he would give testimony for an Israeli documentary about the Tehran Children. But now, starving, the boy slowly reached for the small piece of bread he had been hoarding in his bundle for days and for a split second stared at it, trying to decide whether to eat it at once and squelch his burning hunger, or wait an hour longer. Then he thrust it into his mouth, sliding the wet concoction down his tongue, closing his eyes and for a moment, loosening his constant vigilance and losing himself in the delight of his taste buds.

Janusz had been three when his family fled his hometown of Łódź and had only vague, sensual recollections of his prewar life. The sensation of tasty food was one of them, lulling him back into a world far away from the station. Then his mouth was yanked open, and a man shoved his hand inside, fished out the saliva-covered dough, which Janusz had not yet swallowed, and thrust it into his own mouth. The child opened his eyes quickly enough to see a Red Army soldier, no more than eighteen, walk away.

His earsplitting sobs, howling over the usual sounds of sighing and haggling at the station, rattled the station, Janusz Goldlust, now retired Brigadier General Avigdor Ben-Gal, told an interviewer in the 2007 Israeli documentary *The Children of Teheran*. "I still remember the feeling of the bread, and then of his hand inside my mouth. I think I can even still hear that little boy cry. I also remember his face; he too was hungry," he says of the Russian soldier. Ben-Gal's voice is soft, almost inaudible; his expression a mix of embarrassment and wonder, more of shock than pain, as if he were reliving that moment.

Regina had the same expression, the same low tone, when I asked her about Arys. "Leave it," she said. "It was terrible."

Deportations, evacuations, and the misery of starving refugees stuck in train stations did not exist in our official tour of Uzbekistan, which more or less shifted from the fifteenth century to the present. It skipped over more than five centuries of rule by various empires and two decades of dictatorship: Persian, Mongol, Chinese, Tsarist Russian, Soviet, and other conquerors, kings and empires that predated the creation of independent Uzbekistan, barely a quarter-century ago. "Whatever happened in the past," our guide Kamara, who caught the tail end of my conversation with Sergey, said, "we are all happy now that we are free and have our independence." Uzbeks had lived under Soviet rule—administered by a Sovietized ethnic Uzbek and Tajik ruling class—for seven decades, after which more or less the same people continued to rule it as an independent Uzbek state.

Now all Uzbek tour guides followed an official protocol that was riddled with the words *our, ours,* and *our very own.* "Here I can prove to you how much our own sciences had been developed," Kamara began as we stood at the impressive Ismail Samani Mausoleum in Bukhara, built between 892 and 943. "Let us admire the beauty. The building is perfect. Nothing should be added, nothing should be subtracted. Here we can find sine, cosine, tangent, because our builders were the best mathematicians. And then it is unbelievable that this is the monument which has celebrated its thousandth year. How could it happen? Because the skill of the work, the knowledge of chemistry which they used for the cement of the brick work: tortoises, grape juice, camels' milk instead of water. . . .

"Bukhara was Oxford of the east; all the scholars—philosophers, mathematicians, astronomers—they came here and astonished the world with their knowledge. Biruni from Khwarazm who created the globe; Al Kharezi, who was born in Kiva from this country. This country was the great center of civilization, the cradle of eastern civilization."

Kamara's recitation was relentless and impenetrable. When we asked questions, she answered with brief platitudes ("we are a happy people"), then returned with greater aggressiveness and vigor to her script. Her job, it seemed, was to keep us from asking questions, and to elegantly dodge the few that would come up. Clearly we were not free: our passports had been taken by the clerk at Sasha and Son and would be returned only when we left; our guide and driver were with us nearly all the time.

And yet Bukhara did not feel as tense and uncomfortable as Komi. It felt blessed: the light, the quiet, the pretty young mothers in green, red, and orange dresses, pushing strollers as their older children rode bikes on the mausoleum's park's trails. Even Kamara, relentless and aggressive, was also warm, maternal. I did not feel even the slightest intimidation that I sometimes felt as an Israeli Jew, let's say, in London. Traveling with Salar, whom everyone around me seemed to regard as their friend and brother almost immediately, no doubt helped.

And no one, no Muslim or Jew we met in Uzbekistan, seemed to question or care that the two of us—a Muslim and a Jew, an Iranian and an Israeli—were traveling together. "We welcome all peoples," Kamara repeated ad nauseam. "In my family one of my grandmothers was Polish babushka"—interesting, I noted to myself—"another one was from Ukraine. In such way I used to say that nation is nothing, people are the same. We are all born and die the same way. What distinguishes us is our kindness. As we are used to saying, *bismillah al rakhman*: God is kind. And even more, the Jews have lived here with us for thousands of years."

Roughly fifty thousand Jews out of a population of roughly 6.5 million lived in the Uzbek Socialist Soviet Republic in 1939, nearly all Sephardim from Bukhara; more than a million more arrived during the war, nearly all Ashkenazi Europeans. Central Asian Jews are said to have come directly from the land of Israel, after the Babylonian destruction of the First Temple in ancient Jerusalem. The claim is supported by the remnants of a 2,200-year-old synagogue that Soviet archaeologists discovered in what is now Turkmenistan. By other accounts, Bukharan Jews emigrated from Persia at the time of the persecutions of King Peroz (458–85): they spoke Tajik, a dialect of Persian, which they wrote with Hebrew letters. Jewish merchants on the Silk Road are also said to have settled in Uzbekistan in the seventh century.

Statues of Tamerlane, whom Kamara called "the father of Uzbek nation," "the Great Amir Timur," adorned Bukhara and elsewhere, yet Tamerlane was not an Uzbek at all but a Turco-Mongol conqueror. The founder of the Timurid Empire in Persia and Central Asia, he ruled for thirty-five years, from 1370 to 1405, and by the time of his death, he had conquered all the land from Anatolia eastward to Mongolia and from the Volga River south to Delhi, including much of Iran.

"After the Mongol yoke," Kamara said, "he brought prosperity to our country. Tamerlane has a bad reputation, but in reality he built the architecture, arts, and literature of this country. He was not on the same level as the region's former conqueror, Genghis Khan, who was wild in his violence. He established links to other nations and honored them—there are villages in Uzbekistan called Baghdad, Istanbul, Tehran—and never he killed the rulers of the countries he conquered like the Bolsheviks killed the Romanov family." Kamara continued to heap superlatives upon the father of the nation.

"Tamerlane was a vicious murderer," Salar whispered to me. "He razed entire cities, committed genocide everywhere. His campaigns caused the deaths of something like five percent of the world's population." But Tamerlane did not conquer Jerusalem and was said to have been "good to the Jews."[30]

"Do Uzbek children study the same medieval Muslim scholars as their forefathers?" I asked Kamara.

"Of course, all of them: Biruni, Avicenna, Farabi, who is considered to be Aristotle of the east." Under his sunglasses, I could see Salar grinning. Ismail Samani hailed from a Persian dynasty, the Samanids; Avicenna, aka Ibn Sīnā, was a Persian polymath of the Islamic Golden Age. Much of Uzbekistan's monumental architecture was Persian, and Persian nomads were the first people known to have inhabited Central Asia, which became part of the Persian Empire in the fifteenth century. One of Uzbekistan's spoken languages, in addition to Uzbek and the official Russian, is Tajik. Every exemplar of what Kamara called "our own Uzbek thinker," or "our great Uzbek art" was Persian.

But Salar wasn't angry; he was glowingly happy, and our tour of

Bukhara and its grand Persian culture was an additional layer to his Persian identity. I, on the other hand, was going in the opposite direction, with my father's "identity" increasingly seeming a matter of chance and circumstance. Ernst Gellner and Eric Hobsbawm, those two former-refugees-turned-historians-of-nationhood, wrote developmental accounts of the emergence of nations as products of centuries-long political, economic, and cultural changes. But in the stories I encountered, nations and national identities formed much more arbitrarily, through encounters of one kind or another, rejections and embraces of a group by some and not by others, paths of different groups or persons that converged or diverged. Rogers Brubaker, a sociologist, writes of "nationness" as "a contingent, conjecturally fluctuating, and precarious frame of vision" that may "suddenly crystallize rather than gradually develop." The "contingent events and their transformative consequence," he writes, disappear from the myth of origins of nations once the national identity has been crystalized.[31] I had known my father only through this final "identity," through his point of contact with the Jews of Palestine who embraced him. But he had had other potential fates along the way.

=

Kolkhoz Octoyber, where Hannan and his family were transported from Arys station on a cold November day in 1941, was a barebones settlement forty kilometers from Arys. The refugees were brought there by carts: forty or fifty Polish and Jewish families accompanied by armed NKVD men. In the *kolkhoz* were *kibitkas*, windowless mud huts, and small natural ponds that the children ran to drink from, eating live lizards and frogs, anything they could get their hands on. *Kolkhoz* members were assigned to dig a canal.

"The *kolkhoz* was a very poor one," Hannan said in his testimony.

> And apart from its managers, who had an easy life, everyone there starved [and] walked barefoot. . . . It was already wintertime, so there was no work in the field. The Uzbeks asked us why we had come there. They didn't know what to do with the fresh crop of

200 people and where they were going to get food for such a crowd. In the first days, they gave us a half a kilo of flour per person. A couple of days later, it seems, they reconsidered and only gave us 10 decagram[s] per person and it had to suffice. In the kolkhoz there was also no place where you could purchase something, and even worse: there was no one who wished to buy something from you in exchange for a piece of bread. The Uzbeks go about wrapped in bed sheets . . . and they need nothing, so we literally starved there and many people died of hunger. We lived in a mud hut without windows or doors. No oven, no beds, no table, only a cooking-pot, whose smoke would spread in the hut and evaporate through a hole in the wall. We worked at digging a canal. There were a couple of Polish families with us in the kolkhoz who slaved away and starved just like we did. But we were not allowed to leave the kolkhoz. We were sentenced to sitting there and dying of hunger.

Shocked and weary, leaning against the outside of their smoke-filled hut while their mother tried to bake some sort of thin bread, my father and Regina watched the Uzbeks cook wild plants inside huge pots and eat them with their hands. There was not a single spoon at the *kolkhoz*. There was no common language: most locals spoke Uzbek and knew only a few Russian words. The Uzbeks eyed them with indifference, and at least initially, they did not come near.

In some *kolkhozes*, locals reportedly "ate well" and had better living conditions: plank beds instead of the ground. In a few, Uzbeks oversaw the newcomers or chased them away, shouting that they themselves had nothing to eat. The luckiest among the refugees worked in agricultural *kolkhozes*, harvesting rye or picking radishes or peanuts, which both locals and refugees could periodically steal and eat. In most, including Kolkhoz Octoyber, the two populations starved together yet apart, side by side in the misery inflicted on them by the war and Soviet policies.

The majority of Uzbek *kolkhozes*, some employing as many as fifteen hundred people, were organized around harvesting cotton. Uzbek cotton accounted for two-thirds of all cotton produced in the Soviet Union, and it remains Uzbekistan's main crop today.

Kolkhoz Dimitrov, where Emma Perelgric and her father Adam were sent, was a cotton *kolkhoz*. Sergey had been able to locate it in the vicinity of Samarqand, having been unsuccessful in locating my father's Kolkhoz Octoyber.

It took us four hours to drive from Bukhara to Samarqand. Gliding along with Bilol's calm, competent driving, even the sight of the half-deserted factories and squalid villages along the way could not spoil my mood. I was on vacation, whether I wanted to be or not, on a tour of "breathtaking Uzbekistan." If my father's experience in Uzbekistan had been essentially about hunger, mine was all about food: kebabs in Bukhara; dried apricots and nuts in Samarqand; heaps of rice with and without lentils everywhere; Azia Pilsner beer; black coffee; outdoor cafés in Bukhara; inner courtyards in Samarqand; Korean *bi bim bop* in Tashkent; an endless succession of restaurants, cafés, snacks, food markets, food samplings, and food breaks, as if food were the main diversion, not to mention the main expression of the hospitality of our various hosts.

At Café Zafar, Sergey arranged for us to meet a young man who would take us to the former Kolkhoz Dimitrov near Samarqand. The café looked like a wedding hall, with white upholstered chairs, waiters in bow ties, and wailing Arabic music that blared out of huge outdoor speakers. In the middle of the hall, near a blue fountain surrounded by flamenco statues, sat a young man, Suyun, muscular and smiling, looking like a Maccabee Tel Aviv soccer player in a yellow polo shirt with some kind of symbol and tight jeans.

Because Soviet names of villages have been so methodically erased, Sergey had spent weeks searching for the former *kolkhoz*, scouting the area by foot and talking to people, until he came across Suyun, no older than twenty-five and father to five young children, who worked in timber and helped him make inquiries with the farmers. Suyun was beaming, taking our photographs with a small camera, saying repeatedly that he was very proud we came to see him, and hugging Sergey, whom he called "my best friend." Sergey was reserved and extremely respectful, trying to fend off the succession of dishes that came out of Zafar's kitchen at Suyun's request and despite our protestations.

After some pleasantries and fighting over the bill, which Suyun paid, we drove to Juriyat, a village located twenty or thirty kilometers east of Samarqand, nonexistent on Google Maps. It was formerly named after the Bulgarian Communist politician Georgi Dimitrov, leader of the Communist International from 1934 to 1943 and the first Communist to lead Bulgaria in the postwar era, after whom streets are still named in Bulgaria, Cuba, and Nicaragua.

"You can write a book about each *kolkhoz*," Sergey said as we drove to Juriyat. His own grandparents had been deported from Khabarovsk, a region in the Russian far east, where his grandfather, a tractor driver, migrated from Korea sometime in the late nineteenth century. "Khabarovsk was a vast territory with a climate similar to Korean climate but soil much richer, and he enjoyed the good life," Sergey said. But that life ended in 1936, with the eruption of Soviet-Japanese border conflicts and the deportation of Koreans, who were at the time subjects of the empire of Japan. "They had houses, they had fields, they had crops," Sergey said. "Then came the command: you have twenty-four hours to leave, and if you do not obey you'll be shot. They put you on animal cars, you cannot go to toilet but do everything inside, and many people died around you." A cousin of Sergey's grandmother who was deported with her had told him that during one stop a few children jumped off the car with small pots to fetch water, and they were gunned down. "Just to take water, to bring it to their grandmother," he said.

Sergey's mother, who had been a child like Regina and my father, was exiled along with her parents and 174,000 ethnic Koreans in the first Soviet deportation of an entire nationality. "They were dumped in southern Kazakhstan—my mother's twin sister and older brother died on the way—like beasts into the desert, just to survive. They fought wild animals, and the desert was not fit for humans. It is estimated that forty thousand deported Koreans died in 1937 and 1938 from starvation, exposure, and difficulties adapting to their new environment. Those who survived have succeeded in Central Asia."

"There was a *kolkhoz* near Tashkent called Palitadeh, now Goolistan," Kamara said, "which was established by those Koreans who were thrown to the desert from zero, from nothing. That *kolkhoz* was number one in picking rice and cotton. They were also good in soccer and hockey."

"That's right," Sergey said, without a shred of cynicism. "We are strong people, trained to survive. We didn't have pogroms like the Jews. But this hardship took our soul."

Juriyat, with its gravel roads, barracks, and whitewashed tree trunks, reminded me of an Israeli military base, like the one where my father had spent forty-eight years of his life, only smaller. The *kolkhoz* consisted of different "brigades," Sergey said. The Perelgrics were in "Brigade Number Six: a very large empty house, maybe more like an animal house where they were accommodated." The area was more wooded then than it was now, and less built up; inside, the *kibitka* looked "like army barracks, long and stark."

We parked before a gate. Inside the gate was an Uzbek family: a father in a white cap and a short-sleeve button-down shirt; a pretty, heavyset mother in a blue floral dress, her head covered by a scarf; and three boys, one carrying an iPad.

Their family had lived on this land since the early twentieth century. Suyun led the way; they had known we were coming and walked us to the plot where the barrack was. "The Poles were in terrible shape," the tall farmer, Jamil Boboqulov, said, pointing to the barren patch in his garden where he claimed the refugees, including Adam Perelgric, had lived. "They were thrown off the carts, jumped on the ground, and started eating anything they found. They ate grass, they ate live frogs, they ran after wild dogs and killed and ate them." Jamil looked about forty.

"How did he know this?" I asked.

"His father told him," she said, after asking him. "His father told him that the refugees were too weak to work or even to stand and that many of them just lay down and died. They would cart them to the cemetery and bury them."

"The Muslim cemetery?" I asked.

"Of course," Jamil said, closing his eyes. "They buried them with no name, and that is why since that time we pray for them here. Because of their hunger, because their suffering had been the greatest we have ever seen."

Jamil, tall and handsome with a short, graying cropped beard, and very calm, upright, and composed, with no guile or discomfort, looked more like a scholar than a farmer. "The Uzbeks are a very knightly race," Aleksander Wat had written, a description that felt accurate.[32] His face, elongated, brown-eyed, and radiant, appeared full of grace as he walked us slowly and calmly around his luscious garden, talking to us in a language that neither Salar nor I understood. Yet as Kamara translated, his words conveyed such a deep, simple sympathy that I felt overcome with emotion.

Birds hummed around us. "In the Muslim cemetery there was a separate place for Jewish people," he said.

"Does it still exist?" Salar asked.

"*Da.*" Yes.

"The locals," Sergey said, "didn't know Polish, and of course the Poles didn't know Uzbek—this is a rural area—so they couldn't communicate."

Jamil recited a blessing for the dead, and as he said it, we all stood quietly at the plot. Behind us, his teenage sons—Muhammad Ali and Ali Muhammad—giggled, clueless and bemused, and filmed us with their iPad. I wondered if filming was the iPad's primary use, given they had no Internet.

We proceeded to a covered porch area where the farmer's wife, round-faced and smiling, shelled bread out of a stone oven, a thin pita made of flour, yeast, and water, which was served with bowls of salt water into which we dipped it. It was hot and delicious. The water, Jamil said, came from his own spring. He asked Salar to say a blessing.

Salar touched the bread to his forehead and kissed it several times. Our hosts were ecstatic. I laughed with pure happiness, not at them but with them, with all of us; if there was ever something like a "spiritual moment" in my life, this was it.

As we drove away to Sergey's "best friend" Suyun's house, I saw them standing: the husband and wife, their right hands to their hearts, and one of their sons behind them, still snapping photos of us with his iPad.

Suyun's home seemed slightly more modern than Jamil's. At the entrance Sergey and Suyun hugged profusely: "You are my honored guest," "You are my best friend," "This is the best day of my life." We were invited in as well for a succession of sweets, a display of Suyun's wife and adorable children, and a constant repetition of such phrases and greetings. We sat under the light of a generator—there was no public electricity—thanking Suyun again and again and toasting him with the vodka we had gifted him. My head spun with happiness, nausea, exhaustion, everything.

None of our hosts and helpers asked for any payment. There was no Second World War tourism industry here as there was in Poland, where our guide, Krzysztof Malczewski, though knowledgeable and warm, had charged five hundred dollars a day; there were no financial subsidies of liberal Western foundations for memorialization or reconciliation; there were no grassroots memorialization groups as there had been in Russia; there were no financial or political interests, no guilt, no remorse, no excessive love or hate that dictated the Juriyat farmers' actions. There was, at this moment, a culture of hospitality and compassion, a true feeling of goodness and humility that engulfed us all completely, with full hearts and full stomachs.

Two Tehran Children described Dimitrov Kolkhoz in their testimonies. The first called it "worse than the Posiołek."

> We worked in the cotton fields for 200 grams of grain, even the young children. The day we were given a bit of rye flour was a great occasion for us. After a few weeks the Uzbeks announced they could no longer keep us because they had no food for us, but we begged them, and they let us stay a little longer.

The second described tensions with between the Jewish incomers and the locals.

> In the kolkhoz we worked in the cotton fields together with Mama, for which we got *lepioshki* (a type of flatbread) and sometimes a hundred grams of flour. We were terribly hungry. The Uzbeks taunted us as "Jewish squires" and threatened to throw us out of the kolkhoz. Mama had to beg them to let us stay.[33]

At Kolkhoz Maxim Gorky, NKVD-appointed Uzbek supervisors reportedly kept close watch on the newcomers in order to prevent them from rebelling.[34] There were reports of refugees being chased out, mocked, stolen from, or charged excessive fees for burying their dead.

Stanisław Kot, the Polish government-in-exile ambassador to the USSR, reportedly complained to the Soviet vice commissar for foreign affairs on January 26, 1942 that "the local Mongol population" in Kazakhstan "were behaving very ruthlessly towards [Polish] citizens. . . . Certain of them sent to collective farms have been refused living quarters, they have to camp under the bare sky, or instead of bread they are given gluey cakes in such small quantity that it is quite insufficient to keep them alive."[35]

But Mula Ben Hayyim, a former member of Ha'shomer Ha'tsair who had testified in Israel in the 1970s, called such incidents "exceptional" and reiterated the "deep brotherhood" between locals and him and his friends. After the reduction of the refugees' daily rations to four hundred grams of unprocessed barley, he writes, "the more established local families invited us for meals, which helped a lot. . . . I would even say they appreciated us. They definitely learned things from us that they did not know. . . . The Uzbek members of the *kolkhoz* were very nice and welcoming. They cared for our needs; they really made an effort for us." He added, "I will never forget our *kolkhoz* accountant Akhadadov. When our shoes tore, he took us to the market in Samarqand, one hundred kilometers away, and bought us new ones. He really tried to make things more comfortable for us." Ben Hayyim had been invited to Uzbek celebrations and weddings (which were "interesting"). "Slowly we got used to their music, which was very much like Arabic music. When we got sick with malaria they tried to cure us with sour milk. Of course it was primitive. But their care and worry, during those days, was uplifting.

"They were Muslim," Ben Hayim added, "and they did not pay any heed to the fact that we were Jewish; they called all the non-Muslim foreigners *Orus*." The trouble began only during "the second period," when the starvation and black market dealings deepened.[36]

"These people at Juriyat were formidable," I said to Sergey when we finally drove through the village's dark dirt roads back to our hotel in Samarqand. It was close to midnight.

"Yes, the Uzbeks are very good people, very good," he said, with an emphasis on *very*. "I think Central Asia was the right place to exile the Jews. Because if the Jews could survive anywhere, it was only here. The people were very kind, very hospitable. They shared the last thing they had. It was really like that. Because if it was, say, Ukraine or Belarus or something like that, they would have butchered them. . . . Do you know about pogroms, Professor?" he asked. "I don't know why, but Jewish people were not welcomed anywhere."

That night the cramps came at three a.m., then nausea and shivers such as I had never had before, and an attack of vomiting so strong and violent, it left me unable to walk from the bed to the bathroom and continued throughout the night in intermittent spasms. Within an hour, my fever shot to 104 and I felt as if I were expelling my insides and freezing at the same time. I dialed Salar's room to tell him I was dying for my moment of spiritual bonding with the Uzbek farmers. Why had I let my guard down? Why, despite every prohibition, had I not refused to drink water from Jamil's creek?

One out of four refugees died of dysentery, malaria, typhus, or other starvation- and hygiene-related diseases in Central Asia, and testimonies of those who survived rang in my head: "My father got sick with dysentery and after eight days died in the hospital"; "My mother got dysentery, became terribly thin, and died"; "Mama became sick"; "He didn't cry or groan, just collapsed onto the bed and couldn't get up"; "Papa said that Mama has gone to sleep."

"You'll be fine," Salar said. Our trip had had its tense moments, with his agenda, my agenda, the agendas of our various companions and helpers, and our shared book project: the alternating chapters we each wrote, which did not seem to gel well together. But all night he wiped the vomit off the floors, the sheets, the towels, my clothes, my hair. He dragged me in and out of the toilet, kept me hydrated, and cleaned up when I vomited the little water I drank. He danced, jumped, sang, and made me laugh when I thought I was dying.

In the morning the hotel summoned Dr. Anatoli, who every day made rounds to sick tourists at Samarqand's hotels. Within minutes, looking no older than twenty-five, cheerful and laissez faire, he assembled a mobile IV line that shot massive amounts of Augmentin into my veins, and within an hour, I was revived, still weak but exuberant to be alive and back in the game so quickly.

$$\equiv$$

It was difficult to gauge what the Central Asian landscape and the region's cultural life could have meant to Hannan, Regina, and other Polish refugees. Their social world was Soviet—they worked in Soviet *kolkhozes* and factories, they obeyed Soviet laws, and their lives were administered by Soviet people. But there was also another, parallel habitat, particularly outside the cities: a Kazakh, Kyrgyz, or Uzbek world. In their testimonies and memoirs, Hannan and most of the other refugees made little mention of this world, the silent backdrop to their story of a daily struggle to survive. But some accounts, particularly by those who lived for an extended period in the more rural, less migrant-flooded regions of Central Asia, differed according to geographical settings.

The locals, historian Medvedeva-Nathoo writes, called the newcomers Westerners or *vykovyrennye*, "plucked-out people." The "mutual lack of knowledge" of "Asians" and "Westerners"—and "the resulting lack of mutual stereotypes," she adds—"created an opportunity for both sides to get to know each other."[37] At least to some degree, the "plucked-out people" tried to understand their Asian surroundings, "filling up the vacuum of ignorance with scraps of incidental observations."

"Our first encounter with the locals seemed to us Europeans like a dream," Josek Klapholz, a refugee from Krakow and Tehran Child, wrote of arriving in Aralsk, Kazakhstan: "a nice, quiet city, full of welcoming Kazakhs":

> Those Uzbeks, Kazakhs, Turkmens and the rest of the natives of this vast land, dressed in long, colorful gowns, donning round square shaped caps embroidered with an array of colors reminded me of *A Thousand and One Nights* from my childhood. The camels that we saw for the first time added to the exotic picture. We thought we arrived in heaven.[38]

Alexsander Kovarsky, a teenage Polish refugee, climbed trees and roamed Tashkent's streets with the son of his Uzbek landlord. "I quickly mastered Uzbek and I became the link between the adults and the outside world," he recalled.[39]

"The Uzbeks were pretty nice, hospitable like all Muslims," Shmuel Natanzon, a Tehran Child, recalled of the Uzbek family from whom his parents had rented a room near Samarqand. "Once in a while they treated us to rice, or something. So that even though we were hungry, we didn't starve completely."[40]

"The Uzbeks [are] magnificent horsemen with enormous dignity," Aleksander Wat remembered of his first impressions upon arriving at the Fergana Valley in Uzbekistan. "They were almost entirely in rags, but they had handsome faces, masculine profiles, the faces of real mountain people. Each of them wore a bright, colorful eastern silk sash. They were dressed in rags but their sashes were always in perfect condition. Red silk, blue, green, turquoise." Even their "small horses—I had never seen horses like that before—[had] very beautiful faces."[41]

Wat recalled a "mosque where no services were held"; a mullah "who had been arrested"; and "gray-bearded elders who sat on cushions and drank tea." He continued, "They were very thin from hunger, but they had enormous dignity; I never saw anything like that in all the time I was in Russia."[42] There was something of the European colonist's sensibility in Wat's observations ("all the people in those tribes possessed great subtlety and at the same time great cruelty") but also of the inversion of this sensibility by the powerlessness of the refugees: arrogance mixed with eagerness, desperation even, and closed-mindedness mixed with curiosity and openness toward a people whose "exclusion from the context of their place and time," as Medvedeva-Nathoo puts it, "exacerbated the acuteness with which [they] perceived the world."[43]

Amalia Iosifovna Frajlich, the twenty-seven-year-old Polish-Jewish refugee at the center of Medvedeva-Nathoo's paper, was in Katta-Taldyk (today Kara-Suu), Kyrgyzstan, where she and 1,540 other former Polish citizens worked in agricultural *kolkhozes*. Amalia kept a diary, where she wrote her observations about and interactions with the Kyrgyz people of the Naukat region. In the rural settlements (*kishlaki*) and yurts (*kibitki*), roofs were molded and clay floors were "washed." Quilted blankets also served as mattresses, "an embellishment and pride of the home." The typical kitchen implements were the cast-iron pots that were used for cooking and the stove for baking flatbread (*lapyushka*). She admired the slow Eastern melodies. It was customary to "break cake with a guest." Men wore "traditional quilted robes and [sat] cross-legged or on their haunches." Women "braid[ed] their hair into numerous plaits," and "carried heavy objects on their heads ... with incredible grace." The people had a tradition of "burying the dead in a seated position and leaving a bowl (*piyala*) filled with rice on a grave," which made a great impression on Amalia. They used "hard-working donkeys" and "intelligent camels."[44]

Amalia, formerly known as Malka, had been a teenage member of Ha'shomer Ha'tsair and then of the Communist Party of Western Ukraine. Observations aside, the emotional core of her diary was her loneliness, her daily struggle, and her longing to connect with former comrades.

"Our life is so monotonous, so impoverished, that there is nothing even to write about," she wrote. "Our entire world is the field on which all our interests are inescapably focused." Her diary comes alive only when she receives a postcard from a prewar comrade: "Es[teemed] Com[rade]!" . . . I stumbled across the surname Frajlich on a list. . . . Is that you, Malya? . . . Lord, if this is you, answer at once, write about everything."

"When my hopeless situation had reached rock bottom," Amalia wrote in her diary that night, "a friend stretched out a hand from the distant capital of Kirgizia. . . . I wanted to weep bitterly! Where did we come from? Who are we today? To what depths have we descended? But now we . . . are no longer alone; someone somewhere, even if far away, loves us, someone needs us. . . . We are a particle of something whole!"

Across Central Asia, hundreds of members of political movements wandered in search of each other. Ha'shomer Ha'tsair even tried to publish and distribute a paper—*Baderekh* (En Route)—that would reach its members, who were dispersed across Tashkent, Samarqand, Juma, Bukhara, and into Tajikistan and Kazakhstan. Even after two years in exile, their emotional longing remained for each other.[45]

Newcomer children appeared to make easier, more immediate contact with local children. The liveliest account of such contact appears in the testimony of Eliosha Poznijac (now an Israeli man named Eli Paz), a Polish-born Jewish boy like Hannan who lived with his mother and siblings in the Kazakh village of Dzhambul. Poznijac's account was the basis for the young adult novel *Homeward from Steppes of the Sun* by the Israeli writer Uri Orlev. It is a coming-of-age story of sorts, in which Eliosha becomes fascinated by and eventually befriends the independent, manly Dzhambul children. They teach him how to carry water from the river, pluck bird feathers, ride camels, drink camel milk, and dry camel dung, from which *kibitkas*—huts—were made. Eliosha learns to speak Kazakh and helps support his family by hunting and farming. When news of his father's death arrives, locals pay tribute to his family. "I didn't tell them how Jews mourn," his mother says, "but this is exactly how it was in my home. . . . Everyone who came brought a dish or a drink. I never thought I would get this kind of treatment in Kazakhstan, among the Muslims."[46] By their second year in the village, Eliosha no longer remembers Poland.

When I was next in Israel I visited Orlev at his home in Jerusalem to ask him about his book and about Eliosha Poznijac's recollections. (I also asked him about Emil Landau, the Warsaw-born boy whose travel diary was my guide to my father's refugee experience. Orlev had spent his adolescent years with Emil and was his diary's Hebrew translator.) Poznijac's recollections of Central Asia were unequivocally and uniquely positive, and Orlev said he had been absolutely true to them. Poznijac had been young, highly adaptive, and charismatic, and his village was far from the major refugee centers. And in Kazakhstan, life for the refugees appears to have been slightly better than in Uzbekistan; the Kazakhs, unlike the Uzbeks, were nomadic people, less loyal to the Soviets, more pragmatic and survival oriented, and perhaps more open to the new nomads in their midst.

I wondered whether the Warsaw-born Orlev—who had spent the war years in the ghetto, where his mother died, and then in Bergen-Belsen— had been particularly attracted to this alternate, much happier survival story in which a resourceful boy saves his mother. His book reminded me of the wildly popular children's book series *Khasamba*, which first appeared in the 1950s and continued to feed the imagination of Israeli children like me for decades. *Khasamba* is the acronym of a secret group of brave, independent, and ingenious children who tackle problems of the adult world. Poznijac's recollections—and/or Orlev's retelling—of Kazakh bravery and hospitality (both were eventually raised on a kibbutz) were colored by the same ideology of strength, autonomy, and agency. It was impossible to tell whether witness and writer had superimposed these youthful ideals on their recollection of the past, or whether their own past as child refugee survivors had shaped those very ideals.

=

Unlike Eliosha, Hannan and his family left Kolkhoz Octoyber in Kazakhstan as soon as they could, two weeks after their arrival. "Father realized

that if we didn't get out of there in time, we would be buried there,"
Hannan wrote. He offered "the last 100 rubles [he] still owned" to an
Uzbek resident "to help smuggle us" (in his testimony, Hannan used the
Yiddish word אַרויסגנבֿ'ען—*aroys ganaven*—literally, "to steal us") out of
the *kolkhoz*. The four of them, as Regina would later tell me, left in the
middle of the night, soaked to the bones in a torrent of rain ("so that one
man could not see another," Hannan would write), chasing the Uzbek in
the horse-drawn sleigh that had their belongings on it.

> We had to run with the last strength to be close to the sleigh, and
> no matter how much we asked him to ride slowly, it was in vain. We
> thought he ran fast because he was afraid that someone from the
> kolkhoz would run into him; however, it turned out he wanted to
> be alone with our things, so that he could handle them, "free as a
> bird." Indeed, in the morning, we took away from him a pair of my
> mother's patent leather shoes [Hannan used the Polish word *laki-
> erki*], and a pair of my father's shoes. We couldn't find on him the
> pair of my trousers, which he had taken.

My father narrated the incident with uncharacteristic literariness and
vividness. I wondered if, compared to all misery that surrounded them,
this moment had been a bit of comic relief. Or had his mastery of Yiddish
(*fray vi a foygl*—"free as a bird"—was an idiomatic Yiddish expression), a
language I had never heard him speak, brought out a playfulness in him
that I would never know? It was the only time my father mentioned the
Uzbek locals in his testimony.

In exchange for a few of pieces of clothing, the stationmaster seated Hannan, Regina, and their parents on a train back to Arys, Kazakhstan. At Arys
they stayed for six days, begging Red Army soldiers, who were pouring into
Uzbekistan, for food. "When a train with the military arrived," my father
wrote, "we all grouped by the cars and begged. The civilians had nothing.
The army had all the goods there. The soldiers did not refuse us." The city
of Arys was full to the brim with evacuees and refugees. "It was impossible

to obtain an apartment," my father wrote dryly, factually, "so we went from there to Samarqand." After Tashkent, from which they were banned, Samarqand, the second-largest city in Uzbekistan, was a favored destination.

It was overhelming, with jaw-dropping architecture, incredibly beautiful. "We thought we arrived at the Garden of Eden," another Tehran Child, Josek Klapholz, wrote. "But soon we were disappointed. Continuing south was a fatal mistake. Those who remained in Kazakhstan lived reasonably and did not experience the hellish suffering that would be our lot in Samarqand."

When Hannan Teitel, Josek Klapholz, and hundreds of thousands of other refugees arrived in Samarqand, they found that Registan Square and its surrounding medieval madrassas had become a mammoth refugee camp. They slept amid some of the world's most spectacular works of Islamic architecture under the open sky, in the freezing cold, huddling together and trembling under their shared blanket, an experience that many others also recounted:

> We slept on the streets, like thousands of other refugees. Many died on the street and there was no one to bury them.

> In Samarqand it was impossible to get bread and many refugees were dying on the street.

> We arrived in Samarqand on a cold, rainy day. We spent the night in the mud on the street and were robbed of everything we had.

> After two years of hard labor we didn't have the strength to stand on our feet. We traveled from Tashkent to Samarqand, but there too we lived on the street, sleeping in the mud, and many times we wished we were dead.[47]

Several days after Salar and I arrived in Uzbekistan, Professor Oybek

Bozorov, the mathematician and researcher of Polish refugees in Uzbeki-stan, materialized for the first time and met Sergey Kim and us for dinner at an airy garden restaurant in the outskirts of Bukhara. Bald, potbellied, and wearing jeans and a tight-fitting Abercrombie & Fitch T-shirt with a humongous moose logo, Bozorov declared that he had "devoted [his] life to the project of the Jews." The "project"—copying every banishment or deportation card from the KGB archive in Tashkent onto a USB flash drive that the professor would then hand-deliver to the United States Holocaust Memorial Museum—was a lucrative one. For every card that he manually replicated, he received twenty-five cents. There were "thou-sands, tens of thousands, hundreds of thousands" of cards, Bozorov said.

"All science people in Uzbekistan know each other," Bozorov remarked, "and they all know I'm working on Jewish problem, every Holocaust per-son knows me, every archive." His contract, which he brought in a manila folder to show us, was signed by "the great manager of Holocaust Museum Shapiro" (USHMM's director Paul Shapiro). It had just been renewed for another five years, he said. He had so far made sixteen trips to "Holocaust, Washingtona."

"Is there no problem taking these documents to America?" I asked him.

"A little bit," Bozorov said, appearing very jolly and not even as slightly worried or cautious as Sergey had been. I asked him what had drawn him to the "Jewish question." "In Moscow, where I got my degree, all my mathematics professors were Jewish, so I got curious about the Jews," he explained. He owned a hotel in Bukhara: "Why did you stay at Sasha and Son? Next time you stay in my hotel as my guests, for free. Come every summer, come every fall, bring your children, come live in Bukhara." Bozorov was building a three-hundred-seat restaurant in the old center of Bukhara. "I do many things: mathematics, Jewish research, hotels, res-taurants." He laughed. Twenty-five cents times hundreds of thousands of records: I assumed that the United States Holocaust Memorial Museum was the funder of his recent real estate projects.

"It is incredible the Poles took your father to Iran," Bozorov suddenly said to me, pensively, "because the Polish did not want the Jews to leave with them. There was a tension between the Polish and the Jewish. And why would they take children anyway? Perhaps the women were allowed to take children, but as far as I know, for children they created orphanages here in Uzbekistan. Anyway, it was very difficult to leave; it was the Soviet Union! The Soviets did not want anyone to leave. Even after the war, they took the Poles' passports away so they could not leave. Only sick women and children left because for the Soviet government, it was not worth it to care for them and have to feed them."

Bozorov also said, "You should know that ninety percent of the refugees were Jewish. Some pretended to be Polish, but after the war the documents showed that they were Polish-Jewish."

"What documents are these?" I asked.

But Bozorov clamped down, turning instead to talk to Salar in Tajik about his frequent visits to Tehran (for "conferences"). "I stay in Hotel Mashhad, across from the former American embassy. When I open my window, the first thing I see is 'Down with America.'" Bozorov laughed heartily. Hotel Mashhad was owned by Salar's cousin Madi. "That is unbelievable," Bozorov kept saying, toasting with a glass of vodka, then another glass, and another, "to the days the mullahs will leave Iran forever."

Drinking alcohol in public was allowed in Uzbekistan, but alcohol permits were given only to a few establishments, he said. Around us, groups of local women without men were drinking, laughing, and dancing in their seats to the ever louder Russian and Uzbek tunes that the live band played.

"This is not Iran. Families are free here, women are independent." Bozorov's forehead was shining with sweat as he spoke.

"*Ostad* [professor] says that every year you should come here for two weeks. He says Jewish people know the good cities to visit," Salar translated Bozorov's Tajik for me.

"Today is a very special day. I'm very glad to see you. He is my brother; you are my sister. Bukharans are all brothers: Jews, Uzbeks, Tajiks, Russians. We are not like the Europeans. No problem. No national problem. One thousand years together living Jews in Bukhara, and no problem."

I turned to Sergey. "Is it really true that today Jews have no problem in Bukhara?"

"Ummm," Sergey whispered almost inaudibly, "I wouldn't say that exactly, but they have less trouble than Protestants like me. Bringing non-Muslim religions to Uzbekistan is forbidden. If a Presbyterian minister wants to run a congregation or to minister a people, he breaks the law. The Jews have fewer problems because they are natives. Plus, Judaism is not dangerous for locals: Jews seclude themselves; they want no one else to join. Presbyterians are sometimes more active; they go on the streets and help locals to know God." He said nothing more, but as I would later read, Protestants were deemed "extremist" in Uzbekistan. Registering a church or converting another person was a punishable crime, and there were arrests and torture of pastors and converts.

Sergey fell silent, listening intently to the sad Russian tune the band was playing. "It is about a man who is in the gulag prison, missing his beloved," he translated. "The sadness of the melody is very special. It reminds me of what the Jews have suffered."

"But so many people were deported and exiled," I said, "so many were refugees: your grandparents, your mother, Bozorov's mother; the hundreds of thousands of Uzbeks who were exiled to Siberia and the thousands who were exiled from Siberia to Uzbekistan. And many still suffer from persecution."

"It's true that we suffer," he said softly, "but what I read in the archives about the Jewish people was more terrible: there was no place for Jews; they were discriminated against all the way and everywhere."

"You are my son," Bozorov said, toasting Sergey, who did not drink, and ordered another bottle of red wine.

"You are my father," Sergey replied, wincing. "I never had a father, but you are my father."

"And you are my family"—the professor turned to us—"you, Sergey, Salar, your children, my children, Jews, Muslims, Christians. We are all family!"

=

Friendship of peoples, a term popularized by the Soviet government in the 1930s, was repeatedly used at the outset of World War II to describe relations between Uzbek Soviets and Soviet evacuees from Moscow and elsewhere, many of whom were Jewish. Throughout 1940 and 1941, *Pravda Vostoka* ran articles with headlines like "The Uzbek people have forcefully demonstrated just how strong the friendship of peoples is in our Soviet Socialist State." *Friendship* or *brotherhood of peoples* was, as historian Terry Martin puts it, the "officially sanctioned metaphor of an imagined multinational Soviet community": a lens that substituted the distinction between "locals" and "foreigners" with a picture of distinct but equal parts of a single Soviet system.[48] But the metaphor not only gave rise to an imagined portrait of the Soviet Republic of Uzbekistan; to a considerable degree, it created that reality, a reality whose echoes reverberated in Bozorov's words.

Under the umbrella of the "friendship of peoples," the Moscow State Jewish Theater, whose actors and director, Solomon (Shloyme) Mikhoels, had been evacuated, could perform *Tevye der Milkhiker* ("Tevye the Milkman," the original story of *Fiddler on the Roof*) before a mixed audience of evacuees and Uzbeks, shortly after their arrival in Tashkent. After an ecstatic reception by the Soviet press, which lauded the *Tevye* production as a demonstration of the "close link between the national cultures of the Soviet peoples," Mikhoels commissioned from the Jewish writer Der Nister a Yiddish translation of the Uzbek revolutionary drama *Khamza*, inviting Uzbek actors to consult on the production and an Uzbek dancer, Mukkaram Turgunbaeva, to compose its choreography. "The theatre considers it appropriate," Mikhoels wrote, "to include in its repertoire a play demonstrating the struggle and daily life of the Uzbek people, its heroes, and to thus extract useful lessons about the conditions of life in Soviet Uzbekistan."[49]

The Uzbek director Khamid Almidzhan, who co-directed with Mikhoels, praised the Yiddish director and actor for his "tremendous help to Uzbek dramatic arts." Mikhoels, for his part, rejected a colonial understanding of the contribution of the Yiddish theater to local arts and descriptions of it as "a meeting of East and West," as a British journalist called it, insisting that the influences had been reciprocal and the work was a collaboration between distinct but equal "Soviet theatres."[50]

Under the umbrella of "friendship of peoples," the Uzbek poet G'afur G'ulom published a pro-Jewish, anti-Fascist epic *Men-yahudiy* (I Am a Jew), in which the narrator identifies as a Jew and addresses Hitler:

I am a Jew. . . .
When your ancestors . . . knew not what salt, fire, or Nibelung were . . .
I received the Torah and thundered above the mountains of this world.
I am Jew! . . .
Of my genealogy a million books will tell. . . .
I am Jew!
Verses of the Koran . . . are just shadows of my proud thought.
I am Jew! . . .
When you insult me . . . the world knows it is merely a donkey braying
*   in its barn.*
And when you shout to the world that you, Hitler, are of best of men,
I think how laudable it will be to slaughter you.
How long has the blood of all people mixed?
Mine too has ceaselessly been poured into others'.
Nation, religion, purity of races: what else will you contrive? . . .
The Russian, Uzbek, Jewish, and Belarusian's hand is equally strong in
*   battle.*
We will cleanse this world from rotten fascism forever
And you will vanish in hell together with Pharaohs. . . .
In the name of genius author of Das Kapital, *and by the proud spirit of*
*   the ancestor of nations, I here swear: I am human!*[51]

G'ulom's second poem, *Siz Yetim Emmasiz* (You Are Not an Orphan), arguably the most famous Uzbek wartime poem, is an epic about an Uzbek father who, having adopted an evacuee child, reassures the young boy who has been separated from his parents: "Are you really an orphan? . . . Relax my dear. . . . If your father is alive, let the shadow of worry not disturb him amid the horror and the fire, let him know: his son is with me!"[52] The poem was inspired by the case of the Uzbek blacksmith Shaahmed Shamahmudov, whose family was said to have adopted fifteen evacuee children of all nationalities. It was translated into Russian by the evacuee poet Svetlana Somova and published in *Pravda* to great acclaim. The poem was said to have inspired over a thousand additional adoptions of evacuee children, including by the deputy commissioner of the NKVD and the first secretary of the Uzbek Communist Party. Ordinary Uzbeks wanting to "help the motherland" or "demonstrate a Stalinist care for children" often adopted more than one child.[53] In the adoptions, *Pravda*'s editorial board wrote, "we find the most touching and poetic form of the indissoluble brotherhood of peoples, the foundation of our Soviet system." A "Monument of the Friendship of Peoples," an enormous bronze statue of Shaahmed Shamahmudov, surrounded by his fifteen adoptees, was erected in a Tashkent square that bore the same name.

Images, articles, newsreels, and poems about adoptions emphasized the intermixing of races and the amalgamation of distinct racial features and nationalities in a single adoptive household. "Snub-nosed, blue eyed children from Riazan, dark-eyed Ukrainians, Jewish children from Bessarabia became full-fledged members of Uzbek families," as the writer Lydia Chukovskaya put it.[54] Polish refugees did not, of course, fall under this category of a Soviet brotherhood of peoples, but in a reality of chaos, Polish children would have found their way into Russian orphanages and Uzbek families.

Under the umbrella of the friendship of peoples, the evacuated Russian formalist theorist Viktor Zhirmunsky, a specialist in German Romanticism at the University of Leningrad, taught himself the Kazakh and Uzbek languages and began to research the epics of the Asian peoples of the Soviet Union, in particular the Akyn, improvisational poets and singers of Kazakh and Krygyz culture.

Dmitri Ushanov, the philologist, lexicographer, and creator of the definitive four-volume *Explanatory Dictionary of the Russian Language*, began work on a Russian-Uzbek dictionary.

A group of evacuated historians from the Academy of Sciences' Institute of History began collaborating with Uzbek colleagues on a collective history of Uzbekistan. One of them, Ekaterina Kusheva, described the project as an attempt "to repay the hospitality" of their Uzbek hosts.[55]

"Tashkent's kindness knows no bounds," Kornei Chukosky, an eminent literary critic and leading authority on children's linguistic creativity, wrote in his diary on October 30, 1942, the day the city's commissar of education gave him a room, furnished and in the center of town.

Militsa Nechkina, an evacuee member of the Soviet Academy of Arts, wrote of the "large number of acquaintances and friendships that sprung up between 'honored evacuees' and local Uzbeks in the first months of the war."[56]

The poet Iulia Drunina called Tashkent "the most generous city on earth."

The case of the writer Aleksander Wat, a Polish citizen, is an interesting example of a Polish-Jewish refugee's interaction with the "friendship of peoples." Wat had traveled for a week from Saratov prison to Kazakhstan's capital Alma-Ata on what he described as a "lice-covered" train car full of Polish Jews and "butcher-like" Poles. When he descended, he was still eight kilometers away—as in Tashkent, refugees were not permitted to travel directly to the Kazakh capital. So as the soles of his shoes fell off, he walked nearly barefoot on the snow. His entrance to the city was dramatic. "I will never forget the first impression [Alma-Ata] made. For me the city was a metropolis." The ice-covered poplar trees looked like they were "strewn with diamonds"; the silhouettes of the enormous Pamir Mountains with their snowy tips were "like a fine Chinese drawing against a beautiful Italian sky"; the moon, which came out early that night, was "a silvery half-moon, very Islamic."[57]

In Alma-Ata, Victor Shklovsky, the eminent Russian formalist and now an evacuee, heard about Wat from the poet Vladimir Mayakovsky. As soon as Wat arrived in the city, Shklovsky sought him out and brought him into an illustrious circle of evacuee intellectuals. "Their whole group was there, and I would come see them," Wat wrote. "There was a certain amount of fraternization . . . talk about certain things connected with Russian literature." When Shklovsky saw the condition of Wat's wife, who had been in a Kazakh *kolkhoz* and with whom Wat was reunited in Alma-Ata, "he burst into tears" and "immediately dashed to his room and without a word brought her all his supplies, all the rice he had stored up for his son."[58] The secretary of the Kazakh Writers' Union, a poet in his early thirties, also befriended Wat, who suspected the Kazakh was reporting to, if not directly working for, the NKVD. Wat also hobnobbed with the Kazakh writer Mukhtar Auezov ("something of a Kazakh Alexei Tolstoy"), with whom he discussed nineteenth-century Polish Romantic poetry. "The Kazakhs have the highest opinion of the Polish exiles," Auezov said to Wat.[59]

By mid-November, "after a couple of weeks of searching," Zindel Teitel succeeded in finding his family a place to live in Samarqand: 24 Jangirabackaia Street, "a straw and mud hut below town," as Hannan put it in his testimony. Theirs was the last hut on Jangirabackaia, the outer border of the city. Beyond it, the street spilled into the yellow hilly desert that surrounded Samarqand. I knew their address. It had been scrawled on a postcard I found in the Zionist Archive in Jerusalem, which I sent to Professor Bozorov, who gave it to Sergey, who spent days searching for it in the city whose street names had entirely changed.

Sergey discovered that the name Jangirabackaia had been changed to Ziyukolar Street. He led us there in the heat, humidity, and dust, on the wide dirt roads, in the seemingly empty streets, and past low-rise houses and bricked-up windows. The streets were sleepy and empty but clean and neither slummish nor menacing nor sad. Some of the doors were beautifully ornamented. Sergey said it was the oldest part of the quarter.

We stopped at a dusty, half-empty grocery store, offering tomatoes, watermelon, and eggs.

"*Francia, Franci, Fracuzeh?*" the owner said.

"*Americaneh,*" I said.

"*Americaneh?!*" There were not many American tourists in Samarqand, and probably none had ever appeared in his store.

"Who lives here today?" I asked Sergey.

"Uzbeks, Tajiks, Iranians, Russians, Armenians," he said. "A mix of refugees."

We walked for a while, our footsteps crunching the sand, followed by an entourage of curious children and neighbors who seemed to appear out of nowhere, eager to practice their English. The crumbling buildings were new, but here and there an original wall remained, made of mud and straw and devoid of windows. We knocked on the door of Jangiraback-aia 24 and stood there for maybe five minutes, when a pretty, fresh-faced woman opened the door.

"*Kharashoh*, welcome," she said, unsmiling and visibly nervous. She knew nothing of Polish refugees, she told Kamara in Russian, standing uncomfortably by the door. We stood there too. "*Salam*," Salar said, and shifted to Tajik. She lit up and invited us into the large, unkempt court-yard where her family had lived, she said, for forty years. "When they purchased it," the woman said, Salar translating, "the house had mud walls and no roof. One of the old walls remains." She pointed to an inte-rior wall made of mud and straw. Her *baba* had told her many times that refugees had lived there. The woman was Armenian, a people whom the Soviets exiled from Armenia both before and after the war.

The half-enclosed courtyard, divided into multiple subdivisions, had housed several other refugee families before Zindel, Ruchela, Hannan, and Regina arrived there in early 1942, with their lice-infected down blanket and their dwindling pack of belongings. Only refugees lived on Jangirabackaia—no Russians came near it—and poor Uzbeks who con-gregated and sipped tea in a nearby *chaykhana*. In some testimonies, older refugee boys described hanging around there as well, picking up a little Uzbek from the locals.

The house had—or perhaps I imagined it—a sadness unlike any other I had seen in Uzbekistan, not so much of poverty as of indifference and neglect: half-broken furniture strewn around, empty planters, peeling walls. A mulberry tree that stood at the entrance to the house, a *tut*, as Kamara called it—it was the same word in Hebrew—was the only sign of beauty, its leafy branches penetrating an exterior wall, reemerging, and spreading across the courtyard. I assumed, and was stupidly pleased about it, that the tree must have been there when the Teitels arrived.

═══

In Bukhara, meanwhile, Adam and Emma Perelgric arrived at Kagan station along with thousands of other refugees and evacuees who, as in Samarqand, poured in, multiplying by the day as rumors of the approaching German Army spread. Soon, as in Samarqand, they were all camping out in the open in Bukhara's old center. "Hundreds of people, lying on the streets, the sick with the healthy, the living with the dead," a then-fourteen-year-old Tehran Child wrote of his first days in Bukhara. "People robbed each other—and everyone was robbed by the Uzbeks, who were impossible to chase away. We children got so used to the sight of dead people that we stopped being afraid of them."

> When we arrived in Bukhara, thousands of people were camping out in the open, and prowling among them were Uzbek thieves. Many seriously ill people were lying in the streets.

> In Bukhara we spent our nights at the station because no one would take us in.

> In Bukhara there were many Jews from Poland who were dying from the epidemic, and every day there were dozens of corpses dying in the street.[60]

There are mentions in the testimonies of the local Jewish population, mostly of its goodwill, but inability to extend much help:

> We met Bukharan Jews who knew Hebrew. They could not be of much help, since the rich ones had been exiled long ago and the poor had nothing to eat themselves, but they received us warmly and we prayed with them.

Bukharan Jews were very happy to meet us Jews, but they worried
that the cost of living was going up because of us and that the local
population's resentment would increase.[61]

According to one testimony, a local Jewish man gave up his room to
a refugee family and moved into his stable; in another, a Bukharan man
cared for an entire family ill with dysentery, then for the only member—
a ten-year-old child—who remained alive. Some locals reportedly gave
advice, telling newcomers where to go, what to do, while others charged
exorbitant sums for burying refugees in the local Jewish cemetery.

"The Jews had been with us for a long time and have always been
treated equally," Kamara said the next morning with her usual cheer-
fulness. The night before, in an article titled "Uzbekistan's Long Persecuted Bukhara Jews," I read the long list of grievances against Bukharan
Jews: a sixteenth-century "life sparing" tax; restricted neighborhoods;
prohibition from wearing silk or riding horses; occasional forced conver-
sions. Russian tsarist rule (1876–1917) was something of a golden age for
Bukharan Jews, during which they were deemed a "native" ethnic group
and were permitted to ordain rabbis, build synagogues, and in general
follow their own traditions. Under the Soviets, the city's thirteen synagogues were closed, Torah scrolls were confiscated, and rabbis were persecuted and jailed, forcing the community to hold Shabbat services and
perform circumcisions in secret.[62] By the time the Perelgrics arrived, the
wealthier Jews—merchants who had traded in Russian goods and cotton under the tsar—had been exiled or purged by the Soviets; those who
survived the purges migrated to Afghanistan and Iran or, having surren-
dered their property, continued to live in Uzbekistan in relative poverty.

"In the Soviet period many Bukharan Jews refused to give their property to the collective so they had to flee to Afghanistan, then to Mashhad,
and from there to Tehran," Kamara said. "But the Jews were wealthy even
during the war. We Bukharans still remember how even if they worked in
a factory, they would ask for daily rather than weekly or monthly wages
so they would not be taxed. They had daily money and were very clever.

They knew how to save their gold. And they also worked in professions that were not regulated by the state: barbers, jewelers, dressmakers. They were a very joined community, never they let the outside community know about the life that belonged to them."

"If they were so comfortable during the war, why didn't they help the Jewish refugees?" I asked her.

"Of course they helped them," Kamara answered. To support her claim, she offered to take me to a local synagogue to meet Avram Bakhcicz, a man whose family, as she put it, had lived in Bukhara for generations. Avram was a big, robust middle-aged man in a T-shirt and a large black yarmulke. He was one of 150 registered Jews still living in Bukhara. In the sixteenth-century synagogue where we met, a clean, air-conditioned structure with lovely gold arches and turquoise Stars of David, he was seated nonchalantly in front of the Torah's ark as if it were his office. He remained on his cell phone during most of our visit. Between calls, he told us, alternating between Russian and the local Jewish language Bukhori, a mixture of Tajik and Hebrew, that the synagogue fell into disrepair under the Soviets but had recently been renovated under the current government of Islam Karimov.

"When the Polish Jews came to Bukhara, the local Jews met them with an open heart," Avram said, in Tajik that Salar understood and Kamara translated. "The refugees went to their houses, met their children, learned local crafts. Local traders helped them. They just adopted them." When I looked at him skeptically, he said again with greater emphasis, "According to our traditions we will never let anybody die of hunger. The refugees were not hungry. They were treated very well by the local families."

"Something like a quarter of the refugees in Bukhara are said to have died of hunger," I said cautiously. "They were very ill, and I know the Bukharan community was suffering too and under pressure from the Soviets."

"All I know," Avram said, "is that they created for the refugees very good conditions, maybe not the best but good. As for the Soviets, religious worship was only formally prohibited. The heads of the Bukharan

Communist Party were themselves pious Muslims, so they turned a blind eye on the use of the synagogue, not to mention the fact that there were also Bukharan Jews in the Communist Party itself." His parents had always told him that there was a big flood of refugees and that they were "very kindhearted, very cooperative, very friendly, very educated people."

"That's right," Kamara said, suddenly very animated. "They came to our country and changed our industry. They came from Europe. For example, we had only one kind of ice cream in Bukhara, but when the refugees started an ice cream business, they brought new flavors, new aromas. They liked Bukhara, and after the war most of those who came remained. Even those who left still visit us."

I asked Avram, "When people who lived in Bukhara now come to visit from Israel, does the situation in the Middle East with Israel and

Uzbek and Polish Jews celebrate wedding in Bukhara, 1945

the Palestinians affect the way they're received?" Avram suddenly looked much more aroused and less bored by my questions.

"I can tell you honestly that here we have no discrimination. Not with Jewish, not with Iranian," he said, turning to Salar. "This is a country always welcoming. *Shukran*, we say. Even in our Muslim architecture, we have a Star of David. We have pre-Islam symbols. We are not fanatic or conservative. It has been like that always, since the Great Emir Timur."

"We love Israelis, we love Iranians, and we love the Farsi language: the most beautiful language in the world!" another man, keeper of Bukhara's Jewish cemetery, said when we dropped by his office, prompting a succession of mutual compliments and pleasantries between him and Salar in Farsi. "Here in Bukhara we and the Persians are like brothers. Here Muslims don't even want to hear of Ahmadinejad," he said to me in Hebrew. "Even in Iran, even with Ahmadinejad making problems, the Jews live *beseder gamoor* [just fine]. Plus, our president Karimov has good relationship with the heads of Israel. He knows the Jews well, he went to school in Samarqand with them."

Human Rights Watch and other organizations repeatedly reported on Uzbekistan's long-standing authoritarian president Islam Karimov, who died in 2016. He was known to have imprisoned large swaths of the population; blacklisted and tortured dissidents, immersed some in boiling water; and for forcing millions of citizens, including children, to pick cotton in abusive conditions during high season. He was rumored to have been raised in a Samarqand orphanage, presumably with Jewish refugee orphans.[63]

When I asked the cemetery manager whether he knew of any former refugees who were still living in Bukhara—his brother was said to be the "head" of the Jewish community—he answered that he "had no idea." None of the current 150 registered Bukharan Jewish residents were refugees; nearly all had left, and those who stayed, he said, "do not come to our meetings or pray in our synagogues."

"Ninety percent of the refugees and their descendants have left the area." Kamara was half-running and breathing heavily under the blazing sun. We were heading toward Bukhara's *mahalleh*, a hodgepodge of crooked, unkempt pavements, peeling pink walls, and stinking sewerage running along the buildings. We turned onto Saraffon Street, then onto Levi Boboxonov, where Kamara stopped at number seven.

Here lived a "Bukharan Jew who remembered the refugees," Kamara said. A little black-eyed girl in a pink dress, her hair braided, opened the door, lowered her eyes, and made way for a toothless old man in a Bukharan cap, her great-grandfather. He greeted Kamara with *salam aleikum*, both of them placing their palm on their heart as everyone around here did when they saw us. The toothless man was born in 1935, Kamara told us. He remembered watching the Polish Jews "create things."

"They were using their minds," he said. "They were very kind and helping everybody. Every day they suggested to us something new, any problem we had they found a solution. But it was a very hard time; everybody had been suffering of a shortage of everything. Sometimes when the refugees reached Bukhara, they were so weak they just died. There were a great many children—they were taken to orphanages."

"Polish orphanages?"

"No, common orphanages. All the children, from Ukraine, Poland, Uzbekistan, taken to same orphanages."

"He had been friendly with a Polish refugee named Gershowitz," Kamara translated. "He was a dentist."

"No, no"—the man shook his head—"Dr. Gershowitz was a woman, not a man." Kamara continued, "But she too left a little before the independence. They all left, or died." Kamara smiled sadly, exhausted.

The man's great-granddaughter approached us with a book on the history of Bukharan Jews in English and in Hebrew for which I gave her twenty dollars, then another ten when she kept her palm open.

"The best minds of the country belonged to the Jews, doctors, dentists, teachers, musicians, the best classical music," Kamara said again. "But now they have left us."

Whether and to what extent local Jews helped—"in the beginning Bukharan Jews tried to help us, but eventually they could not deal with such destitution either," a former Tehran Child wrote—within months the food crisis reached such mammoth proportions that no individual or local organization could fight or even contain it. Hunger flattened all social interactions, all encounters between locals and newcomers, all energy, all enjoyment.

"It is a hunger that's a knowledge, not a memory, a bodily knowledge that once you own, it never leaves you," Ilana Landau, the former Tehran Child who had given me her brother Emil's Iran travel diary told me. Hunger dominates all Tehran Child testimonies, both those given to the Polish Information Center in 1943 and those given later in life, including in the interviews I conducted. It dominates my father's testimony: "You could cry your eyes out for a tiny piece of bread; it helped like cupping the dead." The knowledge of hunger, I now knew, was the gulf that had lain between my father and me, the abyss between him and my mother: his and his mother's knowledge of hunger, our ignorance.

I also now knew that there were many types of refugee hunger: Salar's hunger as a young teenage refugee living in the streets of food-washed Los Angeles; my father's hunger in black-market–controlled Siemiatycze; the hunger of a bit of soup and bread at the end of a twelve-hour workday at Arkhangelsk; the hunger of the Soviet evacuees, the hunger of refugee prisoners like Wat, who was released from the prison in Saratov with a fifteen-ruble allowance and two loaves of bread; and the hunger of those, like my father, who was released from a *posiołek* with nothing: the Teitels and roughly 350,000 others. Their hunger in Central Asia, the hunger of having no food at all, was a condition so extreme that it dominated all their memories and dreams and testimonies and memoirs and representations of the period, then and now. When *The Children of Teheran* interviewees speak of this hunger in the film, they visibly breathe faster and more heavily, or they freeze in a kind of pale expressionlessness, or they weep:

In Uzbekistan we lived like animals, with the exception that we did not go to pasture but were confined to our *khusha* [Arabic slang for "mud hut"].

I was horribly hungry, horribly. I couldn't fall asleep; I would swallow my saliva and imagine that it isn't saliva but the hot chocolate Dad used to prepare for me each day before I went to school.

Now I knew, in my body, what the definition of the term *hunger* was, not as a literary or empty romantic notion. True hunger is when a child steals a piece of bread from his brother and a friend stabs his good friend in order to take his breakfast—this is the meaning of hunger, which descends a man toward hell. Whoever did not go through this horrific experience will never understand the suffering of a starving man.

Former child refugee Josek Klapholz recalled that his father would divide the single *lapyushka* (flatbread) the family received into quarters, one for each family member. He would assign himself the smallest piece and within a few months, he died. "Like hundreds of thousands of others," Klapholz wrote, "a pathetic death in filth and lice-infested rags, in a dwelling where a donkey lived before us."

And my own father? I had lived with the aftermath of his hunger: the fanatic injunction against throwing away all, even spoiled food; the six a.m. wake-up calls so that he could make it on time for the free breakfast that was served at his air force base. When I first fasted on Yom Kippur at age twelve, I was shocked to discover how terrible it felt: the muscle ache, the headache, the irritability, the constant thoughts of food.

Hannan's hunger was that of a frantic animal searching through the trash, as my father continued to do, at night, throughout his lifetime.

Sometimes when the kitchen light woke me, I would watch him standing in his striped pajamas and worn-out slippers. His slanted eyes were half shut and so remote that he would not see me. He would be sifting through the garbage can, salvaging the bit of cottage cheese that had stuck to the container. It used to repel me: my father, a cat pawing through the trash. There was an obsessive, almost mechanical quality to his movements that frightened me.

But in Uzbekistan, when I heard the Uzbek farmer Jamil say, "They jumped off the carts. They were so hungry they ate live frogs," I understood what starvation had done to my father. (The writer Ruth Zylberman wrote of her Holocaust survivor mother, "She was crouched like an animal, like a monkey, like a wolf, like a dog . . . in that moment she could have pulled out a rusty bowl, lapped from it without a spoon. But seeing her . . . I realized—and the force of that image was such that my head spun . . . that she had been a monkey, a wolf, a dog.")[64]

By the time Hannan and his family arrived in Samarqand, refugees for two years, their perception of hunger would have been most likely weakened by the partial atrophy of their stomachs. Their body fat and muscle mass would have been used in the service of their vital heart muscle and nervous system. They would have been too weak to feel much thirst and therefore were most likely severely dehydrated; their cracked dry skin and muscle atrophy would have made movement painful. "The refugees were too weak to work," Jamil, the Uzbek farmer, had said, "because of hunger. They were so weak they could not carry the ones who died to the cemetery."

After a few months, my father died of starvation.

Seven of us left Poland. Three died of hunger.

My father died in the night. In the morning Uzbeks came, scooped up his body, and drove away. I don't know where he is buried.[65]

Even the idyllic young adult novel *Homeward from Steppes of the Sun* includes a scene in which a refugee dies of hunger: "We heard murmurs of a hoarse man, begging in Polish for something to eat: 'Just a little food, help me.' . . . In the morning, when we opened the door, we found the man's frozen corpse on our steps."[66]

Soviet sources claim that one of every four people in Central Asia died during the war. The numbers that appear in Tehran Children testimonies appear higher:

Seven of us left Poland, three died.

There were seven of us, and only my twelve-year-old brother Abram and I remained.

Eleven of us left for Russia, and only my two aunts, a cousin and I remained.

Of the fifteen people in our family exiled to Russia, six remained. It was the same in other families.

People died from starvation and from diseases of starving bodies: typhus, malaria, anemia, beriberi (vitamin B1 deficiency), pellagra (B3 deficiency), scurvy, fungi that grew under the esophagus and blocked swallowing, cardiac arrhythmia and cardiac arrest, and the lesser but ever-present others: diarrhea, skin rashes, edema. The death rates from starvation in Central Asia were unquestionably staggering; whether these deaths were intentional, accidental, or the consequence of negligent indifference by the Soviet government—a question that continues to ignite debates in regard to starvation in Ukraine in the early 1930s—has still not been largely examined in relation to Central Asia. At least five million people died of hunger in Ukraine but also, already in the early 1930s, in other farming Soviet republics like Kazakhstan and Uzbekistan.[67]

By 1941, when Hannan and his family and millions of other refugees and evacuees arrived in the Uzbek Soviet Socialist Republic, the land was already famished. Stalinist policy mandated that Uzbek farmers replace nearly all food cultivation with cotton growing. The exception was for small quantities of vegetables needed for the farmers' own subsistence.

Farmers were not allowed to grow rice or wheat and were prohibited from leaving their regions in search of food. After the German invasion, farmers were required to surrender to the Red Army even the little they had, confiscation enforced by routine searches, raids, and arrests. In *Homeward from Steppes of the Sun*, the narrator describes the "women's screams," "children's cries," and men's "clenched fists" as Soviet soldiers extract bags of potatoes from farmers' cellars and drag cows, goats, and sheep into their trucks. After the confiscations, prices for what little was left on the black market shot up to unattainable figures.

The food shortages affected the refugees most; in *Steppes*, refugees began to die immediately after the scenes of confiscation. But everyone—Kazakhs, Tajiks, Kyrgyzs, the Uzbeks whom Wat calls "impoverished knights . . . very thin from hunger," local Jews, and local Russians—was to a degree affected.[68]

In this sense, *The Children of Teheran* documentary, which stages the former Jewish refugees' stories of hunger against footage of heaps of dried apricots and dates at Samarqand's present-day market, paints something of a misleading picture. There would soon be pockets of food in Polish army bases and in the Polish aid delegations established across the Soviet Union. And Kazakh farmers learned to dig holes to hide their crops under a layer of tobacco that repelled Red Army dogs. But death by starvation was widespread and rampant.

Nearly a year after the Teitels arrived in Uzbekistan, on September 9, 1942, the General Council of the Zionist Agency for Palestine, the quasi-government of the Jewish population of Palestine, held a closed meeting in Tel Aviv. Here Moshe Shertok, head of the Agency's foreign office, announced that there was evidence to suggest that the deportations and subsequent starvation of Polish refugees might be a policy and not just a consequence of the war. "I know that I am on unsure ground here and that I must be cautious," Shertok began, "and I am breaching confidentiality and reporting to you with the assumption that you will keep your secrecy and solidarity with me.

But a high-ranking officer of the United States government has told me that when those people [the Polish refugees] were exiled to inner Russia, the policy was to eliminate them. Not to eliminate them by lining them up against a wall and shooting them down with machine guns, God forbid, but the method in which they were deported, their assignment to the snow fields without shelter and a minimal hope for life, and their release from the gulags without any means of subsistence are clear proof that the aim was their demise.[69]

Shertok emphasized that this alleged Soviet policy, whose secret aim was to eliminate the inhabitants of former Polish territories that the Soviet government planned to annex after the war, was not a direct anti-Jewish policy but it de facto disproportionally hurt Jews.

In Uzbekistan, I understood for the first time that hunger may not only have been the source of my father's lifelong neuroses but the actual cause of his death, half a century later. Creutzfeldt-Jakob, from which he died, is transmitted by a protein found in infected animal brains.

"It's very possible that Dad contracted his brain disease in Uzbekistan," my brother Benjamin, a physician, said. We looked closely at photos of our father. Ever since we could both remember, he had had small but noticeable neurological symptoms—ticks and winces, a nervous twitching of the corner of his mouth. "The disease must have been there in some dormant form all these years, until it flared in full force after his retirement," my brother said. And for a moment the image of my father's paper-thin body, spasmodic and flailing on the hospital bed, flashed before my eyes.

6

A POLISH NATION IN EXILE, JEWISH RELIEF EFFORTS

London, New York, and the USSR

Months before their release from their labor settlement, on a frosty day in February 1941, as the Teitels and the Perelgrics and millions of other slave laborers were dragging themselves into the forest feeling utterly abandoned and alone in the world, as if they had dropped off the map, 450 delegates of the Federation of Polish Jews of America met at the Grand Ballroom of the Astor Hotel in Times Square to discuss aiding them. The hotel's owner, Benjamin Winter, was himself a former Polish-Jewish émigré who in just several decades, in addition to the hotel, had managed to acquire the Mrs. William B. Astor House and the William K. Vanderbilt House with monies borrowed from other Polish-Jewish émigrés and the proceeds of twelve years of work as a tenement house painter. Winter spoke briefly about the urgent need to aid Polish Jews and introduced Samuel L. Schneiderman, a journalist who had recently arrived from Europe. Schneiderman gave an overview of the state of European Jews, including those in the USSR. The delegates decided to form a central committee to coordinate all relief activities to Polish Jews in Europe.

In Montreal, the United Jewish Refugee and War Relief Agency held a similar meeting and passed a similar resolution.

In London, the Federation of Polish Jews in Great Britain had by 1940 already incorporated under the War Charities Act. Consisting of local rabbis, lawyers, and professors, as well as prominent Polish Jews who had fled to England along with the Polish government and military elites, its purpose was to "assist Polish Jewry politically and economically." Labor's chief whip Lord Strabolgi (Joseph Kenworthy) and Vice Chairman Baron Josiah Wedgwood, liberal politicians with a reputation for championing the cause of refugees, were among its patrons.

On July 20, 1941, just after the Soviet amnesty of Polish citizens, the federation held a conference at London's Stearns Hotel to discuss aid to the refugees. The conference was attended by ninety delegates of Jewish societies and synagogues from London and Great Britain, as well as several hundred individuals with an interest in Polish-Jewish affairs, including the Polish consul general to Great Britain. The Polish government-in-exile, which resided in London, had two Jewish members on its national council: Ignacy Schwarzbart, a Zionist leader and former member of the Sejm (the lower house of Parliament in Poland) and Szmul Zygielbojm, a Bund leader who was invited to join it later.[1] The federation voted to support the government as the legal representative of Polish-Jewish citizens and to welcome its declared commitment to "restore and maintain the rights and liberties of its Polish-Jewish citizens."[2]

To represent the Polish citizens who had been exiled and just released from gulags, prisons, and special settlements in the Soviet Union, the Polish government-in-exile had dispatched Dr. Stanisław Kot, to Moscow. Dr. Kot, a member of the Polish populist People's Party and a confidant of Prime Minister Sikorski, had been a nationalist, oppositional figure to Józef Piłsudski's multiethnic vision of Poland before the war. But it is to Kot—a professor, editor, publisher, and author of more than fifty books—and to his fondness for documentation and historical record that I owed much of my understanding of the Polish side of my father's story. From his accounts I learned about my father's timeline in Uzbekistan, and about the increasingly divergent paths of ethnic Polish refugees and Jewish Polish refugees. And it is to Kot, who is credited with establishing the Polish Information Center, that I owe my father's testimony.

Kot's *Conversations with the Kremlin* was published in 1963 in Britain, where he remained in exile after the war. The book includes no analysis, only chronologically ordered letters and transcripts of meetings, which he claimed to quote verbatim.[3] Its documents pertain to Polish-Soviet and/or Polish-Jewish relations. From the beginning, they implicitly suggest that the two sets of relations were linked. The Soviet government, which had just entered the war, was strapped for U.S. aid; the Polish government-in-exile, as Kot boasted to Vyacheslav Molotov, vice president of the USSR and people's commissar for foreign affairs, had ties with roughly five million Polish-born Americans who were still "active in defense of Polish aims" and could wield influence in the United States. Among these were Polish-born Jewish American citizens, as well as American Jewish aid organizations that wished to aid the Polish-Jewish refugees in the USSR.[4]

Already in April 1941, on his first official visit to the United States, Polish Prime Minister Sikorski met with Edward M. Warburg, head of the Joint Distribution Committee (JDC) and other officials and updated them on the large number of Jewish Polish citizens in gulags and special settlements. The JDC, the United States' largest Jewish aid organization, would come to play a significant role in my father's life.

≡

The first Jewish organization to give large-scale funding for international relief, the JDC had been founded during World War I by German-Jewish immigrants: "men [who] had become wealthy in America and [whose] religious and moral tradition obliged them to share some part of their wealth with [their] 'co-religionists' and 'less fortunate brethren'," as historian Yehuda Bauer writes.[5] The JDC continued its work in the interwar period, supporting East European Jewish aid organizations, negotiating with governments on behalf of refugees, dispatching delegations of American doctors and other specialists abroad, and creating programs for sending aid packages in Poland and elsewhere. It aided the refugees who fled to Ostrów Mazowiecka during World War I and the subsequent Soviet-Polish war; it most likely helped fund the soup kitchen that Ostrów's Jews set up, the doctor and the pharmacist who had been sent from Warsaw to refugee-flooded Ostrów during the Soviet-Polish war. It may have even helped fund the Bikkur Cholim medical charity, in which the Teitels were involved in their hometown.

As its aid programs grew, the JDC absorbed sectarian Jewish relief organizations—including the Orthodox Central Relief Committee and the Socialist People's Relief Committee—into its fold. But it remained a largely liberal, secular organization with a "strong German-Jewish element," as Bauer puts it. Its chairman at the outbreak of World War II, Edward M. Warburg, was a New York socialite, collector, and champion of the arts, a board member of the Museum of Modern Art and co-founder, with George Balanchine and others, of the School of American Ballet. The war compelled him into the JDC, which his father, the German-born Jewish banker Felix Warburg, helped found. The organization was, in a sense, a continuation of the Jewish aid networks that had been in existence in Europe for decades. But it was bigger, richer, and distinctly American.

"Our course must be to lean over backwards to avoid engaging in any relief work that might infringe [on] the country's laws," JDC vice president James Rosenberg wrote to its members on September 5, 1939, following President Franklin D. Roosevelt's declaration that the United States would remain neutral in the European conflict. "We must not and cannot let our desire to help suffering cause us to lose our moorings. Our rule must be 'When in doubt, ask the State Department.'"[6]

From the rise of Hitler to the outbreak of the war, the JDC's efforts to solve the problem of Jewish refugees through international action had been largely unsuccessful. In 1933 it had collaborated with the League of Nations' high commissioner for refugees, James G. McDonald, later with the London-based Intergovernmental Committee on Refugees; and after that with a plan devised by officers of the German State Bank to set up a foundation that would provide capital to settle Jewish refugees from Nazi Germany (and in doing so making them more acceptable to host countries). "All of these came to nothing," Bauer writes.[7] On its own, the JDC succeeded in placing small groups in Mexico, Jamaica, the Dominican Republic, India, and elsewhere, but largely not in the United States, where in mid-1939 it failed to pressure the government into granting asylum to the 937 German-Jewish refugees aboard the ocean liner *St. Louis.* After the outbreak of the war, the possibility of aid inside Nazi-occupied Europe shrunk even further. Then came the meeting with Sikorski and the news of the Polish-Jewish refugees in the USSR.

Beginning in 1941, rabbis and relatives of refugees who had been exiled in the Soviet Union began sending the JDC pleas for help on behalf, pleas that are still housed at its archive in New York. "I am appealing to you to call attention to the disastrous plight of some thousands of our brethren in Soviet Siberia," Philadelphia's chief rabbi, Eliezer Yolles, wrote on May 21, 1941 to JDC Chairman Edward Warburg. "I am receiving letters, according to which all of the exiles are exposed to strenuous work, but are not provided for with primitive life necessities like food and clothing." He has received reports of "horrifying stories, according to which hundreds of individuals are committing suicide, dying of starvation," and asks whether the leaders of the Agro-Joint, "who have been in the past on good relations with the Moscow government," might not intervene on the refugees' behalf and "persuade the Soviets that these people in Siberia are at least human beings."[8]

The Agro-Joint—American Jewish Joint Agricultural Corporation—was a branch of the JDC that helped create and finance Jewish agricultural settlements in the USSR, particularly in Crimea and Ukraine. At present, though, it notified Rabbi Yolles that it knew "very little" of what was going on in those regions, and though "the masses of Jewish refugees within the Soviet territories . . . are in a tragic situation, . . . little can be done on their behalf."[9]

Two months later, the Soviet government launched its military campaign against the advancing German Army. Exiles like Hannan were released in the amnesty, and Morris Troper, head of the JDC's European Center in Lisbon, declared that "the situation is changed. Russia should openly come out in favor of Jewish relief activities, and these relief activities should now be started."[10]

Hundreds of documents pertaining to the Polish refugees are stored at the JDC archive, a modest operation in midtown Manhattan that does not betray the scope of the organization's activities. Though nothing was ever said to me directly, from my Israeli perspective I had always thought of "the Joint" somewhat condescendingly, as a well-meaning, largely benign organization that took "diasporic" measures to solve the Jewish question: temporary, apolitical alleviations of Jewish suffering, stopgap interventions that differed from and sometimes even impeded Zionism's more radical political project. But JDC officials possessed networks, political clout and acumen, and financial power that, once a decision was taken, enabled them to act forcefully, expediently, and on a huge scale that was awe-inspiring. Between its inception and the 1929 Great Depression, the JDC had raised from American Jewry $78.7 million (equivalent to $1.35 billion in 2018). Those funds were applied to aid abroad, to sustaining strangers.

On the day of Hannan's release from Posiołek Ostrowsky, September 5, 1941, JDC officers met in New York with Soviet ambassador Maxim Litvinov, the Polish consul general Sylwin Strakacz, and the chairman of the American Red Cross, Norman Davies, to discuss what could be done for the newly released refugees. Strakacz presented a list of the refugees' immediate needs. Litvinov announced that his government would not be able to "divert its attention to a refugee problem when it [was] fighting a war for its existence." Davies offered to dispatch a Red Cross official to the USSR "to look into the problem and its various phases."

In view of the fact that substantial American help would not be able to reach Russia "before several months," Strakacz announced that the Polish government-in-exile would begin its relief efforts immediately. A shipment of 676 cases of medicine, clothing, and coffee, he said, was already en route from London to Moscow, where a Polish Relief Commission was being established and a "substantial sum of money" was already pledged by the American Polish Council and Federation of Polish Organizations in the United States "in the name of some five million American Poles."[11]

Conceding that the refugee problem was "nonsectarian" and agreeing that it should be handled by American organizations like the Red
Cross "without reference to distinctly Jewish efforts," the JDC decided
to contribute to the Polish government-in-exile's relief efforts. Immediately, in New York, London, Buenos Aires, and Montreal Jewish presses,
labor committees, synagogues, schools, and private homes mounted a
campaign to collect money to purchase clothing and medicine to ship
to Russia.[12] The U.S. Jewish Labor Committee announced a large-scale
collection of funds to purchase clothing and medicine "on behalf of the
Jewish refugees in Russia." In Montreal, the Canadian United Jewish
Refugee and War Relief Agency met to outline the principles of aid. And
in New York, JDC chairman Edward Warburg wrote a follow-up memo
to Soviet ambassador Litvinov saying that, given the number of Jewish
evacuees and refugees in Central Asia, his organization would be "keenly
interested in any possibility of attempting to cooperate with [his] government in helping the refugees and evacuees to settle in their new locali-
ties."[13] Litvinov answered that his government would gladly "welcome
outside aid."[14]

Ambassador Kot described his first week in Moscow as "a honeymoon."
But within a week the essential rift came to the surface: the number of
Polish citizens on Soviet soil, which Kot had put at 1.5 million, was said by
the Soviets to be a little over 350,000, a figure, as Kot wrote Sikorski, "completely at variance with reality."[15] According to the information received
at the embassy, Kot relayed, the deportees alone numbered 600,000. In
addition, there were the 400,000 resettled farmers from western Poland;
100,000 state officials and their families; and hundreds of thousands of
prisoners and prisoners of war, among them Polish army officers and
prominent Jewish figures like Dr. Moses Schorr, Emil Sommerstein, and
the Zionist "representatives of the Jabotinski Revisionists," as Kot put it.[16]
Andrej Vyshinsky, Molotov's deputy, presented a counterfigure of 291,137
deportees to special settlements; 71,481 prisoners under investigation; and
25,314 prisoners of war, of whom a total of 345,511 had been released. He

dodged the question of the Polish officers and the "prominent Jews" who were still unaccounted for.[17]

In a letter to the Polish foreign ministry-in-exile, dated November 8, 1941, Kot estimated that Jews represented "one third" or "even higher number" among the released Polish citizens in Central Asia.[18] Deported Polish peasants who "were burdened with families" were less willing "to abandon the little villages which they had grown used to," while "the bulk of Jews flow[ed] most swiftly to the south." Though many of them had managed on their own to find placements, "pressure should be brought to bear on wealthy spheres in America" to aid them.

In his letters, Kot also reported on Wiktor Alter and Henryk Ehrlich, two recently released prominent Bund leaders, whom he appointed as "embassy referees on Jewish affairs." Like most other Polish Jews, he wrote, the two had been cured of their Communist sympathies and were now "full of contempt for a system which they know well from personal experience" and "in full loyalty to the Polish government."[19]

===

Sometime in the years that had passed since I began researching the book, my apprehension around Poland significantly subsided. My picture of pre- and postwar Polish-Jewish relations wasn't rosy, but I was no longer overwhelmed by what in the past had felt to me as an enormous, eternal, amorphous horror of the fate of Jews in Poland. I had traveled to Poland. I knew many details about my father's prewar life; I knew his family had lived in the same Polish town for eight generations; I knew that, all things considered, up until the war it had not been a bad life. And so I no longer felt the inhospitable, and maddeningly bureaucratic attitude of a Polish librarian at the Hoover Institution in Stanford or the Sikorski Archives in London as a personal affront to me or to Jews in general.

When I traveled to the Hoover Institution for the second time, in search of materials of the Polish government-in-exile, not even the young Polish man who issued my ID while reading a book titled *Forgotten Holocaust: Poles Under German Occupation 1939–1944* fazed me. I told myself that many other works staged the discussion of genocides and mass murders—of Poles, Cambodians, Palestinians, African Americans— through the framework and terminology of the Holocaust. I was no longer caught up in a competition of suffering, having encountered so much of it, in so many variations and places. At the Hoover I saw plenty of evidence of Polish suffering, testimonies of young cadets of the Polish army-in-exile, of Polish men and women of all professions, provinces, counties: Stec, Boleslaw, doctor, born in Kalusz, Stanislawow; Tonia, Karol, "tailor assistant"; grove keepers, brick layers, painters, artists, technicians. Antoniak, Ignacy, workman; Banaszek, Ignacy, clerk; Dmochowski, Stefan, car mechanic; Godlewski, Jozef, farmer; Goral, Bronislaw, another farmer; Jakubik, Szczepan, forester; and another forester, and another; Pirkel, Adam, forester; Pirkel, Halina, student. There were distinctions but also commonalities with my father.

I also knew the extent to which the fate of Catholic and Jewish Polish refugees was entangled during the war. They had been exiled together. They had suffered together during the frost and hard labor and at the hands of their Ukrainian supervisors at the settlements. In Posiołek Ostrowsky, "they helped one another whenever they could," as my father had written in his testimony. And finally they had been released together, as Polish citizens. I now understood how a blue file folder with a small Star of David could have ended up inside a folder titled "Polish Embasada to the Soviet Union"—a discovery I made on my first visit to the Hoover but couldn't decipher. Inside the blue folder were documents relating to the Polish government's treatment of Jewish refugees. They appeared to be answers to queries.

> The Polish authorities in the Soviet Union profess that according to the rules of the Polish Republic, there is no difference between the Jewish and Polish citizens (as of September 1, 1939) regardless of their nationality, religion and race. Among the released are a big group of Jews and other nationalities. They are treated equally with Poles and regarded as Polish citizens.[20]

In a report that would be published by the Polish embassy in the USSR a year later, the "significant" number of "Jews and other Polish citizens of non-Polish ethnicity" who were released from prisons and camps would be emphasized as proof of the equal treatment of Polish Jews. In particular, the embassy would emphasize the September 1941 release from prison of Wiktor Alter and Henryk Ehrlich "as Polish citizens." The two Bund leaders ("leaders of the Jewish Socialist organization") who were then employed by the Polish embassy, were re-arrested by the NKVD in early December 1941 for "working on behalf of Germany," and the Polish embassy had requested their release.[21] This was not altogether "proof" of equitable treatment of Jews and non-Jews. Still, from Kot's immediate employment of the two men at his embassy and their immediate enlistment for the Polish refugee cause, from Aleksander Wat's Polish memoir, from early entries in Emil Landau's Polish-language diary, and even from my father's recollections of Jews and Catholics at his settlement, I developed a nuanced picture of cautious intimacy, an intimacy of people who shared a language, a long history, and now an exile into foreign territory, a delicate, complicated identity with many shades that no longer existed, but whose traces I was now beginning to feel.

＝

The thaw in my attitude toward Poland can be traced, most significantly, to an e-mail I received three months after I returned from Uzbekistan, from Magdalena (Magda) Gawin, who identified herself as an Ostrów Mazowiecka–born historian. Magda had received my contact information from Krzysztof Malczewski, my Polish tour guide. She wrote to invite me to the seventieth-year commemoration of the death of her great-aunt Jadwiga Długoborska who, as Magda wrote, had hid Jews during the war in two camouflaged rooms in the Wersal Hotel, an inn she owned in Ostrów Mazowiecka. Jadwiga was reported by her maid and was tortured and killed by the Gestapo; now her niece was collecting information to submit to Yad Vashem, the Holocaust Memorial Museum in Jerusalem that recognized non-Jewish rescuers as "Righteous Among

Nations." The niece meanwhile had prepared a local commemoration of Jadwiga in Ostrów, with the presence of the mayor of the city, representatives of Polish institutions, friends, and family. She invited me to the commemoration in Ostrów on behalf of her family and the city. "We will be honored," she wrote.

I politely declined the invitation, not quite sure what to make of it. I had never heard of any rescue attempt of Jews by a Polish resident of Ostrów. But when Magda Gawin invited me to give a paper at the Tadeusz Manteuffel Institute of History of the Polish Academy of Sciences, where she worked as a researcher, and to spend several days together in our "families' hometown," I accepted. When I called her asking what to bring to Poland, she answered, "Mikhal, bring nothing. I just need you."

I was baffled, curious, and a little apprehensive when I saw her at Chopin Airport in Warsaw. Tall and beautiful, with a round face, auburn hair, and lovely smile, she was not what I expected; she was warmer, sweeter, and more familiar, and we hit it off immediately. "After the war," she told me as we drove from the airport to her apartment in Warsaw "young people in Ostrów were not interested in the Jews. Even me, I was informed by my family about the fate of Ostrów Jews, but I wasn't interested. Of course we knew the war was terrible and bad things happened to the Jews, but we didn't talk about it." Now she was interested in every detail of the Teitel family, she said.

I was again in Poland. Again there was the slow stream of cars on the highway from Chopin Airport to Warsaw and later from Warsaw to Brok, the little town adjacent to Ostrów Mazowiecka where Magda and I planned to spend five or six days in her lovely *dacha*. Again the strange calm that engulfed me on my first visit to Poland, lost land of my father. Again the tall pine forests, the River Bug, the stalls on roadsides. Before heading eastward to Ostrów, we stopped at Magda's apartment in a quiet, off-center Warsaw neighborhood, which consisted of Soviet row houses that dipped in green and exuded something of a kibbutz feel. On the walls of her sunny, book-lined apartment were photos of her family: her husband and their two small children, a boy and a girl; in the bathroom was an impressive collage by her eleven-year-old daughter and a sandbox for Pushkin the cat; in the boy's room there were Legos and an Xbox 360, the same as in my son's room. And I realized that even at this late date, I still could not quite grasp that people live ordinary lives in Poland, in this mythical country that for my family had seemingly ceased to exist altogether after the war.

In her interviews with Ostrów residents, Magda told me as we shopped for the food products we would take with us to her dacha, she had come across some who still remembered the Teitels. "They remember them as less traditional, more progressive."

"Do you mean they were less pious than other Jewish families?" I asked her.

"No, I mean that they were on good terms with Poles. Half of their employees were Polish. That was unusual."

Under Magda's patronage Ostrów Mazowiecka became suddenly wonderful: a hospitable and friendly place, much different from the polite, foreign, and slightly dull place it had been the first time I visited with Salar. Everyone, everywhere, was nice to me: at the newly opened Italian restaurant where we dined, at the T-Mobile store where I got my Polish SIM card, at the local grocery store, where Magda asked the owner to prepare kugel for me for the Jewish new year, which was a few days away. At the home of Riczard Ejchelkraut, whom I had met the first time around, and now hugged and greeted me like an old friend. In the two years that had passed since my first visit, Ostrów had become cleaner; more gentrified, with more stores and supermarkets, more renovated apartment buildings. Even Riczard's dull Soviet-era apartment complex had newly planted gardens, new intercoms, and new layers of paint that hid the ugly old graffiti.

Magda's great-aunt Jadwiga Długoborska, was imprisoned, interrogated, and tortured for three days inside the Teitel Broca Brewery, aka Gestapo headquarters, prior to her execution in a nearby forest. "From this we are sisters," Magda said. She had not yet presented Jadwiga to Yad

Vashem because she had not been able to identify the people Jadwiga had hidden. There was a blurry guest list from before the war, which included Jewish names, and the name of a Jewish man who may have been Jadwiga's prewar lover and was hidden by her during the war. The man, Gelberg, was later killed by the Bolsheviks, Magda said.

Magda, like her aunt Jadwiga and her husband Dariusz (Darek) Gawin, a sociologist who worked as deputy director of the Warsaw Uprising Museum and was a regular contributor to *Tygodnik Powszechny*, a Roman Catholic weekly, was a devout Catholic and a Polish patriot. She was not naïve about Polish-Jewish relations, but in her worldview, though there had been problems, Jews and Poles co-existed relatively peacefully in Ostrów until the Nazi and Bolshevik invasions brought an end to this delicately harmonious world. In this world, Jews and Poles were both hapless victims, and Poles, terrorized by the Nazis, bore no responsibility for the fate of their fellow Jewish citizens during the war. It was a narrative that in 2015 would be openly and publicly embraced by Andrzej Duda's Law and Justice government and that for a short while in 2013, as I sat in the evenings by the fireplace in Magda's living room, drinking red wine and listening to her talk about my "great family" ("one of the best families in town"), I too entertained. The Nazi occupation of Poland had been more brutal and violent than anywhere else in Europe, a Polish journalist had told me. They were determined to crush Poland. Was it time to let go, to forgive even?

≡

Beginning in 1941, Jewish aid organizations began to work in tandem with Polish aid organizations and the Polish government-in-exile to bring relief to the refugees. At a December 10, 1941, emergency meeting of the JDC executive committee, Chairman Edward Warburg proposed that an immediate remittance of $100,000 be granted to the Polish government-in-exile for "the relief of Polish refugees in Russia." He reported that the Polish national council had already turned over $150,000 to the Polish embassy and that several shipments of used clothing from the Jewish

Labor Committee had already been sent to the refugees in Central Asia, among whom the number of Jews was said to be "close to 500,000, if not more," according to the Polish ambassador. The $100,000 would be added to a "general fund to be distributed in the form of clothing, medicaments, bandages, [and] concentrated food" to all refugees. The Polish ambassador was "prepared to give absolute assurance" not only in a meeting but also in writing that "Jews will share equally and without prejudice in the distribution of all such supplies," which, Warburg reported, would either be shipped on Russian transports without charge and free of duty, as per the Polish government's understanding with the Soviet government, or bought in Iran and shipped the relatively short distance from there to the care of the Polish embassy in the Soviet Union.[22]

Some committee members hesitated about funneling monies through the Polish embassy. "I know something of the experience of the London Jews in negotiations with the representatives of the Polish government-in-exile. Not a satisfactory state of affairs. They have given promises that have not been fulfilled," one committee member said. But in London, the Federation of Polish Jews in Great Britain was now holding demonstrations of loyalty to the Polish government-in-exile, and in New York, while there were doubts—Kot and even Sikorski were tainted by their illiberal prewar positions, and several members of the Polish government professed outright anti-Semitic views[23]—there was also hope that the blow that had been dealt by the war to Poland and the government-in-exile's need for international recognition, would make mutual cooperation beneficial to both sides. Already in 1940, under mounting pressure, the government-in-exile had issued a declaration on the future of Polish Jewry:

The Jews, as Polish citizens, shall in liberated Poland be equal with the Polish community, in duties and in rights. They will be able to develop their culture, religion, and folkways without hindrance. Not only the laws of the state, but even more the common sufferings in this most tragic time of affliction will serve to guarantee this pledge.

The declaration revealed, as historian David Engel writes, that the Polish government "gradually gave greater credence to Jewish power in the formation of Western public opinion." But it "made a disastrous impression" in occupied Warsaw, he writes, which was conveyed by a secret letter Kot received.[24]

"We are fully aware of all [the challenges of working with the Polish government]," Warburg concluded. "It is, so to say, the best—perhaps not the most satisfactory, but the best proposition that we have to offer." The JDC executive committee approved unanimously the motion to transfer $100,000 to the Polish government-in-exile, with the possibility of making this a monthly sum or extending a much larger amount in the future.

The correspondence between the JDC and the Polish authorities were extremely cordial. By late December, the Polish ambassador to the United States informed the JDC that his government had so far managed to obtain "the sum of $1,292,250," a large part of which came from a Soviet loan. "Six hundred tons of clothing (both new and used), boots, and underwear, as well as needles, threads and material for repairing clothing" had been purchased and would soon be shipped aboard vessels chartered by the Soviet authorities. The relief applied in Russia to Polish citizens under the direction of the Polish Embassy, he assured the JDC, would be "conducted without any discrimination, in an entirely non-sectarian way."[25]

On January 8, 1942, the American Jewish journal Menorah published a call for contributions to aid refugees in the Soviet Union, citing that "representatives of the Polish government" have granted "official assurances" that "the Jews are to be given the same treatment as other Polish nationals now on Soviet soil" and that "a minimum of $100,000 monthly" would be required to match the contributions of Catholic-Polish organizations and aid the Jewish refugees. Henry Hurwitz, general editor for the Menorah, wrote to Joseph Hyman of the JDC that his journal planned to run a symposium of Jewish and Christian historians on "the desired peace and world reconstruction" in the postwar period.[26]

By late February 1942, the Canadian United Jewish Refugee and War Relief Agency added another emergency remittance of $10,000 to the pot of Polish aid.

Meanwhile in Samarqand, as was corroborated by every testimony and memoir, my father continued to starve.

———

During the three days that Magda Gawin's great-aunt Jadwiga was interrogated inside my family's brewery, Magda told me on the second day of our Ostrów tour, another great-aunt tried to negotiate with her captor, a Gestapo agent named Anton Psyk, known as the "butcher of Ostrów." Psyk lived in a ground-floor apartment with two entrances on the brewery's premises."

"That would be my great-grandparents' apartment," I told her. "Two entrances, formal and informal and two kitchens, meat and dairy, as Ze'ev Wolf Teitel described it in his memoir."

"When I was growing up," Magda said, "the word browar—brewery— meant 'Gestapo.'"

In the archives of the Urząd Bezpieczeństwa, or UB—Poland's Office of Public Security—there were many descriptions of what had gone on in the Teitel brewery. Stanisław Szymaski, a man who regularly delivered rice, testified that "the interior—walls, ceiling, floor, tables—was always stained with blood" and that he had seen "dead bodies poked with sticks and iron rods." Andrzej Pęziński, in the unpublished memoir *Ostrów at a Distance*, told of an instance when "German soldiers ordered one Jew to climb up a tall chimney of the brewery and shot at him just for fun."

"The death of Jews at the *browar* was not normal," Magda said. "Torture involved dogs—women who lived in the four houses near the *browar* saw things. Psyk was a sadist, and Jews were tortured in strange ways. He was vulgar, very often drank. He usually addressed Poles as 'Polish pigs.' It is lack of words, what he did with Jews. The act of killing was connected with the play."

Psyk was a Polish citizen. "But he was *Volksdeutsch*, ethnically a German," Magda said.

On November 10, 1939, nine weeks after Hannan and his family fled

Ostrów, roughly five hundred Jewish men, women, and children were arrested under the pretext that a Jew had set the town's main street on fire. The women and the children were placed in the brewery, the men in a large Jewish-owned store. The next day they were executed by machine gun, their bodies left strewn in the field on the outskirts of the city until 1944, when they were transported to be cremated in neighboring Treblinka. It was the first mass execution of Jews in Poland, Magda said. And it was photographed, by those who carried it out.

Three Nazi soldiers who were sent from Warsaw carried out the November 1939 machine gun massacre of Ostrów's Jews. On the way to the execution, Magda told me, a baby was passed to a Polish neighbor, and later raised by her.

"How did these three Nazi soldiers from Warsaw know where the Jews lived? How did they round up over five hundred of them in one night?" I was grateful to Magda for the blanks she was filling in for me, but in the back of my head the words Henryk Grynberg had uttered when Salar and I visited him kept ringing. "How did most of the Jews who were hiding in Warsaw with Aryan papers get murdered? The Nazis themselves couldn't identify an assimilated Jew. . . ."

"The soldiers came with lists," Magda said.

She warded off any suggestion of possible Polish complicity, saying, "Our residents were not like that." And she educated me on the suffering of Poles in "our town"—something I had known nothing about: of the *łapanka* (street roundup), the random arrest and execution of 350 men and boys from Ostrów and neighboring towns in retaliation for the assassination of Ostrów's German mayor. She told me of Kazimierz Warchalski, the director of the *gymnasium* that my great-grandfather Michel Teitel had helped build, the principal of many Teitel children, who died in Majdanek for organizing a network of "secret teaching" after the Gestapo ordered the closing of Ostrów's schools. And she took me to the town's Catholic cemetery, where the names of Warchalski, his wife, Cecilia, and Jadwiga were etched on a black granite plaque at the cemetery's entrance, alongside eighty-five others who were listed under the category *Hitlerowcy* (the

Nazis). For Ostrów's Jewish dead, a black granite stone etched with a Star of David was erected by North American relatives of Ostrów's Jews near the site of the mass execution, just off the highway, in the early 2000s. In other sites in Ostrów, including the grounds of the Teitel brewery, were signs and plaques commemorating Polish resistance fighters.

I had not realized it the first time I visited—and the realization hit me suddenly and in full force—that here was not only the erasure of a Jewish past but its total replacement with a narrative of Polish resistance and heroism. The plaque atop the former brewery for THE MARTYR BLOOD OF POLES FIGHTING FOR FREEDOM DURING THE HITLERITE OCCUPATION was not only silent regarding the owners of the brewery—my father's family—but about the countless Jews who were tortured and died there, the majority of the Gestapo victims.

But I said nothing to Magda, whose great-aunt had been killed by the Nazis, whose empathy for my family's story felt sincere, and whose hospitality was so shockingly generous. One day, she even invited Agata Warchalska-Troll, the great granddaughter of Ostrow's gymnasium principal, who was killed during the war alongside his wife, Cecilia, to drive with us to the Zambrowski forest, where Agata's great-grandmother and other Poles had been shot. In the forest too were many memorials and monuments: for fighters of the *Armia Krajowa* (Home Army), for Russian soldiers who were executed there, for different individuals, but never for Jews. The Zambrowski forest, unlike that in Komi, was peaceful and lovely, and the three of us strolled there at leisure, talking and laughing.

Perhaps violence is like a wave that ebbs and flows, I thought, and even if you get caught in that wave, as my father had, one day your offspring may be walking at the site of your horror with the offspring of other unlikely survivors, or with the offspring of collaborators or perpetrators even. I still had not read the majority of the testimonies and reports; I still did not know what had transpired between Polish and Jewish refugees in Central Asia and Iran.

=

In December 1942, fearing the advancing Wehrmacht, the Polish embassy was evacuated from Moscow to Kuybyshev, a southern Russian town where many embassies and government offices were relocated. By then, the Polish embassy was deluged with work. Thousands of ill and starving refugees poured into Kuybyshev from the settlements and the camps and waited outside for aid. Thousands of letters from relatives of starving refugees pleading for help on their behalf arrived daily, piling up unopened and unanswered on the embassy's floors, as Kot described in his memoir.

The JDC began to send supplies directly to the Kuybyshev embassy. An emergency shipment of clothing and other supplies was sent via the Polish Red Cross from Palestine. The JDC also purchased $30,000 worth of medical supplies—cholera vaccines, tetanus antitoxin and typhoid combined, insulin, spirits of turpentine, quinine sulfate, codeine, aspirin, bandages, surgical dressings, ether for anesthesia, hypodermic needles, and disinfectants, as well as sixty tons of matzo for the upcoming Passover seder, all consigned to the Polish embassy in Kuybyshev.[27]

For expediency, the JDC did not ship anti-tetanus and antityphoid vaccines but airlifted them: from Miami to Lagos to Cairo, where the Polish legation received them and brought them to Kuybyshev. The arrangements, which had been made by the Polish consul general in Washington, were paid for by the JDC.[28] Soon afterward Dr. Harry Gold, a pharmacologist and cardiologist at Cornell University, compiled a more thorough list of "prime materials" that were deemed the most crucial for a war-refugee population, which the JDC immediately began purchasing.[29]

I found long of lists of medical supplies at the JDC archive: 150,000 digitalis tablets for heart failure; 100,000 antibacterial sulfanilamide tablets; 8,000 vials of 5CC typhoid combined vaccine; 10 pounds of antityphoid quinine sulfate; tetanus antitoxin; cholera vaccines; and Squibb insulin. There were orders of nearly 200,000 aspirin tablets and other painkillers. There were orders for surgical supplies: ether, hydrochloride, phenobarbital tablets, thousands of bandage rolls, sterile dressings and gauze; and wards of chloroformic catgut (surgical suture) and surgical silk. For combating starvation, there were orders for vitamin tablets and orders of gallons of brewer's yeast; cod liver oil, olive oil, and cocoa butter; thousands of pounds of liver extract, calcium lactate, magnesium sulfate; sodium powder. There were also orders for methylamine tablets for urinary infections and thousands of ampuls of neoarsphenamine for treating syphilis.[30] The supply list was designed at least in part to accommodate the needs of the army, and I wondered whether the JDC had received it directly from Polish authorities. Regardless, I was amazed by the ingenuity and expediency with which the JDC purchased and shipped the medicines, and by the commitment and urgency with which it acted. I now knew what my father had never known: that in faraway continents and cities—New York, London, Mexico City, Montreal, Buenos Aires, Cape Town, Jerusalem—many highly competent and devoted persons worked incessantly to try to save him.

In addition to the initial $100,000 given to the Polish consulate, and the airlifting of the emergency antityphoid vaccines, the American Jewish Labor Committee shipped tons of clothing and food, including four transports of powdered milk, which were confirmed to have arrived in Kuybyshev. Relief consignments purchased in Palestine and India were delivered to Central Asia via the Polish consulate in Palestine.[31] The Montreal-based United Jewish Refugee and War Relief Agency had purchased its own medications in Canada, which it attempted to ship through the Canadian Red Cross.[32] Five New York–based physicians established an advisory committee to examine additional requests for drugs and medical supplies. The JDC signed an agreement with the American Committee of the OSE— Obshchestvo Zdravokhraneniya Yevreyev (Society for the Protection of the Health of the Jews), a Paris-based organization that specialized in fighting epidemics in Eastern Europe. The OSE made recommendations to the JDC on drugs, suppliers, quantities, prices, and shipping options.[33]

In New York, the Bank Polska Kasa Opieki set up a service for shipping individual food and clothing packages to refugees in Russia. At a charge of $2.50 for a parcel weighing up to 11 pounds and $4 for 11 to 22 pounds, American relatives could now send relief to their relatives, though the Bank Polska maintained that because of war conditions and the frequent movement of refugees, it could not guarantee their delivery to specific addresses and said unclaimed parcels would be given to the embassy to distribute as it saw fit.

In Tel Aviv, the quasi-government of Palestine's Jewish population, the Jewish Agency, formed a Committee for the Rescue of Polish Jews and began to send consignments.

In Argentina and South Africa, fund-raising campaigns took place.

Ambassador Kot cabled New York that supplies arrived in "good condition" and with "minimum damage" and were distributed immediately among "the most needy" Polish citizens—"30 percent in the Northern Russian districts; 30 percent in Kazakhstan; and 40 percent Southern districts."[34] In Washington, D.C., he confirmed to the JDC that the airlifted medications had reached their destination. He also welcomed the idea that labels be placed on the goods informing those who received them of their origin.[35] In May 1942 the JDC offered him a second remittance of $50,000 toward the purchase of "medicines, medical and surgical supplies and equipment."

"The warehouses were bursting with goods," Aleksander Wat wrote in his memoir. "Trainloads of gifts from America and England had arrived . . . countless trainloads of gifts."[36] To distribute the "gifts" to the refugees, Kot writes, in January 1942, an agreement was signed between his embassy and the People's Committee of Foreign Affairs, which permitted the appointment of Polish "men of trust" or "delegates" who would distribute the goods to Polish citizens. Twenty-one regional *delegaturas* (representative office) were opened across Central Asia, with fifteen to twenty branches each (for a total of 381), located near refugee concentrations.

In Alma-Ata, where Wat initially headed, the *delegatura* was situated in a large, "European-scale hotel" that was "almost up to Parisian standards." Inside the hotel, as he describes it, were Red Army officers, evacuated Soviet film stars and starlets, and hundreds of "people with running sores, ulcers, people swollen with hunger" waiting on the staircase leading to the *delegatura* office, which was on the second floor. The head of the *delegatura*, "a Polish prince" who recognized Wat, gave him a bench and a "marvelous Scottish blanket to sleep on." For dinner, he writes, *delegatura* workers drank "excellent wine," ate "cheeses, caviar, ham, and sausage." They even brought caviar over to his sleeping bench while "those poor wretches from the camps were . . . still waiting on the stairs because they had nowhere to go."[37]

After the arrival of the consignments from the United States and elsewhere, I now knew, some Polish refugees did not starve. It was shocking, after having read and heard all the descriptions of hunger—the hunger that had set in my father's bones in Uzbekistan and may have eventually killed him, and that most everyone else in Central Asia shared—to read Wat's descriptions of excess. On Wat's second day in Alma-Ata, he was taken to choose clothing. "I chose some used clothing, a wonderful suit, better than anything I'd had before, a beautiful tan material. . . . I found a winter coat for Ola, a used one, with a fox-fur collar: Maison Neuman, New York Paris."[38] His good fortune did not last long—he fell out of favor of the authorities soon enough—but now I knew that caviar and Neiman Marcus coats existed not far from my father and the other starving, dying refugees and locals.

Aid or the denial of aid from the Polish *delegaturas* was mentioned in some of the Tehran Children testimonies. One said that after the amnesty, a Polish delegation "delivered food and clothing" to a *posiołek*, "but only Poles got them. Jews were given nothing."[39] Others said the child's father got "a job at the *delegatura*" or received stipends:

> Among the officials at the Polish *delegatura* in Bukhara, we met someone we knew, and through him we got an allowance of three hundred rubles a month.

> We received 200 rubles a month and half a kilo of flour each. We were not given any clothes. Non-Jewish Poles got clothes and underwear.

> Mrs. Glancer [a woman from the child's town in Poland] got money for me from the Polish *delegatura*, which I could use to buy food.[40]

Several children mentioned receiving "a little food," "a little flour," or "a few cans of food" from a delegation. One child's father sent a letter to President Roosevelt asking him to help the refugees; the NKVD arrested the man, and a Polish *delegatura* attempted to intervene, unsuccessfully, on his behalf. I read no reports of significant, consistent, life-changing aid. And nothing about coats or caviar.

Overall, little aid seemed to have made its way to the refugees. Wat attributed it to stupidity and mismanagement. "They stinted; they could have given out five times more," he wrote. "Because in the end, when the delegations closed, there were still enormous warehouses packed with goods."[41]

Moshe Kamer, a child refugee whose family found its way to Vrevskaya, near Tashkent, said in his testimony that medications were conserved for the Polish army. When he, his sister, and both his parents were hospitalized, they were not given medications because "the army took all the penicillin, and punished whoever gave penicillin to civilians or traded in penicillin."[42]

As a rule, Jewish refugees were not appointed as *delegatura* heads. In a report on "The Case of Jewish Citizens of Poland in Light of Soviet Official Documents and Practice," which would be sent by the Polish embassy to the Polish Ministry of Foreign Affairs a year later, Kot would attribute this to Soviet authorities. The appointment of two potential delegates—Rozenzweig and Lustgarten—had been thwarted because of their Jewish sounding names, he writes; a recommendation to "avoid controversy" around the identity of appointees had been passed down.[43]

Among those who were appointed were reportedly some who prevented Jews from obtaining any support.[44] A delegate whom Wat described as "a figure in the National Democracy Party" gave Jews "less, sometimes considerably less than Poles," reasoning that because "Jews had come mainly from settlements, they were quite in bearable condition," while the Poles "were mostly people who'd been in the camps or the widows of men who'd died in the camps."[45]

In interviews that would be conducted in Tehran in 1943, all classes of Jewish refugees—Labor, Zionists, Bundists, and even nationalists who were staunch supporters of the Polish government—gave accounts of significant discrimination in access to and distribution of general supplies. So did non-Jewish organizations like the American Red Cross and officers in the British military.[46]

When Kot received complaints from New York and London or from the refugees themselves, he sent staff to make inquiries (and carried out one himself). They produced reports that now are crammed into countless boxes at the Hoover Institution. Among them is a 191-page report "On the Assistance Given to the Jewish Population in the Soviet Union," full of charts, graphs, and numbers. Its purpose, its introduction states, is to respond "to contradictory opinions, including those expressed by international Jewish circles, about the engagement of the Polish government in helping Polish Jews deported to the USSR." This report, produced by the embassy, records that in 1942 a small number of refugees received aid; of them, the number of Jewish recipients is disproportionally small: 3,261 Poles and 726 Jews.[47] Another report, on the relief accorded to *all* Polish citizens in 1943, found that 33.9 percent of those who availed themselves of embassy aid were Jewish.[48] By 1943, however, the majority of Polish citizens had been evacuated to Iran.

Through the documents he included in *Conversations with the Kremlin*, Kot suggests that Soviet authorities interfered significantly and cunningly in Polish matters, including in the distribution of aid and the appointment of "delegates." In New York, Polish officials informed JDC officials that it was the Soviets who prohibited Jewish refugees from serving as delegates.

There were also reports of widespread theft, which suggested that whether as a matter of policy or in the spontaneous acts of individuals, the freight that was brought aboard Soviet ships did not arrive with all their merchandise. "Naturally they did not arrive full. Everyone stole," Wat wrote. "Nevertheless, there was still a lot left for the citizens."[49]

I found it hard to broach the question of anti-Semitism with Magda; she deflected every time. I liked and was grateful to her: she had opened her home to me, fed me, kept me warm, and for days walked me around Ostrów and Warsaw, introducing me to people, driving me to archives, translating Polish documents for me. Her generosity seemed boundless; her vision of our "shared past" genuine, almost touching, seductive. I brought up the subject carefully, tentatively, on our third day together. I told her about the "pogromchiks" that Regina had described to me, which occurred in the years before the war; about the beating my father's cousin Wolf Teitel had received in 1936, after scoring the highest grade in an entrance exam to the Warsaw Polytechnika, a beating that convinced him to leave Poland and study at the Technikum in Haifa.

"When I asked my father about the prewar period," Magda said, "he told me that the instigators were not from our town, but members of ONR"—Opus Naradova Radicalne, the anti-Semitic National Radical Camp—"who came by bus with their badges on their arm. When they entered our own backyard and started to destroy the Sukkot tents of our Jewish leasers, my great-grandmother Anya Mujek took something you prepare the schnitzel with and waved at them. She was a normal woman. The backyard was ours and this family was our residents, and she wouldn't agree to this violence."

"If these were outsiders, why didn't the local police ward them off?"

"When I asked my father, he said, 'My God, in our town there were five policemen. When they saw so many young men coming by bus, they hid in the police station and they feared.' It was the situation where the Jewish people and some Polish people were completely alone with this time of aggression. From the Polish state not enough was done to stop it," Magda said.

And yet I knew from Wolf Teitel's memoir that the ONR had had its own party in Ostrów.

"Even the Radwansky family, who were unequivocal support- ers of Roman Dmowski [leader of the right-wing National Democracy Party] did not support violence against town Jews," Magda said. "Our townspeople were traditional, religious, but not radical, not violent. They were like me. They were like your family, people who were attached to the national idea and to traditional values, not murderers."

Toward the end of my stay, Magda handed me a "surprise" she had prepared for me. At Instytut Pamieci Narodowej (Institute of National Remembrance), where she searched for information on the trial held for her great-aunt's killer, she had found a "Teitel family file," compiled between 1967 and 1971. It contained an investigation against the family on charges of "Syjonism" (Zionism). Among those under investigation were Hannan's grandfather Michel Teitel (who had died before the war), Michel's brother Berek Teitel (both were listed as "owners of the *browar*"); Berek's wife Chaja, "educated and fluent in many languages"; Jacub Teitel, "supplier of furniture and facilities to Komorowo" (a Polish army officers' neighborhood near Ostrów); Hersz Teitel, a "businessman"; and David, Abram, Josef, Bejta, and Suza Teitel, whom I did not know of. All were suspected of "Syjonistic" activities.

"Your great-grandfather was a supporter of Zionism, and the Communists hated the national idea!" Magda did not appear outraged or even surprised by the bogus investigation against a family whose members had been murdered or fled Poland thirty years prior; she alluded to it simply as a routine procedure of the UB, which in the late 1960s helped facilitate massive anti-Semitic purges in Poland. Mostly she was relieved to discover that the Teitels were Zionists, not Bundists or Communists. Magda had been raised with the stereotype of Jews as Communists, she told me, but her research of Ostrów had taught her that "it is absolutely not true that our Jews were typically Communists. In our town, Jews were attached to the national idea, and to traditional values, like everyone. I think Polish historiography does not describe people such as us," she said with a sigh. *Us*: meaning her and me.

At night Magda took me to dinner with her friends: the journalist Bronisław Wildstein, former CEO of Poland's state-owned broadcaster Telewizja Polska; Dorota Skrzypek, wife of the former president of the Polish National Bank Sławomir Skrzypek (who died in 2010 when a plane carrying the Polish governmental, military, and economic elite en route to a commemoration of the murdered Polish officers at Katyń crashed on Russian soil); a prominent Catholic priest; and others. The dinner of Bouillabaisse and top French wine was wonderful. I felt like Aleksander Wat in Alma-Ata, wined and dined by Polish conservatives, and loving it.

Unlike all of my American and most of my Israeli academic friends, my dinner companions did not deconstruct the Polish "national idea," but cherished it wholeheartedly, sentimentally, and uncritically. The nation was for them as Israel had been for me in my youth , as it remains for most Israelis: a thing to love and defend and never question, an absolute safehaven, a guarantee against the violence of others. The violence wasn't abstract either: Wildstein, who in his youth had been a member of an anti-Communist student movement at Jagiellonian University, had been forced into exile after a fellow activist, Stanisław Pyjas, mysteriously fell down a flight of stairs and died. The plane that Dorota's husband had been on is believed by many Poles, and certainly by everyone in the room, to have been deliberately downed by Russia.

I understood their logic. But the problem, of course, was the price that was paid for those who remained outside the fold of the nation, for those who were targeted as its enemies and its threat, for the violence begat *by* the nation.

=

Those questions, of who was a member of the Polish nation-in-exile and who wasn't, came to the forefront in Uzbekistan with debates over enlistment of Polish-Jewish citizens into the Anders Army. Kot had warned Anders to be mindful of the "Jewish question" (he wrote to Sikorski that there should be no problems with the general on this front), and at the outset Anders admitted Jews freely into the Polish army. But when it soon transpired that 40 percent (according to Kot) to 60 percent (according to Anders) of the soldiers in the two first units were Jewish, it became a problem.

In a meeting with Stalin, Kot reports of complaining that "not one of the officers on the staff of General Anders's army, which he commanded in Poland," had been released from the gulags in Starobielsk, Kozielsk, and Ostashkov" and that instead "the first to be released from the camps have been those least physically fit for work, especially the urban Jewish element." Anders, Kot reports, deemed many of the Polish Jews who sought enlistment to be "speculators" or "people who have been punished for smuggling" and stated that in general "the Jewish element does not want to serve in the army." "They will never make good soldiers," he said, an evaluation with which Stalin concurred, claiming "the Jews are lousy soldiers."[50]

Against this conversation, I read dozens of testimonies of Polish Jews who had been disqualified and turned away by the Anders Army.

> My father wanted to join the Polish army, but they wouldn't accept him.

> My father tried to join the Polish army as a driver, but they wouldn't accept him because he was a Jew.

> My older brother volunteered for the Polish army but they wouldn't accept him because he was a Jew.

> I traveled to Tashkent, where a Polish army was being formed. They were happy to accept Polish women for the female detachments but not Jewish women.

> When the news came that a Polish army was being formed, my older brother and uncle Meir went to Samarkand, but they were not accepted. My uncle was in despair and died of starvation, and after him his son Motl.[51]

Admission to the army, as described in testimonies and memoirs, was a question of life and death not only for the soldier himself but for his family members. The army had access to food and medicines. "Unwitting and in desperation, thousands of civilian Poles were turning the military camps into refugee feeding stations," writes Helena Wiśniewska Brow, whose father Stefan Wiśniewski had been a Polish child refugee with a brother in the Anders Army. "Every Pole enlisting in Uzbekistan was a hardened survivor . . . who needed to pass on food rations to starving family members nearby. . . . [Soldiers] would receive accommodations and food, and their rations would be shared with their grateful family." Stefan Wiśniewski, a Catholic Pole, was automatically accepted into the army. Other Catholic Poles mentioned no examination or precondition for entry but simply noted that they or their family members "enlisted in" or "joined" the army. Stefan's older siblings, Roman and Regina, "joined the army," as his daughter put it, in Fergana, Uzbekistan, where thousands of Jews, Poles, and Ukrainians sought to enlist. In February 1942 the army sought to increase its ranks of ethnic Poles by reducing the enlistment age, forming the Polish Cadet Force Junaki. Stefan's fifteen-year-old brother "joined." Stefan recalled "visiting the camp at regular intervals to collect these parcels—mostly sugary, block-like lumps of dried bread" from his "enlisted siblings."

A Catholic former child refugee, Joanna Synowiec, heard that "not too far away, near Fergana, was the Polish army," where "Polish soldiers . . . took care of Polish children who came their way." When we arrived at "a building with a Polish flag . . . it was such an incredible feeling of relief that we had made it; we were with the Poles. . . . Everyone welcomed us warmly, and there was rice to eat."[52]

"The scenes familiar from Poland before the war were here reenacted," Simon Perl, an electrician who was disqualified for enlistment at Fergana, wrote. "The Poles were automatically included among the ranks of the army; the Jews were graded type 'D'—unfit for active military service— and even those who had already been accepted were expelled for trivial reasons. Finally, my turn arrived to appear before the committee; appearing together with me was Richterman, a swimming champion. Both of us received a 'D' grade."[53]

"Maimed, crooked, hunchbacked, and one-eyed Poles were assigned fitness grades that qualified them for military service," Meir Lustgarten, the son of Jewish farmers from western Galicia, wrote. Though he was initially "accepted into the army without any difficulty," he was later ordered to appear before a medical board, given a "D" for physical fitness, and released from the service.[54]

Even Jewish soldiers who had fought in the Polish army at the outset of World War II were disqualified or deterred from enlisting in the Anders Army. Michael Licht, a gymnastics and sports teacher who had fought in the Polish army, was first disqualified, then accepted but expelled ten days later, along with the other Jewish soldiers in his unit. At the outbreak of the war, David Lauenberg, a cadet in the Polish army, waited all night in line at an enlistment center in Kremina ("in essence to re-enlist, because I was never dismissed from the army"), but left when he was insulted. [55]

In his report a year later, Kot would attribute the rejection and de-enlistment of Polish Jews from the Anders Army to Soviet authorities, citing an order issued by the Soviet General Szczerbakov (Schtcherbakov) of Alma-Ata, Kazakhstan, in which the General demanded that all Polish citizens of Jewish ethnicity be incorporated into the Red Army.[56] Yet in the testimonies of young Jewish men turned away or dismissed after enlistment, the rejections and insults reportedly came from the mouths of Polish army men alone. "As I waited in line," David Lauenberg testified, "I heard Polish soldiers say, 'How do we get rid of these filthy Jews? They are shoving themselves everywhere' . . . I was furious to the bottom of my soul. Here I go to re-enlist, and these Poles, with whom we went side by side through the horror of the Gulags, in their eyes I was a filthy Jew again."[57]

There were exceptions. Sixteen-year-old Jocek Shenkelbach was accepted into a Junek school for young army cadets and traveled with it to Iran. When admitted, he was told that there were no other Jews at the school and that he would have to prove himself with proper behavior. "The first two weeks were very hard," he recalled, "but the days passed and they got used to me and I got used to them."[58]

Yehuda Pompiansky served in an all-Jewish Anders Army battalion. In his testimony, he praised the battalion's commander, Colonel Galadyk ("a liberal and a socialist" who treated us "excellent"). The Jewish battalion, which Anders, who opposed the idea, later disbanded, was formed in part because of allegations of maltreatment of Jewish soldiers in other units. "They thought our unit would be a ghetto," Pompiansky wrote, "but the result was the opposite. . . . We were equipped, our camp was organized and trained. Our lieutenants and sub-lieutenants were Jewish. We did lots [of] sports and it really lifted our morale. . . . I never received bad treatment—perhaps because I had a Polish last name and excellent Polish."[59]

A JDC report, composed of interviews with both Catholic and Jewish military personnel in Iran, would state that "anti-Semitism was reported to be widespread in the army among all ranks." It noted exceptional individuals like the army's bishop, Bishop Gawlina, and Colonel Galadyk, but it concluded with a quote from a Polish army officer who said that "unless the Allied Armies occupied Poland after the War, hundreds of thousands of Jews will be pogrommed."[60]

$$=$$

It was in Central Asia, then, on the backs of Polish Jews, on my father's back and on the backs of refugees like him and his family, that the battle for the future of Poland was fought. Would it be a Poland without Jews? A Bolshevik Poland?

For the Soviets, the battle over Poland began with the sentence, "Just as you cannot see your ears, you will never see Poland." Hannan and nearly every other testifier reported being told this repeatedly in the settlements and gulags. It had not been a random act of abuse but a policy, a direct and active Soviet attempt to "de-Polonize" the Polish refugees.

For the Polish government-in-exile, the battle over Poland centered on its Jewish citizens, with their supposed ability to turn international public opinion in favor of the Polish cause. But Polish Jews were also perceived to be Poland's internal enemies, the fifth column who in 1939 welcomed

Soviet soldiers into their Polish towns and villages. And so the picture that emerged from the thousands of documents I read—the corpus of the Polish embassy and *delegaturas*, the responses of the JDC and others in the United States, London, and Palestine—was the one that after my meeting with Magda I hoped to not see, or to see less of: the exclusion of Jews from resources and from their very identity as Poles, and concurrently a denial of this exclusion by Polish authorities.

Polish sources laid the blame for the delays in refugee aid and the obstacles plaguing Polish-Jewish relations on the Soviet side. It was due to NKVD orders, they argued, that 90 percent of the Jews who reported to the enlistment centers were rejected, and that existing Jewish soldiers were subjected to a "re-examination" and dismissed or transferred to support units.[61] These NKVD orders, which were relayed to those in charge of recruitment, they claimed, specified that ethnic minorities should not exceed 10 percent of the recruits and 5 percent of the noncommissioned officers.[62] Kot reports that the Soviet government shot down a proposal to establish regional Polish welfare committees and agreed only to appointing its own "men of trust" whom Polish delegates would assist. Early on the JDC proposed to expedite aid to Polish refugees by buying and shipping supplies from Iran, by shipping the aid to the refugees directly, and by earmarking it separately. The Soviets rejected the plan, Kot writes.[63]

At the beginning of 1942, a little over a couple thousand Jewish soldiers were in the Anders Army, mostly physicians and those trained in essential professions. ("The excess of Jews [in the army] was reduced by the removal of the physically less fit," Kot reported in a January 5 memo).[64] Some Jewish recruits at the army's central recruitment center in Yangiyo'l, twenty kilometers from Tashkent, were told that they could join if they converted to Catholicism, which at least a few hundred, if not a few thousand, did. In some cases, Polish officers accepted bribes from Jews for admittance into the army, which suggests that Jewish enlistment was in fact possible.[65]

The brawls and anti-Jewish incidents, in varying degree of seriousness, continued, despite Kot's simultaneous attempts to curb them and downplay them. Those who did manage to enlist reportedly experienced withholding of supplies, clothing, and equipment; insults, physical injury, and acts of degradation; and frequent and unjustified demands to perform physical labor. The "all-Jewish battalion" was dissolved; its commander, Colonel Galadyk, protested, saying the separation was necessary for the protection of the Jewish soldiers, who "live happier in ghetto barracks . . . than dwell together with anti-Semites and Hitlerites."[66]

The accusations and accounts of anti-Semitism and violence against Jewish soldiers spilled into the Jewish press in the United States and Palestine, which in turn demanded answers from the Polish government-in-exile in London. On November 14, 1941, in order to "put an end to all of the malicious insinuations and gossip being generated behind our backs—which in all likelihood emanates from sources hostile to us—about alleged anti-Semitism in our forces," Anders issued a directive to his commanding officers "to fight relentlessly against any manifestation of racial anti-Semitism."

> The Jew will benefit from the same laws that apply to all Poles; drastic action is to be taken against him only when he does not know how to wear with pride the uniform of a soldier of the Polish Republic and he forgets that he is a Polish citizen.[67]

Two weeks later, in response to a backlash that Anders' order created among the Polish soldiers, a second communiqué from Anders was circulated among Polish commanding officers. After the war, Anders maintained that it was a forgery. In the second memo he reportedly wrote that he was "well aware" of the anti-Semitic outbursts within the army and said they were "a response to the disloyal and often hostile behavior of Polish Jews from the eastern territories during the years 1939–1940." The Polish "raison d'être" required the army at present not to "annoy the Jews," since "anti-Semitism can bring the most disastrous and incalculable effects upon the

Polish cause." But once the Poles were "masters in our own home," they would deal with the Jewish question "as the greatness and sovereignty of our homeland and ordinary human justice demand."[68] By "disloyal . . . behavior," Anders was referring to allegations that the Jews of Polish border towns had welcomed the "Soviet invaders," an allegation that reverberated among the Polish refugees in Central Asia and whose echoes I still heard on my visits to Poland more than half a century later.

═══

During my week in Ostrów, Magda and I visited the memorial for Ostrów's murdered Jews—and the mayor's office, at her request, sent flowers. When she and I returned to Warsaw, she took me to an exhibition on "Polish London" at the Polish History Museum, where I was escorted by its director Robert Castro, another friend. During the war four hundred thousand Poles, including members and families of the government-in-exile, parts of the military, nearly all air force pilots, and large swaths of the Polish intelligentsia, had fled to London and remained there in its aftermath, making Poles England's largest immigrant group. Among them were a number of largely assimilated Jews—newspaper publishers, journalists—whose photos and artifacts were organized with the others' into a cheerful multisensory display of songs, plays, journals, and fashion. On the exhibition's poster was a photo of a bold, decorated, and slightly campy-looking General Anders, who after the war would be stripped of his rank by the Bolshevik Polish People's Republic but was now rehabilitated as a heroic and charismatic figure in Polish history.

We also visited the Warsaw Uprising Museum, an impressive, nifty structure with interactive exhibits of photos, movies, maps, oral testimonies, weapons, a helicopter, and a 3D before-and-after model of the city, all telling a heroic narrative of the Home Army's resistance as the basis for Poland's rebirth. Warsaw's Jews and the Warsaw Ghetto Uprising were absent from the museum, though the razed Jewish ghetto appears as a large black hole in the city's 3D map. The museum had significantly contributed to the rehabilitation of Home Army fighters, who had been repressed in Communist Poland. A German Holocaust historian with whom I e-mailed the night before my visit called the Warsaw Uprising Museum "a Disneyfied version of history." "The Poles are obsessed with the Home Army," she wrote. "The Home Army this, the Home Army that. But the Home Army has a big blemish on its record: it did nothing to support the Warsaw Ghetto Uprising; it excluded Jews from its ranks and did not sufficiently commemorate the ones who did end up fighting for it."

I reiterated my friend's words to Magda. "The purpose of the Home Army was to fight the Germans and the Soviets," she shot back. "Its aim was not to protect Polish civilians, let alone Polish Jews, who were the weakest link." She told me that on the next anniversary of the Warsaw Ghetto Uprising, two beams of light would connect the Warsaw Uprising Museum, of which her husband Darek was deputy director, to the Museum of the History of Polish Jews, linking "our city's two uprisings."

"The Warsaw Ghetto Uprising *was* a military action," the German historian replied in another e-mail. "Yet when Mordechai Anielewicz [head of the ŻOB, the Żydowska Organizacja Bojowa, or Jewish Combat Organization, and a leader of the uprising] begged the Home Army for weapons, they ignored him. Not to mention that some parts of the Home Army didn't just disregard Jews but actively killed them."

When I told Magda's husband Darek what my friend had written, he shrugged as he walked me through the museum, "Germans don't understand this museum and the narrative we are trying to tell," he said. "They fancy themselves post-national, post-history. For them history has ended, but for us and also for you Israelis, history has only begun." Darek was not wrong, I thought.

═══

On December 1, 1941, the Soviet government issued orders that with the exception of ethnic Poles, all Polish citizens who on November 1, 1939, had been residents of areas that formerly belonged to the Soviet Union would be considered Soviet citizens. When a Jewish news agency queried him about the statement, Soviet ambassador to the U.S. Maxim Litvinov (who had been born Meir Wallach-Finkelstein in Russian Białystok) explained that Jews who had lived in regions that formerly belonged to the USSR—like Ruchela Teitel's mother Esthera Averbuch—were now Soviet citizens.[69]

"Sovietization"—stripping Jews and other minorities who had been the borderlands' primary residents of their Polish citizenship and turning them into Soviet citizens—was another step in the battle over the future of these territories. Kot made a case to both Moscow and London that Polish Jews did "not want to be under Russian domination at any price" and should remain Polish citizens.[70] He argued that Polish Jews had suffered so much "injury and humiliation" in the Soviet Union that it had provoked feelings of "contempt and even hatred of Russia," even among the Jews previously most "anti-Polish," and awakened in them "a desire to return at all costs to their little border towns," as they were when they were part of Polish territory.[71]

The Polish government-in-exile, as proof of Polish Jews' attachment to their Polish citizenship and as a defense against claims of anti-Semitism in its ranks, published a letter from six "Polish citizens of the Mosaic Faith" to "the respected rabbis of the United States and England." The letter, which was included in a 191-page report "On the Assistance Given to the Jewish Population in the Soviet Union," produced to appease the protestations of Jewish organizations and presses, decried the accusations of discriminatory treatment by the Polish embassy as "a lie spread by idiots and deliberately provoked in order to break up Polish society" and affirmed that they "want to continue to be Polish citizens," "have not asked for any foreign citizenship," and were begging the rabbis to help the Polish government fight for their rights.

In his report a year later, Kot detailed the timeline that in his words resulted in Jewish de-passportization. After amnesty, he writes, released Polish citizens—both ethnic Poles and others—were issued temporary certificates, which were to be replaced within three months with Polish passports; those passports, due to technical delays, were printed only in March 1942, by which time Soviet authorities began extending the certificates of some and revoking those of others, particularly of non-ethnic Poles. The

Polish Embassy, working under the instructions of the government-in-exile, continued to assert the Polish citizenship of Jewish Poles, Kot maintains, and it was only Soviet propaganda that spread rumors to the contrary. He quoted a Mr. Wiktor Brandes, who while interned in a special settlement was told by the NKVD that the Polish embassy does not care to release him, and another who was told that he was "sold by his government."[72]

Wat's and others' memoirs confirm the desire of many Polish Jews to retain their Polish citizenship. As a recent convert to Catholicism and a prominent intellectual, Wat felt at home in Polish circles and naturally desired to return to Poland. After a series of twists and tribulations, he had been exiled to a Kazakh *kolkhoz*, where, he recalled, "I felt like a Pole in a way I had never felt before, a patriot, almost a nationalist. . . . A Jew, a Polish patriot, a Polish nationalist. . . . I liked that very much. I felt like a fish in water."[73] The other inhabitants—Galician-born Hasidic Jews and Jewish shoemakers, tailors, lawyers, and small merchants—all dreamed of returning to Poland as well. Kramer, a Galician shoemaker who organized the others to resist Soviet passportization, had withstood severe NKVD torture of himself and his son. "Kramer was a passionate Polish patriot. His nostalgia for Poland, his longing for Radom, for Polish life, even with its anti-Semites, was so powerful and genuine that now when I think about it coolly, it's beyond my powers to imagine," Wat wrote in 1977, having returned to Poland after the war, then exiled again in the late 1950s.[74]

≡

On the day before I left Poland, an exhibition of "Old Ostrów" was constructed outside Ostrów's neoclassical municipality building. Eight four-foot posters were hung, the first of which was a photo of the Teitel Brewery, showing my grandfather Zindel Teitel, his brother Icok, and a few other men in long winter coats standing next to their vehicles in the brewery's front yard. The poster's caption was TEITEL BROCA BROWAR, 1885–1940, nothing more, nothing less. I recognized the brewery photo from Regina's album—it was not in the public domain—and wondered who else in town had it. And to whom did the brewery's history belong anyway, to the Jews or the Poles? Next to the poster, a bride and groom posed for a photo shoot: she with dyed blond hair, he in a polyester tuxedo, a little beat-up looking, the future of Ostrów. "I have a fantasy," Magda said as we looked at them, "that we should drink wine and eat kugel on the grounds of the *browar* on the eve of Rosh Hashanah like your family celebrated here before the war." I laughed, touched but also wary. We had been negotiating something, Magda and I, a way back to reconstituting some shared version of history, and each of us would have to give *something*. "Rizcard told me that Ostrówer Jews before the war were 'too nice.' It isn't right that they felt they had to be too nice. They didn't feel natural," she said one night. It was the furthest she could go.

Two years later, in 2015, Andrzej Duda's rightist, nationalist Law and Justice government would be elected, and Magda Gawin would be appointed undersecretary of state in the Ministry of Culture and National Heritage, conserver of National Monuments, and member of the Council for the Protection of Memory of Combat and Martyrdom. "It's because of my aunt Jadwiga," she would tell me when we met again, briefly, in London. "My work on Jadwiga's history taught me what I need to do on this job." In the two years since my visit, Yad Vashem had declined Magda's petition to have Jadwiga Długoborska recognized as a Righteous Among the Nations, citing insufficient evidence. But Duda's government would open its own Museum of Poles Who Saved Jews in the southeastern town of Markowa, and announce plans for two more monuments for the righteous: next to the All Saints Church on Warsaw's Grzybowski Square, and near the Museum of the History of Polish Jews, atop what used to be the Warsaw Ghetto.

In early 2018 Duda's government announced that it was building a dedicated Warsaw Ghetto Museum that would "speak of the mutual love between the two nations that spent eight hundred years here, on Polish land. Of the solidarity, fraternity, historical truth in all its aspects," as Magda's boss, Culture Minister Piotr Gliński, told reporters.[75] Later that year, an Israeli historian, Daniel Blatman, announced that he would be assuming the position of museum's chief historian. I met Magda once more, in London, where I traveled to search at the Sikorski Archive on Princes Gate

and she came on official state business to Westminster. She was a government representative now, and more impenetrable than when it was just
the two of us in Ostrów. When I showed her an article about Polish trolls
who targeted British-Jewish papers, she thanked me for bringing it to her
attention and said she herself had been trolled. When I told her I had been
given the cold shoulder at the Sikorski Archive, she said they were cold to
everyone, even to her. When I said that after everything I had found out
about my father's past, I was deeply sad for what he went through, she said,
"You should not think like that about your father. He survived, he was a
hero. He took part in war for Independent Israel. . . . But I understand how
you feel; we have *both* been robbed of our past." But she opened the door
for me at the Sikorski Archive, whose employees became much more helpful to me after her visit. And she was no less lovely and warm and familiar
than three years prior, and I, warier, was still charmed.

As conservator of monuments, Magda told me, she now oversaw the
restoration of Warsaw's Jewish cemetery, and in 2019 she would begin
reconstructing Ostrów's cemetery, "where all your family is buried." "The
Poles had razed the cemetery," my aunt Regina had told me, "after the
war." Magda also oversaw a large translation project of government-in-
exile documents. "The documents show that the Government had been
100 percent okay," she said. We strolled through St. James's Park, lit a
cigarette, talked about our jobs and our kids. I thought that in the same
way the Polish government-in-exile refused to acknowledge the overwhelming anti-Semitism of its *delegaturas* and army, Magda refused to
face Poland's past; I knew she suspected that that was what I thought. But
I also believed that her efforts were genuine and that in her mind she saw
herself as a true friend to the Jews, as perhaps Kot had thought of himself
in the 1940s. She was both a Polish patriot *and* a denouncer of the extreme
anti-Semitic Polish right. She was, in a sense, on the liberal, pragmatic side
of a right-wing government, as Sikorski and Kot had been, or tried to be,
attempting to balance the desire for a strong Polish state and international
legitimacy. And for this, like them, she too paid a price, trolled by scores
of nationalists and anti-Semites whose actions she continued to downplay.

7

SAMARQAND

City of Refugees

While the "trainloads of gifts" from the United States and elsewhere were rolling into Central Asia, my father was in Samarqand, where corpses were everywhere. Corpses and lice—tiny gray head lice and large white body lice that grew engorged with blood to monstrous proportions. Ruchela peeled them off Hannan and Regina, then off her husband, who would pick them off her and off the blanket on which they slept. Lice feces became a source of typhus that spread across Samarqand and killed thousands, the numbers increasing with each fresh wave of refugees and evacuees who arrived. Josek Klapholz, a former child refugee, describes in his memoir watching a hut mate drown his long beard in a so-called lice repellent he had bought with his last coins from the Uzbeks. Then the hut mate cut off his beard and soon began to die of hunger, his body aching, his mood turning darker and darker, a cruel, slow death of which thirteen-year-old Josek, whose father would soon die of hunger as well, was fully cognizant.

My father, Regina, Ruchela, and Zindel all contracted typhus in Samarqand. "We were in the hospital for what seems to me like a long time," Regina told me. The hospital, which Salar, Sergey, our guide Kamara, and I visited, was a handsome brick structure with arched doors and windows that in the 1940s was surrounded by improvised wood barracks. I did not know whether it carried any of the quinine or the antityphoid medications that had been flown in by the JDC—in some testimonies

Uzbekistan's hospitals were described as empty of medications—but all four of them survived.

They were ecstatic to be alive after their release from the hospital, Regina said, but weaker, hungrier, and more apprehensive. "After the first time, my mother cared about nothing except us not falling ill again. Nothing else broke her—not hunger, not the bread lines—but if your father or I got even a bit sick, she became frantic," Regina told me. Every day she and Hannan stood for eight or sometimes eighteen hours to redeem their ration card for 400 grams of *lapyushka*—Uzbek flatbread—100 grams for each of them. And as more refugees continued pouring in and more food was confiscated, Hannan held the bread tighter under his armpit, terrified of it being snatched away, as it nevertheless was one day as he was on his way from the breadline. "We survived the night, but your father never forgave himself for allowing our bread to be stolen," Regina said. She called it "the worst day of all."

On their way to the breadline one day, they saw a small girl of six or seven, filthy, lice-covered, holding her dress up for sale: she was Hannan's cousin Emma Perelgric. They had not seen her since the day she and Icok's family turned north to Białystok while they had turned south to Siemiatycze. She was alone at the Samarqand bazaar: large brown eyes, oval face, a tiny animal.

The standing water that Emma and her father, Adam Perelgric, had drunk at Kolkhoz Dimitrov—where the uninformed Teitels had arrived in October 1941—turned out to be the habitat of the malaria-carrying anopheles mosquito. Within a week of their arrival, they both lay feverish and shivering on the hard floor of their *kibitka*. In the Samarqand hospital, where they were taken, they lay sweating, their ears ringing, their heads pounding, without any contact with each other for the next several weeks. Emma recovered after a month and was told she would be transferred to an orphanage in Samarqand. No one told her that her father had died weeks before, but she heard the doctors talking. That night Emma walked out of the hospital. "I didn't want to become a little Uzbek girl with a scarf," she said when I interviewed her in Tel Aviv. She survived until Ruchela and Hannan found her, but she did not remember how. She only knew for sure that she did not cry, not when she heard her father had died, and not before or after.

In their testimonies, none of the Tehran Children report crying when they learned that a father or mother or sibling had died. Many memoirs, too, mention the lack of crying. "I didn't shed one tear. I couldn't cry—I didn't know how. I still don't," Joanna Synowiec, a Polish child orphan, recalled. She did not cry when her parents died in Uzbekistan, one after the other, nor when her five-year-old brother Henio, "a beautiful boy with blond hair," to whom she became a "mother," died. Henio died alone in a Tehran hospital at age six: "he died in the early morning. . . . He cried all night, "I want Joanna!" She chastised herself for not having been with him, but still she did not cry.[1]

"Dad died next to me," Avram Raz, an eighty-year-old former Tehran Child, says in *The Children of Teheran* documentary. "But no one cried, not my mom, not me."

"Crying was the worst thing," Lydia Granot, another former refugee who appears in the film, says. Neither she nor anyone else cries in the film, even when speaking about the most harrowing experiences. My aunt never cried during our interviews either, nor did Emma, nor did anyone else.

My father never cried, at least not in public, in all the years we lived together, with the exception of the time we watched *The Deer Hunter*. Back then I had thought he cried because the Russian roulette scene was so tragic, because other people's stories moved him when his own could not. But now I knew that the story of *The Deer Hunter was* his story: the particular inhumanity of the Communist universe; the arbitrariness of life and death in war; the way his own fate had vacillated like a game of Russian roulette.

The lack of crying was also an effect of starvation: dehydration dries up the tear glands; energy deficiency turns one apathetic; and hypoglycemia, the state in which glucose stores are not replenished and blood sugar levels drop, inhibits emotion and diminishes interaction with the outside world. Crying is not only an emotion, it is a bodily action. A starving person cannot cry. Severe childhood hunger can also cause lasting changes in the adult personality: five times more anxiety, decreased sociability, avoidance of new experiences, more hostility than in those who had been even minimally nourished.[2] I wondered if the starvation he had experienced in Samarqand affected not only my father's and others' bodies but also who they had become.

$$\equiv$$

In March 1942, as the violence of starvation and the infectious diseases blanketed the Central Asian cities, violent crime sharply increased. In the streets and around bread-distribution points, gangs of Russian and Uzbek boys ran wild, snatching bread and ration slips and beating people. The breadlines themselves became a hazard, with shoving, squashing, and fistfighting. Even the honored evacuees in Tashkent reported thefts: Alexander Kovarsky's galoshes; Nadezhda Mandelstam's ration of fish; Olga Boltianskaia's bread. "People robbed each other—and everyone was robbed by the Uzbeks and the Russians, who were impossible to chase away," a young refugee testified. The Uzbeks did not "butcher" the refugees, as Sergey had said, but violence against refugees was rising.

In the theater and academy in Tashkent, collaboration and "friendship" continued. But at the bread-distribution points, the Uzbeks were known to sometimes curse the Jews and throw them off the line. And on the streets, as the number of Jewish newcomers rose exponentially, tensions increased, and petty crime began to sometimes be accompanied by anti-Semitic overtones, as did the rarer violent crimes, including three anti-Semitic murders in Tashkent. An August 1942 NKVD report acknowledged that the "arrival of a significant number of citizens of the USSR of Jewish nationality" had led to "problems."

"There's a general dislike for the European Jews," one evacuee wrote. Others reported on "Judeo-phobic sentiments" that escalated into "hatred."[3]

"It's only natural that some hostility would be there when hundreds of thousands of Jewish refugees arrived in the midst of a hungry Uzbek population," I said to Sergey, who did not know about these incidents. As we were talking, the twenty-first-century European refugee crisis that was entering its third year was inflaming xenophobia in Europe, even in Italy, a country with food, without war, and then with a solid pro-immigrant left and a humane culture.[4] Israel, a central player in drafting the United Nations refugee protection treaties of the 1950s, was jailing and expelling its own Sudanese and Eritrean refugees. Complaints against the refugees then and now sounded eerily the same: loitering, exploitation of limited government resources, placing a burden on an already depleted job market.

The refugees and evacuees brought their own forms of xenophobia with them as well, which mixed with fears of a violent Uzbek uprising. "I found out that all the young people had gone off to the mountains to avoid the draft, and some of them had taken weapons and were preparing for an uprising," Wat wrote in his memoir. "The Russians, the Jews, the fugitives, the refugees—everyone is expecting a bloodbath."[5]

"Everyone is afraid," Georgy Efron, the seventeen-year-old evacuated son of the Russian poet Sergey Efron, wrote. "In the event of defeat what will happen in Uzbekistan? Everyone says that a slaughter will begin. The Uzbeks will slaughter the Russians and the Jews."[6]

In Samarqand, near my father's hut, a Ukrainian evacuee family—parents and two young girls who arrived with a trove of belongings—were found murdered in their beds, their hut cleaned of every item. Hannan and his family walked only in pairs now whenever they left the hut.

But life fell into something of a gloomy routine. Across Central Asia, in the areas where the refugees aggregated, the Polish embassy, under special permission and with a loan from the Soviet government, opened Polish schools and orphanages. In April 1943 Polish-Soviet relations would be severed, and these schools would be absorbed into the Soviet school system.[7] Until then, they were run by Polish priests and teachers. Near its recruitment centers, the Anders Army set up its own pre-military schools: the Junkas' Schools for boys and the Schools of Young Volunteers for girls, for young cadets. Elsewhere, children's "orphanages" and "kindergartens" for children of parents working in *kolkhozes* and factories—what Aleksander Wat, who was appointed school supervisor, called "little Polish schools"—were established. Orphanages and schools popped up everywhere, in *chaykhanas* (tea houses) and in local people's residences.[8] As a general rule, Polish-Jewish children were not turned away from them.

In some cases, like that of Emil Landau—the boy who would keep a diary in Iran—a parent would leave their child at an orphanage's door, walk away, and never see the child again. But in most cases, parents kept contact. Nearly a quarter of the children in Polish orphanages, particularly the Jewish ones, were not full or even half orphans.

Some children admitted themselves, without their parents' permission, into Polish orphanages, getting food and schooling during the day, and returning each night so their parents wouldn't notice.

Some were placed in orphanages as a last resort ("when I was left alone in the world I was taken to the Polish orphanage"[9]). Two siblings, Norbert and Zuzanna Kurtzman (now Nathan and Ziva Rom), testified that they were transferred to a Polish orphanage after working as artists' models in the mosques of Samarqand. "Starving children sit there," they recalled, "and they paint you. And then they move you to another mosque, where they make a sculpture out of you. When they wanted to paint Ziva naked we ran away."

In the testimonies, some Jewish children said they were treated well in the orphanages:

Out of a hundred Polish children in the orphanage there were twenty Jews, and we felt very good.

In the Polish orphanage they took all my hair off because we were full of fleas. And they gave me clothes. It was all Poles. They didn't ask me if I was a Jew or non-Jew.

Others said they were mistreated by Polish children:

I was the only Jewish child in the orphanage and during the five months I spent there I suffered quite a bit from the Polish children, although I was polite to everyone and never complained.

In the children's home the Polish children called us dirty Jews.

We suffered a lot from the Polish children, who used to shout "Jews to Palestine!"

We would get food and clothes, but the Polish children bullied us terribly.

The Polish children bullied us a lot, but we didn't care because a piece of bread and a little soup were the most important things for us.

The Polish children treated us badly but we accepted all the abuse, because we knew that by being there we made things easier for our parents.

The Polish children took out all their anger on us and said the Jews were to blame for everything.[10]

In several testimonies, former refugees report praying alongside the Catholic children or having to make the sign of the cross. *The Children of Teheran* documentary dramatizes such moments in a dark, deserted church in Samarqand, with Gregorian chants playing in the background and a blending of tongues in a mixture of the frightening and the exotic, as an elderly Israeli man, a former refugee, wanders quietly inside. But most of the refugee children who had grown up in Poland were no strangers to Catholicism. Some said the hymns, or the image of the Madonna, reminded them of their far-off mothers and soothed them.

There were tensions, there was intimacy. Some recalled secretly holding their own Jewish prayer sessions, or purposefully botching the words
of Catholic prayers. Some said they were permitted to hold Jewish prayer
sessions openly.

Regardless of the children, school and orphanage directors and teachers reportedly stood up for Jewish children and protected them from bullying, in a manner much different from the army and *delegaturas*: "The
older boys were allowed to pray and the director, Mr. Franciszek, would
not allow anyone to harm us." In Poland, as in Ostrów's *gymnasium*,
schools had been among the only public spaces shared by Catholics and
Jews. I wondered whether school directors brought into the scene a different experience and sensibility than others.

Sometime after March 1942, Ruchela and Zindel decided to place Hannan, Regina, and Emma in a children's home in Samarqand.

"They realized they would not succeed in keeping three children
alive, and in the orphanage we would be cared for and fed and had a
better chance of not becoming ill again," Regina told me. "It wasn't a
choice. We had to go where the food was to survive." At the orphanage
too, food was insufficient: Sergey Kim told me he had found many letters
of complaint in the Tashkent archive, including one from K. Kazimer-
chyk, a delegate of the Polish embassy who wrote to the administration
of the Samarkand region that the children did "not receive due provi-
sion" and were in "very hard material state." But the rations were nonetheless larger than those at the breadlines—300 grams of bread for each
child, instead of 100, and a monthly allotment of 0.12 kilogram of rice—
which meant the children could save a little for their parents.[11] Food was
all that was on their mind, when Hannan, Regina, and Emma entered
the orphanage. When its door opened, they nearly ran in, desperate to
get a bread portion without waiting in the dreaded lines. Only after the
door closed behind them did they feel a pang of regret and trepidation,
and worry for their parents, from whom they had not been separated
even for a day since leaving Ostrów.

At the orphanage, "I didn't do much. I sat by the window all day and waited," Regina said. She did not recall any interaction, good or bad, with Catholic children; by the time she and Hannan joined it, most Catholics were no longer there, having evacuated to Iran, along with orphanage directors, in March 1942.

In London, Sikorski complained repeatedly to British and American officials that in Central Asia its soldiers were being decimated, without having fought a single battle, by hunger and disease alone. At a March 18, 1942, meeting, Kot reports, Stalin, despite initial skepticism, agreed as well to the evacuation of forty thousand soldiers and their dependents.[12] On March 24, the first evacuation from the Soviet Union to Iran began.

Rumors of the evacuations to Iran sent Jewish refugees to the *delegaturas*, to army dispatch centers, and to Anders himself, who met with delegations of rabbis and Ha'shomer Ha'tsair members in Yangiyo'l. They pleaded to be able to join the army, but Anders rejected them en masse, making exceptions for individual cases. As trucks and trains departed for Krasnovodsk, some refugees clung to the sides, and some parents threw their children into the trains and ships. But with the exception of Jewish soldiers of the Anders Army, and of random Jewish children who had been in Polish orphanages that were evacuated along with the army, nearly all legal evacuees—there were stowaways, fictitious marriages between Jewish women and Polish soldiers, etc.—were ethnic Poles.

According to Kot and Anders, the Iran-bound Anders Army was closed to Polish-Jewish refugees, as the USSR did not consider them to be Polish citizens.[13] Yurii Zhukov, the head of the Tashkent NKVD, announced that eligibility for evacuation rested entirely with the Polish authorities, who never requested the evacuation of any Jews.[14]

The Polish government-in-exile disputed Zhukov's words, claiming that in his March meeting with Stalin, Anders had already been officially advised that Polish Jews were not regarded as Polish nationals and could not be included in the transports to Iran, while Anders himself requested that an exception be made for immediate family members of Jewish soldiers.

The debate continues today.

In his mammoth 2015 book about the Anders Army, the Polish-British historian Norman Davies contends that Polish Jews "faced rejection," by the army "not as many assumed from naked anti-Semitism, but rather from the working of the Soviet bureaucracy." He asserts that the NKVD controlled the recruitment of soldiers to the Anders Army and even appointed the doctors who served on the recruitment commissions and disqualified Jewish recruits. As evidence, he cites from the testimony of a Jewish Anders Army soldier who reports of no discrimination, calling the charges of anti-Semitism that "bedeviled" the Anders Army in the 1940s and continue to haunt it today "chutzpah."[15]

The Soviets were not particularly interested in enforcing the rule they imposed, the American historian David Engel writes; rather it was Polish military officials who *insisted* that a Soviet liaison sit on recruitment boards so that he could disqualify minority candidates. "Soviet regulations served as convenient means for covering up [the Poles'] own attitude toward Jews in their army," he writes.[16]

"Documentary evidence and eyewitness accounts support the claim that Soviet representatives sat on the recruiting committees—but only on very rare occasions would they investigate the ethnic background of the potential recruit and for the most part refrained from taking an active role in the work of the committees," the Israeli historian Yisrael Gutman adds.[17] Gutman quotes from an April 10, 1942, cable from Kot to Sikorski, in which Kot expresses frustration that the "systematic anti-Semitic policy" of "some officers in the recruitment centers" inadvertently strengthens the aims of the Soviet government. He does not speak of a Soviet policy that binds Polish officers, Gutman writes, but of over-zealous Polish officers.[18]

I read testimonies of the mayhem at the stations and the port, of the crowding, of the shifting of names on lists, and of the British ambassador's ignorance as to how many civilians would arrive in Iran, and the reports of Jewish refugees, including children, being pushed off trains and boats by Polish evacuees. They painted a world where "official" Soviet policy—Kot insisted that there was tight control of exit visas by Soviet authorities[19]—was only one factor in how the evacuation played out.

In Tel Aviv, the head of the Jewish Agency's foreign office, Moshe Shertok, took a "realpolitik" approach to the situation, which he described in a closed meeting of the Zionist General Council on September 9, 1942:

> When the Poles received permission to evacuate, they naturally did not go out of their way to increase the number of evacuated Jews. Man is close to himself, and where there is a crisis and a minority and a majority, the majority takes over all resources. Therefore, in regards to the Jews, two forces worked here towards a single point. The Soviets wished to be rid of Poles but not of Jews; the Poles wished to evacuate more Poles and less Jews.[20]

Shertok did not focus on Polish or Soviet motivations. He did not raise Polish nationalism. He did not elaborate on whether the Soviets considered Jews, but not Catholic Poles, as assimilable into a Soviet commonwealth, or whether their goal was to seize back former territories by Sovietizing the majority of their former residents, who were Jewish Polish citizens. There was no anger in his words, no expectation or demand from either Soviet or Polish authorities. He did not speak of leaning on the Polish government to represent Polish Jews, as American- and British-Jewish organizations were doing. He simply offered an analysis of Polish and Soviet national interests, and the ways the Jewish Agency, aware of these interests, might intervene on behalf of "our brothers and sisters." He was thinking *politically*, as a representative of an independent nation-state. "This is the difference between a stately and a non-stately people: demands and interests. What are our interests? What do we demand?"

=

After the evacuation of the majority of Catholic children from Hannan's orphanage, and the admission of several hundred Jewish children, it became known as the Jewish Children's Home of Samarqand. Across Central Asia, Jewish refugees now began filling positions that were previously closed to them in Polish schools, orphanages. and even *delegaturas*. In Bukhara, a Jewish Tarbut school was even opened.

But by the early spring of 1942, relations between the Polish government-in-exile and the Soviet authorities were fast deteriorating, threatening an end to Polish autonomy in the USSR. Aid was now increasingly under control of the NKVD, the recipient of the many petitions Sergey had found at the Tashkent archive, and decisions were made "from the top," as Sergey had put it.

In early May 1942, when General Anders was on a visit to London, Ignacy Schwarzbart, one of two Jewish members of the National Council of the Polish government-in-exile, met with him to discuss concerns over the nonevacuation of Jewish citizens. Anders assured him that "there were many Jews among the forty thousand Polish soldiers sent from Russia to Persia" and that "some of them even took their families with them to the Near East," but that Soviet as well as British restrictions prevented further evacuations.[21]

The British Mandatory Government, fearing that if a large constituency of Polish-Jewish soldiers made it to Palestine it would upset the equilibrium between Jews and Arabs and potentially contribute manpower and weapons to the Haganah, the Jewish defense forces, which was fighting to overthrow them, was also said to oppose evacuation of Jews. Charles Baxter, head of the Foreign Office's eastern department, emphasized "the necessity for doing the utmost to avoid the transfer of any Polish-Jewish units to the Middle East. . . . Their presence will be a continued source of trouble, and after the war the Poles, who wish to get rid of their Jews, will probably make difficulties about resubmitting them to Poland."[22]

The evacuation of children posed less of a problem. And so it was proposed that one thousand "Jewish orphans" could leave for Iran with the next Anders Army transport. The agreement was said to serve both sides: Jewish organizations would underwrite the expenses of the children's transport and their maintenance; the Polish government-in-exile would be credited with saving the children and supporting them with the amount of four pounds sterling each.[23]

Documents I found in archives in Israel showed that in Iran, after the first March–April 1942 evacuation of Poles, a man by the name of Eliyahu Rudnicki, a Jewish colonel in prewar Poland, tried to negotiate for a greater number of "Jewish orphans," as well as others, including Zionist rabbis, to be included in subsequent transports. These documents suggest that four hundred visas to Palestine had been secured for a list of Jewish refugees even while they were still in Central Asia.[24] Another man, Oscar Hendler, had reportedly tried, and failed, to add adult Jewish refugees to "the list." According to one testimony, a delegation of rabbis met with General Anders, but was refused evacuation (the refusal was attributed to him, not to Soviet authorities). Elsewhere it was claimed that children's parents paid some amount for their transfer. I do not know what or how large a part Anders played in the children's evacuation; a JDC report that was compiled in Tehran after their transfer showed no evidence of any role at all.

"Anders was an old-style Polish anti-Semite," Lauenberg, the former Polish-Jewish officer, wrote.

"Anders was not an anti-Semite," Dr. Valentina Brio, a Polish-born Jewish lecturer in the Russian and East European Studies Program at the Hebrew University of Jerusalem, would reply when I asked her about the general. "He was born a Protestant and was raised in a multiethnic city. If he said certain things, it was because he had to say them to appease his underlings."

In the documents of the Polish government-in-exile, I found reports of Kot's attempts to spread news that General Anders had helped "save one thousand Jewish children from Russia" among different publications, including the Hebrew daily *Ha'aretz*.[25]

A 2015 article in the *Jewish Journal* dubbed Anders "the Polish Moses."

=

In a list of "Osoby Wyewakuowane z Z.S.S.R." ("People Evacuated from the USSR"), which I found at the Sikorski Polish Archive in London, my father was listed as "Henryk Tejtel," born "5.4.28." Hannan's actual date of birth was April 5, 1927—it was listed correctly on his Soviet deportation card but had been changed here, I gathered, so he could be categorized as a child rather than as a near-army-age adolescent. I did not know who changed it, the Jews or the Poles, and I was not sure about the name either. All names on the list were Polish-sounding: Tatur Eugeniusz; Taub Estera; Tawgen Aleksander; Tawgen Stefnia; Tchorzewska Anna; Teitelbaum Bena; Tejtel Henryk; Tejtel Regina. . . .

Did my father pass as a Pole to get evacuated? Later when Zindel and Ruchela sent him letters in Tehran, or when letters were passed to him in Palestine via the Polish Red Cross, they would be addressed to Henryk Tejtel also. I wrote to Magda, asking whether she could inquire if my father had ever used the name Henryk in Poland; his Ostrów-issued birth certificate listed only "Chananja Teitel." Magda answered that she was "sure" that "in Ostrów Hannan was Heniek . . . the shorter version of Henryk." Somewhere in the back of my mind, I remembered that my father's friend Zamek, a Polish-born Auschwitz survivor, would address him whimsically as "Chanek."

"I think he used the two versions, the Hebrew and the Polish. Poles are not able to pronounce such complicated name as Hannan. I think his Polish friends called him Heniek. It is my intuition," Magda said.

On July 18, 1942, the NKVD arrested 118 Polish delegates and *delegatura* employees, many of them Jewish, on charges of spying.[26] *Delegaturas* now fell—if they had not already previously—under Soviet control. At the KGB archive in Tashkent, Sergey Kim said he found "thousands of letters of complaint" ("this family needs bread, this family needs wood to construct something"), which were sent to a centralized location where each petition was rejected or approved and then returned to the *delegatura* with a resolution ("pay this money to this family," "transfer clothing to this region").

Less than a year later, on April 25, 1943, the Polish-Soviet diplomatic relations that began on July 30, 1941, came to an end.

In Tashkent and Alma-Ata, the metaphor of the "friendship of peoples" crumbled as well, as did the collaborative environment between locals and evacuees, which had flourished in cultural and academic circles.

Evacuee historians, rather than chronicling Uzbek history within a wider Soviet context, began to emphasize instances of Uzbek autonomy such as the late-nineteenth-century Uzbek antitsarist movement, creating a de facto historical narrative for a non-Soviet independent Uzbek state long before its creation. Evacuees' self-representations began to focus not on the excitement of collaboration and exchange but on the sadness of exile.[27] "Everyone gazes from some foreign window / Some from New York, some from Tashkent, / And bitter is the air of banishment—/ Like poisoned wine," Anna Akhmatova wrote in a "Poem Without a Hero," in Tashkent, circa 1943.[28]

Solomon Mikhoels, the director of the Yiddish Theater and chairman of the Jewish Anti-Fascist Committee, who in 1942 had traveled to the United States to enlist support for the USSR, returned after the war to Moscow and few years later was assassinated at Stalin's orders.

Amalia Frajlich, the Polish-Jewish refugee who had written her diary in Kyrgyzstan, returned to Poland and emigrated to the United States in the wake of waves of anti-Semitism in the late 1960s.

Aleksander Wat also returned to Poland in 1946, faced additional political strife, suffered a stroke and depression, and migrated to France, a second exile, where on July 29, 1967, he committed suicide.

Mordecai Rozman and Motek Rottman, Ha'shomer Ha'tsair leaders who tried to reconvene their members in Uzbekistan and resume some version of their movement, were arrested, interrogated, and tortured by the NKVD in Tashkent after their pleas for help from Palestine were intercepted. Rozman was smuggled to a safehouse in Bukhara during his interrogation. Rottman continued to be interrogated and tortured in Tashkent for three years, after which he was sentenced and spent the next seventeen years, until his 1961 rehabilitation, in Uzbek, Kazakh, and

Kyrgyz gulags. A reviewer of his 1982 memoir *Gvulot, Makhtarot* (Borders, Undergrounds) called Rottman the "anti-refugee" for having never lost sight of his identity and "having devoted his life to saving his friends and spiritual brothers."[29]

Countless others were arrested for so-called Zionist or American spying, interrogated, tortured, exiled, condemned to hard labor, executed. Some died in exile, some became "prisoners of Zion," some made it to Israel in the 1970s. The majority—hundreds of thousands—were absorbed into the great Soviet patchwork.

Catholic schools closed. Jewish schools closed. Polish schools and orphanages became Soviet schools and orphanages. Polish citizens became Soviet citizens, their grandchildren studying with Sergey in his school in Tashkent, where "there was never a mention of anyone's origin," as he put it.

Catholic and Jewish adoptees remained in Uzbekistan as well. Years after the war, when Faina Barisheva, a Jewish orphan who was adopted at age five by the first secretary of the Uzbek Communist Party, was asked to comment on the "hospitality of Uzbeks," she was said to have replied: "It is awkward to talk about oneself. After all, I am an Uzbek."[30]

For the hundreds of thousands of refugees who died from starvation and disease during the war, only a few graves remained: three Anders Army cemeteries; a few dozen graves in Jewish cemeteries across Central Asia; unnamed gravestones in Muslim cemeteries.

In Avo'i, while we were en route from Bukhara to Samarqand, Sergey, Kamara, Salar, and I visited the two cemeteries for the Anders Army soldiers and their families: a small manicured cemetery and a larger one that was located one hundred meters from the train station because "the Poles were so weak that they died during or immediately after transport and were buried there," as the gentle Uzbek caretaker put it. There were dozens of identical shallow gravestones, each with a cross and a name—Michal Turetzki, Joseph Urbanski—just as in Doulab cemetery in Tehran. They looked newly polished. In 2002 a Polish delegation spent seven months reconstructing the cemetery, the caretaker said.

In the Jewish cemetery in Bukhara, the cemetery's director Emanuel Elnatov pointed to a group of shallow, neglected old gravestones, sunk into the ground with illegible names or no names at all. They "belonged to the Polish refugees who died soon after they arrived," he said. "No one comes to tend to them. It's not that there are no Ashkenazi Jews still in our city still, but they never come to the cemetery. They don't care." The larger, better-kept gravestones with engraved Ashkenazi names such as Esther Goldberg or Lifschitz Eizer ("a great doctor, died in 1999") belonged to former refugees and evacuees who died after the war and whose American and Israeli relatives paid for their upkeep, Elnatov told us. The majority of other gravestones, engraved with lifelike images of the deceased and with Hebrew letters that Sergey, who had studied the Hebrew Bible while training to be a Presbyterian minister, tried to read ("Zayin, Yud . . . Ben Azar") were of local Bukharan Jews. Many were inscribed with Farsi poems, which Salar translated.

Stranger,
Do not step on my ashes
I am here in my home
But you are my guest

"After Independence, Uzbekistan became like Gaza," Sami, the rough, unshaven, and slightly intimidating Samarqand-born barber who regularly cut my son's hair told me when I returned to New York from Uzbekistan. He was quick with the scissors but impatient with Upper West Side moms ("make him a man, cut those long curls off"). At Reamir Salon on Broadway, where he worked, everyone—the barbers and the cleaners and the receptionist—spoke Bukhari, the Bukharan Jewish language.

"In the Soviet era it was more or less good, and all the minorities got along. But after they left, it was different. First they wanted a cut of my profits." Sami owned a cassette store in Samarqand, but I didn't know precisely who "they" were. "Then they wanted my whole store. I burned the store down and fled to the Israeli embassy in Tashkent where I slept for a week, then left for Israel and later to America," Sami told me.

When I said that Uzbekistan had felt to me temperamentally milder than most other places I had been to, he looked at me with condescending pity and rolled his eyes.

In Samarqand, the wife of a local rabbi took me to see Nina Absulov, a Polish-Jewish refugee who had married an Uzbek and still lived there. When I asked Nina why she stayed in Uzbekistan, she said, "I didn't know where to go, to whom to go. I didn't know anyone in Israel. Back home no one was alive, but here was a community."

Seated on a kind of elevated platform in her courtyard, supported by pillows and flanked by a smiling daughter-in-law who rested one hand on her back and with the other held fast to her toddler granddaughter. Nina looked much like my aunt Regina. She dressed like a local—brown wool shawl, a green and brown floral dress, and a matching scarf that loosely covered her hair—but her countenance looked like so many I knew in Israel. She was what Emma Perelgric had feared becoming: a Polish-Jewish girl turned Uzbek.

At eighty-three, blind and widowed, she no longer remembered the name of her Polish hometown. Nina did remember but disliked discussing her life during wartime: the Siberian labor camp, the three-month journey from Arkhangelsk to Uzbekistan, the diet of raw potatoes along the way, the death of her older sister on the train, then of her mother, then of her father, a shoemaker. By age thirteen she was alone; at fifteen she had a head wound and an operation in Tashkent. But from that point on, she said, her life got better. She decided to go from Tashkent to Samarqand ("the refugees could go anywhere, there were no restrictions"), where she stood out as "a beauty among the others," our guide Kamara translated.

At nineteen Nina met a young Uzbek driver at the shoe factory where they both worked. They married, a union that was discouraged by his extended family and neighbors but embraced by the groom's mother, whose older son had died fighting the Germans near the hometown whose name Nina could no longer remember. "God sent me to her as a substitute for her son," Nina said.

"Was it hard for you to enter an Uzbek family?" I asked her.

"She says that it was hard for her to learn the traditions and customs, but that they never hurt or disturbed her," Kamara, who was translating, said, "and eventually she learned the Uzbek language in such a way that she could enter the family as a real member." I had seen this wording— "a real member," "a full-fledged member"—in Chukovskaya's report on Uzbek adoptions: the language of inclusion that contained within it the possibility of exclusion, I thought then. But Nina did appear to be a "full-fledged member" of her family, a Jewish-Muslim matriarch in Samarqand. Had she replaced her Polish-Jewish identity for an Uzbek-Muslim one, while my father and his sister and cousin had reclaimed their "original" Jewish identity in Israel? Or was the identity of the refugee something more fluid?

"Alhamdulillah, when it is time, where will you want to be buried? With the Muslims or the Jews?" Kamara asked her.

Nina said she did not care, whatever her children wanted.

Kamara tried again: "You are almost ninety and have passed through the Second World War. What you think about your life?"

"It was a good life. The beginning was hard, but the rest was better. I am very happy now," Nina said. Watching her speak—seated on a carpet, in an inner courtyard on a peaceful street, with running sewage water and white sheets drying in the late afternoon wind, her daughter-in-law smiling at her lovingly as she rose to fetch a photo of Nina's late husband, a tall, handsome man in a driver's uniform—I believed her.

"If your family cares for you with such tenderness in old age, does it really matter if you end up in a brick house in Samarqand or a luxury condo in Tel Aviv?" I said to Salar when we left. The street was pitch-black now, with only scant streetlights.

"To me she seemed a little out of place," he said, "a little lonely."

"But my father was a little lonely and out of place too, and he was supposedly in his own country, in charge of his own fate," I said, thinking that my father and Regina would have balked at the comparison.

But I was wrong. "It's simply the conditions that dictated our fate," my aunt said a month later when I told her about Nina. We were seated in the living room of her spacious, air-conditioned condo in a Tel Aviv suburb, munching on dietary cookies with Regina's warm, grinning husband, Uri. "You come to a place, you have no one. You meet a guy, and he behaves nicely and accepts you, and brings you to his family, and they are good people. So you ask yourself: what am I going to look for?" I felt a surge of warmth toward her. Both Regina and Emma Perelgric had married into established, landed Jewish families that were native to Palestine. Both had been in long marriages with many ups and downs. Both seemed happy and contented. In her younger days Regina had seemed subservient to her husband, but their relationship seemed to have leveled and flourished in old age.

"Can you imagine your life in Russia or Uzbekistan or in Iran or elsewhere but Israel?"

"Sure I can," she said. "I could have ended up in New Zealand." On a tour of the country they had taken a year earlier, Regina and Uri visited the Pahiatua Polish Children's Camp Museum, where she saw photos of Polish children arriving in Wellington, New Zealand. "They looked just like us," she said.

In Tashkent, Salar, Kamara, and I visited another former Jewish exile who still lived in Uzbekistan. Yasha Shapira, a thin, tall Yiddish-speaking sculptor with a white mane, was born in a village in Volhynia, Ukraine, and evacuated with his mother and two siblings to Margiela, in Uzbekistan's Fergana Valley. His father was recruited into the Soviet army and fought in Stalingrad; his mother worked in a silk factory in a kolkhoz. Meanwhile, the children licked the frost for water, ate turtles, and hunted pigeons for soup ("always, always we dreamt of being full of enough food"). The locals were nice, Yasha said, but after the war the family wanted to return to the Ukraine to reunite with their father in their hometown.

"My father was a war hero, but [Stepan] Bandera [leader of the nationalist party of Ukraine] was on the side of the Nazis, and when my father returned triumphantly to his village, he wasn't respected or honored because he had fought on the side of the Soviets," Yasha said.

"There was a little nationalism," Kamara added. "They were a little discriminated against."

"In Ukraine no Jewish child could enter any school. We needed to find another place to live within the Soviet Union, so we came back here because the heads of this country had suggested the freedom to the Jewish," Yasha said. He decided to stay in Tashkent after independence because Karimov created a civil, not an Islamic state.

"Was there no discrimination against Jews in Uzbekistan after the war?" I asked Yasha.

"It was vice versa," he said. "It was the only place that didn't discriminate."

After he studied art in Leningrad and Italy, the first secretary of the Communist Party in Uzbekistan gave him the small house with the large studio and lovely, blooming garden where he still lives today. "Last week an Uzbek cosmonaut was making pilaf in my garden," he said. "Everyone here is my friend."

His first works were statues of Marx and Gorky, which have since been dismantled. Now, seventy years after the war ended, he created mostly busts of Russian generals ("they gave us the freedom from the Nazis") and of Jewish suffering and survival ("to remind everyone what happened to the Jews"). He made a lifelike statue of the eminent Hebrew poet Hayyim Nahman Bialik (who hailed from Yasha's hometown in Ukraine), and a five-and-a-half-meter statue of a hunched-over woman in a shawl called *Tefilah* (Prayer), a monument to the 1941 Iraqi pogrom Farhud.

His latest project, of which we only saw a model, was a three-and-a-half-meter sculpture of Moses that was to be placed in the Negev desert in Israel. "People will have to walk two kilometers to see it," he said, "to be reminded of the journey we refugees took, without food or water, on our way to the Promised Land."

As for Uzbekistan, he was worried not about the Jews but about the Uzbeks who sought work and were treated badly by Russia. "Uzbeks helped the Russians during the war with the food they needed, their fathers served in the Soviet army, but now when Uzbeks look for work in Russia, they are denied entry as foreign citizens or suffer severe discrimination," he said. My mind drifted to the rugged Uzbek laborers I'd seen at the St. Petersburg airport and the condescending way they had been treated on the plane.

"Uzbekistan was the Babylon of the East during World War II. Great people could survive here—Jews from all over the world, and also Poles, Ukrainians, Hungarians—and then go to the rest of the world. Of course, many found their grave here. . . ." He trailed off and began to cry. His younger sister, he only now told me, died of hunger in the Fergana Valley.

$$\equiv$$

After independence, Uzbekistan revised its memory of the refugees. In 2008 the Monument of the Friendship of Peoples—the large-scale statue, erected by the Soviets in 1982, of the blacksmith Shaahmed Shamahmudov, his wife Bahri Akramova, and their fifteen multinational adopted children—was dismantled and moved from the center to an obscure suburb near the Tashkent beltway. The Palace of the Friendship of People, in front of which the monument had stood, was renamed the Palace of Independence (Istiklol).

The revolutionary street and village names—*Dimitrov, Octoyber*—had been changed as well. Some were renamed after famous former refugees: Avram Tolmasov Street in Samarqand, for the famous Jewish musician; Slonim Street in Tashkent, for an evacuee doctor.

Small reparations to formerly exiled and deported peoples began in the early 2000s. Professor Bozorov's mother, a deported Russian who now lived in Moscow, received vouchers to visit her son in Bukhara. "Because she was deported they try to help," Bozorov said. We were sitting in the inner courtyard of his hotel, near the end of our trip.

"Has your family received reparations?" I asked Sergey Kim.

"We tried to get reparations but have still not succeeded," Sergey said. "They are difficult to get. Only a few people get them, but my mother is stubborn, she is trying. She was getting something: some advantages in taxation, city transport, some kind of sanatorium on the Black Sea where she could go twice a year for free." This was a first phase, but the second phase—getting back the family's original plot of land back in Khabarovsk—was so far unsuccessful.

"Even the Islamic Republic gave our old home back a few years after the revolution," Salar said. "Maybe you can get your land back too."

"But your confiscation was only thirty, not seventy-plus years ago," Sergey said.

"Plus," I said, "part of your family stayed in Iran, and they have now regained some standing. You are dealing with your government, as an Iranian citizen. You have leverage with the government. It isn't the case for Sergey, or for me." The Teitels, and the hundreds of thousands of Polish-Jewish refugees like them who fled east and endured the war in the Soviet Union—in essence, the majority of Polish Jews who survived the war—received no reparations from Germany or from Russia. To receive compensation from Poland for the Teitel family lot that had been turned into a public school in Ostrów—an option I investigated—was likely impossible.

"At least I learned about my family's history of deportation through this process. We Koreans don't have this kind of museum like the United States Holocaust Museum, or memoirs or textbooks," Sergey sighed.

"I'm sorry," I said quietly, suddenly ashamed that I had paid Sergey to research my father's history while he neglected his own. We raised a final glass of beer with Sergey—he drank only water—and watched him walk away slowly, his shoulders slumped, and disappear into the dark.

The next day, our last, walking in silence through the streets of Bukhara, Salar hit his head against a loose nail in a metal gate. Blood gushed out; we disinfected the wound and gave him an Advil before we got in the car and rode in silence through the arid landscape, Salar's face still twisted in pain. Tears suddenly welled up inside me. At the entrance to the airport, an old Tajik man walked over, placed his hand on Salar's wound, and recited a blessing. It was a sweet, moving Uzbek moment, our last in this land, but also a potential menace. "I hope my wound won't get infected now," Salar said, looking worriedly at the Tajik's soiled hand. We laughed, hugged the driver Bilol and guide Kamara, then handed our bags and our passports to the severe, young uniformed border control officers who scrutinized them for a very long time and at last motioned to us to move forward.

≡

First came the announcement, in August 1942, that children in Polish orphanages would be taken to Iran with the Anders Army. Then came the lists: the children of the Jewish Children's Home in Samarqand, where Hannan and Regina were, would be included. In other orphanages, lots were drawn. In nearly all, only a few Jewish children were chosen. Lists were drawn and redrawn, and siblings were separated. Some managed to beg their way with orphanage directors; others were removed at the last minute or on the way.

Some children refused to leave without their siblings and parents, but their parents insisted they go.

> I didn't want to go. I cried in Samarqand until I was told: if you don't go, Nathan (a younger brother) will die. You have to look after him. Because Nathan had already fainted.

> Before we left I was able to run home to say goodbye. Dad stood at the door and said: "I will never see you again. We will never meet." [31]

In others, parents refused to allow their children to leave but they left anyway.

> When it was time for the evacuation our parents came and asked us to stay, but we did not want to.[32]

In many cases, children did not even say goodbye to their parents.

We left without any of our things and without saying goodbye to
our parents.

In the final count, it appears that around 116,000 Polish refugees were
included in the March–April and August evacuations. (According to the
material Bozorov found in the Tashkent archive, the Anders Army took
92,000 civilian men and 17,000 women "for washing and cleaning.")
Among them, 6,000 (roughly 5 percent) were Jews—3,500 military personnel, and 2,500 civilians—though several hundred more, stowaways or
Catholic converts, were included as well. It was a tiny number, less than 5
percent of even the most conservative estimate of Polish-Jewish refugees
who had remained in the Soviet Union. But among this tiny group were
Hannan, Regina, and Emma, who, when told they were about to be evacuated, ran from the orphanage to say goodbye to their parents.

"Our parents decided that we must leave the Soviet Union," Regina
said, "but we knew people who refused to separate from their children
and said, 'Whatever will be our fate will be the fate of our children.'"
Regina's voice shook when she uttered these words, and I wondered what
she was thinking. I did not dare to ask whether in retrospect she wished
her parents had decided otherwise, but she read my thoughts. "Maybe if
they knew what we will endure . . ." she paused. "But our parents wanted
to save us. It was the right thing to do."

Zindel and Ruchela walked the children to the embarkation point at
Samarqand's central train station, then returned to 24 Jangirabackaia, the last house on the last street of Samarqand. If you turned right,
as Ruchela and Zindel did in mid-August 1942, you walked onto sand
dunes and then climbed up a sandy hill, from which you could see the
tips of the domes and minarets of the Registan. Perhaps that was why
Hannan called it "the hut below the town" in his testimony. On the hill,
half-buried in sand, were the train tracks on which their children would

travel from the Samarqand train station to Krasnovodsk, where they would sail to Iran.

They climbed the hill, hoping to wave goodbye when the train passed by. In Samarqand I too climbed it, staging in its original setting a formative moment in my father's life, a formative moment in my life, on these sand dunes. The sun was merciless, and sweat ran down my face, as it must have run down theirs in August 1942. My head pounded. An Uzbek woman, toothless and half-mad, was leaping on the train tracks, shouting at me from afar, in English, "I love, love, love you, I love you, America," then coming closer, she walked right past me, and disappeared down the hill.

I imagined the emaciated Ruchela and Zindel walking up the hill in silence. They had managed to get the children out of the Soviet Union, to save them from starvation. They had sent them penniless and parentless, possibly forever, to an uncertain future and a country they could not point to on a map. Before parting, Hannan gave his mother the shoes he had been given at the orphanage—he said he would get new ones in Iran—and she now wore them, their soles sinking into the sand. Regina told me she and Hannan saw their parents briefly through the window, two waving figures that shrank as the train moved until they disappeared completely.

POLISH AND JEWISH NATION BUILDING IN TEHRAN

Sadness fills the cars, the sadness of parting from relatives. Who knows, we may never see them again. The pain of separation and the deep worry for those left behind fill our thoughts. But happiness also pervades the cars. The happiness of a human being who has been freed after a long incarceration, the sensation of an eagle who has broken through his cage and is beginning a new life of freedom, a magical feeling of which there are no words to describe. After a short struggle, perhaps not long, the sadness is suppressed and makes way for exhilaration and joy. . . . No one mentions the dark past. It was and is gone. . . . The train rushes forward and every second, every turn of the wheel announces the end of the dark nightmare and the dawning of the future.

More than any retrospective testimony, even those that would be granted to the Polish Information Center in Jerusalem less than a year later, Emil Landau's diary, written in real time and without any leading questions, captures most vividly what the moment of departure from Soviet soil must have felt like for my father. Emil—a mature, intelligent writer, with solid historical and geographical knowledge, an adult writer's eye for detail, and the slightly sentimental metaphors of a fifteen-year-old— captured the transient moments of happiness in the sequence of unhappiness. He and his sister Alina were the same age as Hannan and Regina, and they were evacuated from Samarqand with them. Emil also drew a map of their journey, "for my sake, so I could remember," Alina, now Ilana, told me when she handed me his diary at our meeting in Jerusalem.

> A huge engine, huffing and puffing, pulls a long row of cars to the west. The city of T. has long disappeared beyond the horizon. Hundreds of heads of children crowd at the windows to take a last look at the endless fields of the land of angst and suffering, the land that together with Hitlerite Germany has become a symbol of tyranny and oppression, a mass grave for tormented, afflicted people— innocents—who died of starvation, typhus, or dysentery. The wasted body cannot withstand disease, and none of us will forget the death-filled streets of Samarqand.

Hannan, Regina, and Emma, aged fifteen, eleven, and ten, were now children alone. They traveled aboard the train from Samarqand to Krasnovodsk for three days—fifteen hundred kilometers—stopping in Bukhara and Cardzou, crossing the border into Turkmenistan and the yellow expanses of the desert to Ashkhabad, its capital, where their train stopped for several days. From Ashkhabad some passengers continued by bus to Tehran. The train's final stop was Krasnovodsk, the port from which my father, still barefoot, would sail to Iran and where thousands waited, clamoring to board the ships.

At Krasnovodsk my father and his sister and cousin spent their first night alone near the evacuation base, on the ground, and in the morning they were loaded together with four thousand others onto a Soviet cruiser, the *Kaganowich*—the first ship they had ever been on—which sailed daily between Krasnovodsk and Bandar Pahlavi. Soldiers were loaded first, children later, all packed into the ship's cabin. The drinking water stank of kerosene and vomiting. Dozens, children and adults, did not survive the trip.

But those who did watched the contours of the Soviet seashore disappear behind the horizon, and after a three-day sail, they saw the mountain peaks rise above the fog and then the small port of Bandar

Palhavi.[1] I wished I could have seen it; I wished I could have duplicated my father's trip from Samarqand to Pahlavi (now Port Anzali), as I had done in Poland, Russia, and Uzbekistan, and from there continue to Tehran. But my Israeli citizenship and the "Haifa, Israel" birthplace that was printed on my American passport put that out of the question. I had to rely on Salar to scope the city for information, and on the Persian documentary *The Lost Requiem*, on Emil Landau's diary, and on other memoirs and testimonies.

===

In the end, 31,189 military personnel and 12,408 nonmilitary civilians were said to have arrived in Iran with the first evacuation, and 43,746 soldiers and 26,016 civilians with the second, beginning on August 11, 1942.[2] A third group of 2,694 civilians were transferred from Ashkhabad to Mashhad, for a total of 116,131.[3] There were higher estimates: 146,000 (46,000 civilians and 100,000 soldiers) according to the JDC; 400,000 according to a 1943 Iranian census; 300,000 according to some British sources; 117,300 according to Peter Chelkowski, an NYU professor of Middle East studies; and a lower number, 115,000, given by David Engel, an NYU historian.[4]

Both soldiers and civilians in Iran fell under the purview of the British Army, which was said to have been taken aback by the number and the condition of the civilian refugees. Those who descended on Bandar Pahlavi with the first evacuation, in March 1942, were housed in small Pahlavi hotels and in Cinema Shir-O-Khorshid.[5] But by the time of my father's arrival in August, a tent camp had been erected on the Pahlavi shore, a Polish *delegatura* with seventy-five employees was opened at Bandar Pahlavi, and a commission of English doctors had assembled to examine the refugees, isolate the mildly sick, transfer the gravely ill to the town's hospital, and send the rest to be shaved, stripped of their lice-infested clothes, and given a blanket and a new set of clothing and underwear.

Only when I read the descriptions of the refugees' condition when they arrived in Iran and saw a photo of them did I realize how bad their state had become. The photo of three Jewish children at a local hospital looks not much different from photos of liberated survivors: skeletal, dim eyed, one seems to have a stump for an arm, another's eyes are completely shut with trachoma. Regina too had trachoma, an infectious eye disease that roughens the inner surface of the eyelids and that must have prevented her from seeing well for months. If not treated properly, trachoma may cause a breakdown of the cornea and blindness; at least a quarter of the children on their ship had it. All the children—Hannan, Regina, and Emma included—had hair lice, ringworm, scabies, and diarrhea. Some children were gravely ill with malaria or typhus and died during the voyage from Turkmenistan or immediately when they disembarked in Pahlavi. Of the 9,956 children who were evacuated during the August transport, alongside 12,204 women and 3,856 men, Kot reported that 60 percent suffered from malnutrition and 366 died during evacuation.[6] In an earlier transport, on April 2, 1942, reportedly over half of the 131 passengers died: sixteen on the ship, seventeen en route from Pahlavi to the city of Qazvin in northwestern Iran, and thirty-eight in Iranian hospitals.[7]

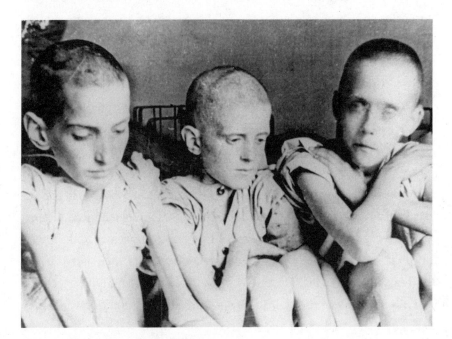

Jewish refugee children in a Tehran hospital

British colonel Alexander Ross, who was charged with care of the Polish refugees, composed an "Urgent Report on Polish Refugees in Persia":

> The physical and mental state of the refugees on arrival in Teheran is generally very bad. The most prevalent diseases are dysentery, diarrhea, deficiency diseases due to prolonged malnutrition, many malarias imported from Russia, and typhoid: 40 percent of the refugees are malaria cases.[8]

General Anders, Ross wrote, expected 25 percent of the refugees to die in Iran.

"They were in very bad condition, thin and ill. . . . They died and were buried the same day," an elderly photographer tells the camera in the Persian documentary *The Lost Requiem*. "There was a strong man who made boxes for them, thirty to fifty boxes a day." Under the tropical mush and grass, Khosrow Sinai's camera captured 639 identical shallow gravestones, the only trace of the thousands of refugees who entered Iran through Pahlavi. That throughout the regime changes and city name changes since then, the graves of 639 foreigners—seventeen of whom were reported to be of Jewish children[9]—remained intact for over seven decades was no small matter, as I, who had traveled through Poland, Russia, and Uzbekistan, now knew.

"In general, the groups of both adults and children who arrived in the second contingent from Soviet Russia are distrustful, apathetic, and sad," a Polish *delegatura* report stated.[10]

"I stood on shore," a Polish Jew who had come from Palestine wrote, "when a group of eight hundred, among them fifty Jews, arrived. The Jewish refugees looked much worse than the Poles. It is difficult to describe the condition of the refugees, the like of which I have never seen before. Swollen from starvation, dressed in rags, spiritually broken, devoid of all hope. There is no strength in a man to stand and look at the faces of the arrivers. One imagines that ours is a world of beasts, not of men."[11]

But over and against the horrified impressions of bystanders, Emil Landau's diary told a different story:

It is possible to find greater luxuries in the world than a refugee camp with dirty sand for a floor. But this bothers no one. Our first lunch: Soup, no! Meat, fresh meat and potatoes! Bread! Everyone is satiated and in seventh heaven. Whoever brought a few things with him trades them for watermelon and other fruits and sweets the scalpers bring. The batons that the Persian police hurl at their countrymen do nothing to stop these "stores" from flourishing in our camp. Whoever has a few pennies buys sweets for ridiculous prices and gobbles them until diarrhea comes. But there's nothing to worry about. There's a hospital!

The Polish *delegatura* reported that it had disbursed allowances to 24,610 evacuees: 60 Iranian Rial for each adult and 30 IR for children, and that all were served ample food: two eggs, hot chocolate or milk, and jam or butter, with the Polish Red Cross providing additional food rations.[12]

Dr. Hayim Hirschberg, one of four rabbis who was allowed to join the August evacuation, recalled:

Immediately a rumor spread about the stores in [Pahlavi] where cakes, sugar, chocolate, and meat . . . are sold. People are mad with desire to buy any of these things. No one has Persian currency . . . but many have some items, or jewelry, and the friendly Persian merchants are willing to buy anything, from sheets and pillow covers to gold and diamond rings. . . . A buying frenzy attacks all of us. . . . Everyone wants pleasure—be it a watermelon, a cup of tea with sugar, an ice cream, or a boiled egg. It's been years since we could buy what we wanted when we wanted. . . . The weather is nice. . . . People bathe in the sea, enjoy the pleasant air. . . . It feels good to lie down on the soil of Persia.[13]

Refugees like Dr. Hirschberg, Emil Landau, and my father, who arrived on the late August transports, remained in Pahlavi for an average of three weeks, after which, unless they were ill, they were transported to permanent destinations in Iran. Some of the Catholic children were taken to Isfahan, where a Polish children's home had been established after the first refugee transports.[14] Others, who had come to Iran by land, were already in Mashhad, where as some children later testified, Persian Jews gave them "a rousing welcome," fed them, and gave them presents.[15] When their turn came, my father and his fellow child refugees in Pahlavi boarded buses and British military trucks to be transported, along with other civilian refugees, four hundred kilometers to Tehran.

They left at six in the morning aboard twenty cars, to arrive the next day at noon. The newly built road along the Caspian Sea passed through green, fertile Gilan province, with well-hydrated rice fields, rivers, and small, tranquil villages. "The villages here are reminiscent, almost to an illusion, of Western European villages," Emil wrote, "wooden houses, straw roofs, everything meticulously fenced. This is the country's wealthiest region. . . . [We pass through] Rasht—a western town. Bustling and moving, stores and artisanal shops wide open. . . .

Dr. Hirschberg's recollections echo Emil's: "Everything [along the way] shocks us; here are open stores with all kinds of merchandise, and yet—there are no lines and no mob storming at them. There are cars and buses, and no one needs to risk his life in order to board them. Our driver takes care of us, offers us cigarettes, generously distributes watermelon and fruit, and regards us as if we were really people, not a human herd. Astonishing!"[16]

From the arrival of the first evacuees in the March 1942 transports, Persian papers reported on the enthusiastic reception of the refugees. The Persian daily *Nahid* stated that "residents of Tehran compete to welcome the refugees into their midst" and that "Iranian government officials in Tehran, Isfahan, Mashhad, Ahvaz and Pahlavi Port" are doing "all in their power to provide support for them," earning the praise of the British liaison Colonel Ross.[17] On June 8, 1942, another daily, *Etelaat*, reported that Prince Sarem od-Doleh placed his one-thousand-square-meter estate and garden in the hands of the Polish Red Cross to be used for Polish refugees.[18]

Those attitudes were still in place when my father's group arrived in Iran. "The Persians were very hospitable. They gave us cakes, and most important of all, water," one child testified.[19] "The population is extremely sympathetic," Emil wrote, "the kids are given candy."

≡

They advanced toward Tehran, climbing the Alborz Mountains, "among domes of Orthodox churches steeped in the rays of the sun," as Emil wrote. The children feared the narrow roads through which the large trucks barely passed, the sharp turns, and the sudden appearance of oncoming cars. "They don't appreciate honking here," Emil noted. "Another second, and our car and its passengers would have fallen into the abyss. But the Persian drivers are experienced and have strong nerves. They accelerate to fifty or sixty kph, until the blood freezes." Emil noted distances, speeds, construction methods of the ancient Persians, regions, bridges, and climate. Along the way, the refugees could glimpse Mount Tochal, with its remnants of late snow.

They made a stop at Qavzin, site of the Shazdeh Hosein shrine, named after a Shiite saint; the Heydarieh mosque, originally a Zoroastrian temple of fire; and the Peighambarieh shrine, where four Jewish saints who foretold the coming of Christ are said to be buried. The next day they continued westward from Qavzin alongside the Persian plateau—"smooth as a table, steaming hot," as Emil wrote—and into Tehran's suburbs.

> Here is the first suburb, but none of us would have believed it is a suburb of the Persian capital—lavish villas, small houses, flower beds, lawns and trees, a general appearance that would not put to shame the most modern city. Cars move along the streets and the wide avenues, everything is paved with asphalt, tall modern buildings, lots of traffic—cabs, carriages and . . . convoys of camels. Tehran was a pleasant surprise. . . . We are awed by the sight of luxurious stores where you can get anything . . . chocolate and other Western sweets, and most importantly, bread and buns made of white flour. No sign of lines. Everything is like a fairy tale, like our dreams of mountains of bread in Samarqand. The heart expands."

"The capital welcomes us with a hubbub of life. The traffic! The roads! The many cars!" Krystyna Wartanowicz, a thirty-something Polish refugee who had become a seamstress in the Anders Army, wrote in her diary of Tehran. Their bus circled the city several times, giving the children a glimpse of the "beautiful, shiny limousines" that "rushed in all directions," the "great edifices, gardens, monuments and squares, window shops that lured the eye, "the orgy of shoes, fruits, sweets, gowns, leather-work," as Wartanowicz described it.[20]

The buses stopped at other Polish refugee camp locations—in the area of Sorkh-e Hessar, where about three thousand elderly men and women were already housed in tents; in a government garden in Yusefabad neigh-borhood, where some three thousand very young children were living; in Manzarieh, in northern Tehran.

Finally they arrived at Dushan Tappeh, seven kilometers to the north of Tehran. Dushan Tappeh, a former Iranian air force base, had been turned over to British authorities for the purpose of housing the refugees. It had a handful of buildings—the air force's Technical University, some aircraft hangers, the artillery regiment building—and rows of barracks and canvas tents. To its north hung the Alborz Mountains.

No accommodations had been prepared for the newcomers on their first night near Tehran. They slept on the ground, under the bare skies, and in the morning were assigned to tents.[21]

=====

I had one undated photo of Hannan in Tehran, the one I first looked at years ago, when I began my search. Now I knew where exactly he was and what he had been through. I knew he was dressed in what looked like an Anders Army uniform—a buttoned khaki shirt tucked inside over-size khaki trousers held in place with a canvas belt. He stood at the top of three rows of boys, his hands tucked behind his back, as they were in his Ostrów Mazowiecka photo from four years earlier. His face was long and narrow and had lost its roundness; his features—cheekbones, fore-head, nose—looked delicate but not quite as emaciated as many of the other boys'. Unlike most of them, Hannan still had a full mane of black hair, which was combed back, as it would be for the next half century. He looked almost normal, a fine-featured and alert child among a sea of shaven heads and contorted faces.

But on closer inspection, I saw that though he was fifteen, his height and his body were those of a twelve-year-old. It was as if he had shrunk since his Ostrów photo: the head disproportionally larger than the body. I also saw his expression: the expression of an old man, simultaneously weary, anxious, and cynical, a sunburned man's face attached to a young child's body, dressed in a dignified, if stained, khaki uniform. Still, as I did years ago, I noted that his eyes were smiling.

Much had happened in Iran in the five months between the March and August 1942 evacuations. A Polish embassy and *delegatura* had opened in Tehran, as well as a Polish Red Cross hospital. Six Polish refugee camps had been established. Camp Number 1, 2, and 3 in the vicinity of Dushan Tappeh ("concentrations of shelters, houses, and bunks, located in an area of two to three square kilometers each) and another (no. 5), for convalescent children, in a villa with a garden near Tehran. Camp Polu, as it is still known in Iran, was set up in Ahvaz, in southern Iran, and another Polish children's camp (Camp no. 4) in Isfahan.[22] Polish refugees began to publish magazines: *Polscy w Iranie* (Polish People in Iran) and *Sami Osobiście* (Ourselves). A Polish board of directors of schools organized and standardized the educational system for Polish schools managing the three thousand children, fourteen and younger, who had come with the April evacuations, and the eleven thousand who would arrive in August. Publishing houses in Jerusalem began shipping Polish textbooks to Iran.[23]

In Isfahan, the initial group of 250 Polish orphans who arrived on April 10, 1942, was soon followed by three thousand more children and adults, giving the entire city the name "Isfahan, the City of Polish children."[24] Isfahan, Iran's former capital, is breathtakingly beautiful, with palaces, mosques, sunny weather, and rows of pomegranate trees. Polish orphans were housed inside fourteen "villas with gardens"[25]: at the Convent of French Sisters; at the Church of Swiss Lazarist Fathers; at the house of Father Iliff, at an English Protestant missionary; and at the estate of the pro-British former governor of Isfahan, Prince Sarem od-Doleh. Within the vast od-Doleh estate, with its whitewashed arched balconies, its shaded gardens, and its pools and fruit trees, the children studied Polish language, history, geography, Latin, religion, history, and biology in what the Persian documentary photographer Parisa Damandan calls "lives lived behind closed doors in a Polish environment."[26]

An Isfahani photographer, Abolqassem Jala, took nearly eleven thousand individual and group photos of the "Children of Isfahan," which Damandan collected and which the filmmaker Khosrow Sinai incorporated into *The Lost Requiem*. Sinai also interviewed the elderly caretaker of the od-Doleh estate, who in 1981 still lived in the now-empty, dilapidated palace; his charge, he says, had been to bring the children "anything they wanted."

"[We lived] in enclosed estates in Isfahan," a former Polish child refugee, now in New Zealand, told Sinai, "in huge buildings, containing up to two thousand children. We were very well looked after and very well fed. We had huge gardens to run around in and play. We had our schools there. We had swimming baths. We had everything that we required." Said another, "We had a happy time in the camps in Isfahan. We played, we studied, we swam. The girls learned carpet weaving. Our governesses tried to amuse us with theater." There were performances, exhibits, clubs; there was access to a radio and Polish magazines, courtesy of a Polish Club at the Teachers Association.

According to JDC and Jewish Agency reports, there were no Jewish children among those in Isfahan, though some could have been secretly Jewish or converts.

———

In the five months that passed between the first and second evacuations of Polish citizens, the Jewish Agency for Palestine had also set up shop in

Tehran. Its first representative, Rafael Szaffar, arrived from Palestine in Tehran on April 29, 1942. He would have come sooner had he not been denied both a transit visa to pass through Iraq and an entry visa into Iran, which necessitated that Szaffar, a Polish citizen who had been living in Jerusalem since the early 1930s, come to Iran as a member of the Polski Czerwony Krzyż (Polish Red Cross). A month later, on May 30, Saul Meirov, head of the organization Mossad LeAliyah Bet (Mossad Immigration), arrived in Tehran as well.[27]

Founded with the outbreak of the war, Mossad LeAliyah Bet sought to bring Jewish refugees to Palestine clandestinely. In May 1939 the British Mandatory Government had published the "White Paper," which restricted annual quotas of Jewish immigration to Palestine to ten thousand. In September, Nazi forces invaded Poland. "We will fight the White Paper as if there is no war, and fight the war as if there is no White Paper," David Ben-Gurion, head of the Jewish Agency, declared.[28] Quietly he gave a green light to the formation of a clandestine immigration arm under Meirov's command.[29]

Born in Tsarist Russia, Meirov had come to Ottoman Palestine as a child and grew up to be a member of the Jewish paramilitary Haganah and member of Kibbutz Kinneret, one of the land's first Jewish cooperatives, where he lived alongside three hundred impoverished yet highly ideological Russian-born migrants like himself. Kinneret was affiliated with the Ha'khalutz (Pioneer) movement—the younger, poorer sister of Ha'shomer Ha'tsair—to which the majority of working-class Jewish youth, many of them women, had belonged in Poland. Kibush Ha'avoda (Conquest by Labor) was the movement's mantra; Jewish autonomy, just and equitable living, and mutual responsibility were its goals. In 1920, after an attack by local Arabs on the Jewish village Tel-Hai claimed the lives of many of Meirov's friends and caused the rest of the villagers to retreat, Meirov resolved to devote his life to fortifying and increasing the military prowess of the Yishuv. To this aim was added, particularly after the rise of Hitler, facilitating Jewish migration to Palestine. The Unified Kibbutz movement, the federation of socialist collective

settlements to which Meirov belonged, subscribed to an "activist" position on immigration, vowing to save as many Jews as possible from persecution by evacuating them, with or without the consent of its British
rulers and in any method possible, to Mandatory Palestine.[30]

In Tel-Aviv, the Foreign Office of the Jewish Agency for Palestine, headed
by Meirov's brother-in-law Moshe Shertok, launched a diplomatic campaign against the British curtailing of Jewish immigration. On November
17, 1941, when the British government announced that even after the outbreak of the war it would not increase White Paper immigration quotas,
Shertok warned Oliver Lyttelton, the British minister of state in the Middle
East, that regardless of any British policy, "millions will swim [to Palestine]
at the end of the war." ("After the pogroms of the last war, Jews swam to
Eretz Yisrael, and this now is much worse.")[31] But as the war progressed,
Shertok, Meirov, Ben-Gurion, and the entire Jewish leadership in Palestine began to slowly comprehend that the "millions" who would be swimming to Eretz Yisrael—those they viewed as the reserves of a future Jewish
state—were actively being murdered. "News about the ongoing genocide
reached the land and spread, causing a mental shock," Yehuda Braginsky, a
Mossad LeAliyah Bet agent, wrote in his memoir *A People Seeking a Shore*.[32]

On February 24, 1942, the ship *Struma*, carrying 769 Jewish refugees
to Palestine, sank in the Black Sea near Istanbul, after Turkish authorities
working under British pressure cut off its fuel supply.

Two months later reports came that Romanian Jews, including women,
children and old people, were being tortured with the gas carbide during
their transport from Romania to Transnistria.

At a May 20, 1942, Mapai (Eretz Yisrael Workers Party) assembly in Tel
Aviv, Braginsky, the Mossad LeAliyah Bet agent, called for the intensifi-
cation of immigration work: "We cannot always act with silk gloves. . . .
We must save Jews from the European hell. We must prepare ships and
operate them. This will be our 'Dunkirk.'"[33]

To intensify "operations," Meirov sent Mossad LeAliyah Bet agents to
Athens, Paris, and Istanbul in complex, daring operations to lease ships,
get entry certificates into the hands of Jews in Nazi-occupied Europe,

and transport Jewish refugees to Palestine. But from the onset of the war until the spring of 1942, Mossad LeAliyah Bet managed to bring in only roughly three thousand refugees—less than the White Paper quota— and was held responsible for the drowning of 250 refugees aboard the ship *Patria*, which capsized because of a bomb that Mossad LeAliyah Bet agents had planted inside it in an attempt to prevent its return to Europe. The day after the disaster, Meirov vowed to go on:

> People like us have no other route to take. The decisions we face are terrible, but my friends and I have concluded that we have no way but to continue.... Our moral right to take such actions—which cost lives—is rooted in the fact that we have been willing to forsake tenfold more of our lives to others.[34]

In late March 1942, after a frustrating period of little action due to the sealing off of Nazi-occupied Europe and the blockage of the Mediterranean's sailing routes, news came that Jewish refugees were being evacuated with the Anders Army to Iran: a few thousand for now, but possibly hundreds of thousands later. "There, in relatively close proximity, are thousands of Jews," Braginsky wrote, "the Jews of Poland and Lithuania whose ties with the Land of Israel are strong, whose youth had in the past populated the Zionist youth movements, and who are even now searching for a route to us."[35]

Inside an agricultural school near Jaffa, a group of Mossad L'Aliyah Bet "emissaries" began training in April for a "mission" in Iran.[36] The intense six-week course was designed for those who would be sent to the "Russian-Persian" front to try to rescue Jewish refugees—"the concentrations of Zionist movement members who sat in Samarqand, Bukhara, in all of Southern Soviet Russia, near the Iranian border," as a participant, Efraim Shiloh, put it.[37] The forty participants—male and female members of kibbutzim across the land—underwent military-style training in weaponry, navigation, camping, physical conditioning, instruction in the topography, history and culture of Iran and

Central Asia, and instruction in the Persian, Arabic, English, and French languages.[38]

Meirov left for Tehran in mid-May, 1942. He drove to Baghdad with two commanders of Solel Boneh, the Jewish labor battalion deployed by the British, under the pretense that they were conducting a supervisory trip of construction sites in the Middle East. From there, disguised as a Solel Boneh technician, he continued by train until he reached Tehran, where he rented a room in the home of an Iranian widow.[39]

At the Alliance Israélite Universelle in Tehran, Rafael Szaffar, the representative of the Jewish Agency for Palestine, opened an "Eretz Yisrael" office to serve as a de facto embassy or *delegatura* for Jewish refugees: to alleviate their suffering, represent them before other authorities, and grant entry visas to Palestine when possible. In mid-May, Szaffar, who continued to double as a Polish Red Cross officer, issued the first "Palestine visas" to four refugees, cabling a request to the JDC to wire four hundred dollars to the Polish *delegatura* for coverage of their travel expenses from Iran, via Iraq, to Palestine, while simultaneously appealing to it more generally to increase its support of the Polish government.[40] Meirov, meanwhile, began independently to put in place rescue operations that would not be tied to the Polish authorities.

By the time of the arrival of nearly one thousand Polish-Jewish children in Iran, an agreement that allowed for the establishment of a separate *Żydowski sierociniec* (Jewish orphanage) inside the Polish refugee camp at Dushan Tappeh had been reached, most likely between Rafael Szaffar and the Polish *delegatura*. An October 12, 1942, Polish report on the organization of camps for civilians, states that "Jewish children, in order to give them an opportunity to study Mosaic religion, are located in camp no 2, with their Jewish tutors." A note is made that it is hard to determine the exact number of Jews, as many of them were leaving the USSR under changed names.[41] Hannan, Regina, and Emma, Emil Landau, his sister Alina, and most other Jewish children on the August transport were taken directly to the Jewish Orphanage. From this point on, and for the rest of most of their lives, they would live in a Jewish world.

To supervise the children and make the rounds to locate new ones, a director and a group of counselors—nearly all twenty-something members of Ha'shomer Ha'tsair—were hired from among the Jewish refugees. The director, the twenty-three-year-old David Lauenberg, who had been a Polish army officer cadet before the war, had arrived in Iran as a stowaway, disguised as an Anders Army soldier, wearing a uniform he had bartered for with a Polish soldier in Samarqand. When he disembarked at Pahlavi, he ran into a well-known Jewish lawyer from his hometown, also a refugee, who pulled him aside, handed him a fresh set of clothes, and told him, "Change your clothes, speak no language but Hebrew, and pretend you are an emissary from Eretz Yisrael." He did as he was told. He discarded his Polish uniform, discarded the Polish that had been his primary language for the first two decades of his life, and became, at that moment, an "emissary" from Eretz Yisrael. "I was no longer a hapless refugee, a migrant without a home, but belonged to a nation," he wrote.[42]

The Jewish Orphanage, with its roughly six or seven hundred children and staff, was located at the edge of Camp no. 2. The Camp housed eight thousand refugees, including mothers and children, men, a small number of orphaned Catholic children who lived in separate quarters, as well as tutors, a doctor, a priest, a "commandant" with a number of deputies, and other camp functionaries.[43] The Orphanage had been allotted three buildings—the general rule in all the camps was that children (and women) were housed in buildings and not in tents[44]—but two of the buildings were reclaimed by Iranian authorities two weeks after Hannan's arrival. In the remaining building—a large open space surrounded by a supply-filled outer corridor—were housed the littlest children, eight and under: ninety-eight, then 120 children slept on cotton mattresses and pillows strewn on bamboo carpets. Older children—Hannan, Regina, and Emma included—as well as counselors, slept inside six large canvas tents, roughly one hundred in each tent. Each child received three blankets, which served as both mattress and cover.

The Jewish Children's Home in Tehran

"[The orphanage] does not evoke much sympathy even among the Jewish refugees, and it is a real find for the anti-Semitic Poles," Emil Landau wrote after just a few weeks in Tehran. "The mess and disorder rule here. Every day new children arrive from all manners of homes and Polish orphanages . . . and the management is unable to get a grip on all the problems." Still, the Tehran photo in which Hannan is smiling was taken inside this camp, with his male peers and counselors besides him.

By the time the Jewish Orphanage had been set up, and even before Meirov and Szaffar arrived in Iran, the Tehran Committee for Jewish Refugees was already assembled and at work. Dr. Ruhollah Sapir was already treating the first ailing refugees—both Jewish and Catholic Poles—who had arrived with the March 1942 transports; Jewish refugees, including Anders Army soldiers who came with the first transport, had been transferred from other hospitals to his clinic, which was full of Catholic refugees as well. Haji Aziz Elghanian had begun to collect clothing, and Elizabeth Kottler, a refugee from Berlin, expanded her activities to include the newcomers. A few years back her teenage daughter, an only child, committed suicide in Tehran; thereafter Kottler turned to public service on behalf of refugees: Bukharans who had been driven away by the Soviets; Afghans, Georgians, Hungarians, and Romanians who had been granted transit visas into Iran and were trying to get to Palestine; and now Polish Jews. Her funds, like those of the committee as a whole, were limited—the majority of Persian Jews lived in the *mahalleh* and were nearly as poor as the refugees—but she resolved to do something. There was another German-Jewish refugee on the committee, Joachim Pollock, a young, extremely pious man who had made a handsome living importing goods and selling them to the Allied forces.[45]

That the Tehran Committee for Jewish Refugees "had been there first, before the emissaries from Eretz Yisrael," was something that I read and heard repeatedly. The historian Dr. Habib Levi describes how he and others "collected donations and provided food and clothing" to the children and "selfless Tehrani Jews took some of them into their homes . . . even knowing that the young war refugees might spread the deadly typhoid fever."[46]

Salar, who over the years continued searching after Hannan's footsteps, was told of a Jewish girl, Suzan Cohan, who "ended up living with locals." From everything he had been told and read, "the Jews of Iran had no real notion of the scale of the murders in Europe," he wrote me from Tehran in 2015.

> They only reacted to what was in front of them, the reality of severely malnourished and typhus-struck brethren who, as if in a dream, had suddenly washed up on the Caspian shore and then been brought down to Tehran. Mansur Meshiyan . . . recalls: "These kids were in some place behind barbed wire. We ourselves were about thirteen, fourteen back then. We put all our money together and bought a bucket of dates for them. Other Tehrani Jews would collect clothes and blankets from their homes and take it to them."

Over the years, I interviewed the Persian industrialist Heshmat Kermanshahi, who as a teen interacted with the Polish-Jewish refugees, and Meir Ezri, scion of a prominent Jewish family in Isfahan and head of the International Federation of Persian Jews in Israel, in Los Angeles, and in Givat Shmuel, Israel, respectively. Both told me they had known of locals who brought refugees fruit and vegetables, transferred refugees to and from bath houses and hospitals, and took them to town, into their homes, and to synagogue, "before the emissaries from Eretz Yisrael even got there." The contribution of Persian Jews to the welfare of the European refugees was, it seemed to me, a point of pride but also of soreness, repeated a little too emphatically in the twenty-first century, as if it still remains a point of contention or has never quite been heard.

＝

Josek Klapholz, who like Hannan was fourteen when he arrived in Iran, recalled a Sabbath dinner at the home of a Persian-Jewish family when I interviewed him in Tel Aviv. Jocek Shenkelbach, who was sixteen, said "Jews from Tehran" who "came to visit us and brought used clothing, food, and sweets and once even took the children to see Chaplin's *The Great Dictator*, most likely at the Grand Cinema in the city center." Meir Ahad, a counselor at the Jewish Orphanage, wrote that after the children's arrival in Tehran, "we witnessed one of the most wondrous expressions of the love of Israel and the feeling that 'all Jews are bound together.'" A convoy of carts passed from town to the tent camp, "bringing food, clothes and blankets donated by Tehran's Jews . . . which not only improved our physical condition but uplifted our spiritual one."[47]

Despite this help, and despite the arrival of the representatives from Palestine, as the children settled into a routine in Dushan Tappeh, their living conditions were "awful," Shenkelbach recalled. "We slept in tents on the ground, without mattresses. We walked around in tatters. We received food, but not enough. The older boys would go to Tehran. The younger children were in a state of malnutrition, and received a supplement of fish oil. A group of the younger children contracted scabies."

And so even in Iran, following a sweet yet brief welcome, my father would have suffered hunger—not the starvation of Uzbekistan, but a nagging never-adequately-full hunger. Clothing and shoes, which like food were supplied by the camp's Polish administration, were also said in testimonies and memoirs to be insufficient, distributed arbitrarily, and therefore never in the right size. Unlike the Polish children at Isfahan, there was no "school board" for the children of the Jewish Orphanage, no books, no curriculum, no school at all. One reason, as an inquiry committee would later find, was the absence of "appropriate people with educational background" from among the Jewish refugees; in essence, all Jewish teachers had remained in Central Asia. And now that the Jewish children had been separated from the Polish children, having non-Jewish Polish refugees to teach them was never entertained, though the Polish refugee population included a disproportionately large number of intellectuals and teachers,[48] from the outset a group of non-Jews who were most likely to have fled Nazi-occupied Poland. Participation in Polish schools was not an option either (due to "fears that the children would be bullied or beaten," as the inquiry committee stated. There was no mention of the other, ideologically obvious reasons).

Much of the Orphanage staff's time was spent collecting Jewish children from the general Polish camps. Lauenberg recounted haggling with the Polish camp directors over the transfer of Jewish children to their care and trying to convince the children themselves to transfer. "They wore crosses on their necks, and swore they were Polish and belonged in the Polish camp. . . . [They had] learned well in the harsh school of their lives in recent years that it was better to be Polish, Russian, Christian, anything but Jewish—because the people of this nation were inferior to all."[49]

In the documentary *The Children of Teheran*, a former female counselor says, with considerable irony, that some children did not want to leave the Polish side and join the Jewish Orphanage because "they had it good there." In her monograph on the Tehran Children, Gadit Shamir, who refers to the counselors not as refugees but as *halutzim* ("pioneers," or members of the Ha'khalutz movement), describes a daily "fight" to identify and retrieve Jewish children. Though the "pioneers" carried "official Polish *delegatura* documents that permitted them to collect all Jewish children . . . the priests did not easily relinquish the opportunity to 'save souls,'" she writes, "particularly those of the pure souls who had not yet been 'corrupted'—the small children." Shamir reports of cases where Jewish children were "kidnapped" or "baptized."[50]

It was difficult, based on what I knew about all that had transpired before their arrival in Iran, to draw a clear line between "kidnapping" the children and aiding them, between their coercion and their consent, between their "forced conversion" and their fear of being labeled as Jews and bullied. Shamir reports a case of a young girl whose older brother, who was in the Jewish Orphanage, tried to convince her to join him, and when she finally relented, "the priests would not let her, and the pioneers were forced to fetch her undercover, at night."[51]

Jocek Shenkelbach, now Zvi Shekel, wrote in his memoir of his dilemma whether to transfer or not to the Jewish Orphanage. At sixteen, he was the only Jewish boy accepted to an Anders Army Junek School in Uzbekistan, where he withstood an initiation of bullying and beating, but was eventually accepted ("they got used to me and I to them").[52] He was evacuated alongside his classmates to Iran, where he received a new uniform, a set of civilian "holiday clothing," and "a plentiful, uninterrupted supply of food": "We were happy. We were free. We ate white bread. We wore clean clothes, an army uniform. We were told that we would be transferred to Kenya for flight training."[53] But after some weeks, a Jewish Agency representative appeared and asked him whether instead of continuing from Iran to Kenya he would not prefer to go with the Jewish children to Palestine. Shenkelbach, who would go on to be one of the founders of Kibbutz Hatzerim in southern Israel, recalls that "immediately after she left, the [Polish] commander appeared and started yelling at me for even agreeing to meet her, since 'it was thanks to [the Poles] that I was even here and not dying in Russia.'" Shenkelbach decided to leave, but when he arrived at the Jewish Orphanage he was mortified by its squalor. "I was disappointed," he writes, "and at times regretted that I agreed to leave the Poles."[54]

I did not know whether Hannan, Regina, and Emma had a say or a choice about their placement. I knew only this: that living conditions in the general Polish camps, particularly at Isfahan, were far superior to those at the Jewish Orphanage and that despite that, the majority of Polish-Jewish child refugees ended up there like them. And I knew, through the reports and letters of the Polish *delegatura* in Tehran that I had read, that hostilities toward the Polish Jews peaked in Iran. A Lieutenant Perkowicz, who in October 1942 discussed with the Polish consul in Tehran the recruitment of civilans into the army, notes that the attitude of Jews toward Poles has "gotten tense, due to their rejection during evacuation."[55] Lieutenant Jan Tabaczynski, in a letter "regarding the conditions of living of Polish refugees in Ahvaz and Karachi," complains in a letter to the head of the Second Regiment of the Anders Army in the East, about Jews vying for resources; about the British choosing to collaborate with "Kikes" over Poles, because the Jews "happen to speak English, French or German"; about "Kikes" doing anything to help "their own breed"; about Jews in Russia who were looking for an easy gain, scheming—sometimes even against Poles—"just to get their life good," and carrying "a lot of jewelry" in their suitcases.[56]

At the Jewish camp, meanwhile, Poland no longer mattered. Two months after my father's arrival in Iran the Polish name of his camp *Żydowski sierociniec* or the Jewish Orphanage was changed to the Hebrew Beit ha-Yeladim ha-Yehudi be'Teheran: the Jewish Children's Home of Tehran. "It was decided," Gadit Shamir writes, "that the children were no longer orphans; the Jewish Nation was now their home!" At the entrance to this newly minted Jewish Children's Home of Tehran, the counselors hung a flag embroidered with the camp's Hebrew name, taught Hebrew songs (Lauenberg reported that only fifty of the children knew Hebrew), and began a weekly Sabbath celebration. Dr. Hirschberg was invited to teach the children biblical stories; emissaries from Palestine told them about Eretz Yisrael.[57]

=

In other sections of Dushan Tappeh, in front of tents and barracks of Polish refugees, white eagles with golden beaks and red shields—the Polish coat of arms—were carved into the ground or built out of rocks and candles. In Isfahan,[58] every Catholic holiday—the Catholic Fathers, St. Nicholas Day, Easter—was elaborately celebrated, and everything from diet (high in protein, especially eggs) to school curriculum was designed to instill a Catholic-Polish national identity in the Polish children. "The 'Poland of Isfahan' was in fact an independent state within Iran," Parisa Damandan observed; the statement was equally true for the Jewish Children's Home.

In both of these "states"—the one that was no more and the one that had not yet come into existence—the emphasis was on the children. Children were deemed the future of the nation and its hope, and national belonging was deemed to be the best way to rehabilitate children. Lauenberg reported that the children were in varying degree of psychological distress. Some did not speak; some screamed "like hunted animals"; one "screamed as though he is back in a northern forest and bears and wolves are chasing him"[59]—and it was only after they entered the "Jewish Children's Home" and "were no longer hapless refugees . . . but belonged to a nation," as Lauenberg writes, that they "had time for memories," for sounding "a cry of relief" and for beginning to share their stories.[60] But niether an ethnically "pure" Catholic Polish state nor a Jewish state were in existence. What was at stake was a future, forward looking identity that had to be simultaneously created and instilled in young future citizens.

Polish nationalism, as the testimonies and archival footage show, flourished in Iran even more than in prewar Poland. And Iran, with its decentralized, multiethnic, multilinguistic makeup, so radically different from the homogeneous European nation-states, tolerated, at least initially, the development of a Polish, and to an extent also a Jewish, independent state within its borders.

But creating "national" content at the Jewish home was harder than in Isfahan. Most of the counselors, barely older than their charges, had had little Jewish education and no pedagogical experience. They ran the camp on a scout-like model: a seven a.m. wake-up call, followed by a wash in cold water, and the singing of the Ha'shomer Ha'tsair anthem:

We sing and rise! Atop ruins and corpses
We stride and pass . . . and in the darkness
And with and without knowing where we go, we walk the path
We rise and sing!

There were daily announcements, and names were called out for special praise or for punishment. Then the children folded blankets and cleaned tents ("to instill in them responsibility for cleanliness and order," Lauenberg wrote) and occasionally heard Hebrew songs and stories.[61] It was an agenda to which many of the children, particularly the older ones, did not relate. "The children and teens at the Children's Home are assembled from disparate social strata of the Jewish world," Emil Landau wrote.

> There are children from Zionist homes, for whom Palestine is their life's aim and ambition, but these are only few. Some hail from observant homes and know some Hebrew. . . . There are working-class children—children of workers and small merchants—who are the majority; and there are the children of the assimilated intelligentsia, more or less, and there are many of these too.

To have gotten this far, it seemed to me, a child would have had to speak good Polish, to have had at least some contact with general Polish society. Emil, whose family belonged to the assimilated intelligentsia, called the camp's teachings "superficial propaganda," derided the singing of the Ha'shomer Ha'tsair anthem, and accused the counselors of bribing the children with candy to join their movement. Jocek Shenkelbach, the sixteen-year-old who had crossed over from the Polish Junek School, writes in his memoir that though "some of the counselors were members of Zionist youth movements in Poland," he was "far removed from these matters" and found the camp routine "terribly boring."[62]

I did not know what my father thought about the Jewish Children's Home. He did not belong to the "assimilated children of the intelligentsia"; the Teitels were neither very observant nor entirely assimilated. They were rooted in Poland while supporting Zionism, but from everything I knew about his prewar life, Palestine had not been Hannan's "life's aim" either. He attended six years of the Tarbut school, had some Hebrew proficiency, and knew not a little about Zionism. His family's worldview was diametrically opposed to the socialist Ha'shomer Ha'tsair, but to a parentless child refugee, those divisions within the Jewish world no longer mattered.

"Everyone knows at least something about Palestine and its aims," Emil Landau wrote. "There are erroneous rumors about collective life in Eretz Yisrael; the nightmare of the *kolkhoz* still haunts us. Still, everyone more or less knows, or has understood that there is no other homeland except Palestine and that it is our collective goal."[63]

"I was sad in Tehran," Regina told me when I interviewed her for the last time in Tel Aviv. "I missed my parents terribly." She was paper thin and dying of cancer but wanted to meet and talk to me.

"Didn't the counselors help or comfort you?" I asked her. David Lauenberg, in his recollections, described counselors who "rushed" to the weepers, "hugged," "calmed," and "caressed . . . the children [who] were thirsty for familial warmth." The counselors, Gadit Shamir writes, granted the children "the first touch of a friend's care, the substitute for mother's and father's love," revived their "faith in humanity."[64]

"The counselors were awful. They were cold, two-faced, they played favorites." Regina, who was eleven in Tehran, told me, lowering her voice as if she were still cautious about offending anyone. "They were only a few years older than us, but demanded that we call them 'Pani' (Miss) this and 'Pani' that. And they had their favorites: the pretty blond girls. I was not blond or pretty." Emil Landau also appears to have had a bone to pick with the Children's Home counselors, calling them a "group of careerists and their appendages—hated by all children."

To corroborate what she was saying, Regina phoned her friend Bracha Mandel, who had also been a child refugee in Tehran and now lived nearby. She dialed her repeatedly, obsessively, her thin fingers punching the numbers until Bracha answered.

"What do you remember of the counselors in Tehran? How were they?" Regina asked a little breathlessly.

"They were 100 percent. Terrific," Bracha said.

"Are you sure you don't remember anything else?"

"Not at all. They were great. We learned songs, they took care of us." Bracha echoed Lonek Jaroslawicz, a former child refugee her age who writes in his memoir that the counselors had been "everything" to him in Tehran: "They were like my parents, my brother, my family. They knew everything, they kept us occupied."[65]

"The counselors were awful," Regina said again, unrelenting. In a psychological assessment that camp director Lauenberg would fill out for her six months later in Jerusalem, he would write that she "adapted herself very well to the camp and presented no particular difficulties to herself or to others." Hannan, on the other hand, would be described by the counselors as "lazy," "unpopular," and "not too developed." I wondered if Regina hated them a little for his sake. "Whenever I was really sad, I would go see Hannan and he would always comfort me," she said, looking me in the eye, as if wishing to "prove" to me my father's goodness before she too was gone.

$$=$$

Some Polish and Jewish refugees in Tehran lived outside the refugee camps: employees of the Polish *delegatura* and the Eretz Yisrael office, and others who could afford it, or who never registered with Polish authorities, having come to Iran as stowaways or in other unorthodox ways. Those who lived inside the camp but wished to leave it were required as per an agreement with the Iranian authorities to apply for a "pass" that would be given for a period anywhere between a day and a month. Long-term passes were issued only to refugees who worked outside of the camps and provided proof of independent earnings. For Catholic Poles, this income mostly came from work at the Polish government, the legation, the Red Cross, the *delegatura*, and other Polish official and semiofficial organizations, which employed all told 1,974 people in Tehran, Bandar Pahlavi, Ahvaz, and Mashhad.[66] "Few, if any, [of these employees] were Jews," a JDC report would later state, "and still fewer who were not converts."[67]

Dr. Hirschberg, one of four evacuated rabbi refugees, moved from Dushan Tappeh to the city of Tehran immediately. First he was a guest of "Reb Haja A.," most likely Haji Aziz Elghanian, who hosted him and the other three Polish rabbis who had come to Iran for the Rosh Hashanah holiday. The home was a "spacious villa, surrounded by a high wall":

> The quiet atmosphere of the home, the garden with the water pools, the tall trees that gave much shade and cooled the air, the polite warmness of the home, improved us. . . . It was after midnight when we went out to sleep on the mats and carpets that had been laid out on the balcony garden. . . . We put our things in the rooms—rooms were not wanting in the villa—but they were superfluous, because according to local custom everyone slept on the garden floor in summer.[68]

Then Dr. Hirschberg took a room in Hotel Persia, a decrepit establishment on Topkhana (Artillery) Square, which was owned by a Georgian Jew and was "a hub for refugees." Finally, after considerable efforts ("finding rooms was difficult as the city was already full of military and guests who have been here for a while"), he found a room inside a villa owned by a Persian colonel.

Some refugees worked for non-Polish employers, mostly for the Allied forces, as artisans, building workers, mechanics, dressmakers, butchers, and barbers. Some worked at Iranian factories and artisan shops and for Iranian contractors. Krystyna Wartanowicz, a widow with two young children, worked as a seamstress in a factory in Tehran; Anna Borkowska worked at a hospital as a doctor's assistant. Aside from a handful of Jewish dignitaries like Dr. Hirschberg, who were supported by small stipends from the Jewish Agency, most Jewish refugees living outside the refugee camps supported themselves from sale of personal belongings.

Some young Jewish women worked as barmaids and waitresses at the bars, cafés, and cabarets of Tehran, a city that had been flung into a state of unprecedented freedom by the Allies' invasion of Iran, where refugees, diplomats, and foreign soldiers mingled in something like the lavish and decadent mood of Rick's Cafe in the film *Casablanca*.[69]

"Seemingly, everything is run here by European costumes," observed Moshe Yishai, a Jewish Agency representative who arrived in Tehran in 1943.

> Black, tuxedoed doormen with long sticks; coat checks; in the lobbies of the restaurants and cabarets—white clothes, black-clad waiters, a jazz orchestra. Couples will go on stage and dance every type of dance. The men, however, will hold their partners at some distance, avoiding too much closeness, though at the bar there are attractive, seductive waitresses. From the bar one can hear the clatter of glasses, a lustful smile. . . . In the morning the cabarets, the fancy restaurants are closed . . . but in the evening everything opens. Colorful lights blink from afar like floating light beams.[70]

"In just a few months after their arrival in Tehran . . . theaters, bars, cabarets, and cafes were built by Polish people for Polish people," historian Lior Sternfeld says, "cultural institutions that later were adopted by the Iranian middle class."[71] Café Polonia on Lalezar Street was a hub where refugees, diplomats, and soldiers bartered, and young Polish refugees kept them company. Twelve movie theaters operated on or near Lalezar Street ("movie theaters are lurking here at every corner," Yishai writes): Cinema Rex, Khorshid, Alborz, Mayak, Metropole, Cinema Crystal, Metro, Shahraz, Sahar, Venus, Cinema Iran, and the Grand Cinema, where the Holocaust refugee children were taken in December 1942 to see Chaplin's newly released film *The Great Dictator*.

"Polish entertainment flourished in Tehran at this time," noted Sternfeld. "It was a part of the war economy." On August 2, 1942, the Theatre du Soldat Polonaise performed its first production at Jardine d'Astoria, followed by a Concert du Soldat Polonaise at the Club Armenien, and Une Soirée Polonaise, a fund-raiser for Polish orphans, at L'Hôtel Palace.

Prostitution was part of the war economy as well, with "young Polish women . . . in high demand by both locals and Allied soldiers."

Krystyna Wartanowicz described this "demand" not as prostitution but as infatuation: "I may safely say that in the streets of Tehran each Polish woman feels beautiful, for so many smoldering, awe-filled masculine gazes pursue her," she testified. "[Iranian] men, and particularly the officers—all very handsome—are very fond of Polish women."[72]

By the year's end, Iranian conservatives would begin attacking the effects of the refugees' "idleness and gay life" on the Iranian population. In their reports on the condition of the refugees to the Jewish Agency and the JDC, Rafael Szaffar and others would also fret about the "dangers" to the morality of Jewish girls and women, "bar maids" and "waitresses" who were reported to be "from very good families." But in those first few months in 1942 at least, erotic fascination that bordered on sexual predation was in the air.

"My father loved the Polish women," Ali Parsa, the son of Asghar Parsa, Persian government liaison to the Polish refugees in the Ministry of Foreign Affairs circa 1942, told me when I met him in New York in 2015. Ali's father, who would go on to become a career diplomat, was a twenty-three-year-old bachelor on his first official assignment when he was charged with supplying the basic needs and supervising laundry services for the inhabitants of Dushan Tappeh. Salar had chanced on Ali in Tehran, and when Ali, an avid jazz lover, next visited him in New York, the three of us met at the Smoke Jazz Club on Broadway. Ali, who expected to meet a Polish woman—he did not know that there had been Jews among the refugees—was surprised that an Israeli would have any connection to the story of his father. "My father just called them all 'the Poles,'" he said.

The Poles—or more precisely, young Polish women—worked for Asghar Parsa. "He employed only women, never men," Ali laughed. "The Polish women got the best clothes, they got the best shoes," and late in life Asghar often mentioned the "blond, blue-eyed Polish beauties" that

descended on Tehran in the 1940s. It was a story that I would read repeatedly in regard to all men in power in Tehran: about Rafael Szaffar, who
was said as well to have employed young women in the Eretz Yisrael office;
about a Persian Jew who in time would run the JDC's Tehran office; about
a Polish doctor and his female assistants.

"The Persians famously adore the beauty of the refugee women,"
Moshe Yishai, who would replace Szaffar as head of the Eretz Yisrael
office, wrote. That young refugee women were given better access to food,
clothing, and working wages was a recurring theme, whether as fantasy
or, more likely, as a reality.

I found no first-person testimonies of incidents of rape, prostitution,
or sexual exploitation by women, but others mentioned such things.
Jozek Klapholz, a former Tehran Child, recalled a neighbor's daughter
who "became a prostitute for the Uzbeks" in Samarqand.[73] Moshe Yishai
reported several cases: a twenty-two-year-old woman who rented a room
from a Persian man and a year later gave birth to twins; a young refugee
who had bartered sex in exchange for evacuation to Iran from a Polish
officer who gave her syphilis; and many women who offered Yishai sexual
favors for entry certificates to Palestine.[74] In other documents, emissaries
noted "rumors" and expressed "concerns" for the level of morality among
certain young women and made indirect allusions.

There were also novels: in Nathan Shakham's *Harkhek mi-Tashkent*
(Away from Tashkent), a retired Israeli accountant learns of the sexual
secrets of his deceased wife, a former Tehran Child, after discovering her
wartime diary in an attic. In the canonical 1947 novel *Hu Halakh ba-
Sadot* (He Walked the Fields), Mika, a blond, blue-eyed former Tehran
Child now living on a kibbutz (collective settlement), is rumored to have
been a victim of sexual assault, twice impregnated, and twice forced to
undergo abortions by a Polish doctor for whom she worked in Tehran and
who used to call her Żydówka ("my Jewess").

Lauenberg describes fending off Persian soldiers who would scout the
Polish camp at night, offering children a few coins and occasionally lur-
ing them away.[75]

"Blond, blue-eyed girls" were what the adults in charge most wanted, Regina told me. "One morning a gorgeous girl with blushing cheeks, a pug nose, blue eyes, and blond hair walked into my office," Lauenberg wrote of the woman he met in Tehran who would become his wife.[76] Race, which was never talked about directly, seemed to have played a significant role in their lives.

≡

I learned the most about the sense of relative freedom of Tehran circa 1942 from the testimony of Dr. Hirschberg, a rabbi and scholar of Middle East Jewry who two years after his stay in Iran would publish the essay "Rosh Hashanah 1942, in Persia."

> It is a special feeling a man has, after an interruption of two years and a quarter, when he goes to pray publicly in a communal synagogue with an ark and a Torah scroll. Only a Spanish *converso* would understand it. It's been twenty-seven months since I have heard the reading of the Torah, months when every public prayer was a crime against the laws of the land. And here a man walks with his head high, a *tallit* under his arm, in a bustling city, amid a crowd of people, dressed festively, walking to the synagogue in the wealthy quarter.[77]

At the holiday meal in the home of "Reb Haja A." ("the first time I am in the home of a Jew from the East"), Dr. Hirschberg was awed by the quantity and variety of foods: "on the table is a large bowl with vegetables, stew meat, lamb's head, and matzo like the one we used to bake for Passover; it was like a Passover feast." He marveled at the unique rituals: "Persian Jews have a special Rosh Hashanah pamphlet, printed in Persian-Jewish letters, as there are Yiddish and Ladino, a mixture of Persian and Hebrew." There was no regular rabbi at his host's synagogue, only "community dignitaries" who led the prayer in succession. Locals gave great importance to *tashlikh*, the custom of symbolically discarding their sins by tossing bread into a body of water, in their case into the little goldfish ponds in

their homes. "Whatever I saw and heard over the days about the past and
present lives of Persian Jews . . . seduced me to know more."[78]

In his recollections, Dr. Hirschberg commented on the prayer style
of the Persians ("they serve fragrant herbs, which they smell and bless,
between each prayer"), the food and the length of the meal (four hours),
and the "special melody" of the prayers. When a custom rang familiar,
he wrote, "It is as with us." He noted the "warm, simple manners of the
household" and their hospitality: "members of the family wait on guests
and do not let the maids near them"). Despite the cheap labor, even
wealthy Persians did not employ nannies—older children cared for the
younger ones. The children were obedient—"every word uttered by the
father is a commandment that should not be questioned"—and, perhaps a
tad ironically, "one can learn of the commandment to respect your father
and mother from the Persians." Though there was no Hebrew language
printing house in Iran, locals spoke the "the Persian-Jewish language of
the Medieval poets." There was little proficiency in Hebrew, but the prayer
melodies were "unique" and had been preserved forever. The Mahalleh's
poverty was dismal—"I have never seen such a slum"—but its synagogues
were "tall, clean, spacious, nicely organized . . . and leave the impression
of generosity and stability."

When he tired during the Yom Kippur prayer at the Mahalleh, Dr.
Hirschberg was shocked when his hosts offered to fetch him a taxi. "Except
for the Ashkenazi synagogue," driving to the synagogue on Yom Kippur
"was the custom of the land." Other local holiday customs were "not to
[his] liking": the writing of donation pledges, even inside the synagogue,
the superficial knowledge of the prayers, and the absence of a congregation
rabbi or a leading public figure. The older refugees warned him, sarcasti-
cally, that "he has seen nothing yet" of the strange ways of the locals.[79]

Iran was the place where Dr. Hirschberg first encountered "Jews of
the East." It was also where the Polish- and Russian-born "emissaries,"
like Szaffar and Meirov, first encountered Persian Jews, an encounter
that the sociologist Yehouda Shenhav would read as a colonial-like meeting of native Middle Easterners and Europeans. "In Iran, at first glance,

I cannot tell the difference between a Jew, an Arab, and a Christian," the Mossad LeAliyah Bet agent Netzer Sirani reported. The locals' religious "sloppiness" was thought to be linked to "an absence of a national instinct."[80] Shenhav likens the emissaries and European Jews who ended up in Iran to "agents of colonial power" on a "civilizing mission," and he points to Iran circa 1942 as the moment in which Zionists "discover ... Arab-Jews," by which he means Persian and Iraqi Jews.[81]

Shenhav's characterization was not untrue; this was perhaps the first substantial encounter between proto-citizens of the Jewish state and the Iranian Jewish and non-Jewish population.[82] But a binary, colonial model that pits colonizer against colonized, Ashkenazi against Sephardi, Jew against Muslim, in an unchanging hierarchical or exploitive pattern was insufficient to describe the complex network of encounters that took place between everyone and everything at that moment in Iran, not just between Ashkenazic and Sephardic Jews but between locals and refugees in general: between Persians and Poles; Palestinian Zionists and Jewish refugees; Polish soldiers and British soldiers; German refugees and Iraqi refugees; Jewish American aid organizations and the Persian Jewish community; the British Empire and the various nationalisms that were about to succeed it. These encounters were not just between so-called colonists and natives but between refugees and locals, between types of refugees, between the wealth of locals and the complete and absolute poverty of the refugees, between one of the oldest Jewish communities in the world and one that had been destroyed.

And so I read Dr. Hirschberg's account of his visit to the "the prayer house of the Iraqis" in Tehran without any preimposed lenses—not the lens of postcolonial theory, or of any other theory—and just let his words sink in:

At the large courtyard of the Alliance school, by the pool, these wealthy "Arabs" arranged a spot for themselves to pray during the High Holidays: they spread carpets, brought in lounge and arm chairs, a Torah Ark, a table for Torah reading, and tents for protection from the sun—and thus a temporary synagogue was erected.

For the women they placed seats in the balconies surrounding the garden so that they too could hear the prayer. I admit that praying in this place left a unique impression on me. There was nothing about it of the atmosphere inside our synagogues during High Holidays. No trace of the seriousness, the high-mindedness, the dread, and the awe that characterized our prayers. The men, dressed in pressed white suits, sat in a half circle around the pool, as if they were at a ball at a country club. The cool air, the pools with the tiny goldfish, and the tent above only strengthened this impression. Many small children, some without a hat, ran around the yard but did not interrupt the prayer. I sat and thought about what I saw. Perhaps these Baghdadi Jews have preserved Yom Kippur prayer in its original form. *Lo hayu yamim tovim le'Yisrael ke'khamisha-asar be'av ve'yom Kippur* (there were no good days for Israel like the fifteenth of the month of Av and Yom Kippur), the Torah says. Perhaps it is appropriate to celebrate Yom Kippur with joy and happiness, to send flowers to each other, and to act not as slaves dreading their rabbi, but as children who have sinned before their father and know that all will be forgiven.[83]

This passage was, I thought, extraordinary. It was the earliest text I had read in which Jews were called "Arab," in essence a precursor of the term "Arab Jew" that postcolonial scholars of Zionism would introduce half a century later. And it demonstrated how a Polish-born rabbi like Dr. Hirschberg both linked himself to his hosts (the shared Yom Kippur holiday) and also differentiated from them ("our synagogues"). A few years back, before I began my research, I would have read the sentence about Yom Kippur and "children who have sinned before their father" much more cynically, if not paranoiacally, as a tad condescending and orientalist observation (natives as "children," etc.). But there was also something else, something subtler, gentler, and more fleeting than the self-assured sensibility of a European colonizer, something that upended categories, hierarchies, national boundaries and just asked for beauty, mercy, forgiveness. Because I knew Dr. Hirschberg was a refugee, because I knew what he had been through and what he and all other refugees lacked—possessions, connections, family, home, ritual—because he had been robbed of everything, I read his words as longing, as fascination, and as openness to the possibility of a lovely, tranquil presence that overtook the European Orthodox rabbi at that moment, because above the national and colonial paradigms that shaped the identities of Poles and Jews in Iran hovered the figure of the refugee: a moving figure, homeless, poor, a bit of a tabula rasa, a particle whose fate was determined by tinier and more arbitrary factors than the larger categories. Dr. Hirschberg's passage was so descriptive, I could almost smell it: the spacious, fragrant garden, the cool air, the pools with the tiny goldfish, the men in white suits, the wealth in funds and in family members that a refugee from Poland like Dr. Hirschberg and my father no longer had, an atmosphere of tranquility in which guilt and dread of the divine presence were suddenly put into question in the face of beauty and a more merciful God.

Something of the same poetic aura crept into the otherwise factual memoir of Dr. Moshe Yishai, the Jewish Agency emissary from Palestine. "Have you ever felt a smile rising from the ground, from flowers, from a garden?" he wrote. "It captivates you, intoxicates you, it seems magical—like the smile of Greta Garbo, Ingrid Bergman, Vivian Lee. That is how you feel in Tehran.

> As you wake up in the morning and go to your garden-facing window, your gaze will fix on the large, round pool. The pool's waters shine against a rising sun that sends its early morning rays onto the ground in the merciful wind, a mother's mercy. From the right of the garden water pours into the pool and the current sends waves that spread across its waters, swaying like a baby's cradle. And amid the waves, small silverfish and goldfish, dotted and undotted, bustle, raising their heads and sinking to the bottom again, and everything is so joyful, everything is filled with delight. . . .

> Once, when I stood near my window with my eyes at the courtyard, a Persian woman sat there holding a small child. The woman's clothes

were simple and faded, full of colorful patches. On her feet were Persian cloth shoes; there were no socks. The boy was dressed in a ripped white blouse and wrapped in brown rag. She shifted her legs from side to side, swaying the sleeping child who suddenly began to sob. The woman tried to calm him, caressing his hair. Her hand slid from his forehead through his hairline to the back of his neck, again and again, countless times, and slowly the boy calmed and stopped sobbing.

And who will caress me? Who will calm me in my difficult moments? I thought.[84]

Yishai, an established Doctor of Jurisprudence and political activist, was not a refugee like Dr. Hirschberg or my father. But he too was Polish-born, having emigrated to Palestine less than two decades earlier, and he too had lost a world, a past, a family—like nearly every European Jew in Iran, refugees and emissaries alike.

$$=$$

Many of the adult refugees, by the time they arrived in Iran, had reportedly lost their religious faith. Nahum Herzberg, who would replace Rafael Szaffar as Jewish Agency representative, wrote that during the 1943 High Holidays, while Russian- and American-Jewish soldiers appeared in Tehran's synagogues, no Polish-Jewish refugees did. "When I asked them why they did not come, and why they did not want a synagogue in Dushan Tappeh, they answered unequivocally. There were among them very intelligent people, with an academic education, very serious, and they said, 'It's our rage at what happened, that no one came to our aid. Our faith, not just religious faith but our faith in the fate of the Jewish people as it is linked to the Jewish God—it has been nullified.'"[85]

The loss or continuation of faith was harder to determine among the children. Even children who hailed from observant homes were distanced from matters of religion and tradition during their trials and tribulations in Soviet Russia. A report published in Jerusalem in May 1943 ascertained that the majority of counselors "belonged to a movement that did not value religious tradition and education," and they were "not interested in grooming religious feelings and religious life among the children."[86] Mostly, counselors and children described religious holidays in the camp at Dushan Tappeh as occasions of deep pain, longing and worry for their families. On Rosh Hashanah, Emil Landau wrote in his diary, "there was a celebration, but no one was in the mood to celebrate. Everyone felt that something, someone was missing; everyone felt a pain that ripped their soul and sought relief and weeping. You could not meet one child that day whose eyes were not filled with tears and on whose emaciated face was not the painful expression of separation. That day, a day of joy in all the Jewish world, was a holiday of sadness and mourning for the children of Tehran." The children's "horrid cry," David Lauenberg recalled, "jolted everyone and swept with it the counselors."

A week later, for Yom Kippur, the children were taken to Tehran's synagogues. The idea was the Tehran Committee's: not only to remove the children from the depressing camp atmosphere but to present them, particularly the young ones, to worshippers at Tehran's synagogues, in order to collect alms for the "young orphans." It was decided that the children would visit a few of the eighteen synagogues inside the Mahalleh, the makeshift Iraqi synagogue at the Alliance, and the Haim and Danial synagogue, which was outside the Mahalleh.

Inside Haim and Danial, a separate section had been built for the Europeans Jews. The older children who were dispatched there—it was decided that the little ones could not walk that far—walked seven kilometers from Dushan Tappeh to get there. They walked north through Tupkhane (now Imam Khomeini Square), and then along Lalezar Street, the "Champs-Elysées of Tehran." Passing theaters, cabarets, and cafés, they reached the Hotel Lalezar, where Iraqi, German, and Polish refugees were housed, On the hotel's façade were red neon signs pointing to a cabaret. Across the street was the Café Pars, and just beyond it was the Grand Hotel. At the Lalezar they turned left onto Reza Shah Avenue (now Jomhuri) and continued until they hit Shahreza (now Enqelab Avenue),

then turned onto Qavam-os-Saltane, where the Haim and Danial synagogue, built in 1913, was located.

Danial, or "the Polish synagogue," as Salar said it became known in
Tehran, had been built as the Ashkenazi extension of Haim synagogue. It
sat up to sixty people and shared with Haim a courtyard into which Hannan and the other children entered. The Persian adults who had begun to
assemble stood and talked quietly, their children playing amid the pomegranate trees. Above the arched front door, a sign in ornamented Hebrew
and Persian letters read THIS IS THE GATE FOR GOD THROUGH WHICH THE
RIGHTEOUS SHALL PASS. Inside was brown, gold, and Persian plum, the
sparkle of chandeliers, and lots of the Persian blue I had seen in the tiles
of Samarqand's mosques and mausoleums. On the cerulean velvet Torah
ark, the words BEIT HA-KNESSET HA'YEHUDIM HA'EUROPIM—Synagogue
of European Jews—were embroidered in gold. The locals gave the children little gifts and sat with them for the Kol Nidrei prayer. Then, when
they noticed the younger children were absent, they sent a car to fetch
them, despite what even their secular counselors knew as the strict prohibition against driving on Yom Kippur.

Everyone was already seated by the time the five- and six-year-olds and
the toddlers walked into the synagogue. "When the worshippers saw the
children, they all began to weep. Tears rolled down the men's cheeks, and
the women wept violently," Dr. Hirschberg recounts.[87]

I knew the exact route my father had taken to the synagogue because in
2015 Salar had purchased a small apartment on Sir-e-Tir Street (formerly
Qavam-os-Saltane) just across from Haim and Danial synagogue. Much
had taken place in the eight years that passed between Salar and my first
conversation in 2007 and the summer of 2015. We had traveled to Poland
and Uzbekistan. We had exchanged hundreds of e-mail messages from
different parts of the world. We had read and edited each other's writings.
We tried to write alternating chapters for what we thought would be a collaborative book on the Tehran Children, which at the end did not gel and
which we discarded. We were both full of obligations and did not see each

other for long stretches of time, and when we did, we sometimes quib-
bled. A subtle yet nagging distrust had settled between us. I did not know
when it happened exactly or what caused it: the separate loyalties we were
each keeping—to Iran, to Israel—or simply the fatigue of a tense intimacy
that sometimes came into conflict. Relations between Iran and Israel had
become even more fraught over the years and often we had distinct inter-
pretations of a situation, two worlds apart, like the Poles and the Israelis,
like the Iranians and Israelis. We had become a bit of a metaphor.

What increasingly plagued us was what had connected us in the first
place: the analogy between "our stories." Under the pressure of my historical research and the facts I was discovering about my father's flight
and exile, it was coming apart. In a chapter titled "Analogies of Trauma"
in our now-defunct joint book project, Salar had compared my father to a
friend of his, a Persian philosopher who had been a refugee and now lived
in internal exile in Iran. I shrieked at the comparison between the lofty,
upper-crust philosopher who had been exiled in Paris and was now back
in his villa in Tehran, complete with two servants and an opium den, and
my starving Soviet-labor-camp veteran father.

"I don't think your analogy works," I wrote to Salar, who was in Tehran. I wanted to say: *How dare you?*

"Do you know what some people here have gone through?" he wrote
back. "You have to allow me to make my own analogies to your father's
experience. . . . I'd like you to be justly critical, but I can't accept your last
criticism. I think there's a blind spot in your thinking." Another time,
when I complained about the erasure of all traces of Jewish life from my
father's hometown in Poland, Salar said, seemingly out of nowhere, "Look
in the mirror. Isn't this what you Israelis do to the Palestinians every day?"
It wasn't so much what he said that opened a rift—I knew all too well of
the erasure of large swaths of the pre-1948 Palestinian past that had taken
place in Israel—but the fact that in his mind I was now "you Israelis" and
he, presumably, "us Iranians."

Increasingly he spent more time in Iran, even contemplating the possibility of moving back there permanently after buying the apartment on

Tir Street. Then he spent time in Syria and Iraq writing about Israel's "unfriendlies," as he called them, and when he returned to New York he was no longer a fervent critic of the regime in Iran. I sometimes called him an Iranian nationalist now when he used expressions like "Bibi wants to destroy *us*" or "*We're* done for," or went ballistic when he felt Iran was demonized by the American press. He was still, of course, sympathetic to my father's story or even to my family in Israel, but his identification lay elsewhere. He was also working on new projects: a novel set in Iran and Syria, an anthology of contemporary Iranian writing. We had begun, you could say, to write very different stories.

I had not wanted this outcome: not with Salar, and not even with Magda Gawin. I had wanted collaboration: to read my father's story alongside theirs, through the widest lens possible: in conjunction with other nations' stories, within the context of large paradigms of theoretization of violence, of movement, of refugees. I had wanted to avoid thinking of my father's fate strictly through the prism of Jewish history. But at the end, there were the facts. And those facts pointed to a fate that was, in the end, though embedded in the larger story of World War II refugees and migrations, distinctly Jewish.

I did not want these facts to harden my empathy towards others. But the only way around being locked in an eternal focus on your own people's victimization, I now knew, was to first and foremost *feel* it, take in the pain of it, the humiliation, the starvation and helplessness that my father never had the privilege of acknowledging, that few Israeli survivors and their offspring had. And after that pain, there should come attention to history, to time, to change: to persons and groups that come together, grow apart, and come together again; to fates that are redealt and reshuffled over the course of history; to dialogues that sometimes, with some people—the challenge is to figure out which—may continue despite rifts and even momentary hatred. It was the only way out of a binary thinking that cast one side as eternal victim and the other as eternal enemy.

And so, after a slump, Salar and I resumed our dialogue, though I no longer needed him as a mediator and a buffer to my father's past. I already

knew that past in minute detail, and while it saddened and sometimes horrified me, it no longer overwhelmed me. Salar and I remained in each other's orbit and continued to correspond when he was in Tehran, using the
words "Colombia" for Israel and "Bogotá" for Tel Aviv. And so it was one
of those truly strange coincidences that in a packed city of fifteen million,
Salar would end up in an apartment from whose third-floor bedroom window he could look down at Haim and Danial's front yard, where a handful
of Jewish children still played and a handful of worshippers still prayed.

Tophkana Square, where the Georgian-owned refugee Hotel Persia was
located, was right by his house. "It's now called Imam Khomeini Square,"
Salar wrote. "It's where I catch the metro." Often he would send me photos of the synagogue, whose arched door and windows were still painted
their original Persian blue and against whose outer wall he now leaned his
motorbike each evening. He met the synagogue's innkeepers, an Afghan
refugee couple who lived there, and on October 12, 2016, on the eve of
Yom Kippur, he sent videos of the worshippers, which he shot from his
apartment. That day was also Tasu'a and Ashura, a Shi'a commemoration
of the martyrdom of Imam Hussein, grandson of the Prophet Muhammad, and so in the series of videos he sent, a procession of self-flogging
men, singing and flaunting their cat-o'-nine tails, was in the foreground,
while Persian Jews sang Kol Nidrei inside Haim synagogue.

"I wanted to share this with you," Salar wrote. "I don't really have the
words. It just feels like I experienced something sublime. During the day
of the holiest day of the Shia, I watched the mourners proceed across my
street just outside the walls of the synagogue, and a few hours later on the
holiest or second holiest Jewish holiday, I filmed the people behind that
wall breaking what I assume was their fast. . . . I heard the saxophone of the
Shia processioners in the day and the shofar of the Jews that same night."

The Shia processioners, self-absorbed as if in a trance, seemed obliv-
ous to the Jewish worshippers; there was no doubt to whom the public
space belonged, and who was praying behind closed doors. But despite
the loudspeakers amplifying the noise of the procession, and despite
the impassioned crowds of men and their flogging (all of which I found

intimidating), the worshippers looked neither anxious nor uncomfortable as they sat and drank their breakfast tea in the courtyard of the synagogue, whose door was flung open.

In a video Salar had shot the next day, in daytime, a singer in a loud megaphone was blasting a eulogy for the Prophet's grandson.

> *Those who shed tears for Imam Hussein are ushered to heaven on*
> *judgment day.*
> *O Hussein, my Hussein . . . May I sacrifice my life for you, Hussein.*

The processions continued, as did the Yom Kippur worship: a man in a Jewish prayer shawl could be seen standing, and women in fitted dresses and loose head scarfs. "It's the only place in the world where there's no security guard at the entrance to a synagogue," Salar joked.

"If only," I e-mailed back. In a conference not long before, I had been told that an Iranian Jew who served as a liaison for Persian Jews wanting to leave the country had been secretly assassinated.

No Shia day of mourning fell on Yom Kippur 1942, when Hannan and the rest of the refugee children—Regina was hospitalized for her trachoma— walked back to Dushan Tappeh along the same route. The children turned on Shahreza and into Lalezar, whose neon lights were now shining and whose cafés, cabarets, and restaurants were filling up with British, Polish, and Persian soldiers, some in uniform, some in suits and dresses. Out of their cars and into the restaurants poured "men in black suits and white collars and women in evening dresses and shiny shoes . . . everything pressed to the last stitch. Everything tightly fitting, the men looking strong and handsome, the women's slender figures suggestive and seductive to you," Moshe Yishai recalled. I imagined my hungry father walking past "countless stores that have everything," past "a ladies' boutique," "a gold and silver dealer," past "a Caucasian restaurant that served real borscht," and especially past "the pastry and ice cream shop, famous in the entire city for its many flavors."

Next to the Hotel Lalezar, the Café Continental, owned by a certain Shamirzadeh and later known as Café Shamirzadeh, served a break-fast meal that "fed the Israelis for three days, before and after the fast," Musa and Azizeh Melamed, Persian Jews who lived near Haim synagogue, tes-tified. Shamirzadeh's daughters Riva Danielpour and Sonia Kashani, to whose recorded testimony, as well as to the Melameds', Salar had listened at the Library of Congress, said that the café "fed the Hebrews"—presum-ably Tehran's Jewish refugees and Jewish Allied soldiers—"for a whole month" around the High Holidays and that their father "had two cows and three sheep slaughtered for them."

The synagogue fund-raiser was a phenomenal success. At the Iraqi syn-agogue, thousands of *tomans* were given, and at the poorest synagogues in the Mahalleh, nearly every worshipper placed a few *tomans* in the *tzedakah* box. "Us children ran home and took out whatever we had in our savings," Heshmat Kermanshahi told me. The total was thirty thousand *tomans*, the equivalent of six thousand dollars, as Dr. Hirsch-berg put it, "an astronomical amount by their standards." It was just the beginning of giving that by the end of 1942, would total $14,500—$4,500 from Iraqi Jews alone—excluding clothing and other supplies that were delivered directly.[88]

Kermanshahi and Habib were right when they said the Iranian Jews had helped first. By the end of 1942, as a JDC report would determine, "the Tehran Jewish community" would contribute to the relief of the Jew-ish refugees in "larger amounts, both in cash and kind, than have the JDC and the Jewish Agency together."

═══

The JDC, which had been busy assisting the refugees in Central Asia, hes-itated before intervening in Iran, where all refugees were legally under the care of the Polish government. On September 13, the day after the Yom Kippur fund-raiser, Rafael Szaffar cabled the JDC in New York, ask-ing for the organization's assistance in maintaining and transporting the children to Palestine. He cautioned that unless the Jewish children immigrated to Palestine, they would soon be transported from Iran alongside Catholic Polish children and "under the auspices of Christian associations" to permanent destinations in Iran, Kenya, and elsewhere.[89]

In Tel Aviv, the Jewish Agency's foreign office head, Moshe Shertok, called for diplomatic efforts to facilitate further evacuations from Central Asia: "Few civilian Jewish refugees have arrived in Iran; people are throwing their children into the trains that depart from Uzbekistan." It was, as he put it to a small group of Agency leaders, "a horrific human problem, a desperate national misery, and a terrible waste of human resources that could be put to use to aid in this war." He did not reveal that as he was cultivating diplomatic channels to evacuate refugees, his brother-in-law Saul Meirov was on the ground in Iran searching for routes to smuggle them across the Soviet border.

Meirov did not visit the cabarets or cafés at Lalezar, or the villas and synagogues of wealthy local Jews. He did not even allow the Agency to purchase a pair of winter socks for him when the winter frost came, rebuffing the extra spending. From his sparse room in the widow's apartment in Tehran, he devised plans, scheduled meetings, scouted near-border locations, and waited for the opportune hour to cross the border into Turkmenistan. He decided to begin with an initial reconnaissance excursion to gauge the terrain as well as the situation in Central Asia: where Jews congregated, what means they had. He especially wanted to identify and locate refugees who were members of Ha'khalutz, Ha'dror, Ha'bonim, Ha'shomer Ha'tsair, and other Zionist youth movements. They were said to be congregating at the borders, clamoring for the homeland. "Our quest for Iran was in actuality Russia," Meirov wrote." Iran was our relatively close vantage point for the hundreds and thousands of Jewish refugees from Poland, Lithuania, and Latvia who had fled to the Asiatic regions of the Soviet Union."[90]

In September 1942 three Mossad LeAliyah Bet operatives who had completed their training—Moshe Agami, Yaacov Dajivensky, and Misha

Notkin—joined Meirov in Iran. They entered as Solel Boneh members via Abadan, then traveled to Tehran, where they received a set of "refugee clothing" and registration cards of deceased refugees, whose names they assumed. Zvi Melnitzer, a refugee member of Ha'khalutz who had come from Uzbekistan with the August transport, was also recruited, sharing information about concentrations of Jewish refugees in Central Asia.[91]

Refugees in Samarqand, Tashkent, and elsewhere had been sending hundreds of pleading postcards and letters to Zionist movement members in Palestine. "People remembered something, some address or name: Degania, Tel Aviv," Shayke Viner, a Mossad LeAliyah Bet agent, recalled, "and we knew people were crowding at the borders."[92] Some refugees moved nearer to the Iranian border, hoping to find a way to cross. "We went to Dedjak," a former refugee, Mula Ben Hayim, testified, "between Samarqand and Tashkent, because we wanted to be nearest to the Persian border. Perhaps, we thought, we would be able to cross." Another refugee, Yaacov Yanai (Jankelowic), said the very proximity of the Iranian border "taunted" him and his friends in the Zionist underground in Tashkent. Eleven of their members who had attempted to cross the border were caught and sentenced to ten years in the gulag. (They served five but remained behind the Iron Curtain for three more decades.) Two attempted to cross into Afghanistan and were imprisoned in Kabul.[93]

Meirov was determined to make contact with the refugees on the eastern side of the Persian-Soviet border, in Central Asia. First he sent Zvi Melnitzer, who had just been evacuated from Uzbekistan, back to Bukhara to deliver a letter and gold coins to Ha'khalutz members and bring back information on the whereabouts of refugees who were movement members. "It was like jumping from the fifteenth floor," Melnitzer recalled, "but it was what Saul [Meirov] decided, and I did not argue."[94] After studying the topography and the activity on both sides of the border, Meirov determined that a nonlocal, particularly a European, could not safely cross from Iran to Central Asia, so he recruited "a local Jew." The recruit (Meirov's biographer gave no name) crossed the border carrying a Yiddish-language letter to movement activists. Neither this recruit nor others who were subsequently dispatched into Central Asia were ever heard from again.[95] "We made tremendous efforts to smuggle ourselves through the border, but we did not succeed. There were casualties. Emissaries were killed. It didn't help. They [the Soviets] guarded the border," Mossad LeAliyah Bet agent Nahum Herzberg later testified.[96]

Having failed to penetrate the Soviet Union, Meirov announced a new priority for Mossad LeAliyah Bet: to maintain uninterrupted contact with movement-member refugees across the border, whose addresses had been obtained through correspondence and information from family members, by sending them letters and packages. In November 1942 the Mossad LeAliyah Bet–friendly travel agency Peltours, which had connections with the Soviet Intourist Agency, delivered the first individual packages, requested and paid for by family and friends of refugees whose addresses were known. Workers organizations in Palestine also mounted fund-raising campaigns to finance parcels.[97]

=

In late October 1942 Moshe Shertok's wife and Meirov's sister, Zipora Shertok, arrived in Tehran to supervise the care of the refugee children and their transfer to Eretz Yisrael. She was the first and only Jewish representative from Palestine to enter Iran with an official visa, granted by A. Isfandiary, consul general for Iran in Jerusalem.[98] On her arrival, she reported that there were 807 children at the Jewish Children's Home in Tehran: 687 were healthy; thirty-six were in Tehran's hospital; thirty were at the camp's hospital; and thirty-nine were in insolation with scabies, eye disorders, and other infectious diseases. Two hundred additional children were in the Polish general camp, together with their parents or other adult caretakers. Shertok did not report on those with lodgings in Tehran, nor on the Jewish children in Polish orphanages or on converts to Catholicism.[99]

By the time Shertok arrived, the "mess and disorder" that Emil Landau had described in his first month at Dushan Tappeh were a bit alleviated, perhaps due to the Yom Kippur fund-raiser. White brick flooring had been installed inside the tents, and a regime of cleanliness was more or less enforced, but the hunger and boredom continued. "The bread portion disappears already after breakfast," Emil Landau wrote, "almost everyone goes to bed without dinner." He describes battles with the Polish refugees over food:

> The food is brought from the relatively distant camp kitchen. The way there passes through several barracks of Polish anti-Semites who tend to block the way. At six a.m., a whole battalion is needed to march there and fetch the food for 700 people. The fetchers sometimes have no shoes, no socks, and no warm shirts. They walk with rattling teeth, freezing.[100]

In her report to the Jewish Agency, Shertok's description of the children's diet and poor clothing echoed Landau's: "the children eat their bread portion at breakfast and are left without bread all day; not a quarter of them have more than one set of underwear; two hundred children are barefoot and the rest wear dilapidated shoes; no one has sweaters." In a letter to her children, she described "half naked children," waiting for their only shirt or undershirt to return from the laundry.[101] In a later report by Moshe Shertok, he confirms that three children died in the camp.[102] To these problems were added the dropping temperatures. "Winter has come," Emil wrote, "and now the cold has been added to the hunger. . . . Filth and scabies are everywhere. Who will go wash their clothing in zero-degree temperatures? . . . You cannot find a place for yourself all day. You feel as if your brain has frozen." "It is raining and extremely cold," another child wrote. "We do not leave our tents."

In mid-November, due to Shertok's pleas, the Jewish Agency transferred one thousand Palestinian liras to the Ottoman bank in Tehran for the purchase of "emergency needs of clothing and bedding for the children," but in the meantime, prices in Iran were rising, and supplies were disappearing from stores.[103]

"There are Agency funds," Dr. Hirschberg, whom Shertok now enlisted as something of an educational director for the children's home, wrote, "and the committee for refugees is also helping with money and with the connections it has with local merchants. . . . But it isn't easy to get large quantities of this merchandise at a reasonable price these days. Every merchant hides his merchandise and reneges on orders even if he agreed to them."[104]

The foreigners' demand for clothing and food products was said to have unhinged the markets: the German-Jewish refugees in Tehran, Dr. Hirschberg reported, told him of a 500 percent inflation since their arrival in the late 1930s. By mid-November, an American-British-Polish-Iranian committee was convened for the purpose of reducing prices of essential food products. They would achieve this reduction, they decided, by decreasing the daily adult refugee ration from 2,952 to 2,565 calories, with anyone over twelve considered an adult.

Prices did not cease to rise, shortages continued, and the local population began turning against the refugees. Persian presses became openly antagonistic, calling the refugees "the parasites of the Allies." In Tehran, antirefugee graffiti began to appear nightly: "all of Persia is hungry as it watches the Poles and the British eat its bread," Emil wrote. Looting followed, the foreign-run bakeries were burned, and demonstrations took place outside the palace of Muhammad Reza Shah. He in turn unleashed his forces against the demonstrators, killing dozens. The local anger was not directed particularly at Jewish refugees, a JDC envoy wrote.[105]

British authorities placed the blame on the Polish *delegatura* and on Polish refugee camp commanders "who purchased large quantities of supplies on the open and on the black markets at any price and contributed very much to driving prices of products in Tehran 'sky high.'" In newspaper reports, American Red Cross officials blamed British forces, attributing the wheat shortage in Tehran and other cities to "the excessive use of the local supplies by the British Army and by the Poles," to "hoarding," and to corruption.[106]

At the Archives of Diplomatic History in Tehran, Salar found dozens of documents regarding the day-to-day dealings of Polish refugees in the city, about their illnesses and treatments, about their workplaces. He found complaints about the damage Polish refugees had done to an apartment, and about Polish officers buying in the black market and causing prices to rise. At an August 22, 1942, meeting, Iranian ministers discussed moving Polish refugees out of Tehran and dispersing them across Iran to combat food shortages.

The Poles, on their end, denied the accusations. On October 21, 1942, in the Iranian newspaper *Setareh,* the Polish embassy in Iran refuted the allegations that the scarcities and price hikes in Tehran had to do with the presence of refugees. On October 27 the recently appointed commander in chief of the British Persia and Iraq Command, General Henry Maitland Wilson, complained to General Anders about "civilians living independently in Tehran and spending considerable sums of money there." Anders answered by blaming the NKVD and the Jews:

> [Anders] explained that there were a number of these, Jews in particular, who have probably deserted from trains, convoys, etc., and are living here without permission . . . General Anders explained that during the evacuation from Russia, the Russian NKVD had secretly sent people out with the Polish troops, and it was known that these were living in Tehran and have at their disposal considerable sums of money. It is known also that a number of Russians who came out with the second evacuation were discovered. . . . It is thought possible that these are the people who are spending considerable sums of money and not the Poles.[107]

Only ten thousand refugees were to remain in Iran after December 1, 1942, according to the original agreements between the British and the Iranian government, and within days, the British ambassador Sir Bullard announced that his government was "most anxious" to move twenty-six thousand Polish refugees out of Iran "if for no other reason than to placate the Iranians."

At Dushan Tappeh, Zipora Shertok too pressed her husband, who was in London, to facilitate the children's transfer to Palestine immediately, warning him that if the Agency waited until spring, the children might not survive the Tehran winter, or they could be sent to other destinations of Polish refugees. By September 30, 1942, 8,727 refugees had already been transferred to Nairobi, Tanganyika (now Tanzania), and Uganda.[108] Negotiations were in full swing for transferring the rest to India, Mexico, and Lebanon.[109] By late December 1942, roughly three thousand people remained at Camp no. 2 in Dushan Tappeh, including nearly one thousand at the Jewish Children's Home.

By September 1942, the Jewish Agency managed to secure from the British Immigration Department in Palestine eight hundred B3 certificates— for students who had been accepted at educational institutions and whose maintenance was guaranteed. The JDC had pledged to cover transport costs and confirmed in October that it was "working with [the Zionist women's organization] Hadassah to bring eight hundred orphan Jewish children from Tehran to Palestine," and that it would meet "the entire cost of [their] transportation."[110] The Agency's Youth Aliyah (Youth Immigration) department, under the leadership of Hadassah founder Henrietta Szold, had begun to prepare for the children's future in Eretz Yisrael. "There is tremendous willingness in the public to help in any way: with money, with adoption of children, with any preparations," Szold wrote Zipora Shertok. "We follow the news from Tehran directly. We feel your cold in Tehran, and all the discomforts that you are unable to appease."[111]

Twelve hundred miles separated Tehran from Tel Aviv. But the road passed through Iraq, whose government, though under British control, refused to issue transit visas to the Palestine-bound Jewish children. Eighteen months earlier British forces had defeated the pro-Axis government of Rashid Ali al-Gaylani, an Arab nationalist who had volunteered Baghdad as a base of Nazi intelligence operations in the Middle East. The anti-Jewish pogroms known as Farhud followed, after which a pro-British government was installed. Al-Gaylani's strongholds and his imprint were nonetheless still tangible in Iraq and other Arab countries that opposed Zionist aims in Palestine.

In a meeting with Szaffar, the British chargé d'affaires in Tehran explained that Britain's treaty with the Iraqi government did not give it the right to grant transit visas and that doing so would weaken the position of the pro-British prime minister Nuri as-Said, who would be perceived as caving in to British and American pressure.[112]

In New York, the JDC appealed to the Polish ambassador to request Iraqi transit visas "on behalf of Polish children." It further asked the U.S. ambassador to Turkey, Laurence A. Steinhardt, to facilitate direct meetings with the "Iraqi Minister in Washington" or approach "friendly" foreign legations who might present the matter to the minister.[113]

Hadassah had independently appealed to Eleanor Roosevelt, whose husband was close to Steinhardt. The first lady appealed directly to the Iraqi prime minister on behalf of the children.[114]

As-Said, according to the British chargé d'affaires, was "annoyed and surprised" that such an appeal was made to him "at a time when it was important not to rouse Arab feelings." He replied that out of humanitarian concerns, he would have no objections to bringing the children to Iraq for the remainder of the war, "provided they would not be a burden on the Iraqi Government."

In late October, the State Department informed the JDC that "despite intervention by British and American representatives in Baghdad," the Iraqi government had issued a final refusal of transit visas. Unofficially, it was said that the Iraqi prime minister acquiesced to Jewish children quietly being transported on Polish or British Army trucks through Iraq. Rafael Szaffar, after a meeting with General Anders, announced that such a transport was "within the realm of possibilities." But the British chargé and the American ambassador told Szaffar that they were skeptical about the genuineness of the offer, and suggested that if it were accepted, it would be withdrawn. Moreover their respective armies would not supply the trucks to transport the "500 children." ("They always referred to 500 children and were surprised to learn that there were 1,000 children and 200 adults," Szaffar wrote.)[115] It was unclear who had caused the blockage: the Poles, the British, the JDC (which reportedly refused to pay bribery), or the Jewish Agency, which, anticipating future evacuations from Iran into Palestine, preferred to negotiate for an openly secure route of transport rather than a covert operation. In a report he would deliver six months later, Moshe Shertok would say that even David Ben-Gurion was not in favor of the children being transported through Iraq.[116] And so the option of a semi-clandestine transfer of the children through Iraq fell through.

The JDC reported on three more aborted proposals. A proposal to transport the children by land through Turkey fell through because Turkey was "in tacit support of the Moslem countries [and] would not grant transit visas." A sea route through the Mediterranean was considered but scrapped because a blockade would first have to be removed. And the notion of an airlift on any British planes "as can be commandeered for this purpose" was rejected by the British ambassador to the United States, Lord Halifax.[117]

In London, where Moshe Shertok had gone to bolster up attention to the extermination of European Jewry and efforts to allow Jews in danger to immigrate to Palestine, he discussed the children's transport with British Foreign Secretary Anthony Eden.[118]

"Could we perhaps evacuate [the children] with the Arabs who are going on pilgrimage [to Mecca]?" Zipora Shertok wrote.[119]

"There is no more talk of Palestine" Emil Landau summarized in his diary. "And anyway, during these days of war and peril, who will want to harbor a band of riff-raff? Never mind. We have suffered so much, we will suffer a little more. And after the war . . . these were the thoughts of the older and younger children. Apathy, an acceptance of fate, and a tiny sliver of hope, very small. Like anyone who has been through so much: we tolerate the situation."

===

In November 1942, the JDC dispatched Harry Viteles to Tehran to produce "a full report on the situation there" for the JDC, which, viewing

the children to be under the care of Polish authorities, had so far allo-
cated only limited funds to the Tehran Children's welfare.[120] Viteles, who
was the American general manager of the Central Bank for Cooperative
Institutions in Palestine, interviewed ninety people in Tehran, including
American, British, and Polish diplomatic and military personnel, Jewish
Agency workers, and members of the Iranian Jewish community.

The result of his research was a forty-seven-page, extremely detailed
report. The American Red Cross, he wrote, had distributed 750 tons of
food, two hundred tons of clothing, and roughly sixty tons of medica-
ments in the fall and winter of 1942. Out of an estimated $3 million worth
of aid, $1.6 million was earmarked for Polish refugees—including Polish
Jews—and stored in warehouses belonging to Poles.

The JDC had turned over ninety-eight separate consignments of supplies from relatives and friends of refugees to Polish authorities in the
United States, who were said to have shipped them to the USSR through
Tehran.[121] The Jewish Agency and the JDC gave $10,500 to the children's
home. The local Iranian and Iraqi Jewish community raised $14,500. In
addition to providing clothing, housing, and food, the Polish *delegatura*
paid an individual monthly stipend of $3 to each adult refugee and $1.50
to each child refugee.

Still, Viteles reported on December 31, 1942, that "the children were
hungry and clamored for bread."

The American Red Cross and nearly all non-Polish sources confirmed
to Viteles that "the Poles did discriminate against the Jews in granting relief in Tehran both as regards food and clothing"; that "the Polish administration was less concerned with the welfare and comfort of
the Jewish refugees than they were with that of non-Jews"; that non-Jews
were given "improved housing facilities," while Jewish children at Camp
no. 2 continued to "live under canvas"; that the Polish camp authorities
may have known in advance that two out of the three buildings they had
allotted for the Jewish Children's Home in Dushan Tappeh would be requisitioned by the Iranians two weeks later; that efforts to improve overcrowding and reduce the cold were undertaken first for non-Jews; and

that the best-equipped facilities for children, which were in Isfahan, were given to Catholic children.

I had hoped against hope to uncover a better story of Poles and Jews in Iran, but the evidence Viteles cited was unequivocally damning: the American Red Cross representatives, who routinely visited all five Polish refugee camps in Tehran, "insisted" on being quoted in the JDC report that in all the camps, non-Jews, particularly children, had "more blankets" and "more suitable clothing," than did children in the Jewish Children's Home. They drew particular attention to the unequal distribution of sweaters and to the fact that "Camp no. 1 gets better food" and "children in Camp no. 1 look better than those in the Jewish children's camp."

The Red Cross representatives also cited rampant "dishonesty, unfairness, inefficiency, waste and extreme selfishness" in the administration of all Polish refugee camps where, they said, administrators tried to pass off a shortage of three hundred tons of white flour with false receipts. They did not know the whereabouts of 147,000 sweaters that the American Red Cross and the British military had given the Polish Red Cross. And medicines and other supplies that had been given to the refugees "were later found being sold at high prices by the stores of Tehran," the Red Cross workers reported.

In March 1943 the British journalist James Aldridge confirmed the allegations in Viteles's report.[122] In June the Iranian consul in New York also confirmed Aldridge's findings to the Iranian Foreign Ministry. The consul had been waiting for a year to say something, he wrote, about abuses of "well to do women" and "officers" who used aid supplies "to better their situation."[123] Eight thousand British Army uniforms that had been given to refugees were seen being sold in a bazaar, and were still being sold there, he wrote. In his diary, Emil Landau alluded to the possibility of corruption among the Jewish home counselors. "The lack of clothing does not concern [the counselors]," he wrote, perhaps unfairly. "It is much easier and more profitable for them to go about their dealings and dark business, with which everyone is familiar."

Refugees from "all classes" of Jewish society in Tehran—Labor, Zionist, Bundists, and even Nationalists who were "staunch supporters of close cooperation and collaboration with the Polish Government"—told Viteles about discrimination in the distribution of aid in Central Asia. Iranian and British soldiers testified that during the March–April 1942 transports, Polish children had arrived in Pahlavi with boxes of Manischewitz matzos, and that refugees in general were wearing clothing with Hebrew trademarks allegedly sent for Jewish refugees from Palestine.

The Polish embassy for its part, submitted to the Polish Foreign Ministry in London a report on its treatment of Polish-Jewish refugees in which it continued to maintain that the law of the Republic of Poland was to not differentiate between Polish citizens based on ethnicity, religion, or race. Any such differentiation, it said, had been implemented by Soviet authorities, who had prevented Jews from enlisting in the Anders Army and from being evacuated to Iran. Anti-Semitism in the Anders Army had been treated by General Anders, as was evident in his November 10, 1941, orders to commanding officers to battle anti-Semitism. The Polish embassy had tried to facilitate the evacuation to Iran of four hundred additional Jewish refugees, it said, but Soviet authorities had blocked the effort. Still, it had managed to add to the lists some prominent Jews. Furthermore, it had tried to intervene on behalf of Polish Jews who had not been released from camps and prisons and others who had been arrested, and it had tried to appoint Jews to the *delegaturas* in the USSR but was prevented by Soviet authorities (citing several examples). As a whole, the Polish embassy had been the victim of Soviet propaganda and censorship that often erased references to the Polish ambassador's efforts on behalf of Polish Jews from briefs to foreign correspondents.[124]

The NKVD may have indeed worked to destabilize Polish authorities in Iran; Polish authorities may have even been scapegoated for the actions of the British or Soviet forces. But Viteles noted that even the director of the Polish Red Cross had admitted that much of the aid intended for Polish refugees in the USSR had not been delivered. Twelve hundred tons of supplies, including 1,250 individual food and clothing parcels from

the United States and Palestine, had been waiting for transportation for
five months or more, stored in Polish Red Cross warehouses in Tehran.
Another one thousand tons were waiting at the Persian Gulf port to be
transported to Tehran, and one thousand tons were en route from America.[125] Polish authorities claimed they lacked the trucks to transport supplies from Tehran to Ashkabad—most trucks had been requisitioned by
the Allied forces. But they had reportedly rejected American Red Cross
offers to itself deliver and distribute the aid in the USSR.

Combating the situation, Viteles wrote, was difficult. Trying to force
the Poles to "correct the injuries" would "take months of unpleasant
negotiations" and most likely have "negative consequences" for the Jewish
refugees themselves. The American Red Cross discouraged earmarking
supplies for Jews alone, and the Soviets prohibited it. As for the Jewish refugees in Iran, including the children, "the Jews must either supply what is
necessary," or accept that "the Jewish refugees, children and adults, have
to get along with insufficient and unsuitable food and clothing" until they
are evacuated to Palestine.

Unlike Zipora Shertok, Harry Viteles did not consider the conditions
under which the children lived to be dangerous or life threatening, even
in the winter months. If irregularities in the supply department and camp
kitchens were eliminated, he wrote, even the newly reduced daily food
rations, though not ideal for the younger children, would be sufficient for
maintenance. He included all manner of graphs, figures, and compari-
sons between the camp's children and the normal curve of development
of "Palestinian (Jewish) children" and "school children from Central
European countries." He found that 67.8 percent of all camp children
under the age of fourteen (238 out of 351) were "lower in height than the
prescribed size," while only 49.3 percent of the older children were "less
than normal," hypothesizing that the younger children, who were in the
midst of growing, suffered more from the lack of nutrients and were also
prone to more serious illnesses.

"Viteles has left Tehran armed with all kinds of charts, but is too busy
to offer real help," Zipora Shertok complained to the Agency in Jerusalem,

requesting more help.[126] But it wasn't just the American Viteles who was producing reports. So was the Jewish Agency: Rafael Szaffar, Dr. Hirschberg, David Lauenberg, the head of the Refugee Department at the Jewish Agency Eliyahu Dvorkin, the head of Youth Immigration Henrietta Szold, and even Zipora Shertok herself all wrote reports. Shertok not only submitted a final report of her stay in Tehran but also wrote long weekly letters to her own children in which she detailed everything the Tehran Children did, said, sang, wore, and complained of, every emotion they displayed, every anecdote.

Even after I read all the various reports—by Viteles, by the Polish embassy, by the Jewish Agency, Hirschberg, Herzberg, and Shertok—it was still not entirely clear to me why the children in Tehran continued to go hungry, cold, and barefoot. Perhaps having been rescued alive from the Soviet Union, and in light of increasing knowledge about the extermination of European Jews, their temporary welfare was no longer a priority to anyone, including Jewish organizations. Perhaps even the children themselves were too traumatized for self-care. After distributing shoes to the two- to seven-year olds, Zipora Shertok writes, "the children were so happy that they hid their shoes under their blankets and continued to walk barefoot."[127]

But regardless of how Hannan, Regina, Emma, Emil, and Alina now saw themselves—Polish citizens? Refugees? Saved children? Future children of the Land of Israel?—*they* were now being seen: observed, inspected, supervised, classified, routinized, in what David Lauenberg and others described as "care" and a "return to normal life" and what the philosopher Michel Foucault might have called "discipline." Lists, reports, assessments, classifications by age and gender, by degree of Zionist affiliation, by health and sickness, height and weight, intelligence and socio-economic background. It was a body of knowledge that not only assessed the one thousand children as potential citizens in a Jewish state but also constituted them as such citizens. And even more so, it was a process through which the counselors, emissaries, and adult refugees, as representatives of the Jewish state-in-becoming, were asserting *their* own new power as a body authorized to assess and dispense knowledge about their charges.

Reports and descriptions of the children's behavior in Tehran tended to focus on their unsocial behavior and psychological instability—"horrible state"; "like homeless people"; "full of suspicion"; "have learned that only the strong survive"; "they steal," "cheat," "lie"—as compared to "normal" behavior of children their age.[128] It was, in a sense, the most ordinary example of what Foucault called the "normalizing judgement," an impersonal exercise of agents of the liberal nation-state assessing and policing their subjects.[129]

Only there was no a priori nation-state, no liberal subject, only children without parents, without homes, vomited out by Polish-Catholic nationalism. The children were to fortify the nation, and the nation was to psychologically fortify them. Much of what plagued them was articulated by their caretakers as loss of identity. (Nahum Herzberg, an emissary from Palestine, reported that "most of the children, even fifteen and sixteen year olds," remembered no special Passover rituals that had been celebrated in their homes, and when told of new ways of celebrating Passover in Eretz Yisrael, they asked what the "old ways" had been.) And so, as it would be in displaced persons (DP) camps and other refugee centers in postwar Europe, rehabilitation of the children was tightly linked to a reclaiming of identity. "Within seven months, the miracle occurred, their self-respect was restored, and their longing for Israel emerged," Lauenberg observed.

It was difficult to read his and others' reports not only because by now I knew what my aunt and others truly thought of their supervisors but because this collective, nationalistic way of treatment seemed so limited, so impersonal, and so out of sync with my father's slightly mysterious, multifaceted identity. I had wanted to carefully trace this through his prewar life and his refugee journey rather than presuppose it, to "follow the actor himself," as the sociologist Rogers Brubaker writes. I had wanted to avoid labeling it, either as primordial and unchanging, or as "socially constructed." I had wanted my careful tracing of my father's footsteps—the turns and twists, the roads taken and not taken—to dictate my understanding of who he was and the options that had been available to him.

But now, at this juncture, there was only one option. "Maybe it's not good pedagogy to present only one side of a case," a Zionist teacher at a German DP camp would write several years later. "But we can't afford such luxuries. The children have nothing, nothing. What should we talk about—the blessings of Poland? They know them. Or the visas for America? They can't get them. The map of Eretz Yisrael is their salvation."[130]

≡

In Tehran, Saul Meirov's crew continued to send postcards, letters, and parcels across the Persian-Soviet border to refugees in Iran and Central Asia who were movement members. "The letters and the packages meant that Eretz Yisrael did not abandon them and that people are risking themselves for their sake," Shayke Viner testified.[131] The effort started small, as friends and family in kibbutzim in Palestine sent the men in Tehran the names and addresses of relatives they knew were in Central Asia, but it grew quickly. Mossad LeAliyah Bet people sent thousands of personalized postcards in Yiddish, Polish, and Hebrew, including, for morale, movement leaders' signatures or mentioning specific names that the recipient might know from prewar life in Poland, all while trying to avoid the Soviet censor. As Viner recalled,

> Every name raised associations. I knew if the person I am writing to is from a certain group, or an area in Poland, I would send that person regards from someone who would make him feel safe. If they were from Vilna, I would mention someone from Vilna who was in Eretz Yisrael. . . . It was a person they identified, and it was an expression of the solidarity of all of Israel. When they wrote back, I asked for more addresses, and I always asked that they share what they received with their 'family,' meaning their group members . . .[132]

During those months, Soviet authorities tolerated these exchanges.

By the middle of 1943, Mossad LeAliyah Bet was shipping roughly one thousand parcels per month from Iran to Central Asian refugees, the

Relief packages en route from Iran to the USSR

maximum the Soviet authorities allowed to enter, and the maximum the Iranian government allowed to be exported. The contents of the packages were designed for their exchange value. Recent evacuees from Central Asia who had made it into Tehran taught the senders that small things had the greatest value there: needles, buttons, string, shoes all had enormous resale value. Oils and butter were valuable too, boiled with large quantities of salt to preserve it. This became the standard package, which soon was being assembled by a crew of Persian-Jewish women who worked alongside Mossad LeAliyah Bet.

Many corners of the Jewish world, mostly in "Palestina" but also in America and South Africa, and members of all movements, sent Meirov's operation the last-known addresses of their refugee friends and family members, as well as funding. The Mossad sent packages "knowing that refugees moved often and that their addresses were far from secure," Viner wrote. "We shipped and hoped it got there. . . . Recipients would write back, confirming that, say, 'the piece of soap they had received was a holiday for them,' and in this way their address was confirmed."[33]

"From the moment Saul [Meirov] started sending us packages from Teh-ran, we began to feel better," Yaacov Yanai testified years later, of receiv-ing a parcel in Bukhara. Yanai's sister was a member of Kibbutz Degania and had written to Meirov personally to aid her brother. I read dozens of such testimonies: men and women who often knew each other intimately, former members of Zionist movements and later in Israel members of kibbutzim who in their interviews referred to each other as close friends: Viner, Agami, Dvorkin, Herzberg, and Leybaleh Slovah, Yonah Rosen-feld, Zvi Hassa Goldfarb, Zipora Feldman Nussbaum, Ziskind Mitkovsky, Bronca Zlotincky. Rescuers—those who risked their lives to steal across the Russian border and those who packed and sent life-saving packages— and refugees who had received the aid, often knew each other, if not by name then by association. Theirs was a story of commitment, solidarity, love even: packages that "rescued from illness, death, and arrest," pack-ages that "kept people alive and helped them maneuver their situation."[134]

It was a story of Zionist self-reliance. From the outset, Meirov objected to shipping any aid to refugees in the USSR via the Polish *delegaturas* and strove instead for an autonomous assembly line of shipping letters and packages through Soviet and Iranian customs and messengers who were recruited from time to time to personally transfer them. (Jewish-American soldiers delivered Lend-Lease supplies from the United States, through Iran, and into the Soviet Union. A Polish colonel, Josef Rudnicki, was said to have acted as liaison to "friends" in the Soviet Union.) But it was also a story of solidarity and self-sacrifice: those who were caught were jailed and tortured for their Zionist activities, and would spend years in the gulags, particu-larly after the war. People like Bronca Zlotincky, who would be so broken by years of starvation and torture that once she made it to Israel, would be hospitalized for the rest of her life. Those who belonged to movements and communes had friends who kept in contact with them and risked their lives to feed them. Their testimonies read much differently from those of unaffili-ated refugees like my father, but often they also paid a greater price.

═══

On December 29, 1942, a cable stamped by the Iranian censor was delivered to Zipora Shertok who, afraid to open it in front of the children, delayed reading it until she had returned to her room in Tehran at night.

AM INFORMED TRANSPORT AVAILABLE EARLY JANUARY. GET READY. SENIOR NAVAL OFFICER IN THE GULF INSTRUCTED CONTACT YOURSELF AND SZAFFAR. CABLE JERUSALEM WHETHER YOU INTEND ACCOMPANY THE CHILDREN OR RETURN OVER LAND. LOVE—MOSHE SHERTOK.[135]

Moshe Shertok, a pragmatic politician who favored diplomacy over armed conflict and in later day Israel would be remembered as a "weak," "unrealistic" politician, had been able, while in London, to solve the quandary of the children's transport.[136]

The child refugees of the Children's Home of Tehran, among them my father, were to be evacuated to Palestine by sea. "Thursday, January 1, 1943, isn't different from any other weekday," Emil wrote in his diary:

> Early wakeup, measly breakfast, frost. Nothing suggests any drama.... Suddenly, an announcement is made: "We leave for Palestina." The news bounces like thunder off the walls of the Children's Home and is carried on everyone's lips. Shouts of joy ... are heard from every corner. We run to the office like drunks to get the details. There will be two transports, and the first leaves already tomorrow. We are filled with joy. A sudden, unexpected happiness!

There were last-minute difficulties: after the children's transports were announced, Polish authorities demanded that seven male counselors be drafted into the Anders Army, including head of camp David Lauenberg and Zvi Melnitzer, who had joined Meirov's organization in Tehran: these young men had only been "lent" for work at the Jewish Orphanage, said the authorities.[137] Within days, Meirov had put the seven army-bound counselors on a train to Baghdad, where Mossad LeAliyah Bet agents and

Three girls on the day of leaving Tehran. Regina is in the middle.

local Iraqis hid them for six weeks. They were then driven to Palestine in British Army uniforms, as Solel Boneh soldiers headed home on leave.

The Polish authorities also summoned roughly one hundred of the boys born in 1926–27 to be examined for potential enlistment in the Anders Army's youth division. Also within days, those hundred children (my father was not among them because his year of birth had been listed as 1928) were released, reportedly through the intervention of the head of the Polish *delegatura*, a converted Jew named Bader.

The children had to pass examination by a British medical committee: those with scabies had to wait for a second transport and were negotiated over. "There is complete chaos. The Poles complain that they've not seen such a transport. But whatever happens, Palestine isn't Africa!" Emil Landau wrote. "Our cars drive through the empty streets of Tehran, which are now under curfew. Once in a while police guards stop us. In the train station, modern and elegant . . . there is the same chaos as in the camp."

Upon hearing news that the Jewish children were to be evacuated to Palestine, other Jewish refugees—living in the Polish camps or in Tehran—rushed to join: "the cars are packed, and every minute new passengers arrive. Names are read out of order," Emil wrote. Some Jewish soldiers of the Anders Army got their children onto the train; some jumped onto the train themselves.

"At nine the engine blows and we are on our way: the last leg of the Great Journey," Emil wrote in his diary. Zipora Shertok cabled her husband: 600 CHILDREN 60 GUARDIANS LEFT LAST NIGHT FOR AHVAZ BY TRAIN. OTHERS LEAVE NEXT FEW DAYS. GOD HELP YOU . . . CONVEYS THANKS ON BEHALF OF YOUR EFFORTS CROWNED SUCCESS.[138]

The children, including my father, arrived at Ahvaz, in southwestern Iran, on January 4, 1943. There they were told that the journey to Palestine had been canceled; Egypt was reluctant to allow them to pass through the Suez Canal. The children would instead sail to India, where they would remain until the end of the war.[139] Zipora Shertok refused to allow the children to be moved and insisted that they stay in Ahvaz for the remainder of the war if they had to. The children remained at the train station in Ahvaz for five days, when Moshe Shertok cabled from London to confirm that they would sail to Karachi but would continue from there to Palestine.[140]

My father and the other children traveled to Bandar Shahpur (now Bandar-e Emam Khomeyni) on the Persian Gulf, where an out-of-service British cargo ship, the *Dunera*, was docked. On shore were three Solel Boneh men from Abadan—Meirov's recruits—who were to help those without proper documentation board the ship. They pulled aside two Indian soldiers and asked them to bring back the documents of children who had boarded so they could be given to others. "Each of them would take two children, then return their documents to us. They did it without any payment or promise of remuneration," Zalman Schar, one of the handlers, testified. At the end they simply shoved undocumented refugees—roughly 140 of them—through the ship's windows. Some were able to hide quickly; others were moved into a British police boat, screaming and weeping.[141] When the *Dunera* disappeared, Szaffar cabled the JDC offices in New York:

1231 REFUGEES INCLUDING 836 CHILDREN LEFT FOR PALESTINE. ON BEHALF OF THE REFUGEES I WISH TO EXPRESS TO YOU OUR THANKS FOR YOUR HELP.[142]

=

After the Jewish children's departure from Iran, thousands of sweaters and articles of clothing appeared in the bazaars of Tehran, Isfahan, and Mashhad, a shocking sight that elderly Persians like Heshmat Kermanshahi and others confirmed in testimonies and interviews.

Polish officials, including all five heads of Polish refugee camps in Tehran, were arrested for charges of corruption, embezzlement, and abuse of power, Viteles reported.[143]

Roughly 120 children remained in the Jewish Children's Home, including those deemed too ill to travel. Others were new arrivals, including thirty who had traveled from Turkmenistan to Mashhad on December 6 as part of a transport of 250 Polish children, then continued on to Tehran. Among the newcomers was Hannan's cousin on his mother's side, Sarah Halberstadt, whose parents had died in Samarqand and whose older brother remained there. These remaining children would be shepherded to Palestine through Iraq by the Polish Red Cross, according to an agreement negotiated by General Sikorski.[144]

Four to five hundred adult Jewish refugees waited in Tehran for certificates to go to Palestine; three hundred others who had certificates waited for transport. At least two hundred, Viteles reported, remained in Tehran and did not wish to go to Palestine.

Saul Meirov also remained in Tehran, continuing his efforts to reach the Jewish refugees in Central Asia. He recruited a Jewish-American soldier named Mendelsohn to deliver dispatches to Ha'khalutz members aboard American military supply convoys. He also approached Soviet officials in Tehran with a proposal that the kibbutzim in Palestine would

contribute food and supplies to the Red Army in exchange for the evacuation of Ha'khalutz members. Nothing bore results. "We understood
finally that the dream to open a crack through which our friends could
escape from Russia was unattainable," Meirov wrote. And so, in the pragmatic and unrelenting manner that characterized him, he turned to an
attainable goal: persuading Jewish soldiers of the Anders Army to desert
for Palestine and join the Haganah.[145]

After Viteles's report, the JDC announced that it was halting its cooperation with the Polish government-in-exile and was considering new tactics of
aid. In Montreal, the Canadian United Jewish Relief purchased medicines
that would be transferred to the USSR via the Canadian Red Cross. In New
York, the JDC signed an agreement with the Œuvre de Secours aux Enfants
(OSE), a French-Jewish humanitarian organization that specialized in medical assistance to war-stricken areas and that had "intimate familiarity with
the refugee conditions in Russia," as the JDC stated.[146] And it began paying
for up to 50 percent of the cost of each parcel sent by the Jewish Agency,
adding 90,000 Palestinian liras (46,000 of which were collected from relatives in the United States) to the 35,000 liras collected from relatives, workers unions, and Va'ad ha'Hatzala (the Rescue Committee) in Palestine.

By the end of 1943, fearing that the Jewish Agency would get booted
out of Iran for political reasons, the JDC took over operations of the package program. It reportedly reached a deal with the Iranian government
according to which it would be allowed to import into Iran supplies from
any part of the world without having to pay customs duty; it terminated the
agreement with the shipping company Peltours and opened its own parcels office; it accredited JDC warehouses in Tehran as customs branches so
that parcels would not have to be removed elsewhere for inspection before
leaving Iran; it arranged with Russian military authorities in Tehran to
facilitate transport of supplies arriving at the Iranian borders; and it negotiated a fixed, simplified system of paying a Soviet duty based on the price
of the goods purchased and not on their value in Iran. It bought supplies
in India, Palestine, Egypt, and South Africa. It contacted the Jewish Relief

Association in Bombay, the South African War Appeal, and the United Jewish Relief Fund in Melbourne, which each contributed connections and funds. It created an advisory committee in Jerusalem, where fund-raising campaigns continued.

All this reduced shipping time to three weeks, and by the beginning of 1944, the monthly package shipments increased from one thousand to ten thousand. As of March 1945, the JDC spent $2 million to pay for individual parcels from Iran to the USSR, in addition to $500,000 for commodities shipped in bulk from the United States to the Russian Red Cross, to be distributed in areas where Jewish refugees and evacuees were concentrated.[147] As it confirmed in a June 25, 1944, letter, the JDC's "Tehran Office" continued to work in "full cooperation" with the Polish Red Cross; as a result, it sent relief parcels to a "considerable number of Polish refugees of non-Jewish origin."[148]

Although some feared that the JDC would receive sole credit for the package program that the Jewish Agency had started, Meirov gladly relinquished his organization's list of roughly sixty thousand names and addresses in Central Asia to the JDC and lauded its ambition to reach a greater number of refugees. He did not, like some others, reject the nonpolitical, purely charitable ideals at the heart of the JDC's efforts. But his own ideals, and those of all strands of the Zionist movement, were much different: the desire for what the philosopher Sir Isaiah Berlin had called "positive freedom": Jewish self-determination, action that would lead to the Jewish people taking control over their own destiny.[149]

At the beginning of the twentieth century, "this mere will to action [of the Zionist Movement]," Hannah Arendt wrote, had been "something so startlingly new, so utterly revolutionary in Jewish life, that it spread with the speed of wildfire."[150] Hundreds of thousands of Jewish youth joined the various Zionist movements in Poland. Now that Poland was under Nazi occupation, Meirov and the Agency knew that these youth would likely not be coming to Eretz Yisrael after the war, or ever; many would also perish in the Soviet Union, and those who survived might remain behind its hermetically sealed wall or be lost to Communism. The pain of the situation was personal: like most members of the Jewish population of Palestine, Meirov, Shertok, and others had family in Europe. But the problem of replenishing the reserves of the Zionist movements was also a national and political one. Most European Jews had been lost, but another group stood before Meirov free and unencumbered: the Jews of Iran whom he "discovered" when coming to the aid of Polish refugees like my father.

Ironically it was Tehran, as one Mossad LeAliyah Bet and Ha'khalutz member put it, that became "the beginning of Zionism as a 'movement of the masses.' Like all youth movements we spoke about 'the masses' . . . but our notion was of an anonymous mass. . . . We were an elite group. The real meaning of the masses, just regular Jews, we saw for the first time in Tehran." In Tehran, as well as in Hamadan, Isfahan, and Abadan, Mossad LeAliyah Bet agents established Hebrew study groups and translated Zionist booklets into Persian.

After British intelligence intercepted information about German plans to incite Persian pro-Nazi groups to commit acts of violence against Persian Jews, Efraim Shiloh, a Haganah commander, began training local youth in face-to-face combat and handling the few pistols they had. When

Persian-Jewish children celebrating the agricultural holiday of Tu BiShvat, *1944*

it was reported that pro-German underground activities were intensify-
ing among the Bakhtiari tribe of Luristan, in southeastern Iran, Shiloh
developed a self-defense program—with "5–6 pistols, 2 or 3 guns, a few
homemade bombs . . . and rocks, loud noises, and boiling oil and water"—
for nearly one hundred young volunteers, students at Tehran University.[151]

The JDC's worries that the Jewish Agency would get booted out of Iran
were not realized. There were problems, tensions, and setbacks, but Hebrew
teaching was intensified, new emissaries came who continued to organize
the local community, and some local youth themselves joined Mossad
LeAliyah Bet. In March 1943 the Eretz Yisrael office threw a Purim party
and invited Polish and British officials—and any non-Jews who wanted to
join. From that point on, Meirov, and later his replacements Nahum Herzberg and Moshe Yishai, began to develop the Agency's diplomatic ties with
British, Soviet, and Persian officials in Tehran.[152] Notably, relations and
cooperation with Polish intelligence and diplomatic staff thawed considerably in Tehran once Jewish refugees began to be represented by the Jewish
Agency and Mossad L'Aliyah Bet. In late 1944, a memorial service for Jews
killed by the Nazis in the Warsaw ghetto took place in a Tehran synagogue,
most likely at Haim and Danial, in which Yishai sat side by side with the
Polish Consul and translated the Yiddish speeches for him.[153] In late 1944
Yishai would meet with twenty-four-year-old Reza Shah, "as a Jew, an
emissary from Eretz Yisrael, and a representative of the Jewish people." "I
knew that a simple visit would not be viable," Yishai recalled in his memoir, "and that when all Muslim countries are opposed to our movement,
it is unfathomable and would appear as a provocation against the Arab
world if the shah would honor the Agency." Instead Yishai presented the
shah with "a token of the cultural ties between the two ancient nations":
Hebrew translations of Omar Khayyam and Firdausi. The parchment on
which the bilingual poems were copied was delivered inside a silver box
engraved with a phrase from the Book of Ezra: "This is what Cyrus king
of Persia says: 'The LORD, the God of heaven, has given me all the king-
doms of the earth and he has appointed me to build a temple for him at
Jerusalem in Judah.' "[154]

"Yishai did a tremendous thing," Heshmat Kermanshahi, the Persian industrialist I interviewed in Los Angeles, told me. "His visit with the shah changed everything."

Kermanshahi, and the Persian-Jewish community as a whole, would prosper in the postwar years. The JDC, which had come to Iran to aid Polish refugees, would continue supporting its poor, its schools, and its various initiatives. And starting in the 1960s, Israel itself would have a significant presence in Iran, as its engineers, military experts, architects, artisans, businessmen, laborers, and agricultural specialists replaced Germany's as the country's modernizers. In the summer of 1978, the Israeli embassy would run a film festival, screening Israeli films on the outer walls of its building. The highlight of the festival would be *Operation Thunderbolt*, a film about the Entebbe Rescue. "Thousands of Persians sat around us and watched," a former embassy worker recounts in the documentary *Before the Revolution*. "In the scene in which Israeli forces storm the Entebbe terminal, they clapped, and in the scene when Yoni [Yehonatan Netanyahu, brother of Benjamin] dies, a cry was heard from all the roofs above us." A month later revolutionaries would begin to clash with royalists, the Israeli embassy closed, and the Israeli workers were gone. But wounded revolutionaries who were denied care at government hospitals would be treated at the Jewish Mahalleh Hospital, which, after the war, would be renamed Sapir Hospital and Charity Center after Dr. Ruhollah Sapir. Sapir died in late 1942 from the typhus he contracted while treating the refugees.[155]

Scores of refugees, among them my aunt Regina who was ill with trachoma, were cared for at the Mahalleh and other hospitals in Tehran. Many, like Sapir, died of typhus. When Salar visited Beheshtieh, Tehran's Jewish cemetery, he lit a candle and sent me photos of the graves of ADLER ADOLF 1912–1942; RUBINSTEIN RACHELA 1875–1942; MIGDAL TERESA 1941–1942; KLEIN HELENA 1928–1942; SIERAKOVSKA SOLA 1940–1942; BEDER SZLAMA 1905–1942; and many more, graves that still stood in Tehran, unvisited. On all the graves was the letter *J*, a Star of David, and the letter *P* for Poland. On all were the Hebrew letters תנצבה: MAY THE SOUL BE BOUND UP IN THE BOND OF EVERLASTING LIFE.

HEBREW CHILDREN

Kibbutz Ein Harod

W hat might have been a forty-eight-hour drive from Tehran to Tel Aviv took forty-eight days by sea.

After boarding in Bandar Shahpur along with a few thousand British soldiers, my father and the rest of the children sailed through the Persian Gulf into the Strait of Hormuz, where their ship, the *Dunera*, fearing German torpedoes, dropped anchor and waited to join a convoy of other ships that snaked slowly into the Gulf of Oman. It rained, the sea was choppy, and waves washed on deck and pounded against the cabin windows, where the children slept on hammocks. Up ahead, smoke rose from the chimneys of the first ships in their convoy. In an attempt to circumvent possible torpedoes and landmines, the *Dunera* zigzagged constantly. On the second day of sail, the children were given life vests and ordered to carry them at all times. On the fourth day, an alarm went off, and they were ordered to wear their life vests and descend into the cabin. There was panic, crying, screaming. The chaperones, as an inquiry would later find, were helpless, anxious, even violent. Nearly all were seasick and vomiting.[1]

Sixteen-year-old Jocek Shenkelbach saw a burning ship from afar, and a British Red Cross ship sailing past them carrying soldiers wounded in Burma. None of the children could eat much—nearly all were contorted on the floor, vomiting—nor even drink the cans of sweet milk they had been given by the British soldiers, who dumped tons of spoiled food into the sea each night—"if only we could send it to our parents in Russia."[2] On January 22, 1943, they reached Karachi, where Polish refugees and Anders Army soldiers, who had come there directly from Central Asia or arrived from Iran before them, were already housed in an enormous British-American military camp. In Karachi, as well as in Lahore and other cities in Colonial India, there were Jewish refugees from Germany and elsewhere, as well as civilian Polish refugees.[3]

My father was taken straight into a special "Jewish" section that had been prepared in advance for him and the other children. They underwent the now routine disinfection, examination, and quarantine, transfer of the sick to hospitals, and return to life under canvas. But the tents, unlike those in Iran, were clean and comfortable, with eight to ten children in each; cans of fried fish, sardines, and Australian cheese were plentiful. The clothing was improved—ten truckloads of khaki uniforms and cork helmets, courtesy of the Bombay-based "Rothschilds of the East" Sassoon family. And the camp's leadership, in the person of Sergeant Major Joe Berger, an American, was friendlier.

"We could hardly believe our eyes: a Jewish camp commander from Brooklyn in an American military camp in India," Josek Klapholz wrote in his memoir. "He spoke good Yiddish, and we immediately told him about the battles over food and the beatings we suffered from the Polish children. Joe listened, and we knew our day of revenge had come." Within a day, Joe Berger appointed a "militia" from among the Jewish boys sixteen or older, who wore Military Police armbands and conducted daily inspections of cleanliness and order. "It was found, not once or twice but in truth every day, that the tents of the Poles, including those of the families of Polish officers, were untidy, in which cases the entire tent would be collapsed on top of its inhabitants. There was shouting and crying, but it did not matter. Our revenge was justified by any scale of justice."[4]

Seventeen-year-old Klapholz (now a Tel Aviv lawyer named Yosef Etzion) had a great time in India. On my visit to his palatial Tel Aviv apartment, the elegant, whimsical eighty-something-year-old man gave me a draft of his memoir, in which he described his adventures in Karachi's streets, bazaars, and Buddhist temples. Young Klapholz admired "the sari-clad women," "the cows that strode peacefully on Karachi's streets," the "sad Indian music," the "dances with snakes." He had money ("one of the boys received a sum from an American relative") and stocked up on soap ("we heard there was a shortage in Palestine"). His narrative, in India, changes from refugee memoir to the travelogue of a cosmopolitan tourist.

I wondered what had propelled the change: the sufficiency of food? The reassuring presence of Sergeant Major Joe Berger, "the father and mother of the camp"? Klapholz's urbane Krakow upbringing? His naturally cheerful nature or a basic "resilience," a term that in 2018 was increasingly used to classify those who emerge less scathed than others from traumatic events? And I wondered where Hannan had been in India. There is an iconic photo of the children in the camp in Karachi, in shorts and cork helmets, doing jumping jacks, but Hannan is not in it. Did my father share some of Klapholz's adventures in the fourteen days they spent in Karachi? He loved to travel; I hoped he did.[5]

On February 6 Klapholz, my father, and 857 other children—one girl remained in India after being reunited with relatives—and 358 adults boarded the *HMS Neuralia*, a 500-foot World War I cargo vessel owned by the British India Steam Navigation Company, which was packed with Indian laborers, "large, rude, redheaded Irish" sailors, and military supplies and equipment.[6] Again they sailed in a convoy: cargo ships, merchant ships, "heavy artillery destroyers," and "nimble mine plucking ships" sailed ahead, scouting for deep-water sea mines that were said to have been planted in the Indian Ocean by Japanese torpedoes. "It was a breath stopping, awesome sight: petrifying warships with their cannons aimed at the sea expanse, gliding on the quiet waters," Klapholz wrote. Both Japanese submarine cruisers and German raiders were patrolling the Indian Ocean; seventy Allied ships were sunk there in 1942 alone.[7]

Japanese planes bombed their convoy but caused little damage and were chased away by British fighters. A typhoon dumped torrents of rain on their ship: "It looked like the windows were exploding; it got darker, and the waves pounded the boat with tremendous force." But they sailed through the storm and made it to the Port of Aden, Yemen, a city built on a cliff, where the *Neuralia* was refueled and repaired.

At Aden, fearing a hostile local Arab population, the children were told to hide in the lower cabin, but within minutes they were surrounded by dozens of local children, not at all hostile but emaciated and begging for food.[8] "We went to the kitchen, fetched leftovers and tossed them at the kids," Klapholz recalled. "They caught what they could and dived into the sea to collect the rest." It was the first time on their three-and-a-half-year ordeal that they contemplated that there could be fates in this world that were worse than their own. After a two-day stop in Yemen, they sailed aboard the *Neuralia* for six more days, arriving at El Qantarah el-Sharqiyya, a town at the northern terminus of the Suez Canal, on February 18. Their journey from Poland to Palestine had covered roughly thirteen thousand miles, half the earth's circumference.

$$\equiv$$

El Qantarah el-Sharqiyya, or El Kantara, as the Allied troops called it, was a main supply hub for the Allies' North African Campaign and was swarming with soldiers. Amid them, the sight of 859 children and toddlers in British military sweaters and old Macy's blouses and jackets presented a strange and pathetic sight that many Jewish Engineering Corps soldiers, who knew of the children's arrival and waited for them, later described in various recollections. "We are waiting at the port, tense and silent. Soon they will arrive," Lieutenant A. Ben Moshe wrote in the February 1943 issue of *Ba-makhaneh* (The Camp), the battalion's journal. "When the first boat approaches, a tragic spectacle reveals itself before our eyes: children, babies, barefoot and half naked; adolescents jumping on shore with torn bags, looking at us fearful and suspicious when we approach to help them. . . . We are shaken . . . tears choke us. They're our flesh and blood."[9] Lova Eliav, a future Israeli Labor party politician, recalled that at El Kantara, "we began to feel truly and deeply that this war had a Jewish aspect and that our service had an aim that was unique and particular only to us." He and others reported that they were overcome with emotion, hugged the children, showered them with fruit and candy, and after several hours helped them board the Palestinian railway train that would transport them to their new life.[10]

In New York, Montreal, Argentina, and London, champagne poured, ecstatic phone calls were made, and congratulatory and thankful letters were exchanged. Hadassah president Gisela Warburg wrote to Eleanor Roosevelt, while the children were still in transit:

> You will be delighted to know that the 835 Polish Jewish refugee chil-
> dren who had been stranded in Teheran, and in whose fate you took
> such a deep interest, are about to arrive in Haifa. . . . [Today we won-
> der] what will be most retained in the minds of these children—the
> hatred that sought to destroy, or the love that sought to save them?[11]

The children's train traveled from night to dawn along the northern peninsula of the Sinai desert, through Al Arish and the Gaza Strip, stopping first in Egyptian towns, then, and after crossing the border at Rafah, in Palestinian and Jewish villages. I had been in the Sinai desert many times in my youth—it was my favorite landscape—and I imagined them staring at the long stretches of sand dunes, then at olive trees and prickly pear bushes, which they had never seen before. In Artuf, an Arab village, a reporter for the typically restrained Hebrew daily *Ha'aretz* boarded the train, publishing his impressions on the front cover of the next morning's issue under the giant headline CHILDREN OF ISRAEL SAVED FROM ORPHANHOOD AND BROUGHT TO ERETZ YISRAEL. "When [the train] stopped at the station, with a full moon hanging above, I saw hundreds of faces looking through the windows and shivers ran through my body," the reporter wrote. "The children asked: 'Do Jews live here?' I answered, 'Not here, but you'll soon stop in Rehovot. There only Jews live.'"[12]

By the time of my father's arrival, the Yishuv (the Jewish population of Palestine) had a quasi-government (the Jewish Agency), labor unions, and ties with Zionist youth movements that had swept up hundreds of thousands of eastern and to a lesser degree western European Jewish youth.

It had already erected universities, factories, banks, moshavim (villages), kibbutzim, and cities like Tel Aviv and Rehovot, where the crowds lined up on either side of the tracks, waving and shouting at the children in Hebrew. The Yishuv was already locked in deadly conflict with the local Palestinians and the British government of Palestine.

In Hadera, a second Jewish town they passed, local children rode on their parents' shoulders trying to reach out and touch the children inside the trains, and adults asked for their names, hoping to find an acquaintance or a family relative. Some of the children inside the train craned their necks to get a better look at the scene outside or to grab some of the candy and peanuts that were thrown at them. The *Palestine Post*, an English-language daily, reported on an older woman who was crying hysterically and pushing away the candy and the nuts, and on a boy who, when "asked innocently about his parents" by a girl who had recognized him as a former neighbor, answered, "choked by sobs," that he had "seen them murdered by Nazis."[13] *Ha'aretz* as well reported of "astounding, uplifting spectacles at receptions" in towns and villages along their route.[14]

Crowds waiting for the children's train in Hadera, February 19, 1943

I have a photo of Regina from the day of her arrival in Palestine, February 19, 1943, the one Henryk Grynberg had given me years earlier, on the cover of *Children of Zion*'s German translation. I did not know then that it was taken on the train that transported Regina, Hannan, and Emma to a British internment camp in Atlit, a small northern coastal town near Haifa. I now knew that the oversize woman's jacket Regina was wearing must have been donated to the JDC, which had shipped it to Iran or to Karachi. I knew she was wearing a headscarf because her scalp was infested with lice. I saw that she was leaning a tiny, sharp chin on the train's windowsill, and noted that above her were an adult woman and three girls, with only one of them smiling a nervous half-smile. The adult, whose age could have been anywhere from thirty to fifty, was squinting as if blinded by strong sunlight, although the photo was taken in early dawn. Regina did not look jubilant. She looked despondent, anxious, her blue eyes half shut, her forehead wrinkled.

The new arrivals looking out the train window. Regina is at the bottom left.

The testimonies in *Children of Zion* revealed nothing of the ecstatic celebrations and receptions of the children. They were merely factual:

I was in Tehran for several months and from there I came to Palestine with a group of Jewish children.

In February 1943, after several months in Tehran, we arrived in Palestine.

We left Tehran, and in February 1943 I arrived with my sisters Miriam and Zipora in Palestine (Palestyny).

I came to Palestine with my younger brother Joseph. Saul, my younger brother, remained in Tehran because he was gravely ill.[15]

But a seven-minute newsreel titled *Tehran Children Arriving in Atlit, 1943* shows children huddled anxiously and excitedly together inside the train. The footage was taken from a special edition of *Carmel Diary*, a newscast that in the 1940s was screened before main features in movie houses at major Jewish cities. It was shot from within the train as it moved through Jewish cities. It shows no Arab villages or cities. It shows local preschool children lined up with bouquets of wildflowers and adults holding Hebrew banners: KI LANU HA-ERETZ HAZOT (For this land is ours), ERETZ YISRAEL AKHREI HAKOL (The Land of Israel, after all), and BRUKHIM HA-BA'IM (Welcome). The children are then shown descending from the train in Atlit and being boarded onto buses in a melee of flags, speeches, and a singing of the national anthem, "Hatikvah" (The Hope). The footage is silent and narrated by an elated voiceover: "Full of happy feelings as their wanderings have ended, they have arrived at their longed-for destination. These Hebrew children will receive a Hebrew education in the free environment of the budding Homeland. A Hebrew teacher meets them, a Hebrew policeman chats with them. . . . [They] are *olim* from Tehran."[16]

Olim is Hebrew for "ascenders," a term for newcomers "ascending" to the Land of Israel. *Olim* are the opposite of refugees: displaced persons who have been forced to flee from their home and who cannot return to it safely. *Olim* are those who have come home.

Waiting at the Atlit internment camp for them was Henrietta Szold, head of the Jewish Agency's department of Youth Aliyah (Youth Migration). Now age eighty-two, Szold had been involved in Jewish refugees aid since survivors of the Kiev pogroms arrived in her hometown of Baltimore in the 1880s. In Palestine, where she moved at age sixty, she founded hospitals, food distribution programs, mother-infant wellness stations, social service networks, and with Judah Magnes, Ernst Simon, and Martin Buber, a binationalist political party called Ichud, which advocated the creation of an Arab-Jewish state within a broader Arab federation. As head of youth immigration, Szold prepared placements in schools, foster homes, and kibbutzim for children and adolescents who arrived in

Children waiting to be transported to the Atlit internment camp

Palestine unaccompanied. She had been a major voice for bringing the Tehran Children to Palestine. "These children are not refugees," she said in a public lecture in Tel Aviv shortly before my father's arrival. "They are *olim*, and our attitude and commitment toward them should be as it is for *olim*. We are all *olim*; the country (*eretz*) needs *olim*."[17] Now she was assembled alongside Moshe Shertok and other Zionist politicians, activists, and even members of the local British administration to welcome the children she fought to care for.

≡

The Atlit internment camp, where my father spent his first night in Palestine, was a British detention facility for illegal immigrants. For days Szold had fought the Mandatory government against interning the children there on their first night; having lost, she and her staff cleaned and swept the floors and covered each military cot with a starched sheet and a blanket. When the first Palestinian Railway train stopped at Atlit, the crowds on the platform burst into spontaneous singing of "Hatikvah," the national anthem. Szold's staff and medics helped the ill into Magen David ambulances, and the healthy into buses donated by a Haifa bus company, where each child received a small plastic Israeli flag that some waved through the windows at the crowds.

In the camp, the children were welcomed "home" by Dr. Bernard Joseph, acting head of the Jewish Agency's political department, and by other officials of the Agency's immigration department. Szold, who spoke last, greeted them in Hebrew: "I hope we will see each other on many occasions in the future, and I sincerely hope that you will become good citizens of Eretz Yisrael."[18] Two children, a girl and a boy, handed her the flowers they had just received from the crowds. A huge pile of oranges was laid out in the open—orange groves were plentiful in Palestine—and was consumed within seconds and expelled shortly afterward in a bout of collective vomiting that many of those I interviewed remembered vividly. Then the children were once more washed, disinfected, and immunized—the standard protocol for all immigrants entering British

Palestine—and were left to their own devices inside the barbed-wire camp, which is now the Museum of Illegal Immigration at Atlit.

In 2017 I visited the museum. I was, after all these years, now a tourist in my homeland, following my father's footsteps to places I had never been, or to ones I had visited but never quite seen. In my childhood, my father had driven us by the internment camp countless times, but he never pointed to it nor mentioned that he had been interned there. The museum seemed to me like a miniature Auschwitz-Birkenau, which I had visited on my first trip to Poland: rows of identical wooden barracks, a barbed-wire fence, a disinfection barrack. My son, who came with me, immediately wanted to leave and wait for me in the car.

I walked in and out of the rows of sleep barracks and into the brown, bare sanitation barrack where my father was stripped, washed, and sprayed with DDT. There were no other visitors that day. Then I walked along the barbed-wire fence, trying to see what they had seen on their first night in Palestine. On their second day in Palestine, my father's cousin Ze'ev (Wolf) Teitel would come visit his young cousins Hannan, Regina, and Emma. "As I approached the camp, I saw the three of them: hanging on the fence, miserable and pitiable."

In the *Ha'aretz* article, a ten-year-old boy was quoted as saying to the reporter: "It isn't true that we have come home. I don't have a home anymore."[19] And I wondered if my father, despite sleeping for the first time in over three years on a bed with a sheet and a blanket, felt the same or differently. A sliver of the Mediterranean Sea was visible from the yard between the barracks, and to the west was the lovely silhouette of the Carmel hills. But as I glanced at my teenage son, seated in the parking lot, singing and listening to Eminem, I wondered if it was possible really to know what my father felt when he arrived here.

In the museum's database were "Letters of Thanks to the Jewish Agency," including one from my father. His letter was opposite in tone and emphasis to the testimony he had given to the Polish Information Center. It was a succinct summary of his prewar and wartime experiences

and a long, detailed account of his arrival in Eretz Yisrael. He wrote the
letter in antiquated, ungrammatical Hebrew that nonetheless bore the
signature of his prose. It ended on an uncharacteristically emotional note:
"In the evening we came to Atlit. There we descended the train and felt
that from this moment on our lives will be different. No longer will we be
nomads and people without a roof on the hearth, for in our Homeland are
we." Signed "Teitel, Hannania, 21 February, 1943."

In the museum was also a database of certificates of arrival issued by
the British government during its thirty-one-year rule (1917–48) over
Palestine. My father's, Regina's, and Emma's B(3) entry certificates into
Palestine—given to school-age children whose sustenance was secured—
were there. Each had a fresh photo. All three of them look clean, almost
sparkling in the used sweaters and collared undershirts they must have
received on that February 1943 day. Regina's straw-colored hair is combed
back neatly and covered with a clean new scarf, and she is smiling, laughing even: a full-toothed smile with her large top incisors protruding.
Emma, looking sweet with her large brown eyes and dimples, is giggling.
My father, who seems a little feverish, is laughing too, his eyes twinkling.
They appear genuinely, wholeheartedly happy at that moment, despite
what their cousin Wolf had written.[20]

Hannan, Regina, and Noemi, Atlit, February 19, 1943

The next morning, the children were given letters addressed to them from relatives in Central Asia, sent to Iran and forwarded to Palestine. The children who received none cried or fell into gloomy silence. I do not know whether Hannan and Regina received a letter from Zindel and Ruchela. I do know that a letter from their parents had been sent to Iran and could have been forwarded to them in Atlit.

Nahum Herzberg, the Agency representative in Tehran, wrote to Zindel from Tehran, in Yiddish, on behalf of the "Yiddishe hilps cam-mitat par plitim fon Polin, Tehran" (the Jewish Agency Committee for Aiding Refugees from Poland, Tehran):

Mr. Z. Teitel
Uzbekistan
Samarqand
Esteemed Sir,
  Your letter of 15.2.43 was delivered to us. In response we inform you that your children, Regina and Henik, have left for Palestine on 6.1.43.
  They are well, are being well taken care of and are in good health.
  We have provided them with your address and we believe they will write to you soon. It is possible to write them at the below address (of Youth Aliyah in Jerusalem).
With good wishes,
N. Herzberg[21]

The handful of parents who were in Palestine came to Atlit to fetch their children; those became a cause célèbre and the greatest source of envy. The rest of the children fell into two subtly distinct groups: those with and without relatives in Palestine. Hannan, Regina, and Emma had two relatives: Ze'ev (Wolf) Teitel, Hannan's revered older cousin, who had been a civil engineering student at the Technikum in Haifa and remained in Palestine after the war broke out, and Riwka Zwykielski, a cousin of Zindel's who had emigrated to Palestine from Poland in 1928 to join Kibbutz Ein Harod. Both came to visit the children in Atlit.

≡

A year after my father was evacuated from Iran, 733 Polish "Children of Isfahan" and 102 caretakers were also evacuated. They were sent to New Zealand on the *USS General Randall*, along with returning New Zealand soldiers. Like my father in Palestine, they were met in Wellington by caretakers, nurses, and politicians. For these children too, thousands of locals lined up in the streets, waving white scarves and shouting as they rode to Pahiatua, the former foreign aliens prison camp that had been transformed into their housing. "The little girls and the boys with the shaven heads touch the hearts of New Zealand's people," a television broadcaster announces against the backdrop of New Zealanders hugging and carrying children in the 1966 documentary *Poles Apart: The Story of 733 Polish Orphans*. "New Zealand's children wave as their train passes. . . . The youngsters are fascinated by New Zealand's green countryside." Both the narration and the footage, shot from inside the children's train, look and sound remarkably like the *Carmel Diary* newsreel that had been made during my father's arrival in Palestine. The mass of young children huddle inside the train, looking curious and tired, then carry little plastic New Zealand flags they received while onlookers cheer. This too was presented as a "national" story of rescue: local children who were waving at the newcomers, and the children who "could not believe" their welcome.

There were no Jews among the "Children of Pahiatua." But Jadwiga Kowalska, deputy keeper of the Sikorski Archives in London, told me during my visit that among Polish refugees evacuated from Iran to other places, there were at least "some Jewish people" in Pretoria, Mexico, Argentina, Lebanon, South Africa, and . . . in Palestine, where hundreds of Catholic adults and children would find refuge along with my father.

After my father's departure from Tehran, non-Jewish civilians lined up in the Agency office, hoping to obtain entry certificates for Palestine. "In Tehran, I noticed an interesting phenomenon among the Polish refugees: they were jealous of the Jews for immigrating to Palestine while they were being forced to emigrate to India or Kenya," Jewish Agency representative Yishai wrote. As far as the climate, the standard of living, the cleanliness, the people, Eretz Yisrael, particularly its Jewish part, was like a heaven to them. They would often express their jealousy with anti-Semitic remarks like "with the money they amassed in Poland, our homeland, the Jews are now building a thriving garden in Palestine, where to us there is no entry."[22]

Yishai did not distribute the certificates in his possession to non-Jews, nor to Jewish converts to Christianity who offered to return to Judaism if they were to immigrate to Palestine. "Our certificates were for our people; the people who were part of us and supported our cause," he wrote. But there were exceptions: a woman whose daughter had helped Jews board the ship from Turkmenistan to Iran ("we are not ungrateful, and we forever remember those who aided us"); another who was deformed by a rare bone disease and was transferred to Hadassah Hospital in Jerusalem ("a human life was on the scale: if she stayed, she'd die; if she left, she'd live"). Now, for the first time, in an ironic twist of fate, the Jews, who had been granted a batch of British entry visas to distribute in Iran, controlled the border crossing.[23]

At the end, approximately seventy thousand Anders Army soldiers evacuated to Palestine, including family members and hundreds of Polish orphans. The army traveled from Iran to Khanakin in Iraq, then continued in a month-long trek to Palestine. "The Army's march from Iraq has begun," a Polish soldier, Marian Czuchnowski, wrote in his diary. "They walk with their war machines through the deserts of Syria and trans Jordan and into the peaceful land, the land filled with grapes and oranges: Palestina."[24]

Yehuda Pompiansky, a Jewish soldier in the Anders Army, testified that en route to Palestine, Polish commanders referred to their destination as "the Land of Israel" and as the country of the Jews. In no testimony, Jewish or Polish, was the Arab population of Palestine mentioned.[25]

Once they were in Palestine, Anders Army soldiers joined other Polish refugees already there. A February 18, 1942, news dispatch by *New*

York Times correspondent Joseph Levy notes that thirty thousand Jewish and non-Jewish peoples had been admitted to Palestine since the war began two and a half years earlier. By year's end, Palestine would become a "principal center for the absorption of Polish refugees."[26]

$$\equiv$$

Hannan, Regina, and Emma spent three days at the British detention camp in Atlit, then were formally released to the care of Youth Immigration, which distributed all the children among various dormitories and resorts for purposes of "recuperation and evaluation," as Szold called it. Hannan, Regina, and Emma were placed at Beit Ha'khalutzot (Pioneer House), a beautiful stone house in Jerusalem that had been built the previous year for lodging and training single female immigrants. There they slept in comfort, for the first time in years, between four walls, on real beds and mattresses. They were doted on, as people came from everywhere to see the "children who were rescued." They were assigned local "buddy" families who invited them to their homes. They visited sites and were visited by their cousin Ze'ev, who took them to buy new shoes. They gave testimonies to representatives of the Polish Information Center, who transcribed them and compiled them into the collections that Henryk Grynberg and I would later unearth at the Hoover Institution and at Ginzakh Kiddush Hashem seven decades later. When his Information Center interviewer asked Hannan about the current whereabouts of his father, he gave the family's address in Uzbekistan and said: "It seems to me that he lives in the mud hut [in Samarqand] until this very day." There was a quiet, tragic undertone to those words, which ended his testimony, as if son and father were now separated not only by continents but also by decades.

In Jerusalem, each child underwent a physical. Their height and weight were measured—twelve-year-old Regina was four foot three and 28.9 kilograms; Hannan's measurements were unavailable. Their past diseases were documented: Regina's sheet listed typhus, scabies, and proctitis. Their eyes, ears, skin color, urine, and lungs were examined for further medical treatment, and Regina was found to have a murmur in her upper right lung; an X-ray was recommended. And they underwent a psycho-academic evaluation, in which Regina—who now went by her middle name, Rivka—was found to be "superior" in her "preparedness for academic study," "quick to grasp matters," "honest and well behaved," and excelling in "her treatment of her brother."

Emma, now "Noemi Perelgric, 11," was described as "age appropriate," "pleasant," "very polite," "compliant," "smart," "alert," "eager to study," and possessing a "rich imagination": "she claims to have once been stolen from her parents' home and to have lived for a year and a half among gypsies." Her "unusual ability to calculate her steps wisely" was also noted.

The Agency's head psychologist, Dr. Moshe Brill, found my father, "Teitel Channania, 15," to be socially maladapted and underdeveloped. His height was that of a thirteen-year-old, as were his "general understanding and everyday behavior." His Tehran counselors described him as "cross-eyed," "two-faced," "not too developed," "unpopular," "unwilling to work," "attention seeking," and "lying." This last characterization seemed absurd for the man I knew to be uncompromisingly truthful and hardworking. But it wasn't just he who received such a harsh assessment. Many of the older boys were labeled as "mean," "lazy," "argumentative," "refusing to complete chores," "extraordinarily agitated," "lying," "overly critical and never content," "dirty," and suffering from "moods of depression" and "rage."

Such descriptions of child refugees as wild, uncivilized "wolf children" would become almost standard in postwar reports on survivor children. "They have known no parental authority," the British-American author Alice Bailey wrote in 1946; "they run in packs like wolves; they lack all moral sense . . . they know no laws save the laws of self preservation."[27] The word *trauma* does not appear in my father's assessment—it would be decades before post-traumatic stress would be officially acknowledged as a psychological disorder—nor any reference to starvation, violence, or separation from parents. And though I knew the assessment was commonplace, I wondered what effect it had on the rest of my father's life.

It predicted, for example, that Channania Teitel would "accomplish only ordinary achievements academically" and should be directed to a "technical" career path. My father was in fact much more passionate about, say, history, than about anything technical, for which he had no special talent. Did the assessment's prediction set in motion the subsequent placements and decisions that would result in his forty-eight-year career at the Technical School of the Israeli Air Force? I noted that Brill assessed Hannan's friend and fellow Tehran Child Moshe Druker, who became a highly successful tax lawyer in Tel Aviv, as "able to reach outstanding achievement." Had his assessment been a prediction or the trigger to *his* success? I wondered.

While Hannan was recuperating in Pioneer House in Jerusalem, he visited the home of the local "buddy" family that had been assigned to him, the family of the gynecologist Yuval Bdolach, who would reach out to me seven decades later. There he told Bdolach's grandmother of the murder of her sister and four nieces, which he had witnessed. "They did not really know yet what was happening in Europe," Bdolach told me when I met him in Jerusalem. "It was a terrible moment. But they always said what a sensitive, polite boy your father was, and how well he cared for the two little girls, his sister and his cousin."

From Pioneer House, Hannan and the other children were taken on excursions to villages and kibbutzim across the land. "The children thought of a kibbutz as some kind of *kolkhoz*," Szold wrote, "and *kolkhozes* they knew very well." In the beginning, they all preferred to remain in cities, "but after a few trips, their attitude changed, and not one of them wished to stay in town any longer." Central to Youth Immigration was the belief that "children's best interests" were better served in collective settings, and after the war agencies and social workers treating children in DP camps and elsewhere would adopt the belief as well.[28] But in the Yishuv at large, it was far from consensual.

Already in Atlit, an intense clash broke out between different political parties that wanted to lay claim to the children, particularly the secular-socialist Mapai (Workers of Eretz Yisrael), the party of the kibbutzim, the ultra-Orthodox Agudath Israel, and the religious Zionist Mizrahi Party. (The Mizrahi was a movement that historian Tchiya Nedivi-Horovitz calls "a midway stance between religion and Zionism.") It was a competition over funding—Hadassah had pledged to pay for the maintenance and education of each child, and in principle, each refugee child was also entitled to a monthly subsidy of four British pounds from the Polish government, funds that would be a lifeline for impoverished Jewish institutions and people in Palestine.[29] And it was a competition over political power, as each party sought to increase its base, particularly after it was rumored that thousands more children would soon come.

There were complaints by the religious parties about what was claimed to have been neglect of the children's religious life in Tehran. There were inquiry panels and interrogation of the counselors. The accusations and infighting lasted for months, provoking such bitterness that the daily *Ha'aretz*, in its November 26, 1943, issue, published a cartoon under the heading "The Yishuv Welcomes the Children of Tehran." The cartoon featured a heap of fighting people piled up next to two crying children, a boy and a girl, with a caption that read: "Don't worry, Sarah. We survived our haters, we'll survive those who love us too."

In Jerusalem, Henrietta Szold called for the "public" to stop "intervening" in the children's rehabilitation. "There are curious incidents: people who insist on asking the children whether they prefer to be rabbis or pioneers, political party rivalries. . . . I cannot tolerate such contacts and do my utmost to prevent them. In many cases, however, people have succeeded in getting hold of one child or another." In his memoir, Josek Klapholz wrote that his younger brother disappeared, to be subsequently retrieved from an ultra-Orthodox yeshiva in a yarmulke and side curls.

The ultra-Orthodox Agudath Israel insisted that "any child of Jewish origin who has no parents or was separated from his or her parents be given a religious education," and requested for its group half of the children. Rabbis in the United States and Palestine signed a petition to prevent the children from transferring to kibbutzim, "where their religion will be abolished, whether by indoctrination or by force." In Jerusalem,

I interviewed Ayala Rottenberg, who was an ultra-Orthodox counselor at Kfar Hasidim, a Hasidic village where some of the children were sent for the intermediary period. She told me that members of the socialist party Mapai "took the children on trips to kibbutzim and tricked them into going there." The ultra-Orthodox parties called to fight the Jewish Agency, even violently, for "refusing to give the children a religious education in accordance with their places of origin."

At the end, the children were divided more or less equally between kibbutzim and institutions of the Mizrahi. In August 1943 a second transport arrived from Tehran with 120 children, and Youth Aliyah assigned nearly all of them to Mizrahi-affiliated families and institutions, in an attempt to divide them equitably. Among this second group would be Hannan's and Regina's cousin on their maternal side, Sarah Halberstadt, whose family in Poland, as Regina told me, "had been less religious than the Teitels."

The ultra-Orthodox parties received only thirty-seven of the refugee children to their care, which would remain a sore point decades later. Ayala Rottenberg, the former ultra-Orthodox counselor, wrote a memoir in which she devotes many chapters to the story of the Tehran Children. For her they were not child Holocaust refugees but Jewish children who were persecuted by the secular Zionists. It was rumored that children had been driven against their will to a Tehran synagogue on Yom Kippur; counselors had misused funds to buy wine instead of kosher food; children were prohibited from praying or wearing a yarmulke; their *peyos* (side locks) were cut off secretly at night; and they heard antireligious sermons and socialist indoctrination in Tehran and in Palestine. "The Torah- and Mitzvah-following portion of the people of Israel were a tiny group with little means then, unable to fight for the souls of the children," Rottenberg wrote. Her memoir went through at least five printings.

"We had no political power then," Rottenberg, elegant and welcoming, told me when we met in Jerusalem. "But we learned from our loss in the fight over the Tehran Children how to organize politically." As I wrote the final chapters of the book, Agudath Yisrael was a major power broker in Israeli politics, at the center of a large right-wing coalition.

While they were at Atlit, Hannan, Regina, and Emma met Zindel's cousin, Riwka Zwykielski, for the first time, and this meeting changed the course of their lives. She had been a classmate of Emma's mother, Sura, and had left Ostrów for Warsaw at eighteen to enroll at the University of Warsaw. She studied education and psychology, planning to intern with the famous Polish-Jewish pedagogue Janusz Korczak at his Warsaw orphanage. Then she quit her studies unexpectedly and returned to Ostrów, pregnant and alone, refusing to abort or relinquish her infant daughter for adoption after she was born. The father, who was rumored in the family to be a fellow Polish student who had impregnated and abandoned her, would turn out—we learned, nearly a century later, long after her death—to have been a close relative. Her insistence on keeping the baby sparked a war with the family. She moved to the Baltic port city of Danzig (now Gdańsk), with her infant daughter Mia, took a job as a teacher, then returned to Ostrów when she could no longer sustain the two.[30]

There she met a distant relative who was visiting from Palestine. David Drozdowski had lost a leg fighting in the British Army at Gallipoli in World War I and in return had received British-Palestinian citizenship for himself and for any family he might have. "My father had no leg and my mother had no husband," their now seventy-plus-year-old son would tell me when I interviewed him, "and so they married." In 1928 Riwka and her toddler daughter sailed with David Drozdowski to Palestine and settled in his newly founded Kibbutz Ein Harod, a 287-member cooperative settlement in the northern Jezreel Valley.

In May 1943 Riwka took Hannan, Regina, and Emma to visit Ein Harod. The children apparently liked it, and she asked that they be added to the list of seventeen children who were already designated to be housed there.

Hannan, who was older than fourteen, was allowed to choose his own placement. But younger children like Regina and Emma, it was decided, would be questioned to help determine whether they belonged in a religious or secular setting. In an interview whose transcript I read, "Teitel,

Rivka" was said to have "remembered nothing about her home and its atmosphere." She said that she "did not remember what her father used to do when he got up from his bed in the morning." And in answer to the question "What did your mother do with the meat after she bought it?" she replied that back home, "she was never in the kitchen." The placement committee noted that she "wished to be sent together with her brother Channania (15) and her relative Noemi Perelgric (10) to Kibbutz Ein Harod," and recommended a "non-religious education."

Immediately, a man presenting himself as the children's "uncle" entered the picture, writing to Szold that he was "shocked to discover" that the boy "Channania Teitel" and the girls "Rivka Teitel" and "Perelgric Nahama" from "Ostrow Maz" were transferred to Ein Harod. The man, a distant relative by the name of Abraham Czukerman, claimed that "their parents are begging in a letter sent to [him] from Russia that [he], their uncle, be a parent to them, look after them, and educate them according to their parents' spirit, the spirit of tradition and Torah." He continued requesting guardianship over the children ("Esteemed Madame! Have pity on these children and give an immediate order to transfer them") and protesting their transfer to a location that "fills their bodies with treif and their souls with heresy . . . against the will of their parents."

Szold answered Czukerman that the children were "wholeheartedly attached to their relative Riwka Zwykielski and insist on remaining in Ein Harod." She asked him to forward the letter he claimed to have received from their parents. "There was no such letter. It was a lie," Duban Simchoni, Riwka Zwykielski's son, would tell me when I visited him in Kibbutz Ein Harod, where he still lived in 2018. "The religious parties did what they could, including lying, to get the children out of the kibbutz and into their institutions." But in the Zionist Archive in Jerusalem was an undated "summary of a letter by Mr. Zindel Teitel," as it was titled, which had no addressee:

> *I wrote you several letters a while back. How are you?*
> *Our children Channania and Rivka, as well as Emuchka, daughter of our*

sister Sarah, traveled to you as part of the children's brigade. . . . Please write
and cable how they are. They traveled to you, and I am certain that you will
try to welcome my dear children in the best way possible so that they will not
be lonesome. I trust that you will receive them truly as your own and be to
them as true parents until we meet them again.

We are fine. I am also writing to Wolf. I know nothing about Icok. Do you
know?

Regards from my wife. Regards to all our acquaintances.
Your friend, Zindel Teitel

Reading my grandfather's letter, with its energetic, somewhat hopeful
tone and its double plea to treat the children "truly as your own" and "to
be to them as true parents until we meet them again," was both moving
and terrible. Moving, because the bond between parents and children
had not dissipated, as it had in so many families, and because Zindel
still assumed his paternal role from across the Iron Curtain. Terrible,
because it was a letter from beyond the grave. Zindel would never meet
and be a parent to his children again. And by the time he wrote the letter inquiring about his brother Icok, or soon after, Icok, Icok's wife Leja
(Abraham Czukerman's daughter); their daughters, Ruchela, Szulamit,
and Pesja, his mother, Fejge, his sister, Sura, and her son, Danek, his
mother in law, Estera, and brother in law, Daniel—they would no longer
be alive.

The way Icok and his family died is unknown; their traces disappeared in Białystok after Nazis invaded the Soviet Union on June 22,
1941. They could have been burned to death inside Wielka Synagoga w
Białymstoku, Białystok's Great Synagogue, where Nazi soldiers locked
up two thousand Jews and set it on fire on June 27. Or they could have
died in the grenade attack and shooting that killed a thousand more
that day. They might have been deemed "NKVD collaborators" and
executed in a field in nearby Pietrasze village, assembly line style, and
alongside five thousand others in a joint operation of Einsatzgruppe B,
Kommando SS Zichenau-Schröttersburg, and Kommando Białystok,

on July 12, 1941. Or they might have remained inside Białystok's Jewish ghetto for a year or so before being sent to their deaths at Treblinka or Majdanek.

Sura Perelgric's death certificate, which the International Red Cross would supply to Emma after the war, would list as her cause of death "shot near Warsaw," with no date attached. Whether Emma's brother, Danek, was shot with his mother, or was murdered elsewhere, in the ghetto or in Treblinka, we did not know.

Hannan's paternal grandmother, Fejge Teitel—Regina told me that her cousin Ze'ev Teitel had told her—died before the Nazi occupation of Białystok, but when I visited Białystok, I did not find her name in the Jewish cemetery where she would have been buried.

Hannan's maternal grandmother Estera Averbuch and her son Daniel were deported to Auschwitz, where they were murdered on February 25, 1943, a week after Hannan, Regina, and Emma arrived in Palestine.

I had lived in the same household with my father and grandmother for my entire childhood yet knew nothing of their murdered family members. I was not alone in this respect. In nearly every house of my friends and neighbors in Haifa, and in thousands of households across the country, I now know, lived uncles, aunts, cousins, sometimes brothers and sisters and parents' ex-spouses, about whose life and death no one of the next generations ever knew.

But reading Zindel's letter did not only evoke horror. It was not only a painful trace of his cruel fate and that of his murdered clan. It was also a direct connection to his past. And because I knew a great deal about this past, I could hear it: the particular manner of writing, speaking, and being of my grandfather, the dignity and energy that would soon disappear but in 1943 still existed in his words, which I, who had grown up without them, now heard, familiar, from beyond the grave.

The same dignity, energy, and respectability were in the words of Henrietta Szold, who in early August 1943 wrote to Zindel in Samarqand, in Yiddish—a language that would soon disappear from the vernacular—to ask for instructions regarding his "*kinderlach Channania on Rivka Teitel on aiyner krova* [your relative] *Noemi Perelgric.*"

Herr Teitel,
. . . Your children ask us to inform you about their lives: that they are happy with their life, are learning in school, and are healthy and happy. But today we are not only informing you that the children are well. We also want to tell you that your relative Riwka Zwykielski, a secular laborer, is supervising the education of Hannan, Rivka, and Noemi, who have told us they . . . wished to be in [her] care. Later we received a letter from a man who presented himself as the children's trustee, Mr. Abraham Czukerman, and who has written that the children have been given to his care and should be sent to an institution of religious education.

We are now contacting you to ask for your opinion whether you agree with the adoption of the children by Ein Harod. We believe that you have already received a message from your children that they are happy with their placement, and would be very thankful if you could give us an answer. We greet you and wish you "ales gut" (all good).
Henrietta Szold

I was moved that Szold had addressed the man who she well knew was now a starving, lice-ridden refugee as "Herr Teitel." I was moved that his address—Jangirabackaia 24, Samarqand, "the mud hut on Jangirabackaia Street," as my father called it—was typed according to convention on the upper-left-hand corner of the letter like any other address. I was moved by the neatness of the page that was without typo or blemish. Most of all, I was moved by the letter's content: the polite report, the solicitation of parental consent for the education of their offspring. The letter was shocking in its ordinariness. It was as if Szold was still preserving, in 1943, the contours of a world of legal norms, logic, politeness, and cordiality, while every norm, every convention, and life itself would soon be completely annihilated.

=

The expectation that thousands more Polish-Jewish children who were currently in Central Asia would possibly follow suit after the arrival of the Tehran Children began with negotiations in London, where Moshe Shertok met with various British, Soviet, and Polish officials, including Sikorski, to discuss the matter.[31] Then, in a chance meeting between Shertok and Stanisław Kot in Palestine, Kot informed him that secret talks were taking place between the Soviet and Polish governments that could potentially result in the evacuation of an additional fifty thousand Polish refugees, among whom would be Jewish children. The former Polish ambassador to the USSR who was now minister of state in the Middle East, now resided in Palestine. He was recovering from an illness at Carmel Sanatorium, a twelve-acre hilly resort overlooking the Mediterranean in Haifa, and was cared for by Dr. Wilhelm Bodenheimer, a German-Jewish refugee who together with other German physicians had built it a decade earlier. Shertok reported on the encounter in an Agency meeting in Tel Aviv shortly after, and from there his words spread across the land.[32]

Tens of thousands of Catholic Poles were now living in Haifa, Gedera, Rehovot, Castina, Tel Aviv, Nazareth, and Jerusalem. They were soldiers and civilians, government officials, Red Cross workers, and children. "It was," as historian Valentina Brio would tell me in Jerusalem in 2018, "the largest concentration of Poles in the East. Here is where they trained and built their army, but more importantly, here is where they built their largest cultural center outside Poland. Larger than London, larger than anywhere." Brio spent years reading poetry, fiction, memoirs, and newspaper and journal articles written by Poles in Palestine. "In Palestine was the meeting of political, cultural, and social minds," she said. "It was the place of exile where the Poles stayed the longest."[33]

In Palestine, the Anders Army prepared for what would become known as the Battle of Monte Cassino: in a large-scale drill they "conquered" Mount Sinai, Nazareth, and other locations. Poles also had a great deal of civilian life in Palestine, with hospitals, sanitoriums, courses for administrative officers in Tel Aviv, and meetings of authors and journalists, like the poetry reading that the Hebrew poet Shaul Tchernichowsky organized with the Polish poets Władysław Broniewski and Marian Czuchnowski.

There were multiple Polish-language periodicals in Palestine: the *Gazeta Polska*, a daily paper for Poles in the Middle East, a soldiers' journal, a women's paper, a youth magazine, and a biweekly literary review called *Drodze*. Polish presses published books of poetry, anthologies, textbooks.

Hebrew University advised the Polish publishing centers, which published new editions of Polish books that were already in the university libraries; local Polish-born Jews and Catholic refugees collaborated. Polish journal articles that were thought to interest the local population were immediately translated into Hebrew in local papers. Articles about Hebrew poets like Shaul Tchernichowsky, who had ties to Polish literature, were translated from the Hebrew and published in Polish journals. Local Polish-born musicians played in Polish orchestras and in the jazz band of Henryk Wars, a pioneer of Polish jazz who had arrived with the Anders Army.

Valentina Brio, who had been a lecturer at Vilnius University in Lithuania before she joined the faculty at Hebrew University, did not focus on the tensions between Jews and Poles that occasionally flared up in Palestine. In Tel Aviv, there were reports of two murders by Polish soldiers, a fistfight at a technical school, and an attempted arson at Beit Ha'am, the largest auditorium in Tel Aviv.[34] The Polish commandant of the Tel Aviv regiment, Major Wróblewski, categorically denied that Polish soldiers had committed any murder and attributed the unrest to "a drunk Polish soldier" who stirred a small argument that was blown up; the major claimed that in fact a Polish soldier had been murdered in Tel Aviv.[35]

Brio ignored all this, as well as the anti-Semitic Polish presses in London that warned of "the Jews of Palestine" who possessed "no pro-Polish feelings" but awaited "the opportunity of returning to Poland." Instead she emphasized the close cultural cooperation between the Yishuv and the Polish refugees: the makeshift theater in Jerusalem's Edison House, where Polish-Jewish actors from Palestine performed alongside Catholic actors; Polish-Jewish journalists like David Lazar and Paulina Apenszlak, editor of a prewar feminist paper, who wrote for the Polish papers; and dozens of memoirs and diaries, like the one by the poet and Anders Army officer Bronisław Brzezicki, in which he described trips to holy sites, to Tel

Aviv, and to the sea. "I have realized," Brzezicki wrote in his diary, "that the Jews of Palestine have nothing against the Poles."

In Palestine then, something of the vision of harmonious relations between Jews and Poles was finally realized. It seemed predicated, as the Polish Consul in Tehran had insinuated to Moshe Yishai, on the fact that Eretz Yisraeli Jews now had their own, autonomous aims, separate from Poland. (The consul, who had visited Palestine, told Yishai that he admired the "different Jew"—not a "merchant or a peddler"—that Eretz Yisrael has borne and that he respected the "enterprise," but added that his "change in thinking [about Jews] only applied to the Jews of the Land of Israel.")[36] And those national aims, as Brzezicki noted, spurred new, more immediate conflicts that shifted the focus away from Poland.

In an April 25, 1942, meeting of the Zionist Agency executive council, Moshe Shertok, who had met with Sikorski and with the Jewish Polish government council member Ignacy Schwarzbart, praised the Polish government for its public dispatch on the "Mass Extermination of Jews in German Occupied Poland." The dispatch had been based on the reports of the Polish soldier and resistance fighter Jan Karski, who, escaping Poland, informed the Polish government-in-exile and others about the extermination of Jews in Nazi-occupied Poland. "We had already received news of the slaughter in Poland . . . of the systematic extermination, of the transport by trains . . . from eye-witnesses who have made it to Palestine," Shertok stated. "But, until the official declaration of the Polish government there was a pact of silence between the British government and the British press. . . . What has elevated the urgency of the matter was the Polish dispatch. . . . I do not analyze the Polish motives, what they are thinking or not thinking. . . . But [Anthony] Eden's declaration (in which Eden read a statement about the extermination of Jews in the House of Lords) would not have happened without the dispatch. It is a historical fact, the first international act to place the slaughter on the global agenda."[37]

In 1943 the Hebrew University in Jerusalem invited Kot for a tour and a meeting of its general assembly.[38]

At the Polish Information Center in Jerusalem, Jewish and Catholic

Poles—including a Polish aristocrat, Teresa Lebkowsky, and the journalists David Glazer and David Flincker, the latter of whom interviewed my father—worked together to collect the testimonies of all Polish refugees in Palestine, including the children's. "It was Anders who on his visit to Polish troops in Palestine said that Jewish testimonies should be collected as well," Brio told me. And it was he who gave orders not to search for Jewish soldiers who left the Anders Army. In Palestine, "Anders did not oppose to us leaving, only the British searched for us," Yehuda Pompiansky, a Jewish former soldier, wrote in his testimony.

Two-thirds of the Jewish soldiers in the Anders Army deserted in Palestine: "Why should we have stayed in the Polish army given how we were treated," Pompiansky wrote.[39] One-third remained and fought at Monte Cassino. At least one Polish-born local Jewish man enlisted in the Anders army and fought as well.[40] The song "Red Poppies on Monte Cassino," which would be recorded shortly after the battle, was sung by the Polish-Jewish singer Adam Aston. Another song, "Blue Scarf," one of my favorites in the repertoire of the Israeli singer Arik Einstein, would be written by the Polish lyricist Jerzy Petersburski in Palestine and later be translated to Hebrew. Josef Lejtes, a Polish screenwriter and director, would make Palestine's first English-speaking feature drama, *My Father's House*, with Polish-born Jewish actors. His next two films would be made in Israel, in Hebrew: the 1949 *Ein Brera* (No Choice), and 1952's *Faithful City*, a film that according to IMDb "depicts some of the courage, patience, bravery and understanding that attended the birth of Israel as a free and independent nation."

The Polish Institute and Sikorski Museum is housed in a dark, stuffy townhouse on Princes Gate, London. Its walls are lined with medieval Polish suits of armor, all manner of Second World War weaponry, and photos of Sikorski and Anders. Here I found the traces of Polish lives in Palestine: expense report books, including lists of flowers, typewriters, dresses, bills for tuition at the Hebrew University, at the Technikum in Haifa, and at more than a dozen other schools, for courses and training programs, receipts for rooms at the Julian Hotel in Jerusalem, recommendation letters for Polish students at the Eretz Israel Conservatoire of Music in Jerusalem, and lists of leisure and self-improvement items and activities for non-Jewish Polish refugees in Palestine.

In the archive I found lists upon lists compiled by the representative of the Polish Ministry of Labor and Social Care in Jerusalem, Dr. Lubaczewski. Lists of Polish refugees in Palestine were categorized by cities (Tel Aviv, Jerusalem, Haifa). Notations indicated marital status: *S* for single; *Ż* for married, wife in Palestine, too; *s/1* for single with one child; *s/2* for single with two children. A pink circle indicated a soldier; a pink underline meant a Jewish refugee; a black underline meant a Catholic; a short black underline meant a Protestant. I found details of financial support, either recurring or one-time stipends. There was report of a soup kitchen in Tel Aviv and the amounts of sugar it required.

There was a letter from the main physician regarding the health status of refugees: soldiers and female refugees who needed urgent dental care, glasses, and orthopedic tools. An August 20, 1942, letter from the Association of Polish Lawyers in Jerusalem said they wanted to be more active,

Students, both Catholic and Jewish, in a Polish high school in Tel Aviv

and a report and bylaws followed. There were reports on the activities of the Association of Lawyers, the Association of Technicians and Engineers, the Society of Biologists, a group of economists, a Higher Education lecture series, the Association of Technicians, and the activities of the Polish Red Cross in Tel Aviv. There were lists of specialists in the field of health care, education, farming, engineering, accounting, and translation, and lists of available English courses and lectures.[41]

Jewish Palestine would become another center from where aid would be shipped to the refugees in Central Asia and Africa. The Polish government-in-exile would commission the production of anti-typhus vaccines in Palestine, which would then be sent to other places of exile; vitamins and medicines would be bought. In Tel Aviv, a sweater knitting circle and a soup kitchen would collect food for shipment. Doctors— Poles, Jews, and nonrefugees—were enlisted to go care for Polish refugees in Nairobi. School supplies, textbooks, notebooks, pencils, pens, Polish books, prayer books, song books, records with Polish songs, dictionaries, typewriters with Polish font, and national symbols to be hung at cultural centers were bought. These efforts, according to Polish sources, were done jointly with the Jewish Agency, which contributed 250,000 British pounds for relief that was sent to the refugees in Central Asia.[42]

I read all these documents with astonishment. In the end it was Palestine—and primarily its Jewish side—that would become the most hospitable and longest place of refuge of Polish citizens: a chapter in Jewish and Polish history that seems to have been erased from both Jewish and Polish memory. "I never understood and no one ever told me how come my mother's birth certificate was issued in Tel Aviv," a Polish MIT professor would tell me in a casual conversation in 2018.

Krystyna Orłowska, a former Polish refugee in Palestine who now lives in Denver, had been evacuated to Palestine in November 1943 and remained there until October 1947. Polish schoolchildren studied in Nazareth and Jerusalem, where at a Catholic church in the Ain Karem neighborhood, a plaque still hangs with the Polish words HERE IN AIN KAREM, CHILDREN FROM THE POLISH SCHOOL OFFER THEIR THANKS TO GOD FOR DELIVERANCE

FROM EXILE IN SOVIET RUSSIA. "It was the best years of my life," Krystyna told me when I called her from New York. She boarded and studied at the School of Young Volunteers in Nazareth, "with Poles and Jews and Arabs," as she put it, who on weekends and breaks traveled together to Tiberius and Tel Aviv to see movies. "Once my friends and I walked all the way to the Carmelite Monastery in Haifa," she said. "The priests were so friendly, and the Arab boys were so polite." The father of one of the Arab boys had a car, she said, and would drive them all to the beach, and "we'd get ice cream, play ball, tan." She asked me what had happened between Jews and Arabs in the past decades since "in those days everyone got along."

Listening to Krystyna speak about "the best years of [her] life" in Nazareth, and the ways Jews and Poles and Arabs got along, I thought about my father, living nearby in impoverished, swelteringly hot Kibbutz Ein Harod. Because of his strict work and study schedule, and because he was penniless, Hannan could not travel to the beach or to Tel Aviv to see movies, let alone live, like some of the Polish refugees, in Bakaa, Katamon, or Rehavia, Jerusalem's loveliest neighborhoods. From the kibbutz, Hannan also wrote to an addressee in Youth Aliyah that he was not able to travel because of the tense "state of things" (*ha'matsav*) between Jews and Arabs.

But Poles came to kibbutzim. The poet Marian Czuchnowski took classes at an agricultural school in Kibbutz Givat Brenner and wrote a book about Degania. The poet Władysław Broniewski held readings in kibbutzim, most likely even at Ein Harod; once when a generator failed and he had no light by which to read, a young kibbutz member continued, reciting Broniewski's poem by heart.[43] I wondered what my father, whose muted anger at Poland I would sense years later, thought of it all then. I also wondered what would have happened if he had been not an *oleh* but "a Polish refugee": would he have received a living stipend from the Polish *delegatura*, studied at the Herzelia Gymnasium in Tel Aviv, then at the Hebrew University, as some Poles did in Palestine? If that had even been possible, it was no longer even fantasizable without a hefty dose of pain. Hannan's home was now the kibbutz.

Ein Harod, alongside several other kibbutzim, was built on a plot of seventy *dunams* of land in the Jezreel Valley that had been purchased in the early 1920s by the World Zionist Organization (WZO). Whether to call such purchases "a return to the Land of Israel," "legitimate moves in a free market," "colonial," "partially colonial," "colonial practices that were necessitated by the national movement," or by any other description—the historian Yishai Rosen-Zvi calls it "colonization of refugees"—remains a point of painful debate. In practice, the dramatic changes in British real estate law that enabled, for example, the dispossession of farmers in Great Britain when sheep herding became profitable, enabled the purchase by the WZO; Arab farmers viewed them as illegitimate.[44]

From the 1920s to the 1940s, waves of peace, friction, and violence between local Jews and Arabs ensued, but tents and later permanent structures were built, generators were acquired, and a large communal dining hall was built in Ein Harod. Richard Kaufman, the German-born architect, designed the modernist, concrete communal building that towered over a "boulevard" that afforded an uninterrupted view of the valley and Mount Gilboa; in the kibbutz, he had sought to create an antithesis to the industrial European city. More than a place, the kibbutz was a technology for reengineering European-Jewish existence. "We left the past behind us," as one kibbutz founder put it, "with all its complications and wars; it was as if we were done at once with all our dilemmas . . . and the extra baggage that had tied and weighed us down."[45] But the kibbutz also demanded enormous sacrifices from its first members, among whom was Riwka Zwykielski. In 1928, when Riwka first arrived at the kibbutz, delicate-featured and dreamy (as she looked in the photos Duban showed me), she set aside her education, deposited her dresses in the communal clothing warehouse, placed her three-year-old daughter Mia in the communal children's home, and became a laundry woman.

During my childhood, my father often took us to Kibbutz Ein Harod. I swam in its pool and ate peaches in the two-room home of Riwka, a small, elderly woman with a long braid. Duban, her son, was born a decade after she arrived there. He embodied for us children, and also for Hannan and Regina, the quintessential kibbutz-born *sabra*: tall and blond, a farmer and a decorated soldier, always busy elsewhere. I had not seen him for decades and now, when I visited as an adult, stood alongside him on the dining hall balcony, overlooking the Jezreel Valley, sweat blinding my eyes, fumes of heat rising from the steaming valley. Cheerful and friendly and seemingly oblivious to the heat and the stark landscape that were weighing on me, Duban shepherded me around the kibbutz, pointing to different landmarks, including the barracks where my father lived. Like most other cooperative settlements, Ein Harod was now privatized, and the kibbutz movement as a whole wielded little political power in 2018 Israel. But in 1943, regardless of the meager living conditions, my father had arrived at the seat of political power.[46]

The Unified Kibbutz movement had voted to adopt four hundred of the "1,000 Tehran orphans" even before their arrival from Iran. Youth Aliyah had sent a list of supplies and clothing needed for each child: two blankets, two sheets, four towels, a pair of work shoes, a pair of sandals, and several articles of clothing for "work," "after work," and "Sabbath." Details about specific locations, counselors, and living arrangements were discussed, and a proposal for how to raise the children was voted on. There had been two options: to assign children to individual families or to educate them as a group. The latter prevailed. The younger children, including Regina and Emma—whom "it [was] necessary and possible to root into our children's homes and way of life so that they view Ein Harod as their home forever"—would be raised alongside kibbutz children, while adolescents like my father would live, study, and work in their own distinct group.

On the day of their arrival, the twenty children who were assigned to Ein Harod were welcomed with music and singing and a banner that said, YOU ARE NO LONGER "TEHRAN CHILDREN" OR "REFUGEE CHILDREN" BUT EIN HAROD CHILDREN LIKE US. The next day, in a meeting with his peers and teachers, Hannan's group decided to call itself Etz, the Hebrew word for "tree." "We are all hopeful," their teacher announced, "that this tree will become entrenched within us and grow deep roots and abundant branches."

Hannan's group of twenty Tehran Children consisted of five girls and three boys in the ten-to-thirteen age group; and eleven boys and one girl in the fifteen-to-seventeen age group. Two of the younger children entered school immediately at grade level with kibbutz children. The rest were grouped in a dedicated class for studying Hebrew and making up for the lost years of study, with the intention of integrating them into regular classes the following year. The older children like my father, members of Etz, studied separately under a dedicated teacher and, like all older kibbutz children, worked after school in the different agricultural or industrial branches of the kibbutz.

In theory if not always in practice, the newcomers were educated under educational principles that had been developed in kibbutzim during their first decades. Education was egalitarian, and the children had unmediated contact with "nature" as part of the curriculum. Early twentieth-century, central European progressive pedagogical and psychological theories were incorporated, especially those developed by Janucz Korczak, with whom Riwka Zwykielski had contact in Warsaw. Korczak visited Ein Harod twice, in 1934 and 1936, meeting with children and teachers and lecturing on "the child, his life and his rights." After he returned to Warsaw, he composed an essay on the "Ein Harod child": "This child will create the epic of our times. He senses . . . that he is born to a new Hebrew life, but also that many around him are tied to the past. . . . He must be helped in creating this new epic." Korczak's closest associate, Stefania Wilczyńska, immigrated to Ein Harod in 1938, but the next year, fatefully, she returned to Poland. Her protégée and fellow proponent of democratic, child-centered education Fejge Biber became my father's teacher.

Education was central to kibbutz life, and in its archive I found dozens of documents about how to best educate the Tehran Children, how to educate Holocaust survivors and immigrant children generally, and how to educate all children. There were discussions of adolescents' moods, of improvised educational toys, music, hygiene, optimal bedtimes, and "nature as a vehicle for developing the senses." Every minuscule aspect of collective education was analyzed. "The teachers are excellent, real educators, and we worship them," Josek Klapholz, who was sent to Kibbutz Ganigar, wrote.

The teachers, for their part, commended the children's ambition and discipline. "The children who arrived from Tehran . . . are absorbing quickly and advancing in their studies in large strides," someone wrote anonymously in the May 21, 1943, issue of *Ein Harod Diary*, less than a month after Hannan's arrival. "Their attitude toward work is equally serious." Two years later teacher Fejge Biber summarized the success they had

Noemi and Rivka, Kibbutz Ein Harod

achieved through the force of their discipline—the trait by which I knew
my father.

> For months they worked night and day, in the sweltering summer,
> without psychological equilibrium, full of tremendous longing for
> their distant families—an extraordinary effort, an extraordinary
> adjustment, a kind of repression of all desire for this goal. Their real-
> istic attitude to life—a product of a harsh war of survival—and their
> enormous willpower: these are what propelled them forward. They
> have retrieved what was lost and are in constant improvement.

Biber also noted the children's physical improvement: the diseases they
overcame, the imprint that nature and physical labor have made on their
bodies. "We now have before us fresh, joyful children, tall, lovely girls, tall,
erect, broad-shouldered adolescents. . . . I am so deeply saddened for the
mothers and fathers who could not accompany their children and see with
their own eyes how much they have grown and developed." I found photos
at Ein Harod showing Hannan in a white "Sabbath" shirt, locking arms
with his cohort; Hannan riding a horse; and Hannan with Regina-Rivka
and Emma-Neomi, who both look tall, tan, and blooming.

But there were also difficulties, particularly for the older boys: teasing, harassment, occasional nightly beatings, ideological arguments that
ended badly. "They [the kibbutz members] worshiped Stalin," Klapholz
recalled. "We tried to explain to them how cruel the government in the
Soviet Union had been, how artificial the path they are choosing was, but
our opinions were dismissed." I met Arye Drucker, a member of Hannan's group, at his home in Holon. "Kibbutz members were terribly rigid,"
he told me. "They wouldn't allow me and your father to take a trip to Tel
Aviv because we couldn't miss a day's work. They were stingy on stamps
we needed for writing our parents."

The writer Uri Orlev, who was raised at Kibbutz Ganigar with Klapholz,
Emil Landau, and his sister, Alina, told me when we met in his home in
Jerusalem about the "class differences" between the kibbutz locals and

the newcomers. "The parents of the local children often came from small shtetls and brought narrow-minded attitudes with them. They insisted on rigid practices—mandatory afternoon naps, mandatory eating, co-ed showers—that were contrary to Korczak's teachings. Mostly they had little understanding of what we had been through during the war."

"The newcomers say, 'What do you know of the misery of diaspora Jews?'" wrote an anonymous writer in *Ein Harod Diary*. "But could it be that a feeling of inferiority is mixed in with this condensation, a jealousy of our children's joyfulness, their carefree lives?" Recalled Klapholz, "Not everything was ideal in the children's society. We felt discrimination or more accurately an inability to live up to and connect to the kibbutz's children," who were "taught to view themselves as an elite group, born in a free country and free of the neuroses of the diaspora. We were the opposite."

"In the area of their merging with the locals there has been little progress," Hannan's teacher Fejge Biber conceded. "These sons of the diaspora remain alone, isolated and isolating, while the large camp of locals stays tranquil behind a tall, locked wall."[47]

"They didn't want us contaminating their children," a kibbutz "adoptee" who arrived at the kibbutz from Syria a decade later told me. She and her sister "just sat there" in the kibbutz where they were sent, barred from associating with kibbutz children. It was a wound that continued to haunt Israeli society seven decades later: the "abuses" inflicted by the kibbutz "Ashkenazi establishment" on later waves of (mostly North African) immigrants. At the heart of the matter was the raison d'être of the Jewish state in general and the kibbutz in particular: to create a space that would be free of suffering and humiliation, a place where Jewish children, no longer a minority, no longer scared, would grow into free, autonomous citizens. Kibbutz-born children were to be the realization of this goal; for the refugee children, the goal was unrealizable, which meant they potentially could "disillusion" their native peers.

When I asked him about the tensions, Duban, mild-mannered and careful with his words, felt that kibbutzim had been unfairly attacked. "People talk about how supposedly elitist the kibbutzim were, about our pools and our horses, but they forget how harsh living conditions were, how tough you needed to be to survive here, how many committed suicide." After the war, Ein Harod became a transitional home to thousands more refugees. "Every time I came home from my army vacations, a stranger would be living in my room. . . . There was no other empty space in the kibbutz," Duban said. Most of the refugees left; some, including three Tehran Children, settled in Ein Harod, with branches of their families still living there. This is "Mikhal Dekel-Teitel," Duban introduced me to the few we encountered, "daughter of the kibbutz."

It wasn't just the past that weighed down on Klapholz, Drucker, and my father. It was also, perhaps mostly, the present. Biber noted her students' "psychological confusion and sadness" over having "left their parents behind in the war," and their frustration over the inability to help them. In his diary, Jocek Shenkelbach put it directly: "We arrived in Eretz Israel. . . . We have been told that our wanderings have ended and that now we will receive permanent placements and begin our lives; but at the same time all of this is of no importance. The war continues, and our families are far from us."[48] Biber observed, "Writing letters to Russia or receiving them agitates them and throws the children off track for a long time." I wondered whether it was not only "stinginess" that drove the kibbutz to ration stamps.

Only now did I understand that the food hoarding of which Tehran Children were often accused was not—or not only—a consequence of their wartime starvation but an attribute of their desperate desire to feed parents "who were in Russia and could barely get bread," as Shenkelbach recalled. Only now did I understand that for my father, the war did not end in Ein Harod.

=

On June 10, 1943, three months after their arrival, Hannan and Regina received the first two letters from their parents. The letters had been forwarded from Iran by Polski Czerwony Krzyż (Polish Red Cross) Tehran to Polski Czerwony Krzyż Jerusalem, which passed them to the Center for Aiding Polish Jewry, which forwarded them to Youth Aliyah, which sent them to Ein Harod. My father thanked Youth Aliyah from "the bottom of his heart" for its "great effort" and asked that his parents be notified that he and Regina were "at peace in Ein Harod." He asked that they be told that he had entered the eighth grade and Regina the fourth, and that their cousin Noemi Perelgric was "also well" and "prepares for school."

Hannan was also able to arrange for a parcel to be sent to his parents from Iran to Jangirabackaia 24, Samarqand, USSR, an address that Zindel confirmed in a postcard. Ein Harod officials notified the Agency office in Tehran that the father of children who were currently under the care of the kibbutz movement was "ill with tuberculosis and cannot work" and asked that he receive "free parcels" according to the "agreement between the Agency and the Joint." And so, even though they did not belong to Ha'khalutz or Ha'shomer Ha'tsair, Hannan managed to add his parents' address to "the list" in Tehran, and they reportedly "received several packages while they were in Russia," as a letter from him later confirmed.

Ruchela and Zindel survived the war. They remained in Uzbekistan, as did the majority of Polish-Jewish refugees. It's unclear if they worked. According to some testimonies, after the initial bout of starvation, some refugees found work as drivers, teachers, doctors, healers, or employees of the *delegaturas*, positions that became vacant after most Catholic Poles were evacuated.[49] Refugees also worked in Polish orphanages and schools, which continued to function in Central Asia until they were absorbed into the Soviet education system.[50] Or perhaps Zindel, as Hannan wrote in his pleas for help, was too ill to work and lived off packages he received and other aid. But they did not perish. After the war ended, through a repatriation agreement for Polish citizens, Zindel and Ruchela returned to Poland. "Of course they released your grandparents," Professor Bozorov had told me in Bukhara. "The Soviets did not release everyone, only the old and the weak." Both Zindel and Ruchela were in their forties.

I did not know what they felt, but in another memoir, that of Ze'ev Katz, I read of jubilation: "The day of our repatriation arrived at last, the day we hoped and suffered for." Katz, a young man who had survived in Kazakhstan, decided to return to Poland even after having studied and done fairly well.[51] "Our overwhelming desire to return to Poland," he wrote, "was colored by idyllic memories of our prewar 'fine' life there. We also knew from various sources that despite Poland's pro-Soviet government, it had incomparably more freedom." It was a 2,850-mile reverse journey: "Again, we were packed in a very long, primitive goods train, with much the same arrangements as the one that exiled us to Siberia years ago. . . . But we now cheered as our train set off on the long journey home."

When Katz and his family arrived at the Polish-Soviet border, he writes, a Polish border control officer glanced at them and said: "Well, well, this is the last thing we need now." "This was our welcome to our beloved 'patria' Poland, and it gave us a truthful indication of what awaited us in our beloved homeland," Katz wrote. He was enthralled, nonetheless, by Poland's "European atmosphere"—"so different from the drab 'Asian' look of Russia"—and only slowly, gradually began to notice the pieces of desecrated Torah scrolls strewn on the streets and the belongings of mur-dered Jews in the homes in which the returnees were temporarily housed: "To us it seemed as if the souls of our martyred brothers and sisters still haunted these rooms."[52]

In Ostrów Mazowiecka, where I assumed Zindel and Ruchela returned, Magda Gawin told me that retreating Nazi soldiers had burned down their brewery and homes. Perhaps a former business acquaintance or neighbor warned them that it was dangerous for them to remain in Ostrów; perhaps they were driven out immediately, even threatened or beaten like many others. If an apartment or two that had belonged to the family was left standing, they were unable to sell it, as Katz and others had done. I knew nothing of what happened to them in Ostrów. When I asked Regina about it, she told me only, "My mother wanted to hear nothing more of Poland."

On August 26, 1946, a postcard that Zindel sent Hannan from Poland listed Dolny Śląsk in Lower Silesia, three hundred miles southwest of Ostrów, as his and Ruchela's new address. In Dolny Śląsk was Komitet Żydowski in Wolbrzycki, an organization that represented surviving Polish Jews to Polish authorities and international Jewish organizations. Mossad L'Aliyah Bet people were in time also there. Zindel and Ruchela left immediately. I was told that they walked with hundreds of others through the Dolomite Mountains, with Zindel carried or supported, in the direction of Ebensee, in Austria. There a former concentration camp now served as a displaced persons camp. Like most Polish Jews who survived the war in Central Asia, returned to Poland, and then left again, Hannan's parents would spend years in DP camps; their lives as refugees were only at their midpoint.

Hannan, Ein Harod

Barrack 22 in Ebensee Displaced Persons Camp would be my grandparents' home for the next four years. During these years, Hannan would continue pleading for aid to be sent to them—pleas that, as refugees began flooding Europe in the postwar period, became more desperate. "As you know, I live in Ein Harod and have no means of helping my parents, and therefore, though I am uneasy, I must ask for your help again," Hannan wrote Hela Gerlich, who replaced Henrietta Szold after her death in 1945. He requested items his parents had asked for—"a few food packages of oils, sugar, soap" and "lard, canned goods"—and confirmed when they received a package. Shortly after Youth Aliyah wrote him that they "could not guarantee that there would be any more free parcels," my father left the kibbutz.

His plan was to enlist in the British Army "in order to return to Europe and reunite with the parents," Arye Drucker, who had also planned to enlist, told me. He and Hannan traveled together to the Enlistment Agency in Haifa, but then Drucker received news of his mother's imminent arrival and bailed out. Hannan left with him and enrolled in the Tiez Technical School in Kibbutz Yagur, near Haifa, a competitive placement that required the permission of Youth Aliyah and major string-pulling by Riwka Zwykielski and her husband. He left Ein Harod with an excellent recommendation—"one of the best students in the class, serious and a quick study, and a good worker, responsible and serious"—much different from his first assessment. But the kibbutz also asked that Hannan return the clothing he had received, and upon arriving at Tiez, he requested from Youth Aliyah funds for the purchase of "a second shirt." "All money from the little work I have found," he wrote, "I must send to my parents in Russia, who are elderly people and need my help." He also asked for funds to cover his stay at the school on weekends and school holidays, writing "I have nowhere to go."

Regina and Emma, now Rivka and Noemi, stayed at Ein Harod until the early 1950s. "To us the kibbutz was truly good," Rivka told me the last time we spoke. "We studied with their children; we were just like kibbutz children—and Riwka was there, looking after us from afar. She was a human being, and Duban, he is like his parents, a mensch," she said, her eyes dimming. A mensch and a human being was what she was as well, I thought, distraught and heartbroken, when she died shortly after. The book had brought us into an easy intimacy with each other, the ease I never had with my father.

≡

By 1947 most of the Catholic Poles in Palestine had left. The Polish children who had been studying in Nazareth and Jerusalem, the Polish civilian refugees, the noncombatant personnel, and the workers at the Polish *delegatura*, the Polish Red Cross, and the Polish Information Center in Jerusalem were gone, but very few returned to postwar Poland, which was now the Communist People's Republic of Poland. Many left for England, some continuing on to DP camps in England and Wales. And some went to New Zealand, where the former Children of Isfahan were now adult New Zealanders, smiling, suited teachers and lawyers, flanked by families, in the images presented at the end of the *Poles Apart: The Story of 733 Polish Orphans* documentary. "The past is behind them. . . . The children of 'the Polish children,' these bright-eyed young New Zealanders, prove that their migration into this country back in 1944 has been a success, for them and for us," the film's narrator says.

Some Catholic Poles, like the Polish aristocrat Teresa Lebkowsky, who collected, during the war, Jewish testimonies for the Polish Information Center, stayed in Palestine and then in Israel. She became a mathematics teacher in a Haifa school.[53] Some Polish artists, like the filmmaker Josef Lejtes, continued coming and going to Israel; others left only traces behind them. Among these traces were 340 Polish-language books printed in Palestine, which were housed in the National Library in Jerusalem; an archive of Polish soldiers' memoirs; books about Eretz Yisrael written by Poles during their stay; a neatly manicured section allotted to Polish soldiers and refugees at the Catholic cemetery in Jerusalem; Polish graves in Jaffa, Ramallah, and Haifa; Polish plaques in churches in Nazareth and

Jerusalem, in the Via Delarosa, and in a monastery in Tiberius; and spontaneous engravings in stones in Latroon and elsewhere the Anders Army trained. Until I started looking, I had never seen them; they were invisible to me in the Jewish Israel in which I was raised.

Like the New Zealander documentary *Poles Apart*, the Israeli documentary *The Children of Teheran* also ends with images of contented Israeli men and women, well dressed and well spoken, flanked by children and grandchildren. Among them are two generals, a famous television host-turned-executive, a writer, a painter, the head of the Israeli Insurance Agents Board, and the former head of the Israeli Securities Board. Every one of these better-known Tehran Children was educated in a kibbutz. The film did not track the hundreds who had been educated in religious institutions, among whom were some prominent rabbis; their "success" was still largely invisible to the filmmakers' secular imagination and my own.

Emma, now Noemi Arison, would become head of the Sheba Hospital and Medical Center Nursing School near Tel Aviv; Regina, now Rivka Binyamini, would become a draftswoman at an architectural firm and an amateur painter; and Hannan Teitel, now Hannan Dekel, would hold various technical, educational, and management positions over a forty-eight-year career in the Israeli Air Force. Hebraizing "diasporic" sounding names would be the norm in 1940s Israel, but my father would not change his until much later, when as a public servant representing the air force on a delegation to France he would be asked to take on a proper Israeli name. They would go on to have children and grandchildren, as would the fourth Tehran Child, Hannan's cousin Sarah Halberstadt, who arrived with the second Tehran Children transport, was placed with an adoptive Orthodox family, and remains pious today.

———

From August 1946 on, Hannan petitioned for Palestine entry certificates for his parents, first with the Jewish Agency, then, on their advice, directly with the British chief secretary of the Government of Palestine, to whom he and Regina wrote:

We arrived in Palestine from Teheran in the year 1943 after having passed
through many terrible sufferings. . . . Recently we received word that our
parents are alive. . . . They have succeeded leaving Russia and coming to
Poland, and subsequently to Austria. . . . Our father had a brewery in Ostrów
Mazowiecki, Poland, which belonged to the family for generations. He is
an expert brewer. . . . It is more than five years since we saw our father and
mother, and now that they have escaped death and come out alive through
all they had to live through, shall we stay separated? . . . I hope you will be so
kind as to let us meet our parents yet and maybe to forget, at least partly, the
horrors we were subject to.
We are, Sir,
Your obedient servants,
Hannan Teitel (age 18). Rivka Teitel (age 15)

The letter was followed by dozens of other exchanges with Youth
Aliyah, with the Jewish Agency, and with Eretz Israel in Germany. Han-
nan and Regina sent letters in Hebrew and English, while Zindel and
Ruchela wrote in Polish. Letters from third parties vouched that "Zindel
Teitel is a good Zionist who used to be a significant donor to foundations
in his town." The letters were beautifully handwritten or officially typed.
But all were met with similar replies.

Hannan was eligible to apply for a D-1 "dependent visa," he was told,
but "the line is long for requests of this kind," or "more patience" was
needed. "Thousands" of such requests were waiting to be "handled by the
Government's Immigration Department." Others said that he and Regina
were "too old now," with Hannan being "over eighteen," to request dependent visas.

From Ebensee DP camp in Austria, and later from Eschwegge camp
in Germany, my grandmother wrote neat, handwritten letters in Polish, where she described the "sad, hard life of the *Lager*," the longing
of her children "who after so many years of separation can no longer
wait to meet their parents," and her and Zindel's desire "to be together
with [their] children and start a new life of normalcy." She begged for

"connections" to hasten their petition, suggested they had been approved for an entry visa, and implicitly blamed the Agency for sending others before them.

At some point Ruchela hinted that she and Zindel planned to travel to neighboring Cyprus and from there try to enter Palestine. At the Central Zionist Archive, I found an "Oleh card" issued to Zindel Teitel, which referred to a file of prospective candidates for "aliyah."[54] Whether because the line was invariably long (the British government issued few entry certificates to Jews after the war), or because Zindel had tuberculosis (a reason that was never stated directly), or because family reunification was not a priority for postwar refugee aid workers, and possibly because reunification was not even deemed to be in the children's "best interests"[55]—Zindel and Ruchela were unable to enter British-controlled Palestine after the war.

In September 1947 the British government announced that in six months its Mandate over Palestine would be terminated. That month an Agency worker wrote Ruchela that she hoped the number of certificates would be increased the next year, but warned of "the terrible sacrifices" that lay ahead.

On November 29 the United Nations voted on the partition of Palestine. The next day the war began, first between Jewish and Palestinian inhabitants, then after the end of the British Mandate and the declaration of Israel's Independence, between Israel and Egypt, Jordan, Syria, Iraqi expeditionary forces, and the Arab Liberation Army, an army of volunteers from Arab countries, led by the Berlin-based, Nazi-allied Arab nationalist Fawzi al-Qawuqii. Hannan was enlisted, first to the Military Police ("his job was to go to people's homes and round up young men who would fight," Regina told me before she died. "It was a terrible thing. Many Holocaust survivors hid their children and refused to let them go. He had to argue with them.") Then he was enlisted into the air force, where he threw bombs manually out of a Black Spitfire made from abandoned spare parts of British planes.

Thirty Ein Harod members were killed, 978 in the Unified Kibbutz movement.[56] Among them was Gur Meirov, Saul Meirov's seventeen-year-old son. Meirov, whose organization, Mossad LeAliyah Bet, would continue to play a key role in DP camps and postwar Europe, was out of the country and did not attend his son's funeral. When he returned to what was now an independent State of Israel, he changed his name from Meirov to Avigur (father of Gur).

Emil Landau, whose diary had guided my search, was also killed. A delivery of grenades and rifles had been sent from Lebanon to Arab forces in Haifa, who then had the upper hand; he stopped it by jumping on top of the delivery truck and blowing up the weapons convoy with his own body. A year later, when the fighting halted, Emil's fourteen-year-old sister Ilana received, all alone, her brother's posthumous Medal of Valor, the highest Israeli medal of honor awarded for "an act of extreme bravery done during battle and involving extreme self-sacrifice," and one of only twelve given for the war. "I had no one left in the world," Ilana told me when she gave me Emil's diary. She missed Emil every day, she said, and she missed Poland.

Zindel Teitel died in 1949 at Sanatorium Gauting, a TB hospital just to the southwest of Munich. He had died in the West, in Germany of all places, and therefore his death, unlike his life and especially his war years as a refugee, was well documented. In 2018 I received his highly detailed, ninety-five-page medical file from Gauting Hospital. It noted "coma hepaticum" (liver failure) as the cause of death, and April 5, 1949, Hannan's twenty-second birthday, as its date.

Five weeks later, along with hundreds of thousands of refugees from displaced persons camps across Europe, from British detention camps in Cyprus, and from Egypt, Yemen, Iraq, Morocco, and Iran—Jewish refugees and migrants who could now enter freely into the newly established State of Israel—Ruchela disembarked in Haifa.[57]

Regina was eleven when she had last seen her mother. She was now eighteen and a member of Kibbutz Ein Harod. When I asked her about their meeting, she did not elaborate about it. She said, very quietly, in the passive voice, "*Hayta simkha gdola*" (There was great happiness). She also said, "When I saw my mother, I suddenly didn't know who I was. I had grown accustomed to thinking of myself as an Israeli. My mother was a refugee." Ruchela moved to Ein Harod with Regina, "but kibbutz life wasn't for her," my aunt had said, and after a few months Ruchela moved in with Hannan. They lived in a one-room apartment in Kiryat Hayyim, a squalid Haifa suburb; then in a two-room apartment at a better address in Haifa; and after my parents' marriage, in the apartment where six of us— my parents, us three siblings, and my grandmother—would live together for nearly two decades. It was in that dark apartment, with its quiet yet breathtaking views of the Mediterranean, that a girl of six or seven, raised in what I now knew were relative privilege and safety and care, asked her father why he loved his mother more than her.

Acknowledgments

*T*ehran Children was written over a decade, across three continents and in many cities: from New York to Warsaw to Tashkent to Tel Aviv. It is the kind of book that could not and would not have been written without the support of collaborators, institutions, translators, archivists, funders, without generosity and hospitality, without connections, without family, without friends and colleagues—without all those things that people who are thrust from their homes into a hostile wide world lose. It is a tragic book, because it tracks that loss—and worst—in minute detail. But it is also a hopeful book. Hopeful not only because I, the daughter of a refugee, have access to those things in abundance, but also because, as my research taught me, even the most dejected refugee had access to a bit of them, be it from Jewish aid and rescue organizations across the globe or from an anonymous Persian man dolling out a piece of candy. What is lost is lost and cannot be retrieved. What is lost will project into the lives of future generations. But this book, ultimately, is not only about the unmaking of the world of Holocaust refugees during World War II, but also about its imperfect remaking.

Tehran Children would not have been written without Salar Abdoh, who first turned me to this project and accompanied it in different ways from start to finish. It would have been much impoverished without the words of the "Tehran Children" themselves: first and foremost of my aunt Rivka Binyamini (Regina Teitel), whose superb memory and intelligence were crucial, and of Noemi Arison (Perelgric), Yosef Etzion, Tamar Peleg,

Bracha Mandel, and Ilana Karniel. It would have been a very different book without the boundless generosity, excellent meals, and fascinating conversation provided by my hosts across the globe: Viktor Aslanov, Sergey Kim, Magda Gawin, Mikhail Rogachev, Oybek Bozorov, Duban Simchoni, and Henryk Grynberg. And it surely would have been a much rougher (and longer) book without the input of my superb W. W. Norton editor, Alane Mason, aka "the R.B.G. of editing," who believed in the project from the start and did so much to help shape it.

The book draws on extensive research, conducted in far and near archives by other scholars before me: Stanley Diamond and Michael Richman of the Ostrów Mazowiecka Research Family Foundation, Israel Bartal, Valentina Brio, Rebecca Manley, Katrin Stoll, Lior Sternfeld, Daniel Tsadik, and also Anne Applebaum, Atina Grossman, Timothy Snyder, and Tara Zahra to name just a few. The book also draws on many languages—Polish, Yiddish, Russian, German, Farsi, Bukhori, Hebrew, as well as English—many of which I do not read. And so I am grateful to my translators: Agata Tumilowicz, Malgorzata Bakalarz Duverger, Agi Legutko, Grazynia Drabik, Peter Tsvetkov, Faina Tsvetkov, Elik Elhanan, Andreas Killen, and Roy Greenwald. Librarians at many archives, particularly Daniela Ozacky-Stern of Moreshet Archive, Misha Mitsel of the JDC, and Irena Czernichowska at the Hoover Institution at Stanford went out of their way to help. Jamie Fine and Nicole Alexeeva were superb research assistants, with Nicole doubling as a babysitter in the early years. Jody Schwartz, Eliyana Adler, and Alek Nadan intervened in critical moments and made miracles happen. Kevin Kanarek, a kindred soul and fellow author, built the Tehran Children website. Sarit Arison, Yuval Bdolach, Gideon Benyamini, Yael Benyamini, Uri Benyamini, Naomi Benyamini, Marissa Brostoff, Alex Dancyg, Maiken Derno, Meir Ezri, Vilma Gabbay, Lucy Gold, Dalia Guttman, Hannan Hever, Yana Joseph, Alyssa Katz, Heshmat Kermanshachi, Erec Koch, Orly Lubin, Moe Liu-D'Albero, Krzysztof Malczewski, Elizabeth Mazzola, Alan Melowsky, Abbas Milani, Roy Mittleman, Dee Dee Mozeleski, Jessica Papin, Iris Pappo, Ali Parsa, Barbara Rifkind, Peter Rosenblatt, Sarah Senk, Yaakov Sharett, Khosrow Sinai, William Willis, Dassi Zeidel, and Sari Zvi—all assisted the project in various ways.

Without the financial backing of the institutions that supported the long making of *Tehran Children*, I could not have written it. These were the National Foundation for the Humanities; the Provost Office and Research Foundation at the City College of New York; CCNY's Michael and Irene Ross Program in Jewish Studies; the Lady Davis Foundation at the Hebrew University in Jerusalem; CCNY's Office of the Dean of Humanities and the Arts; and the Mellon Foundation and Committee on the Study of Religion at the CUNY Graduate Center. The Sabbatical from CCNY and other gifts of time from my home institution were crucial.

Every exchange at lectures I was invited to give at Columbia, CUNY Graduate Center, and the Paris Yiddish Center-Medem Library propelled my thinking forward. I am grateful to Marianne Hirsch, Victoria Rosner, Francesca Bregoli, and Tal Hever-Chybowski for inviting me. Victoria also published an early introduction to the book. The wickedly smart and perennially fun members of my reading group—Daniel Gustafson, Robert Higney, Andreas Killen, András Kiséry, Václav Paris, and Harold Veeser—read parts of this manuscript in its various stages. I am especially thankful to Robert, who not only read, but also put down his own project to edit mine. Other smart friends and colleagues have been essential interlocutors: Natalia Aleksiun, Beth Baron, Elissa Bemporad, Emily Greble, Tamar Hess, Hannan Hever, Michele Kahane, Ben Lapp, Nancy K. Miller, and Daniel Rosenblatt.

I am grateful, finally, for the unrelenting support of my family: My mother, Zipora Dekel, who is not a protagonist of this book but is nonetheless a huge and constant protagonist of my life; her partner Yosef Rosenthal; my siblings, loves of my life, Benjamin Dekel and Sharon Tsvetkov; my brother-in-law Peter Tsvetkov; my nieces, Shira Dekel and Anna, Sophia, and Daniela Tsvetkov; my nephews, Itamar and Michael Dekel. I am grateful also to Amir Halfon for the years of support, encouragement, and the long journey we two took together. And finally to my son, Daniel Halfon, who has tolerated his mother's absences, has read and traveled, and who is such awesome company—Daniel is to me the greatest proof that a world can, indeed, be remade.

Archives

CZA	Central Zionist Archives, Jerusalem
EH	Ein Harod Archive
GKH	Ginzakh Kiddush Hashem (Sanctification of the Name Archive), Bnei Brak, Israel
HI	Hoover Institution, Stanford University
IPN	Instytut Pamieci Narodowej (Institute of National Remembrance), Warsaw
JDC	Joint Distribution Committee, New York
LOC	Library of Congress, Washington, D.C.
MAMAM	Moreshet Archive, Mordechai Anielevich Memorial, Givat Haviva, Israel
MS	Moshe Sharett Archive, Tel Aviv (online)
PISM	Polish Institute and Sikorski Museum, London
SMO	Syktyvkar Memorial Organization, Syktyvkar, Russia
USHMM	United States Holocaust Memorial Museum, Washington, D.C.

Notes

Introduction

1 "Revealing Errors: Iran, Jews and the Holocaust: an Answer to Mr. Black," *Iranian*, February 23, 2006, http://web.stanford.edu/group/abbasmilani/cgi-bin/wordpress/wp-content/uploads/2016/03/Revealing-Errors.pdf.
2 Quoted in Hall, *Gellner*, 59.
3 Arendt, "We Refugees," 110–11.

Chapter 1: "Each of Us Feels as If He Is Born Again"

1 Sinai, "A File," 172, trans. Salar Abdoh.
2 The questionnaires' main focus was on refugees' life in the Soviet Union, as their unstated goal was to collect documentation that would hinder the creation of a satellite Soviet Polish state at the end of the war, but other questions on resistance, religious life, and the experience of women were added over time. As many of the refugees were Jewish, many of the testifiers were Jewish as well. But identification of religious belonging began only in 1943, when as minister of state and representative of the Polish government-in-exile in the Near East, Stanisław Kot created the CIW, the Center of Information in the Near East, which collected Hannan's and others' testimony in March 1943. See Siekierski and Tych, *Widziałem Anioła*, 30–31.
3 Earlier Irena Grudzinka Gross and Jan Gross compiled a book of testimonies of mostly non-Jewish Polish child refugees collected in Iran. *War Through Children's Eyes: Soviet Occupation of Poland and the Deportations 1939–1941* was published by the Hoover Institution in 1981.
4 Roy Chicky Arad, " Meet the Iranian embassy in Jerusalem," *Ha'aretz*, July 11, 2015, https://www.haaretz.co.il/magazine/tozeret/.premium-1.2679611.

5 Reza Shah Pahlavi, founder of the Pahlavi dynasty, was Iran's king from 1925 to 1941. His son Muhammad Reza Pahlavi ruled from 1941 until 1979, when a popular Islamic Revolution supplanted Iran's 2,500-year-old monarchy.

6 Beeta Baghoolizadeh, "Lior Sternfeld on Polish Refugees in Mid-Century Tehran: War and Migration in the Cosmopolitan City," Ajam Media Collective, January 22, 2015, https://ajammc.com/2015/01/22/lior-sternfeld-polish -refugees-iran/.

7 *Life*, August 23, 1943. American-made industrial vehicles that had been converted for military use represented a large part of U.S. aid to the Allied forces, some of which were assembled in Iran.

8 Hirschberg, "Yerakh ha'eitanim," 44.

9 Quoted in Ziolkowska-Boehm, *Polish Experience*, 1510.

10 Rosenberg, 112.

11 Ailreza Asgharzadeh, *Iran and the Challenge of Diversity.* New York: Palgrave, 2007:91.

12 Foreign Ministry to the Ministry of the Interior, September 1936, letter no. 25691: "As you may be aware, ever since the regime of the National Socialists has come to power in Germany the Jews of that country have met a difficult condition and are emigrating from Germany to other countries." Rā'ī Gallūjah, *Bar'rasī va*, 2015.

13 See Yishai, 1949.

14 Published in Rā'ī Gallūjah, *Bar'rasī va*, 2015.

15 Jenkins, "Iran in Nazi Order."

16 Hersh Cynowicz to JDC, May 9, 1941, JDC Archives, Collection 1933–1944, file # 712.

17 Rafael Szaffar to the Jewish Agency, Jerusalem, August 20, 1942, quoted in Saadoun and Rappel, *Ba-makhteret*, 100.

18 Grynberg, *Children of Zion*, 162.

19 Siddiqui, *Hospitality*, 27.

20 More secular Jews expressed *tzedakah* (charity), which shares a root with *tzedek* (justice), through a general will for charitable giving. The religious expressed it through specific commandments, like one requiring farmers to leave the corners of their fields unharvested so that "the poor and the stranger" could pick the crops there.

21 Tsadik, "Legal Status," 380.

22 Tsadik, "Legal Status," 401.

23 Bird, *Journeys*, p. 2:155.

24 Lewis, *Jews of Islam*, 166.

25 Hirschberg, "Yerakh ha'eitanim," 54.

26 Quoted in Tsadik, "Legal Status," 108.

27 Sternfeld, *Between Iran and Zion*, 23.

28 Yishai, *Tsir beli*, 90.

29 Quoted in Dan, *Unpaved Road*, 176.

30 Shenhav, *Arab Jews*, 19.

31 Report of Elizabeth Kottler for the Jewish National Fund. Shamir, *Yaldei Tehran*, 45.

Chapter 2: "A Liberal Family"

1 Bartal, Polonsky, and Ury, *Jews and Their Neighbours*, 10.

2 Data compiled by Michael Richman for the Ostrow Mazowiecka Research Family organization. www.Ostrów-mazoweicka.com.

3 Hundert, *Jews in Poland*, 22.

4 Levin, *Megilat Polin*, 150–51.

5 Arye Margolis, in the Ostrów Mazowiecka Yizkor Book, www.Ostrów -mazoweicka.com.

6 Dziennik urzedowy Guberni Augustowskiej Suwalki, December 31, 1849– January 12, 1850, in Bartal, Polonsky, and Ury, *Jews and Their Neighbours*, 75.

7 http://ohd.huji.ac.il/holocaust/project241/project241pdf/241-16.pdf.

8 As I learned from Pęziński, *Ostrów Mazowiecka*, chapter "On the Co-Existence of Jews and Poles."

Chapter 3: Border Crossing

1 All testimonies collected by the Polish Information Center were called protocols.

2 Grynberg, *Children of Zion*, 16.

3 Grynberg, *Children of Zion*, 10.

4 Grynberg, *Children of Zion*, 21.

5 Grynberg, *Children of Zion*, 17–49.

6 Grynberg, *Children of Zion*, 55–56.

7 Bugaĭ, *Deportations of People*, 194.

8 Grynberg, *Children of Zion*, 72.

9 Solzenitsyn, *Gulag Archipelago*, pt. 1, chap. 4.

Chapter 4: *Ukazniks*

1 Grynberg, *Children of Zion*, 75–77.

2 Solzenitsyn, *Gulag Archipelago*, pt. 2, chap. 3.

3 Gross and Gross, *Children's Eyes*.

4 Grynberg, *Children of Zion*, 77–78.

5 Bugaĭ, *Deportations of People*, 194.

6 Solzenitsyn, *Gulag Archipelago*, 237.

7 Gross and Gross, *Children's Eyes*, xxiii.

8 Collected by the Syktyvkar Memorial Organization (SMO).

9 Sura to Emma, September 5, 1940, courtesy Noemi Arison. The letter, written in Polish, was translated into Hebrew by Noemi Arison.

10 Sura to Adam and Emma, March 10, 1941, courtesy Noemi Arison. The letter, written in Polish, was translated into Hebrew by Noemi Arison.

11 http://www.shoa.org.il/image.ashx?i=79378.pdf&fn=35.pdf.

12 Grynberg, *Children of Zion*, 115–16.

13 Jewish Agency for Palestine to the WJC, memo, September 24, 1942, JDC.

14 Grynberg, *Children of Zion*, 90.

15 Grynberg, *Children of Zion*, 89.

16 Solzenitsyn, *Gulag Archipelago*, 208.

17 Grynberg, *Children of Zion*, 121–23.

Chapter 5: "I Am a Jew"; "I Am an Uzbek"

1 Polish government-in-exile to Polish embassy in Washington, cable, September 5, 1941, in Kot, *Conversations*, 2.

2 Kot's Conversation with American Red Cross; Kot, *Conversations*, 40.

3 Meeting of the JDC Executive Committee, minutes, December 10, 1941, transcript, JDC.

4 A. I. Vyshinsky, vice-commissar for foreign affairs, in Kot, *Conversations*, 63.

5 Meeting of the JDC Executive Committee, minutes, December 10, 1941, transcript, JDC; Jewish Agency for Palestine to the World Jewish Congress, memo, September 24, 1942, JDC.

6 Kot, *Conversations*, 31. This is confirmed by children's testimonies. One child reported that his family "had no money for the journey and walked three hundred kilometers," while another reported that his family "received red papers—for criminals," which supposedly entitled them to a stipend. Grynberg, *Children of Zion*, 124.

7 Anders, *Army in Exile*, quoted in Davies, *Trail of Hope*, 10.

8 Kot, *Conversations*, 146.

9 Kot, *Conversations*, 1.

10 Laub, "Failed Empathy."

11 Wat, *My Century*, 8.

12 Wat, *My Century*, 91.

13 Wat, *My Century*, 138.

14 "Władysław Broniewski," Culture.pl, n.d., https://culture.pl/en/artist/wladyslaw-broniewski.

15 Brauda, "Tashkent."

16 Mordecai Rozman testimony, in "Zionist Undergrounds in the USSR," A.1532.01, MAMAM; Ben Hayyim Mula Kaciasky testimony, in "The Holocaust in the USSR," A.1493.12, MAMAM.

17 Manley, *Tashkent Station*, 1.

18 Manley, *Tashkent Station*, 230.

19 Manley, *Tashkent Station*, 26.

20 "Uzbekistan Soviet Republic Becomes New Home for Hundreds of Thousands of Evacuated Jews," Jewish Telegraphic Agency, February 18, 1942, JDC.

21 Wat, *My Century*, 344.

22 Wat, *My Century*, 27.

23 Wat, *My Century*, 307.

24 As told to Ziolkowska-Boehm, *Polish Experience.*

25 Władysław Kot to Polish Ministry for Foreign Affairs in London, telegram, November 8, 1941, in Kot, *Conversations*, 97.

26 Medvedeva-Nathoo, "Certificate of Birth."

27 Kot, *Conversations*, 30.

28 Kot, *Conversations*, 31.

29 Wat, *My Century*, 309.

30 Shterenshis, *Tamerlane*, xvii.

31 Brubaker, "Rethinking Nationhood," 9–10.

32 Wat, *My Century*, 336.

33 Grynberg, *Children of Zion*, 136.

34 Grynberg, *Children of Zion*, 136.

35 Kot, *Conversations*, 206.

36 Ben Hayyim Mula Kaciasky testimony, in "The Holocaust in the USSR," A.1493.12, MAMAM.

37 Medvedeva-Nathoo, "Certificate of Birth."

38 Etzion, *Yeladim*, 84.

39 Manley, *Tashkent Station*, 227.

40 Ben Michael, *Yaldei Tehran*, 63.

41 Wat, *My Century*, 336.

42 Wat, *My Century*, 336.

43 Medvedeva-Nathoo, "Certificate of Birth."

44 The diary was transcribed by Medvedeva-Nathoo.

45 Brauda, "Tashkent."

46 Orlev, *Habyta*, 116.

47 Grynberg, *Children of Zion*, 128–29.

48 Martin, *Affirmative Action Empire*, 432.

49 Manley, *Tashkent Station*, 221.

50 Manley, *Tashkent Station*, 221.

51 G'ulum, *Mukammai*, translated from Russian by Sergey Kim.

52 Guliam, *Izbrannyre*, 1:54.

53 Manley, *Tashkent Station*, 226.

54 Manley, *Tashkent Station*, 224.

55 Manley, *Tashkent Station*, 222.

56 Manley, *Tashkent Station*, 227.

57 Wat, *My Century*, 334.

58 Wat, *My Century*, 335.

59 Wat, *My Century*, 332.

60 Grynberg, *Children of Zion*, 129.

61 Grynberg, *Children of Zion*, 129.

62 Mansur Mirovalev, "Uzbekistan's Long Persecuted Bukhara Jews," *Aljazeera*, May 6, 2015.

63 Human Rights Watch, Islam Karimov, https://www.hrw.org/tag/islam-karimov.

64 Zylberman, *Missing Persons*, loc. 881.

65 Grynberg, *Children of Zion*, 131.

66 Orlev, *Habyta*, 55.

67 Applebaum, *Red Famine*, 205.

68 Wat, *My Century*, 336.

69 Moshe Shertok, Meeting of the Zionist General Council, Jerusalem, minutes, September 9, 1942, MS, http://www.sharett.org.il/cgi-webaxy/sal/sal.pl.

Chapter 6: A Polish Nation in Exile, Jewish Relief Efforts

1   Engel, *Shadow of Auschwitz*, 122. The Sejm is the lower house of parliament in Poland.

2   "Relief for Jewish War Victims in Russia," *London Jewish Chronicle*, September 5, 1941, JDC Archives, Collection 193–1944, file # 421.

3   Kot, *Conversations*, 4.

4   Kot to Molotov, September 10, 1941; Kot, *Conversations*, 9.

5   Bauer, *American Jewry*, 22.

6   Quoted in Bauer, *American Jewry*, 35.

7   Bauer, *American Jewry*, 30–31.

8   Ephraim E. Yolles (rabbi, United Orthodox Congregations) to James Rosenberg (JDC), May 21, 1941, JDC Archives, Collection 1933–1944, file # 421.

9   JDC Archives, Collection 1933–1944, file # 1055.

10 JDC Archives, Collection 1933–1944, file # 421.

11 Sylwin Strakacz, "Report About the Actual Situation of Relief Work for Former Polish Exiles in Soviet Russia," September 24, 1941, JDC Archives, Collection 1933–1944, file # 421.

12 Saul Hayes to National Offices of the United Jewish Relief and War Relief Agency, memo, September 18, 1941, JDC Archives, Collection 1933–1944, file # 421.

13 Warburg to Litvinov, memo, February 25, 1942, JDC. JDC Archives, Collection 1933–1944, file # 421.

14 United Jewish Refugee and War Relief Agency, memo, September 18, 1941, JDC Archives, Collection 1933–1944, file # 421.

15 Kot, *Conversations*, 15.

16 Kot, *Conversations*, 41.

17 Kot, *Conversations*, 67. Approximately 22,000 Polish officers and POWs had been mass-murdered a year earlier at Katyń.

18 Kot, *Conversations*, 102.

19 Kot, *Conversations*. 60–61.

20 "Polish Embasada to the Soviet Union," December 8, 1942, HI. KOL-25-33A, USHMM.

21 Kot, *Conversations*, 159.

22 Meeting of the JDC Executive Committee, minutes, December 10, 1941, JDC.

23 During Sikorski's tenure as prime minister from December 1922 to May 1923, he publicly pronounced Poland's Catholic essence and expressed doubts about Jewish loyalty. See Engel, *Shadow of Auschwitz*, 52.

24 Engel, *Shadow of Auschwitz*, 54–55.

25 Meeting of the JDC Executive Committee, minutes, December 10, 1941, JDC Archives, Collection 1933–1944, file # 421; Kot, *Conversations*, 173.

26 January 8, 1942, JDC Archives, Collection 1933–1944, file # 421.

27 Edward Warburg to Judah Magnes (Hebrew University, Jerusalem), cable, January 22, 1942, JDC Archives, Collection 1933–1944, file # 421.

28 Consul General of Poland to JDC, March 10, 1942, JDC Archives, Collection 1933–1944, file # 421.

29 Herbert Katzki to Dr. J. J. Golub and Alfred S. Cohn, February 24, 1942, JDC Archives, Collection 1933–1944, file # 421.

30 JDC Archives, Collection 1933–1944, file # 421. Alongside a relatively small amount of antityphoid medications, much of what the JDC initially purchased seems geared toward the needs of the army, not the civilian population: 150,000 anesthesia tablets, 100 pounds of ether, 100,000 sulfanilamide tablets, a powdered antibacterial medication commonly used by the Allies, and 3,700 ampuls of syphilis medication. I did not read of any cases of syphilis in the refugee testimonies, but documents Sergey Kim found at the Tashkent archive referred to 49,411 cases of contagious diseases treated by the Anders Army.

31 Yitzhaq Gruenbaum to JDC, March 17, 1942, JDC Archives, Collection 1933–1944, file # 421.

32 JDC to United Jewish Refugee and War Relief Agency, April 17, 1942. JDC Archives, Collection 1933–1944, file # 421.

33 JDC to Ose, April 20, 1942, JDC Archives, Collection 1933–1944, file # 421.

34 Kot to JDC, cables, May 7 and 12, 1942, JDC Archives, Collection 1933–1944, file # 421.

35 Kot to JDC, May 7, 1942, JDC Archives, Collection 1933–1944, file # 421.

36 Wat, *My Century*, 340.

37 Wat, *My Century*, 323.

38 Wat, *My Century*, 340.

39 Grynberg, *Children of Zion*, 141.

40 Grynberg, *Children of Zion*, 141.

41 Wat, *My Century*, 340.

42 Ben Michael, *Yaldei Tehran*, 27–28.

43 Kot, report "On the Case of Jewish Citizens," August 11, 1942. KOL-25-33A, USHMM.

44 Litvak, 1997:139. Converts like Wat served as delegates; Wat reports that he was appointed as delegate to Fergana to replace a Jewish dentist, which suggests that there may have been at least a few such appointees.

45 Wat, *My Century*, 342.

46 Harry Viteles, *Report on Visit to Bagdad (2.XI-9.XI, 1942) and Tehran (11.XI-2.XII, 1942*. 12.31.1942. JDC Archives, Collection 1933–1944, file # 712, 713.

47 Produced in London, November 17, 1944, A-7-307-40, HI.

48 Box 28, HI. See Gross and Gross, *Children's Eyes*, 254.

49 Wat, *My Century*, 340.

50 Kot, *Conversations*, 141.

51 Grynberg, *Children of Zion*, 143–44.

52 Ziolkowska-Boehm, *Polish Experience*, 379.

53 Gutman, "Jews in General Anders' Army in the Soviet Union," 237.

54 Gutman, "Jews in General Anders' Army in the Soviet Union," 237.

55 Ben Michael, *Yaldei Tehran*, 101.

56 Kot, report "On the Case of Jewish Citizens," August 11, 1942. KOL-25-33A, USHMM.

57 Ben Michael, *Yaldei Tehran*, 101.

58 Shekel, *Nomadism and Soil*, 74.

59 Yehuda Pompiansky testimony, A.1492.02, MAMAM.

60 Viteles, *Report on Visit*. JDC Archives, Collection 1933–1944, file # 712, 713.

61 The Polish position is summarized at length in Engel, *Shadow of Auschwitz*, 133.

62 Engel, *Shadow of Auschwitz*, 134.

63 At the October 1, 1941, Moscow Conference, British and American envoys Lord Beaverbrook and Averell Harriman signed with Stalin the Lend-Lease protocol

that would supply food, oil, and weaponry to the Soviet Union. Kot reports that the Jewish-American ambassador Laurence Steinhardt, a staunch Roosevelt man, opposed Lend-Lease, feeling that it gave Stalin too much in return for too little. He preferred that aid to the Polish refugees be shipped and distributed separately from aid to the USSR, and he even facilitated direct meetings between Poles and representatives of the American Red Cross. Lord Beaverbrook, a loud proponent of the Lend-Lease agreement, opposed this idea. Kot, *Conversations*, 53–54.

64 Kot, *Conversations*, 82.

65 Yishai, *An Emissary without a Title*, 98; Tamar Peleg testimony.

66 "Jews in General Anders' Army," 237.

67 Engel, *Shadow of Auschwitz*, 135.

68 Engel, *Shadow of Auschwitz*, 136.

69 Maxim Litvinov to Jacob Landau (Overseas News Agency), July 10, 1942, JDC Archives, Collection 1933–1944, file # 1056.

70 Kot to Polish minister of foreign affairs, January 5, 1942, in Kot, *Conversations*, 185.

71 Kot to Polish minister of foreign affairs, January 5, 1942, in Kot, *Conversations*, 185.

72 Kot, report "On the Case of Jewish Citizens," August 11, 1942. KOL-25-33A, USHMM.

73 Wat, *My Century*, 233.

74 Wat, *My Century*, 359.

75 Reported in "Poland: Warsaw Ghetto museum will show the 'mutual love' between Poles, Jews," *Times of Israel*, March 8, 2018, https://www.timesofisrael .com/poland-warsaw-ghetto-museum-will-show-the-mutual-love-between -poles-jews/.

Chapter 7: Samarqand

1 Ziolkowska-Boehm, *Polish Experience*, 436.

2 Maia Szalavitz, "How Childhood Hunger Can Change Adult Personality," *Time*, April 11, 2013, http://healthland.time.com/2013/04/11/how-childhood -hunger-can-change-adult-personality/.

3 Manley, *Tashkent Station*, 232.

4 As Italy struggled to accommodate an influx of a half-million people between 2014 and 2017, formerly moderate Italian cities saw the rise of right-wing, anti-immigrant politicians, while migrants complained of being turned away from medical clinics and schools. "In Once-Welcoming Italy, the Tide Turns Against Migrants," *Washington Post*, August 25, 2017.

5 Wat, *My Century*, 336.

6 Efron, *Diaries*, entry for August 29, 1942.

7 Translated by Sergey Kim from Документы и материалы по истории советско-польских отношений (*Documents and Materials on the History of Soviet-Polish Relations*), T. VII, Moscow, 342.

8 Translated by Sergey Kim from Государственный Архив Самаркандской области /ГА Самаркандской (State Archive of the Samarkand Region / General Archive of Samarkand) Obl., F. 942, Op. 1, D. 58, pp. 14–18.

9 Grynberg, *Children of Zion*, 153.

10 Grynberg, *Children of Zion*, 153–55.

11 Translated by Sergey Kim from ГА Самаркандской. Обл., Ф. 74, Оп. 1, Д. 1039, л. 4 (General Archive of Samarkand, Regional, F. 74, Op. 1, D. 1039, l. four). The letter pertained to the Narlay district of Samarqand. But the same conditions, its author wrote, prevailed in several districts of the Samarqand region and in the city itself.

12 Kot, *Conversations*, 152.

13 Kot, *Conversations*, 183.

14 Engel, *Shadow of Auschwitz*, 140.

15 Davies, *Trail of Hope*, loc. 1207.

16 Engel, *Shadow of Auschwitz*, 138. When it was revealed that the Soviets would be transferring four hundred Jews to the Anders Army, Engel writes, Anders even wrote in a secret memo to division commanders that they should be disqualified for medical reasons.

17 Gutman, "Jews in General Anders' Army," 242.

18 Gutman, "Jews in General Anders' Army," 244.

19 Kot, report "On the Case of Jewish Citizens," August 11, 1942. KOL-25-33A, USHMM.

20 Meeting of the Executive Committee, minutes, September 9, 1942. Shertok put it poetically: "I was still a young man when I read *Anna Karenina*, and I remember how in the salons there was talk of *Obrussia Polski* [Sovietization of Poland]. It seems that history has returned. But things have also shifted: Germany invaded Russia, Russia has joined the Democratic Front, and an agreement has been signed between the Soviet and the Polish governments, [which] has been granted a certain permission to evacuate its people out of Russia as military personnel, and also not only as military personnel." September 11, 1942, MS.

21 Engel, *Shadow of Auschwitz*, 140.

22 Engel, *Shadow of Auschwitz*, 144.

23 Simon Mirelman, Letter to Mundo Israelita, October 24, 1942, correcting statement made by the South American Jewish World Congress on October 10, trans. from Spanish by Lolita Goldstein, AR33/44-347, JDC. Polish sources confirm the payment of four pounds. Report on the distribution of funds by the Polish Refugee Aid Office in Jerusalem. s, 271, USHMM.

24 Letter from Eliyahu Dobkin to Lous G. Dreyfus, Jr., American Minister, Tehran. C.54.02.01, MAMAM. Kot maintained that only one of the people on this list received a Soviet exit visa. Report "On the Case of Jewish Citizens," August 11, 1942. KOL-25-33A, USHMM.

25 Reported by Dr. Lubeczewski on November 5, 1942, Report on the distribution of funds by the Polish Refugee Aid Office in Jerusalem. KOL-25-39A, 158–59, USHMM.

26 Litvak, 1997:141

27 Martin, *Affirmative Action Empire*, 432.

28 Anna Akhmatova, "Poem Without a Hero," *The Complete Poems of Anna Akhmatova*, expanded ed., trans. Judith Hemschemeyer, ed. Roberta Reeder (Boston: Zephyr, 1989), 575.

29 Brauda, "Tashkent," 180.

30 Manley, *Tashkent Station*, 227.

31 Testimonies given in the documentary *The Children of Teheran*.

32 Grynberg, *Children of Zion*, 156.

Chapter 8: Polish and Jewish Nation Building in Tehran

1 Grynberg, *Children of Zion*, 159.

2 Kot, report "On the Case of Jewish Citizens," August 11, 1942. KOL-25-33A, USHMM.

3 Damandan, *Children of Isfahan*, 278.

4 As Lior Sternfeld writes, "Every state or organization had a motive to inflate or deflate numbers; the Soviets wanted to show that not that many were put in internment to begin with, so they provided low numbers (the lowest estimations from them are 40K), the Red Cross wanted to show and justify the huge budgets they received to treat refugees and they talk about 500K, Iran had interest in greater numbers because it got its food supply based on numbers of refugees, and the British showed bigger numbers because they operated the transportation from Central Asia to Iran and India and then to East Africa. There is no certainty that any of the numbers are accurate." Sternfeld, "'Poland Is Not Lost.'"

5 "But at the last moment we learned that more were coming than we expected," Sir Reader Bullard, the British ambassador to Iran, wrote in a letter to London, "that they were to arrive in a much shorter time than had been foreseen, and that some thousands of civilian refugees—women and children and old men—whom we had never expected at all, would arrive with the troops." Bullard, *Letters from Tehran*, 128.

6 Kot, Report "On the Case of Jewish Citizens," August 11, 1942. KOL-25-33A, USHMM.

7 Damandan, *Children of Isfahan*, 277.

8 Alexander Ross, "Urgent Report on Polish Refugees in Persia," Box 420, File "Ewakuacja obywateli polskich z ZSSR, 1945," HI.

9 Netzer, *Padyavand*, 87, also reports that a four-year-old boy named Yehuda vanished.

10 Polish Delegatura in Tehran, *Report on the Organization 1942*.

11 Anonymous observer, August 21, 1942, quoted in Saadoun and Rappel, *Ba-makhteret*.

12 Polish Delegatura in Tehran, *Report on the Organization 1942*, pp. 42–78.

13 Hirschberg, "Yerakh ha'eitanim," 44–45.

14 Wasilewska, *Suffer Little Children*, puts the number of evacuated Catholic children at 22,688. See also Gross and Gross, *Children's Eyes*, 24.

15 Grynberg, *Children of Zion*, 162.

16 Hirschberg, "Yerakh ha'eitanim," 47.

17 Damandan, *Children of Isfahan*, 278. The article was published on April 17, 1942.

18 Bullard cynically attributed Persians' embrace of the refugees to their schadenfreude: "The Russians are always preaching about the wonderful conditions in Soviet Russia, and I have seen newspapers which were distributed in Persia by Soviet troops, showing the delights of collective farm life in the Soviet Union. So if the Persians now find pleasure in helping people they probably consider victims of Bolsheviks one cannot be surprised." Bullard, *Letters from Tehran*, 130.

19 Grynberg, *Children of Zion*, 162.

20 Quoted in Ziolkowska-Boehm, *Polish Experience*, 66.

21 Hirschberg, "Yerakh ha'eitanim," 47.

22 Polish Delegatura in Tehran, *Report on the Organization 1942*, pp. 42–78.

23 Władysław Banaczyk, minister of internal affairs of the Polish government-in-exile, asks in a letter to Viktor Styburski of the Office of Labor and Social Welfare in Tehran for data about schoolchildren in Iran in order to determine how many books to send. Documents of Viktor Styburski. KOL-25-33A., USHMM.

24 Polish Delegatura in Tehran, *Report on the Organization 1942*.

25 Polish Delegatura in Tehran, *Report on the Organization 1942*, pp. 42–78.

26 Damandan, *Children of Isfahan*, 274.

27 Boaz, *Alum*, 151.

28 Quoted in Blum, *Brigade*, 5.

29 Boaz, *Alum*, 114.

30 Boaz, *Alum*, 106–7.

31 Quoted in Shapira, *Haapala*, 204. *Alum akh nokhakh bakol* (Absent yet present in everything) are the words engraved on Meirov's gravestone in Kibbutz Kinneret.

32 Braginsky, *Am khoter*, 290.

33 Braginsky, *Am khoter*, 292.

34 Quoted in Boaz, *Alum*, 130.

35 Braginsky, *Am khoter*, 293.

36 Boaz, *Alum*, 147–8.

37 Efraim Shiloh testimony, A.1584.14, MAMAM.

38 Braginsky, *Am khoter*, 293–4.

39 Boaz, *Alum*, 141.

40 Rafael Szaffar to JDC, cable, May 26, 1942, JDC.

41 Polish Delegatura in Tehran, *Report on the Organization 1942*, pp. 42–78.

42 Ben Michael, *Yaldei Tehran*, Interview with David Lauenberg, 108.

43 Minute details of their living conditions are found in Polish Delegatura in Tehran, *Report on the Organization 1942*.

44 Polish Delegatura in Tehran, *Report on the Organization 1942*, pp. 42–78.

45 Hirschberg, "Yerakh ha'eitanim," 50.

46 Levi, *History of Jews of Iran*, 545.

47 Quoted in Saadoun, *Iran*, 104.

48 Intelligentsia were 10 percent of the total refugees according to Polish Delegatura in Tehran, *Report on the Organization 1942*.

49 Omer, *Ha'takhana*, 168.

50 Shamir, *Yaldei Tehran*, 43.

51 Shamir, *Yaldei Tehran*, 43.

52 Shekel, *Nedudim*, 74.

53 Shekel, *Nedudim*, 76.

54 Shekel, *Nedudim*, 78–79.

55 Shekel, *Nedudim*, 156.

56 Polish Delegatura in Tehran, *Report on the Organization 1942*, pp. 152–54. The letter is included in a report on Poles' living conditions.

57 Shamir, *Yaldei Tehran*, 47.

58 For an account of daily life in Isfahan, see Polish Delegatura in Tehran, *Report on the Organization 1942*.

59 Omer, *Ha'takhana*, 181.

60 Omer, *Ha'takhana*, 171.

61 Omer, *Ha'takhana*, 172.

62 Shekel, *Nedudim*, 79.

63 Landau, *Diary*, entry for December 1, 1942.

64 Shamir, *Yaldei Tehran*, 39.

65 Whiteman, *Escape*, 109.

66 Polish Delegatura in Tehran, *Report on the Organization 1942*.

67 Viteles, *Report on Visit*.

68 Hirschberg, "Yerakh ha'eitanim," 50.

69 Viteles, *Report on Visit*, puts their number at "around twenty." A Jewish Agency
    report "The Human Element in Tehran" noted the moral degradation of some
    young women among the Jewish refugees. September 24, 1942, JDC.

70 Yishai, *Tsir beli*, 260.

71 Many of these cultural institutions would remain in operation until the 1979
    revolution. Beeta Baghoolizadeh, "Lior Sternfeld on Polish Refugees in Mid-
    Century Tehran: War and Migration in the Cosmopolitan City," Ajam Media
    Collective, January 22, 2015, https://ajammc.com/2015/01/22/lior-sternfeld
    -polish-refugees-iran/.

72 Ziolkowska-Boehm, *Polish Experience*, loc. 1520.

73 Etzion, *Yeladim*, 96.

74 Yishai, *Tsir beli*, 102.

75 Omer, *Ha'takhana*, 180. As I write, a study shows rising levels of "sexual
    exploitation of unaccompanied migrant and refugee boys" in Greece and
    other refugee hosting countries. Julie Freccero et al., "Sexual Exploitation of
    Unaccompanied Migrant and Refugee Boys in Greece: Approaches to Preven-
    tion," *PLOS Medicine*, November 22, 2017, https://doi.org/10.1371/journal.pmed
    .1002438.

76 Ben Michael, *Yaldei Tehran*. Nahum Herzberg, an Agency representative and
    Mossad agent, reported about a Jewish woman who was coaxed into marriage
    with "a Tehrani professor," with whom she had twins. She would not care for
    them, and Herzberg prided on separating them from her. Herzberg testimony,
    A.1583.03, MAMAM.

77 Hirschberg, "Yerakh ha'eitanim," 49.

78 Hirschberg, "Yerakh ha'eitanim," 50.

79 Hirschberg, "Yerakh ha'eitanim," 53–54.

80 Shenhav, *Arab Jews*, 103.

81 The term "Arab-Jews," which Shenhav uses to highlight the contrast with
    "European-Jews," isn't an accurate description of the ethnicity of Persians. Nor
    were Persian Jews "discovered" in 1942, having had links to the international
    Zionist movement by 1917.

82 In November 1942 David Ben-Gurion, head of the Jewish Agency, announced
    in a speech in Rehovot his plan to bring a million Jews from Middle Eastern
    countries to Palestine: "The Jews of Europe will perish, and the Jews of Russia
    are locked in."

83 Hirschberg, "Yerakh ha'eitanim," 53.

84 Yishai, *Tsir beli*, 272–74.

85 "Report of the Inquiry Committee Regarding the Treatment of Children and
    Refugees in Tehran," p. 12, D.1.5589, MAMAM.

86 "Report of the Inquiry Committee Regarding the Treatment of Children and
    Refugees in Tehran," p. 12, D.1.5589, MAMAM.

87 Hirschberg, "Yerakh ha'eitanim," 54.

88 Viteles, *Report on Visit*.

89 In a confidential Mossad L'aliya Bet report dated September 9, 1942 the writer suggests that some Jewish children had been transferred to Kenya already and suggests that local Jewish organizations be contacted to aid them. C.54-02-01, MAMAM.

90 Boaz, *Alum*, 146.

91 Moshe Agami Averbuch testimony, A.1583.01, MAMAM.

92 Shayke Viner testimony, D.1.1003, MAMAM.

93 Efraim Shiloh testimony, A.1584.14, MAMAM. In Tehran circa 1942, all Mossad LeAliyah Bet operatives were members of kibbutzim. Most remained members until their deaths. At the United Kibbutz archives, situated inside the Center for Shared Living in Givat Haviva in northern Israel, historians collected their testimonies, as well as those of movement members with whom they made contact across the Soviet border.

94 Zvi Melnitzer testimony, D.1.5929, MAMAM. Boaz, *Alum*, 153.

95 Boaz, *Alum*, 149.

96 Nahum Herzberg testimony, A.1583.03, MAMAM.

97 Boaz, *Alum*, 150.

98 E.E. (possibly Eliyahu Abulin) to A. Isfandiary, Consul General for Iran, Jerusalem, thanking Isfandiary, June 3, 1942, A245\121-10, CZA. In a June 15, 1950, lecture, Shertok would note that "only one woman in the entire country managed to obtain a visa to Iran." Speeches file, MS.

99 Zipora Shertok, letter to Bernard Joseph, November 1942, A245\121-31, CZA.

100 Accounts of Polish refugees taunting and bullying the Jewish children on their way to fetch food from the camp's communal kitchen also appear in the memoir of Yosef Etzion, *Yeladim*, 8.

101 Zipora Shertok, letter to her children, November 14, 1942. A245\121-23, CZA.

102 Moshe Shertok, meeting of the Zionist Agency Executive Council. April 25, 1943. Shertok states that these deaths were omitted from the report in order to not upset the Polish authorities with whom the Agency was dealing.

103 Moshe Shertok to Zipora Shertok, November 23, 1942, A245\121-7, CZA.

104 Hirschberg, "Yerakh ha'eitanim," 54–55.

105 Viteles, *Report on Visit*.

106 James Aldridge, "Abuses by Poles in Tehran Reported: Correspondent Says Refugees Even Sold Relief Good Supplied by Americans," North American Newspaper Alliance, March 13, 1943.

107 "Meeting at Tehran on 27 October, 1942 between the C.-in-C. and General Anders. Lt. Colonels Szymanski and Hulls were also present." AXII.65/1, PISM.

108 Kot, Report "On the Case of Jewish Citizens," August 11, 1942. KOL-25-33A, USHMM.

109 The first transport to Africa of ten thousand refugees began transports on Sep-
     tember 2, 1942. Polish Delegatura in Tehran, *Report on the Organization 1942*,
     pages 83–112. Non-Jews were evacuated to India, though many were disappear-
     ing between camps and trains, as Indian camps rumored to be worse than
     those in Tehran. Charles Passman to Harry Viteles, July 29, 1943, JDC.

110 Saul Leavitt to Harry Viteles, November 12, 1942, JDC.

111 Henrietta Szold to Zipora Shertok, December 10, 1942, A245\121-32, CZA.

112 Viteles, *Report on Visit*, 14–16.

113 Paul Baerwald (JDC) to Laurence W. Steinhardt, October 27, 1942, JDC.

114 Whiteman, *Escape*, 131.

115 "The general feeling of the American community in Iran," a JDC representa-
     tive reported, is that "if the British really wished to arrange it and see the chil-
     dren in Palestine, it could be done." Viteles, *Report on Visit*.

116 Meeting of the Jewish Agency Executive Board, April 25, 1944. Sharett (Sher-
     tok), *Moshe Sharett and his Legacy*.

117 The option to fly the children on British or American planes is mentioned in a
     secret Mossad L'Aliyah Bet memo dated 9/29/1942. C.54.02.01, MAMAM.

118 Shertok reported on his conversation with Eden after his return from London,
     in an April 25, 1943 meeting of the Zionist Agency Executive Council. Sharett
     (Shertok), *Moshe Sharett and his Legacy*.

119 Zipora Shertok, letter to Bernard Joseph, November 1942, A245\121–31, CZA
     A245\121-31, CZA.

120 By December 31, 1942, the JDC had spent only $9,000 in Iran: $3,000 for Pass-
     over seder needs for Jewish soldiers in the British and Polish armies as well as
     for the first refugees in Tehran (for which it received no receipts or account-
     ing,) and $6,000, which it cabled on September 23, 1942, at Szaffar's request. It
     had pledged another $5,500 "towards financing relief programs for the Jew-
     ish refugees" at the request of Zipora Shertok on December 7 but had not yet
     cabled them. "It is our understanding," JDC head Paul Baerwald wrote, "that
     these refugees are being helped by the Polish Red Cross with Lend-Lease sup-
     plies of our own government. Unless there is a special need for the children,
     which cannot be met through the general relief activities of all refugees, we
     would question the advisability of stepping into this picture financially."

121 Viteles, *Report on Visit*. "Statement of Relief Activities of the JDC for Refugees
     in the USSR."

122 James Aldridge, "Abuses by Poles in Tehran Reported: Correspondent Says
     Refugees Even Sold Relief Good Supplied by Americans," North American
     Newspaper Alliance, March 13, 1943.

123 Salar found this June 20, 1943, memo in the Diplomatic Archive in Tehran.
     KOL-25-33A, USHMM.

124 Polish Embassy in Kuybyshev, *Case of Jewish Citizens*, 42–78.

125 Viteles, *Report on Visit.*

126 Letter from Zipora Shertok to Youth Aliyah, Jerusalem, December 12, 1942. A245\121-30, CZA.

127 Letter from Zipora Shertok to her children, November 14, 1942. A245\121-23, CZA.

128 Lauenberg in Ben Michael, *Yaldei Tehran*, 109.

129 Foucault, *Discipline and Punish*, 184

130 Quoted in Zahra, *Lost Children*, 135.

131 Shayke Viner testimony, D.1.1003, MAMAM.

132 Shayke Viner testimony, D.1.1003, MAMAM.

133 Shayke Viner testimony, D.1.1003, MAMAM.

134 Viner testimony, A.1492.03, MAMAM.

135 Cable from Moshe Shertok, London, to Zipora Shertok c/o British Consulate of Tehran, December 28, 1942. A245\121-44, CZA.

136 Shertok reports on this after his return from London, in an April 25, 1943 meeting of the Zionist Agency Executive Council. Sharett (Shertok), *Moshe Sharett and his Legacy.*

137 A report on anti-Jewish incidents and practices in the Anders Army had resulted in an article by a United Press reporter documenting incidents of violence, demotions of Jewish soldiers, and the segregation of 240 Jewish soldiers in Tehran who were made to wear a letter C (civil) armband on their uniforms. The article reportedly caused an uproar among the Polish authorities, who issued the punitive demand to recruit those who were about to leave. Viteles, *Report on Visit.*

138 Cable from Zipora Shertok to Moshe Shertok, London, January 3, 1943. A245\121-15, CZA.

139 Cable from Zipora Shertok to Moshe Shertok, London, January 2, 1943. A245\121-22, CZA.

140 Cable from Zipora Shertok to Moshe Shertok, January 17, 1943. A245\121-2, CZA.

141 Zalman Schar testimony, A.683, MAMAM.

142 Cable from Zipora Shertok to Moshe Shertok, January 17, 1943. A245\121-2, CZA.

143 Viteles, *Report on Visit.* Documents of the Polish government-in-exile also mention receiving bribery from Iranian sources. Documents of Viktor Styburski. KOL-25-33A, USHMM.

144 Charles Passman to Harry Viteles, July 29, 1943, JDC. Polish authorities asked that as many non-Jewish adult companions as possible (twenty were authorized) accompany the children on the journey.

145 Boaz, *Alum*, 156.

146 JDC, OSE, Collaborate in Medical Supply Planning. Press Release. JDC?

147 Evelyn M. Morrissey (treasurer, American Jewish Joint Agricultural Corporation, Assistant treasurer, JDC), memo, March 23, 1945, JDC. Since June 1941,

the JDC had spent $33 million. "Statement of Relief Activities by the JDC for Refugees in the USSR," May 31, 1944, JDC.

148 Letter from Charles Passman, NY, to George Washington, Office of Lend-Lease Administration, Tehran. 6/25/1942. JDC.

149 Berlin distinguished positive freedom from a liberal, "negative" definition of freedom that emphasizes individual liberties and minimal state intervention. Isaiah Berlin, *Two Concepts of Liberty* (Oxford: Clarendon Press, 1958).

150 Arendt, *Jew as Pariah*, 166.

151 Efraim Shiloh testimony, A.1584.14, MAMAM.

152 Diolomatic meetings are described at length in Yishai's memoir *Tsir beli*.

153 Yishai, *Tsir beli*, 90. Dealings between the two are detailed in a secret Mossad L'Aliyah Bet memo dated 9/29/1942. C.54.02.01, MAMAM. In his memoir, Yishai even describes how the Polish consul comes to bid him goodbye at the airport upon his return to Palestine. Yishai, *Tsir beli*, 326.

154 Yishai, *Tsir beli*, 282.

155 Sternfeld, *Between Iran and Zion*, 23.

Chapter 9: Hebrew Children

1 Shekel, *Nedudim*, 75.

2 Shekel, *Nedudim*, 81.

3 The Forward and Gabe Friedman, "When Jews Found Refuge in an Unlikely Place: Pakistan," *Ha'aretz*, October 19, 2014, https://www.haaretz.com/jewish/when-jews-found-refuge-in-pakistan-1.5317022.

4 Etzion, *Yeladim*, 145.

5 For more on life in the camp in Karachi, see Shamir, *Yaldei Tehran*, 62.

6 The numbers were reported in a *Palestine Post* article: "Wandering Refugees Reach Journey's End." February 19, 1943, page 1.

7 Etzion, *Yeladim*, 148.

8 Aden was considered hostile. On November 29, 1947, when the United Nations would declare the end of the British Mandate over Palestine and the establishment of Jewish and Arab states, it would be the only Arab territory where anti-Jewish violence would erupt, resulting in the murder of thirty-eight and vast destruction to property. Moshe Shertok lecture, June 15, 1950, Speeches file, MS.

9 A. Ben Mosheh, *Ba'Makhaneh: Pluga 745* (in the Camp. Battalion 745 Journal) [in Hebrew] (February 1943), 2.

10 Eliav, *Haruakh*, 101.

11 Quoted in Whiteman, *Escape*, 131.

12 "Children of Israel Saved from Orphanhood." *Ha'aretz*, February 19, 1943, page 1.

13 "Touching Reunions at End of Long Trail." *Palestine Post*, February 19, 1943, page 3.

14 "Children of Israel Saved from Orphanhood." *Ha'aretz*, February 19, 1943, page 1.

15 Grynberg, *Children of Zion*, 164.

16 *Tehran Children Arriving in Atlit, 1943*, https://www.youtube.com/watch?v= a7F2eDNhGJk.

17 *Tehran Children Arriving in Atlit, 1943*, https://www.youtube.com/watch?v= a7F2eDNhGJk.

18 Shamir, *Yaldei Tehran*, 65.

19 "Children of Israel Saved from Orphanhood." *Ha'aretz*, February 19, 1943, page 1.

20 All three names appear in a list of *olim* who arrived in Palestine on February 19, 1943, ISA1\15491\6, CZA.

21 This and all subsequent letters to and from or pertaining to Hannan Teitel, Regina/Rivka Teitel, Emma/Noemi Perelgric, Zindel Teitel, and Ruchela Teitel are taken from their personal files at CZA.

22 Yishai, *Tsir beli*, 133.

23 Yishai, *Tsir beli*, 134.

24 Czuchnowski, *Cofniety czas.*

25 Yehuda Pompiansky testimony, A.1492.02, MAMAM.

26 "Inside Palestine," news release presented through CZA, February 18, 1942, JDC.

27 Quoted in Zahra, *Lost Children*, 4. David Lauenberg described the children as "in a horrible state, homeless, full of suspicion," in Ben Michael, *Yaldei Tehran*, 109.

28 Zahra, *Lost Children*, 134.

29 Polish sources state that these monies were paid directly to Youth Aliyah. At some point, complaints were made that in return for this funding the children should be required to study Polish. Report on the distribution of funds by the Polish Refugee Aid Office in Jerusalem, KOL-25-39A, USHMM.

30 Riwka Zwykielski, diary, entry for May 26, 1930, courtesy of Dov (Duban) Simchoni, in Polish.

31 Shertok reports on these meetings after his return from London, in an April 25, 1943 meeting of the Zionist Agency Executive Council. Sharret, *Moshe Sharett.*

32 Moshe Sharett (Shertok), *Moshe Sharett and his Legacy.* Diary entry for November 11, 1942. Sharett, *Moshe Sharett.*

33 Brio, *Polish Muses*, 15.

34 "Poles attack Jews in Palestine." Jewish Telegraphic Agency, February 7, 1943.

35 Report on the distribution of funds by the Polish Refugee Aid Office in Jerusalem, KOL-25-39A, 214–15, USHMM. There were hundreds of typed documents detailing funds allotted for each person and institution in the archives, perhaps as a response to misuse of funds in Iran.

36 Yishai, *Tsir Beli*, 90.

37 Shertok, meeting of the Zionist Agency Executive Council. April 25, 1943.

38 Brio, *Polish Muses*, 227.

39 Polish authorities blamed Jewish Agency representatives for encouraging Jewish Anders Army soldiers to desert and for conducting interviews to prove that they had deserted due to bad treatment of Jews in the army. Yehuda Pompiansky testimony, A.1492.02, MAMAM.

40 Such was the case of eighteen-year-old Julian Bussgang, who enlisted in the Anders Army in Tel Aviv on November 10, 1943. Museum Photo Archive #73240, USHMM.

41 File on Palestine A19II/116, SA, and also: Report on the distribution of funds by the Polish Refugee Aid Office in Jerusalem, KOL-25-39A, USHMM.

42 File on Palestine A19II/116, SA, and also: Report on the distribution of funds by the Polish Refugee Aid Office in Jerusalem, KOL-25-39A, USHMM.

43 Mikhail Krutikov, "When Polish Intellectuals Thrived in Pre-State Israel," *The Forward*, March 29, 2017.

44 Ishay Rosen-Zvi, "The Big Denial of Zionist Colonialism," *Ha'aretz*, October 18, 2018, https://bit.ly/2DQoJzq; Ishay Rosen-Zvi, "Yes, We Can Afford to Acknowledge Our Colonial Past," *Ha'aretz*, October 23, 2018; and Alexander Yacobson, "If Zionism Were Colonial It Would Have Ended Long Ago," *Ha'aretz*, October 20, 2018, https://bit.ly/2Pa1zJo.

45 D. Meletz in Gilad and Tsizling, *Ein Harod*, 70.

46 Libman, *State of Shock*, shows that in the pre-state period the Unified Kibbutz movement sought to endlessly defer the goal of establishing a Jewish nation-state. It wished to realize its utopian ideals outside the clutches of state bureaucracy and to avoid being in a constant violent struggle.

47 "Two Years with the Young Olim," *Ein Harod Diary*, March 2, 1945.

48 Shekel, *Nedudim*, 83.

49 In April 1943, the *delegaturas* employed 3,847 people who were Jewish. "Report on the Relief Accorded to Polish Citizens by the Polish Embassy in the USSR," April 25, 1943, Box 128, HI; Gross and Gross, *Children's Eyes*, 254.

50 Some eventually did work for Polish *delegaturas*—after most of the Catholic Poles left—as well as in Polish orphanages and schools, which continued to function in Central Asia until they were closed and merged with the general Soviet education system. *Wolna Polska* 24 (1943); Gross and Gross, *Children's Eyes*, 237–38.

51 Katz, *Gestapo to Gulag*, 115.

52 Katz, *Gestapo to Gulag*, 115.

53 The inclusion of negative accounts of the treatment of the children by Poles and the fact that these accounts were not edited out of their testimonies are attributed to Lebkowsky. See Gross and Gross, *Children's Eyes*.

54 *"Oleh Card"* (S6C) issued to Zindel Teitel by the Jewish Agency. S6P\1701\T, CZA.

55 Zahra, *Lost Children*, 19.

56 http://kanisrael.co.il/19420/.

57 Ruchela Teitel appears in a list of *olim* who arrived in Israel on May 11, 1949, ISA1\15493\7, CZA.

Bibliography

Books, Articles, and Reports

Adamczyk, Wesley. *When God Looked the Other Way: An Odyssey of War, Exile and Redemption*. Chicago: University of Chicago Press, 2004.

Amitai, Enat. *Shai li-yeladenu : tarbut li-yeladim ba-ḳibutsim* (A Gift for Our Children: Children's Culture in Kibbutzim). Ein Harod: Mishkan Le'Omanut, 2012. In Hebrew.

Anderson, Benedict. *Imagined Communities: Reflections on the Origins and Spread of Nationalism*. London: Verso, 1983.

Applebaum, Anne. *Gulag: A History*. New York: Anchor Books, 2004.

———. *Red Famine*. New York: Penguin, 2017.

Arendt, Hannah. *The Jew as Pariah: Jewish Identity and Politics in the Modern Age*. Edited by Ron H. Feldman. New York: Grove Press, 1978.

———. *The Origins of Totalitarianism*. New York: Schocken, 1951.

———. "We Refugees." In *Altogether Elsewhere: Writers on Exile*. Edited by Marc Robinson. 1943; reprint London: Faber and Faber, 1994.

Auerbach, Erich. *Mimesis: The Representation of Reality in Western Literature*. New York: Princeton University Press, 1954.

Bartal, Israel. *Jews of Eastern Europe, 1772–1881*. Philadelphia: University of Pennsylvania Press, 2005.

Bartal, Yisrael, Antony Polonsky, and Scott Ury. *Jews and Their Neighbours in Eastern Europe Since 1750*. Vol. 24 of *Polin: Studies in Polish Jewry*. Jerusalem: Littman Library of Jewish Civilization, 2012.

Bauer, Yehuda. *American Jewry and the Holocaust: The American Joint Distribution Committee*. Detroit: Wayne State University Press, 1981.

Ben Michael, Gideon Raphael, ed. *Yaldei Tehran* (Tehran Children). In *Bit'on Forum le'shmirat Zikaron ha'Shoah* (Forum for the Preservation of Holocaust Memory) 33 (October 2010). In Hebrew.

Benjamin, Jessica. *Beyond Doer and Done To: Recognition Theory, Intersubjectivity and the Third*. New York: Routledge, 2018.

Bhabha, Homi. *Nation and Narration*. London: Routledge, 1990.

Bird, Isabella, *Journeys in Persia and Kurdistan*. London: John Murray, 1891.

Blum, Harold. *The Brigade*. New York: Harper Perennial, 2002.

Boaz, Aryeh. *Alum ve'nokhakh ba'kol* (Unseen but Present in Everything: The Life of Shaul Avigur). Tel Aviv: Office of Defense Ministry, 2001. In Hebrew.

Braginsky, Ychuda, *Am khoter le'khof* (A People Seeking a Shore). Tel Aviv: Habibutz Ha'meukhad, 1965. In Hebrew.

Brauda, Ruth. "'Tashkent City of Bread': The Polish Ha'shomer Ha'tsair in Central Asia, 1941–1945." *Israel* 23 (2016): 157–81. In Hebrew.

Brio, Valentina. *Polish Muses in the Holy Land. General Anders Arm: Place, Time Culture*. Jerusalem and Moscow: Gesharim, 2017. In Russian.

———. "Polish Literary Newspaper in Jerusalem (*W drodze*: 1943–1946)." *Jews and Slavs*. Edited by Wolf Moskovich and Irena Fijalkowska-Janiak. Jerusalem-Danzig: Hebrew University, 2003.

Brubaker, Rogers. "Rethinking Nationhood: Nation as Institutionalized Form, Practical Category, Contingent Event." *Contention* 4, no. 1 (1994), http://works.bepress.com/wrb/17/.

Bugaï, Nikolaï Fedorovich. *The Deportations of People in the Soviet Union*. Hauppauge, NY: Nova Publishers, 1996.

Bullard, Reader. *Letters from Tehran*. London: I. B. Tauris, 1991.

Czuchnowski, Marian. *Cofniety czas* (Times Past). London, 1945. In Polish.

Damandan, Parisa. *The Children of Isfahan: Polish Refugees in Iran: Portrait Photographs of Abolqasem Jala, 1942–1945*. Tehran: Nazarpub, 2010.

Dan, Hillel. *The Unpaved Road: The Story of Solel Boneh*. Tel Aviv: Schocken, 1963. In Hebrew.

Davies, Norman. *God's Playground: A History of Poland*. Vol. 2, *1795 to Present*. New York: Columbia University Press, 2005.

———. *Trail of Hope: The Anders Army, An Odyssey Across Three Continents*. Oxford: Osprey, 2015.

Dekel [Teitel], Chanania. Testimony. *Ginzakh Kiddush Hashem*. 1943. In Yiddish; translated to English by Agi Legutka. Unpublished.

———. *In Memoriam*. 1993. Unpublished.

Dekel [Teitel], Ze'ev (Wolf). *In Memoriam*. 1990. Unpublished.

Dror, Yuval, ed. *Interdisciplinary Studies of the Legacy of Yanusz Korczak*. Tel Aviv: Tel Aviv University Publications, 2008.

Drucker, Moshe, and Arye Drucker. *Drucker: Sipura shel mishpakha* (Drucker: The Story of a Family). Tel Aviv: Sipurei Savta, 2009. In Hebrew.

Dwork, Deborah, and Robert Jan Van Pelt, *Flight from the Third Reich*. New York: W. W. Norton, 2009.

Efron, Georgy. *The Diaries of Georgy Efron, August 1942–August 1943 (The Tashkent Period)*. Translated Olga Zaslavsky. Lewison, N.Y.: Edwin Mellen, 2010.

Eliav, Arye Lova. *Haruakh lo tikakh* (The Wind Will Not Blow Away). Tel Aviv: Am Oved, 1974. In Hebrew.

Engel, David. *Facing a Holocaust: The Polish Government in Exile and the Jews, 1943–1945*. Chapel Hill: University of North Carolina Press, 1993.

———. *In the Shadow of Auschwitz: The Polish Government in Exile and the Jews, 1939–1942*. Chapel Hill: University of North Carolina Press, 1987.

Etzion (Klapholz), Yosef. *Yeladim la'netsakh* (Children Forever). Tel Aviv: Docostory, 2013. In Hebrew.

Flincker, David. *Warsaw*. Jerusalem: Rabbi Kook Institute, 1947. In Hebrew.

Foucault, Michel. *Discipline and Punish*. Trans. A. Sheridan, 1977. New York: Vintage, 1995.

Gellner, Ernest. *Nations and Nationalism*. Ithaca, N.Y.: Cornell University Press, 1983.

Gilad, Zrubavel, and Neria Tsizling, eds. *Ein Harod: Semi-Centennial*. Hakkibutz ha'Meuchad Press, 1972. In Hebrew.

Gitelman, Zvi, ed. *Bitter Legacy: Confronting the Holocaust in the USSR*. Bloomington: Indiana University Press, 1997.

Gross, Irena, and Jan Gross. *War Through Children's Eyes: The Soviet Occupation of Poland and the Deportations, 1939–1941*. Stanford, CA: Hoover Institution Press, 1981.

Grynberg, Henryk. *Children of Zion*. Trans. Jacqueline Mitchell. Evanston, IL: Northwestern University Press, 1997.

Guliam, Gafur. *Izbrannyre proizvedeniia*. Edited by Akhmatova and R. Farkhadi. Tashkent, 1983.

G'ulom, G'afur. *Mukammai asarlar to'plami.2-tom*. Tashkent, 2014.

Gutman, Yisrael. "Jews in General Anders' Army in the Soviet Union." *Yad Vashem Studies* 12 (1977): 231–96.

Hall, John. *Ernest Gellner: An Intellectual Biography*. London: Verso, 2010.

Hever, Hannan. *El ha-khof ha-mekuveh: ha-yam ba-tarbut ha-ivrit veha-sifrut ha-ivrit ha-modernit* (Toward the Longed-For Shore: The Sea in Hebrew Culture and Modern Hebrew Literature). Jerusalem: Van Leer Institute, 2007. In Hebrew.

Hirschberg, Hayim Zeev. "Yerakh ha'eitanim tashag, be-Paras" (Rosh Hashanah, 1942, in Persia). *La'mo'ed* [Journal of ha'Mizrahi Religious Movement]: Literary Collections for Three Holidays, vol. 1 (1944): 44–58. In Hebrew.

Hobsbawm, Eric. *Nations and Nationalism Since 1780: Programme, Myth, Reality*. Cambridge, UK: Cambridge University Press, 1992.

Hundert, Gershon David. *Jews in Poland Lithuania in the Eighteenth Century: A Genealogy of Modernity*. Berkeley: University of California Press, 2004.

Jenkins, Jennifer. "Iran in the Nazi New Order, 1933–1941." *Iranian Studies* 49, no. 5 (2016): 727–51.

Jolluck, Katherine. *Polish Women in the Soviet Union During World War II.* Pittsburgh: University of Pittsburgh Press, 2002.

Katz, Zev. *From the Gestapo to the Gulag.* London: Vallentine-Mitchell, 2004.

Klein, Melanie. *Love, Guilt and Reparation and Other Works, 1921–1945.* New York: Free Press, 1984.

Koselleck, Reinhart. *Sediments of Time: On Possible Histories.* Stanford, CA: Stanford University Press, 2018.

Kot, Stanisław. *Conversations with the Kremlin.* London: Oxford University Press, 1963.

Landau, Emil. *Diary, 1941–1944.* Courtesy of Ilana Landau Karnie. In Polish; translated to Hebrew by Uri Orlev. Unpublished.

Laub, Dori. "Failed Empathy—A Central Theme in the Survivor's Holocaust Experience." *Psychoanalytic Psychology* 6, no. 4 (1989): 377–400.

Levi, Habib. *Comprehensive History of the Jews of Iran.* Los Angeles: Mazda, 1999. In Persian and English.

Levin, Yehuda Leib. *Megilat Polin: Ostrów Mozovyechk* (The Scrolls of Poland: Ostrów Mozovyechk). Jerusalem: Dfus Da'at, Tashkhav. Yad Yahadut Polin, 1965. In Hebrew.

Lewis, Bernard. *The Jews of Islam.* Princeton, NJ: Princeton University Press, 1978.

Libman, Lior. *A State of Shock: Representations of the Kibbutz in Israel 1948–1954.* Ph.D. diss., 2014.

Litvak, Joseph, "Jewish Refugees from Poland in the USSR, 1939-1946." Gitelman, Zvi, ed. *Bitter Legacy: Confronting the Holocaust in the USSR.* Bloomington: Indiana UP, 1997.

Manley, Rebecca. *To the Tashkent Station: Evacuation and Survival in the Soviet Union at War.* Ithaca, NY: Cornell University Press, 2009.

Margolis, Julius. *Masa le'eretz ha'asirim* (Journey to the Land of Ze Ka). Translated by Idit Shaket [Hebrew translation of Russian manuscript]. Jerusalem: Magnes, 2014.

Martin, Terry. *The Affirmative Action Empire: Nations and Nationalism in the Soviet Union, 1923-1939.* Ithaca, NY: Cornell University Press, 2001.

Medvedeva-Nathoo, Olga. "Certificate of Birth, Certificate of Survival." American Association for Polish-Jewish Studies (2003), http://www.aapjstudies.org/index .php?id=192.

Nail, Thomas. *The Figure of the Migrant.* Stanford, CA: Stanford University Press, 2015.

Naor, Mordecai. *Makhaneh ha'maapilim be'Atlit* (The Immigration Camp in Atlit). Atlit Museum, 1987. In Hebrew.

Netzer, Amnon, ed. *Padyavand: A Study of Iranian Jewry.* Costa Mesa, CA: Mazda, 1997.

———. *Yehudei Iran be-yamenu* (Iran's Jewry in Our Days). Jerusalem: Shazar Library, Institute for Contemporary Judaism, Hebrew University, 1981.

Ngũgĩ wa Thiong'o. *Decolonizing the Mind: The Politics of Language in African Literature.* Heinemann Educational, 1986.

Omer, Devorah. *Ha'takhana Teheran* (Tehran Station). Netania: Amichai Press, 1991. In Hebrew.

Orlev, Uri. *Ad Machar.* (Till Tomorrow). Tel Aviv: Am Oved, 1968. In Hebrew.

——. *Habyta me' arvot ha'shemesh* (Homeward from Steppes of the Sun). Jerusalem: Keter, 2010.

O'Sullivan, Adrian. *Espionage and Counter Intelligence in Occupied Persia: The Success of the Allied Secret Service, 1941–1945.* London: Springer, 2015.

Pęziński, Andrzej. *Ostrów Mazowiecka z dystansu* (Ostrów at a Distance). In Polish; translated to English by Agata Tumilowicz. Unpublished.

Polish Delegatura in Tehran. *Report on the Organization of Lodging, Food, Clothes, Education and Cultural Life for Children, etc. for the Period Between July 16 and September 15, 1942.* KOL-25-33A, USHMM.

Polish Embassy in Kuybyshev. *The Case of Jewish Citizens of Poland in Light of Soviet Official Documents and Practice*, signature illegible, August 11, 1942, KOL-25-33A, USHMM.

Polonsky, Antony, Jakub Basista, and Andrzej Link-Lenczowski. *The Jews in Old Poland, 1000–1795.* London: I. B. Tauris, 1993.

Rā'ī Gallūjah, Sajjād. *Bar'rasī va taḥlīl-i ravābiṭ-i Īrān va Ingilistān: bar pāyah-i asnād-i ārshīv-i Vizārat-i Umūr-i Khārijah-i Īrān* (Study and Analysis of Relations Between Iran and England, 1941–1953: Based on the documents of the Iranian Ministry of Foreign Affair's archives). Tehran: Idārah-i Nashr-i Vizārat-i Umūr-i Khārijah, 2015. In Persian.

Rosenberg, Alfred, *Der Mythus des zwanzigsten Jahrhunderts (The Myth of the Twentieth Century.* 1930; reprint Invictus Books, 2011.

Rottenberg, Ayala. *Dapim shel Etmol* (Pages of Yesterday: Recollections of the Daughter of Beis Yaacov in Eretz Yisrael). Jerusalem: Feldheim, 1999.

Saadoun, Haim, ed. *Iran.* Jerusalem: Ben Zvi Institute, 2005. In Hebrew.

Saadoun, Haim, and Joel Rappel, eds. *Ba-makhteret me-artzot ha-Islam* (In the Underground in Muslim Countries). Jerusalem: Ben Zvi Institute, 1997. In Hebrew.

Sadok, Haim. *Yahadut Iran be-tkufat ha-shoshelet ha-Pahlavit* (The Jews in Iran During the Shah Pahlavi Era). Tel-Aviv: Meyatseg, 1991. In Hebrew.

Shaham, Nathan. *Harkhek me'Tashkent* (Far Away from Tashkent). Tel Aviv: Dvir, 2007. In Hebrew.

Shamir, Gadit. *Yaldei Tehran* (Tehran Children). Tel Aviv: Yaron Golan, 1989. In Hebrew.

Shapira, Anita, ed. *Haapala: Studies in the History of Illegal Immigration.* Tel Aviv: Am Oved, 1990.

Sharett (Shertok), Moshe. *Moshe Sharett and His Legacy.* Edited by Yaacov Sharett. http://www.sharett.org.il.

Sharshar, Houman. *Esther's Children: A Portrait of Iranian Jews*. Los Angeles: Center for Iranian Jewish Oral History, 2002.

Shekel, Zvi. *Nedudim ve'adama* (Nomadism and Soil). Kibbutz Hatzerim, 1999. In Hebrew.

Shenhav, Yehoudah A. *The Arab Jews: A Postcolonial Reading of Nationalism, Religion, and Ethnicity*. Stanford, CA: Stanford University Press, 2006.

Shterenshis, Michael. *Tamerlane and the Jews*. London: Routledge, 2002.

Siddiqui, Mona. *Hospitality in Islam: Welcoming in God's Name*. New Haven, CT: Yale University Press, 2015.

Siekierski, Maciej, and Feliks Tych, eds. *Widziałem Anioła Śmierci. Losy deportowanych Żydów* (I Have Seen the Angel of Death: The Fate of Polish Jews Deported to the USSR During World War II). Warsaw: Rosner & Partners, 2006. In Polish.

Sinai, Khosrow. "A File, a Story: 'The Lost Requiem.'" *Pole-e-Firuzeh: Journal of the Dialogue Among Civilizations* (Turquoise Bridge) 4, no. 13 (Autumn 2014): 171-82. In Persian.

Snyder, Timothy. *Bloodlands: Europe Between Hitler and Stalin*. New York: Basic Books, 2010.

Solzhenitsyn, Aleksandr. *The Gulag Archipelago*. New York: Basic Books, 1997.

Specter-Simon, Reeva, Michael Menachem Laskier, and Sara Reguer, eds. *The Jews of the Middle East and North Africa in Modern Times*. New York: Columbia University Press, 2003.

Sternberg, Cecilia. *The Journey*. London: Collins, 1977.

Sternfeld, Lior B. *Between Iran and Zion: Jewish Histories of Twentieth Century Iran*. Stanford, CA: Stanford University Press, 2018.

———. "'Poland Is Not Lost While We Still Live': The Making of Polish Iran, 1941–1945." *Jewish Social Studies* 23, no. 3 (2018): 101–27.

———. "The Revolutions Forgotten Sons and Daughters: The Jewish Community in Tehran During the 1979 Revolution." *Journal of Iranian Studies* 47, no. 6 (2014): 857–69.

Tsadik, Daniel. "The Legal Status of Religious Minorities: Imāmī Shī'ī Law and Iran's Constitutional Revolution." *Islamic Law and Society* 10, no. 3 (2003): 376–408.

———. *Between Foreigners and Shi'is*. Stanford, CA: Stanford University Press, 2007.

Viteles, Harry. *Report on Visit to Bagdad (November 2-9, 1942) and to Teheran (November 11 to December 2, 1942)*, December 31, 1942, AR33/44-212, JDC.

Wasilewska, Irena. *Suffer Little Children*. London: Maxlove, 1946.

Wat, Aleksander. *My Century*. Edited by Czesław Miłosz. New York: New York Review of Books, 2013.

Whiteman, Dorit Bader. *Escape via Siberia: A Jewish Child's Odyssey of Survival*. Teaneck, NJ: Holmes & Meier, 1999.

Yishai, Moshe. *Tsir beli to'ar* (An Emissary Without a Title: Impressions from a Mission and Travels to Persia). Tel Aviv: Taversy Press, 1949. In Hebrew.

Zahra, Tara. *The Lost Children: Reconstructing Europe's Families After World War II.* Cambridge, MA: Harvard University Press, 2011.

Ziolkowska-Boehm, Aleksandra. *The Polish Experience through World War II.* Lanham, MD: Lexington Books, 2013.

Zylberman, Ruth. *Department of Missing Persons.* New York: Arcade, 2017.

Films and Videos

Before the Revolution. Directed by Dan Shadur and Barak Heymann. Heymann Brothers Films, 2013.

The Children of Teheran. Directed by Dalia Guttman, David Tour, and Yehuda Kaveh, 2007.

The Lost Requiem. Directed by Khosrow Sinai. Narrated by M. Bayandor. In Persian; subtitles by M. Crawley. Cini, 1983.

Poles Apart: The Story of 733 Polish Orphans. Directed by Mary-Jo Tohill. Polish Association of Christchurch and CTV, 1966.

Yaldei Tehran magi'im le'Atlit, 1943 (Tehran Children Arrive in Atlit, 1943). Directed by Nathan Axelrod. In Hebrew. Nathan Axelrod Newsreel Collection, Jerusalem Cinematheque, Israeli National Archive, https://www.youtube.com/watch?v=a7F2eDNhGJk&t=12s.

Interviews

Arison, Noemi (Emma Perelgric)	8/27/2009; 12/15/2009; 7/20/2018
Beck, Anton	6/6/2013
Ben Ezri, Meir	8/20/2009
Binyamini, Rivka (Regina Teitel)	8/20/2009; 12/15/2009; 8/13/2010; 7/3/2012
Drucker, Arye	7/13/2014
Etzion, Yosef	8/21/2009
Ejchelkraut, Riczard	6/2/2012; 9/20/2014
Givol, David	8/5/2010
Grynberg, Henryk	1/24/2010
Dr. Kermanshahi, Heshmat	1/25/2018
Landau, Ilana	8/25/2010
Mandel, Bracha	12/25/2009
Nitzan (Halberstandt) Sarah	6/7/2017
Peleg, Tamar	12/22/2017
Pęziński, Andrzej	6/2/2012
Shapira, Yasha	6/14/2013
Simchoni, Duban	7/9/2012; 7/15/2018
Yaron, Yehudit	1/3/2012

Illustration Credits

Index

400 INDEX

Dmochowsi, Sefean, 180

Dmowski, Roman, 50, 196

Dolny Śląsk in Lower Siles, 348

Dominican Republic, resettlement of
Jewish refugees in, 175

Doulab cemetery, 12, 226

Drodze, 333

Drozdowski, David, 327

Drunina, Iulia, 157

Duda, Andrezej, 184, 209

the *Dunera*, 300–301, 307

Dushan Tappeh, Iran, 245–46, 251,
255–56, 258–59, 263, 265, 272–73,
278, 282, 286, 289–90

Dvorkin, Eliyahu, 293, 297

Dzhambul children, 147

Dzieci Syjonu (Children of Zion), 13

Eastern European historiography,
35–36

Eben Ezer, 129

Ebensee Displaced Persons Camp,
348–49, 352

Ebriyat Hamziqat Sefet Eber, 30

Eden, Anthony, 105, 288, 334

Edison House, 333

Efron, Georgy, 215

Efron, Sergey, 215

Egypt, 300, 302, 311, 353–54

Ehrlich, Henryk, 96, 179, 181

Ein Harod Diary, 342, 344

Einsatzgruppen, 57, 65, 329

Elghanian, Haji Aziz, 30, 32, 253, 263

Eliav, Lova, 310–11

El Qantarah el Sharqiyya (El Kantara),
310

Endecja (National Democracy Party),
50. *See also* National Democracy
Party

Engel, David, 186, 220, 239, 372n

Entebbe Rescue, 306

Eretz Yisrael (Israel), 249, 252–55, 258, 261,
262, 282, 286, 295, 303, 311, 314, 316–18,
321, 345

"Eretz Yisrael" office, 251, 262, 266, 305

Eschwegge camp, 352

Etzion, Yosef, 308–9, 377n. *See also*
Klapholz, Josek

Eugeniusz, Tatur, 224

Evacuation Council, 119, 125, 130

evakuirovannyy (evacuees), 119–20,
126–27, 155–56, 166, 178, 214–15
starvation of, 166–70
Uzbek kindness toward, 155–57
violence against, 214–15

exile colonies, 79–112

Ezri, Meir, 255

the Farhud, 24, 286

Fawzi al-Qawuqii, 353

Federation of Persian Jews in Givat
Shmuel, Israel, 255

Federation of Persian Jews in Israel, 255

Federation of Persian Jews in Los
Angeles, 255

Federation of Polish Jews in Great Britain, 172–73, 185

Federation of Polish Jews of America, 172

Federation of Polish Organizations in
the United States, 177

Fergana, Uzbekistan, 145, 200, 230, 232

"fifty Austrian Jews," petition from,
22–23

Flincker, David, 56, 335

forced labor, 16, 70, 79–80, 82–85, 88,
97–98, 104, 113, 172

Foucault, Michel, 293, 294

Frajlich, Amalia (Malka) Iosifovna,
146–47, 225

friendship of peoples, 153–56, 157, 225, 232

FSB, 83

fungi, 169